OXFORD MONOGRAPHS IN INTERNATIONAL HUMANITARIAN AND CRIMINAL LAW

Series Editors

SALVATORE ZAPPALÀ
Professor of International Law, University of Catania

PHILIPPA WEBB
Professor of Public International Law, The Dickson Poon School of Law, King's College London

The Arms Trade and International Criminal Law

OXFORD MONOGRAPHS IN INTERNATIONAL HUMANITARIAN AND CRIMINAL LAW

This series emerged through the vision of the late Antonio Cassese. Since then the series has published original and innovative works on challenging issues in international humanitarian law and international criminal justice, primarily by emerging authors. Given the ever-growing intersection of these areas with other fields of international law such as the jus ad bellum, and disciplines such as criminology, sociology, and history, the scope of the series also incorporates these perspectives. Fresh approaches and new ideas for improving conceptual and practical challenges are welcomed. The series editors encourage submissions from around the world, and will consider edited collections, although the primary focus is on authored works.

ALSO PUBLISHED IN THIS SERIES

International Criminal Tribunals and Domestic Accountability
In the Court's Shadow
Patryk I. Labuda

The Morality of the Laws of War
War, Law, and Murder
Marcela Prieto Rudolphy

Accountability for Mass Starvation
Testing the Limits of the Law
Edited by Bridget Conley, Alex de Waal, Catriona Murdoch, and Wayne Jordash KC

The Defence of Mistake of Law in International Criminal Law
A Study on Ignorance and Blame
Antonio Coco

The Use of Force against Individuals in War under International Law
A Social Ontological Approach
Ka Lok Yip

Non-Binding Norms in International Humanitarian Law
Efficacy, Legitimacy, and Legality
Emily Crawford

The Arms Trade and International Criminal Law

Reframing Accountability for Complicit Weapon Suppliers

TOMAS HAMILTON

OXFORD
UNIVERSITY PRESS

OXFORD
UNIVERSITY PRESS

Great Clarendon Street, Oxford, OX2 6DP,
United Kingdom

Oxford University Press is a department of the University of Oxford.
It furthers the University's objective of excellence in research, scholarship,
and education by publishing worldwide. Oxford is a registered trade mark of
Oxford University Press in the UK and in certain other countries

Published in the United States of America by Oxford University Press
198 Madison Avenue, New York, NY 10016, United States of America

British Library Cataloguing in Publication Data
Data available

Library of Congress Control Number: 2024949663

ISBN 978-0-19-286867-1

DOI: 10.1093/oso/9780192868671.001.0001

Printed and bound by
CPI Group (UK) Ltd, Croydon, CR0 4YY

MIX
Paper | Supporting
responsible forestry
FSC® C013604

The manufacturer's authorised representative in the EU for product safety is
Oxford University Press España S.A. of El Parque Empresarial San Fernando
de Henares, Avenida de Castilla, 2 – 28830 Madrid (www.oup.es/en or product.safety@oup.com).
OUP España S.A. also acts as importer into Spain of products made by the manufacturer.

Foreword

'Once weapons were manufactured to fight wars', Arundhati Roy has said, 'Now wars are manufactured to sell weapons.' Although perhaps somewhat overstated, the great Indian novelist's aphorism captures well the profound role the transfer of arms plays in fomenting armed conflict and rendering it increasingly brutal. In the modern era, it is the rare conflict indeed in which the weapons combatants use to kill each other have not been provided by those who watch the conflict from the sidelines. Far more often, the purveyors of the means of war are states interested in seeing one side prevail or persons—legal and natural—concerned solely with maximizing profit. In both cases, the consequences are almost always as dreadful as they are predictable: more unnecessary killing, more needless suffering.

Much ink has been spilled on the extent to which various areas of international law prohibit arms transfers that lead to unlawful violence, such as the *jus ad bellum*, the *jus in bello*, the law of neutrality, and international human rights law. By contrast, and surprisingly, the writing powder remains largely dry concerning the status of such transfers under international criminal law, the one area of international law in which the consequences for unlawful behaviour are the most striking—and the most corporeal.

No longer. In this groundbreaking book—part dispassionate study, part *cri de cœur*—Tomas Hamilton provides a synoptic and historically informed overview of international criminal law's potential to limit the catastrophic consequences of the transnational arms trade. The first half of the book highlights that potential by showing how international criminal law can enhance the effectiveness of the areas of international law that are more familiar in the arms transfer context. International criminal law can have that effect, Hamilton convincingly explains, because a wide variety of 'arms transfer conduct' qualifies as criminal facilitation when causally connected to the commission of an international crime—particularly under Article 25(3)(d) of the Rome Statute, which prohibits 'contribut[ing] to the commission or attempted commission of such a crime by a group of persons acting with a common purpose'.

By itself, the concrete blueprint Hamilton provides for how to use international criminal law to combat the arms trade represents a significant advance for scholarship in this area. But instead of resting on his doctrinal laurels, Hamilton dedicates the second half of the book to providing an empirical explanation for why, despite Article 25(3)(d), the ICC has shown little interest in prosecuting arms traders for facilitating crimes in the various situations the Court is investigating. Based on extensive ethnographic work with lawyers and judges at the ICC, Hamilton identifies two different explanatory frames, neither of which is convincing. The first, 'Frame 1', is that practitioners are not only sceptical that arms traders can be held individually responsible under the Rome Statute for facilitating international crimes, they actually reject the very idea that it is the Court's job to 'regulate' the arms trade. The second, 'Frame 2', is that even if both of Frame 1's assumptions did not hold, it would simply be too practically difficult, for reasons such as evidentiary availability and personal security, to prosecute arms traders as accomplices. As Hamilton points out, such non-legal rationales for inaction strike a dissonant chord given the legalistic culture that pervades the ICC.

It is a pleasure to write this Foreword, because Hamilton's book represents the very best of international criminal law scholarship. Many scholars in the discipline excel at doctrinal analysis. A smaller but still not insignificant number are skilled empiricists. Very few, however, are able to combine the two. Hamilton is one of the happy exceptions—and the net result is a book that draws on both doctrinal analysis and ethnography to build a compelling argument that international criminal law provides powerful tools for combating the arms trade. I hope the judges and lawyers who work at the ICC—and those who work at cognate institutions, both international and national, who share their hesitation—will read the book and pay heed to the lessons it contains.

Kevin Jon Heller
Professor of International Law & Security
University of Copenhagen, Centre for Military Studies
7 November 2024

Series Editors' Preface

The monograph '*The Arms Trade and International Criminal Law*' by Tomas Hamilton is a most welcome contribution to a very sensitive area of international law, which needed profound analysis such as the present one in order to reflect on and fill what is rightly perceived as a serious accountability gap.

It may seem obvious to state that 'those who [...] provide weapons could also be authors of the crimes' (see the quote by the first ICC Prosecutor, Luis Moreno-Ocampo, cited by the author at the outset of his book). Nonetheless, reality shows that capturing through the lens of criminal law the level of contribution (or complicity in some cases) the providers of weapons lend to mass atrocities is never easy.

Despite the fact that since World War II there has been clarity as to the proximity of the industry, and in particular the weapon industry, to the perpetration of international crimes (and in this regard the author appropriately refers to the various post WWII efforts), the role of international criminal law in this area was never central. Difficulties emerge every time one tries to become more concrete as to the responsibilities of manufacturers and traders in weapons.

This has been experienced for decades at the domestic level, and it is even more complex in the transnational dimension, where exporters and traders can exploit loopholes and gaps in the applicable regulation, as well as complicities by political supporters of parties to a conflict.

At the international level there has always been awareness of the nefarious impact of arms trade for fuelling conflict and mass atrocities. It is well-known that preventing the acquisition of weapons by warring factions can be an instrument to try to prevent or reduce the impact of fighting. In this vein, the Security Council, when intervening in situations which pose a threat to international peace and security, has almost systematically resorted to imposing arms embargoes, which many times unfortunately have proved unsuccessful. Moreover, negotiations leading to the conclusion of the Arms Trade Treaty highlighted the need to address human rights abuses and international crimes in such an instrument.

However, ultimately, even if in the past decade there has been increasing attention (with some focus on corporate responsibility), there still seems to be no or too little accountability in this area. It is precisely this accountability gap that is the main object of this excellent book which we are very pleased to publish in this series. In particular, this book—apart from its numerous academic qualities in terms of being seriously researched, rigorously argued, and well-written—fits extremely well with the spirit of the series in trying to make the world a better place.

The Editors

Acknowledgements

I would like to express my gratitude to those who contributed to this book in different ways, whether instigating, encouraging, or providing the means to ensure its completion.

First and foremost, I would like to thank my doctoral supervisors Dr Nicola Palmer and Professor Philippa Webb for their advice, support, and wisdom. Without Dr Palmer's unwavering enthusiasm for the project's blend of doctrine and empiricism, it would not have come to fruition.

I am especially grateful to the scholars who taught me law or discussed my research over the years, including Professor James Crawford, Professor Kevin Jon Heller, Professor Nina HB Jørgensen, Professor Sarah Nouwen, Professor Nicola Padfield, Ambassador Stephen J Rapp, Professor Göran Sluiter, Professor Carsten Stahn, Professor James G Stewart, and Professor Sergey Vasiliev. I owe a longer-standing debt to Professor Peter Mitchell, my undergraduate tutor at St Hugh's College.

The book is partly a product of working at the international criminal tribunals, often for lawyers who shaped my ideas of justice and accountability through their practice, their writings, and informal discussions. My thanks go to Dr Gilbert Bitti, Dr Sylvia Fernández de Gurmendi, Michael G Karnavas, Dr Alejandro Kiss, Dr Rod Rastan, Dr Simon de Smet, Mr So Mosseny, Ms Suzana Tomanović, Professor Ekaterina Trendafilova, and Professor Christine van den Wyngaert.

I am most grateful for the support of the Economic and Social Research Council, which continues to champion interdisciplinary legal scholarship in the United Kingdom. I wish to thank King's College London and the other institutions where the book was developed: Columbia Law School, the University of Amsterdam, the Grotius Centre for International Law, the Chinese University of Hong Kong, and the Asser Institute.

Lastly, I am deeply grateful to the many friends and family whose patience and encouragement sustained me through a decade of spare evenings and weekends spent working towards this book. Above all, I would like to thank Dounia Hattabi for her love, kindness, and inspiration.

This doctorate is dedicated to the two people who taught me most about academic integrity: my parents, Professor David Barton and Professor Mary Hamilton.

Tomas Hamilton
London
March 2024

Contents

Table of Cases xv
Table of Primary Sources xix
List of Abbreviations xxvii

1. Introduction 1
 1.1 Introduction 1
 1.2 Arms Traders as Accomplices 3
 1.3 Unpacking the Global Arms Trade: Items, Actors, Conduct 6
  1.3.1 Types of 'Items' 6
  1.3.2 'Actors' in the Arms Trade 8
  1.3.3 'Arms Transfer Conduct' 10
 1.4 The Arms Trade in International Criminal Law Scholarship 12
 1.5 Overview of This Book 17

2. Complementing Export Regulation with Criminal Accountability 18
 2.1 Introduction 18
 2.2 National Arms Export Regulations 19
  2.2.1 National Export Criteria in Relation to International Crimes 19
  2.2.2 The Netherlands: Unlawful Exports as Complicity 21
  2.2.3 The UK: Challenging the 'Lawful' Trade 23
  2.2.4 Export Regulations Are Constrained by Foreign Policy 25
  2.2.5 Limitations to Specified Types of Item 27
  2.2.6 Ineffective Brokering Regulation 28
 2.3 International Agreements on the Arms Trade 29
  2.3.1 The Arms Trade Treaty is Limited in Scope 30
  2.3.2 International Agreements and Accountability for Atrocity Victims 31
 2.4 Conclusion 35

3. 'Arms Trade Law' and the Potential of International Justice 38
 3.1 Introduction 38
 3.2 Arms Embargoes 39
  3.2.1 Arms Embargoes Do Not Provide Criminal Accountability 39
  3.2.2 Arms Embargoes Are Limited to Specific Categories of Item 41
  3.2.3 Arms Embargoes Are Used Selectively 43
  3.2.4 Integrating International Criminal Law and Arms Embargoes 45
  3.2.5 Targeting 'Embargo Busters' Using International Criminal Law 47
 3.3 The Plurality of 'Arms Trade Law' 49
  3.3.1 The Law of State Responsibility 50

3.3.2 Law on the Use of Force 51
3.3.3 The Law of Neutrality 53
3.3.4 International Humanitarian Law 55
3.3.5 International Human Rights Law 56
3.3.6 Counter-Terrorism Law 58
3.3.7 Other Subsidiary Areas of Arms Trade Law 60
3.4 A Potential Role for International Criminal Law? 62
3.4.1 Limitations of Existing Arms Trade Law 63
3.4.2 Complicity in the 'Lawful' and 'Illicit' Arms Trade 65
3.4.3 Expressing the Seriousness of Complicity 65
3.4.4 Context and Content in an Expressive Prosecution 67
3.5 Conclusion 68

4. The *Actus Reus* of a Complicit Arms Transfer 70
4.1 Introduction 70
4.2 Complicit Assistance in the Rome Statute 71
4.3 Preliminary Remarks on Interpretation 72
4.4 The Quiet Primacy of Article 25(3)(d)(ii) of the Rome Statute 74
4.5 Basic Requirements of Article 25(3)(d)(ii) 75
4.6 'Significant' Arms Transfers (Degree of Contribution) 77
4.7 Causal Relationship with the Arms Transfer 81
4.8 Remoteness as a Useful Juridical Concept 83
4.9 The Significance of a Particular Shipment 85
4.10 Transferring Arms from Outside the Group of Perpetrators 88
4.11 Conclusion 89

5. The *Mens Rea* of a Complicit Arms Transfer 91
5.1 Introduction 91
5.2 Article 25(3)(c) Aiding or Abetting 91
5.3 Contributing to a Group Crime under Article 25(3)(d) 94
5.4 Specificity of Knowledge: 'Essential Matters' 95
5.5 Sources of Knowledge: Awareness of a UN Embargo or Fact-Finding 98
5.6 Degree of Knowledge: 'Occurrence in the Ordinary Course of Events' 100
5.7 Aligning with Arms Trade Law: A Risk-based Approach 104
5.8 Appropriate Labelling of Arms Transfer Complicity 104
5.9 Conclusion 107

6. Observing ICC Legal Culture on the Arms Trade 111
6.1 Introduction 111
6.2 The Concept of 'Legal Culture' 111
6.2.1 Interpreting 'ICC Legal Culture' 114
6.2.2 Beyond 'Law versus Politics' 116
6.2.3 Identifying Legal Culture at the ICC 117
6.3 Frame 1: Obscuring the Arms Trade through an Arms Trade Law Lens 118
6.3.1 The ICC is Not a 'Regulator' of the Arms Trade 119

6.3.2 The Arms Trade is 'Already Regulated' 120
6.3.3 The ICC 'Must Defer to National Authorities' 122
6.3.4 Delineating Frame 1: International Criminal Law's Role Seen as Distinct from Arms Trade Law 123
6.4 Frame 2: Excluding the Arms Trade Due to Pragmatic Constraints 124
6.4.1 Arms Traders Pose Dangerous Security Risks to the Court 125
6.4.2 Obtaining Evidence Would Be Exceptionally Challenging 126
6.4.3 Arms Trade Investigations Involve Complex Business Structures 128
6.4.4 Delineating Frame 2: Arms Trade Cases Not Seen as Pragmatic 130
6.5 Conclusion 131

7. Imagining the Arms Trade in ICC Case Selection 133
7.1 Introduction 133
7.2 The Indeterminacy of Rules on ICC Case Selection 134
7.2.1 Case Selection 134
7.2.2 OTP Policy and Regulation 33 135
7.2.3 Legal Reasoning for Not Selecting Arms Trade Cases 136
7.2.4 Weakly Articulated Legal Grounds 137
7.3 Legalism in ICC Case Selection 140
7.3.1 Concepts of 'Legalism' 140
7.3.2 Legalism versus Aspiration in ICC Case Selection 142
7.3.3 Cognitive Dissonance: Legalism versus Aspiration 143
7.3.4 Constructing Case Selection Decisions through ICC Legal Culture 145
7.3.5 ICC Legal Culture in the Narrowing of Actors Considered in Case Selection 147
7.4 Conclusion 149

8. Investigating the Arms Trade in the Second Congo War 151
8.1 Introduction 151
8.2 A Case Study of the Second Congo War 152
8.3 Analysing Arms Flows in the Second Congo War 153
8.3.1 Background Levels of Arms Proliferation in the Great Lakes Region 154
8.3.2 Arms Transfers within the 'Pro-DRC Alliance' 155
8.3.3 Arms Transfers from Rwanda and Uganda in the 'Anti-DRC Alliance' 156
8.3.4 Weapons Followed Transnational Alliances 157
8.3.5 Arms Transfers from Outside the Great Lakes Region 158
8.3.6 The Pivotal Role of Arms Brokers 160
8.3.7 Linking Arms Transfers to Atrocity 162
8.4 Arms Export Regulation During the Second Congo War 164
8.5 Arms Embargoes During the Second Congo War 166
8.6 Politicization Critiques of Arms Embargoes 167
8.7 The Panel of Experts: Resource Extraction and Arms Trafficking 170
8.7.1 The Resource Extraction Mandate 170
8.7.2 Initial Findings on Arms Supplies 171

8.7.3 Revising the Annexes 173
8.7.4 A New Mandate on Arms Trafficking 173
8.7.5 Implicating Rwanda and Uganda 174
8.8 Conclusion 175

9. Overlooking Arms Brokers in the ICC's Situation in the DRC 177
9.1 Introduction 177
9.2 Recognizing Potential Arms Trade Cases in the DRC Situation 178
9.3 Blind Spot 1: Politically Viable Arms Trade Cases 180
9.4 Blind Spot 2: Pragmatic Arms Trade Prosecutions 183
9.5 Blind Spot 3: Imagined Victims, Imagined Perpetrators 185
9.6 Blind Spot 4: Horizontal Selectivity 190
9.7 Conclusion 193

10. Conclusion 196

Bibliography 199
Index 219

Table of Cases

INTERNATIONAL COURTS AND TRIBUNALS

ICC

Prosecutor v Ahmad Al Faqi Al Mahdi (Confirmation Decision) ICC-01/12-01/15-84 (24 March 2016) 75, 76, 80, 92–93
Prosecutor v Bosco Ntaganda (Confirmation Decision) ICC-01/04-02/06-309 (9 June 2014) 75, 76
Prosecutor v Callixte Mbarushimana (Confirmation Decision) ICC-01/04-01/10 (16 December 2011) 73, 75, 76, 77–78, 79–80, 81, 84, 85–86, 88, 91–92, 106
Prosecutor v Callixte Mbarushimana (Defence Filing) ICC-01/04-01/10-451 (26 October 2011) 194
Prosecutor v Callixte Mbarushimana (Judgment) regarding the normative and causal links to assess the actus reus of contribution: ICC-01/04-01/10-514 (30 May 2012) 88–89
Prosecutor v Charles Blé Goudé (Confirmation Decision) ICC-02/11-02/11-186 (12 December 2014) 92–93
Prosecutor v Dominic Ongwen (Confirmation Decision) ICC-02/04-01/15-422 (23 March 2016) 75, 76, 80, 92–93
Prosecutor v Germaine Katanga (Defence Filing) ICC-01/04-01/07-3369 (15 April 2013) 86, 88
Prosecutor v Germaine Katanga (Trial Judgment) ICC-01/04-01/07-3436 (7 March 2014) 73, 75, 76, 81, 82–83, 84, 85–86, 88, 95, 96–97, 101, 105, 186–87
Prosecutor v Jean-Pierre Bemba Gombo and others (Appeals Judgment) ICC-01/05-01/13-2275 (8 March 2018) 74, 92–93
Prosecutor v Jean-Pierre Bemba Gombo and others (Confirmation Decision) ICC-01/05-01/13-749 (15 November 2014) 92–93
Prosecutor v Jean-Pierre Bemba Gombo and others (Trial Judgment) ICC-01/05-01/13-1989 (19 October 2016) 74, 86, 92
Prosecutor v Laurent Gbagbo (Confirmation Decision) ICC-02/11-01/11-656 (12 June 2014) 75, 76
Prosecutor v Laurent Gbagbo and Charles Blé Goudé (Defence Filing) ICC-02/11-01/15-1198 (28 September 2018) 96–97
Prosecutor v Laurent Gbagbo and Charles Blé Goudé (Prosecution Filing) ICC-02/11-01/15-1207-Anx1 (8 November 2018) 106
Prosecutor v Laurent Gbagbo and Charles Blé Goudé (Transcript) ICC-02/11-01/15-T-223-ENG (3 October 2018) 85–86
Prosecutor v Thomas Lubanga Dyilo (Trial Judgment) ICC-01/04-01/06-2842 (14 March 2012) 84
Prosecutor v Uhuru Muigai Kenyatta (Notice) ICC-01/09-02/11-983 (5 December 2014) 125
Prosecutor v Uhuru Muigai Kenyatta (Summons Decision) ICC-01/09-02/11-1 (8 March 2011) 75, 76
Prosecutor v William Samoei Ruto and Joshua Arap Sang (Confirmation Decision) ICC-01/09-01/11-373 (23 January 2012) 75, 76, 77–78, 84, 107–8

Situation in the Democratic Republic of the Congo (Decision) ICC-01/04-1 (5 July 2004) 151–52
Situation in the Democratic Republic of the Congo (Decision) ICC-01/04-02/06-20-Anx2 (10 February 2006) 191
Situation in the Democratic Republic of the Congo (Judgment) ICC-01/04-169 (13 July 2006) 191
Situation in the Democratic Republic of Congo (Judgment) ICC-01/04-556 (19 December 2008) 185–86
Situation in the Republic of Kenya (Authorization Decision) ICC-01/09-19-Corr (31 March 2010) 134

ICJ

Application of the Convention on the Prevention and Punishment of the Crime of Genocide (Bosnia and Herzegovina v Serbia and Montenegro) (Judgment) [2007] ICJ Rep 43 50
Legality of the Threat or Use of Nuclear Weapons (Advisory Opinion) [1996] ICJ Rep 226 52–53
Military and Paramilitary Activities in and against Nicaragua (Nicaragua v United States of America) (Merits) [1986] ICJ Rep 14 52–53

ICTY

Prosecutor v Anto Furundžija (Trial Judgment) IT-95-17/1-T (10 December 1998) 81, 97–98
Prosecutor v Duško Tadić (Decision) IT-94-1-A (2 October 1995) 47
Prosecutor v Momčilo Perišić (Appeals Judgment) IT-04-81-A (28 February 2013) 4–5
Prosecutor v Pavle Strugar (Trial Judgment) IT-01-42-T (31 Jan 2005) 97
Prosecutor v Tihomir Blaškić (Appeals Judgment) IT-95-14-A (29 July 2014) 97

STL

Prosecutor v Akhbar Beirut SAL and Ibrahim Al Amin (Judgment) STL-14-06 F0262 (15 July 2016) 5
Prosecutor v Ayyash and others (Decision) STL-11-01/1 F0010 (16 February 2011) 58

SCSL

Prosecutor v Charles Ghankay Taylor (Appeals Judgment) SCSL-03-01-A-1389 (26 September 2013) 77–79, 84–85
Prosecutor v Charles Ghankay Taylor (Trial Judgment) SCSL-03-01-T (18 May 2012) 4–5, 77–78

ECtHR

Van Anraat v The Netherlands, Decision on Admissibility, App no 65389/09 (ECtHR, 6 July 2010) 21

DOMESTIC COURTS

Netherlands

Public Prosecutor v Frans Cornelis Adrianus van Anraat (Judgment) Court of Appeal of The Hague (9 May 2007) ECLI:NL:GHSGR:2007:BA4676 . . . . 21–22, 94, 99
Public Prosecutor v Frans Cornelis Adrianus van Anraat (Judgment) District Court of The Hague (23 December 2005) ECLI:NL:RBSGR:2005:AU8685 21–23

Public Prosecutor v Frans Cornelis Adrianus van Anraat (Judgment) Supreme Court of the Netherlands (30 June 2009) ECLI:NL:HR:2009:BG4822 21
Public Prosecutor v Guus Kouwenhoven (Judgment) Court of Appeal of The Hague (10 March 2008) ECLI:NL:GHSGR:2008:BC6068.........22, 100, 102–3
Public Prosecutor v Guus Kouwenhoven (Judgment) Court of Appeal of 's-Hertogenbosch (21 April 2017) ECLI:NL:GHSHE:2017:1760, English translation: ECLI:NL:GHSHE:2017:2650 22
Public Prosecutor v Guus Kouwenhoven (Judgment) District Court of The Hague (7 June 2006) ECLI:NL:RBSGR:2006:AY5160........................22
Public Prosecutor v Guus Kouwenhoven (Judgment) Supreme Court of the Netherlands (18 December 2018) ECLI:NL:HR:2018:2336............... 22, 23

UK

Johnson v Youden (1950) 1 KB 544 (KB)..98
National Coal Board v Gamble (1959) 1 QB 11 (QB)...........................91, 101–2
Re B (A Child) [2013] UKSC 33...80
R v Bryce [2004] EWCA Crim 1231 102
R v Jogee [2016] UKSC 8.. 73, 102
R (Campaign Against the Arms Trade) v Secretary of State for International Trade [2019] EWCA Civ 1020.. 23, 24
R (Campaign Against the Arms Trade) v Secretary of State for International Trade [2017] EWHC 1726 24
Trial of Bruno Tesch and two others (1947) 1 Law Reports of Trials of War Criminals 93 ....4, 66

US

Holder v Humanitarian Law Project [2010] 561 US 1................................59
United States v Alfried Krupp and others, 'Opinion and Judgment of Military Tribunal III' (31 July 1948) (1950) 9 Law Reports of the Trials of War Criminals 1327 3–4
United States v Carl Krauch and others, 'Opinion and Judgment of Military Tribunal VI' (30 July 1949) (1953) 13 Law Reports of the Trials of War Criminals 1081 4–5
United States v Victor Bout (Appeal Judgment) 27 September 2013, United States Court of Appeals for the Second Circuit, United States, 12-1487-cr 20
United States v Victor Bout (Trial Judgment) 2 November 2011, District Court for the Southern District of New York 20

Table of Primary Sources

INTERNATIONAL TREATIES AND CONVENTIONS

Arms Trade Treaty (adopted 2 April 2013, entered into force 24 December 2014) 3013 UNTS . . . 1–2, 12, 13, 16, 18, 19, 24, 29, 30, 35, 57, 60, 68, 104, 152–53, 164–65, 166
Art 1 . . . 31
Art 2 . . . 6
Art 2(1) . . . 6
Art 2(1)(h) . . . 6–7
Art 2(2) . . . 31
Art 5(2) . . . 31
Art 6 . . . 1–2, 19, 31
Art 6(1) . . . 30
Art 6(2) . . . 30
Art 6(3) . . . 30, 31
Art 7 . . . 19, 30, 31, 33–34
Art 7(3) . . . 108–9
Art 10 . . . 31
Art 14 . . . 31
Charter of the United Nations (adopted 26 June 1945, entered into force 25 October 1945) 1 UNTS XVI
Ch VII . . . 39–40, 42–43, 44–45, 46–47, 63–64
Art 2 . . . 51–53
Art 2(4) . . . 52–53
Art 2(5) . . . 51
Art 27 . . . 39–40
Art 39 . . . 39–40, 99
Art 41 . . . 39–40, 46
Art 51 . . . 52
Convention for the Protection of Human Rights and Fundamental Freedoms (adopted 4 November 1950, entered into force 3 September 1953) 213 UNTS 222 . . . 56
Convention on the Prohibition of the Development, Production, Stockpiling and Use of Chemical Weapons and on their Destruction (adopted 13 January 1993, entered into force 29 April 1997) 1975 UNTS 45
Protocol I . . . 7
Protocol II . . . 7
Protocol IV . . . 7
Protocol V . . . 7
Convention Relative to the Slave Trade and Importation into Africa of Firearms, Ammunition, and Spiritous Liquors (adopted 2 July 1890, entered into force on 31 August 1891) (Brussels Act)
Preamble . . . 32
Art 8 . . . 32
Art 10 . . . 32
Convention (V) Respecting the Rights and Duties of Neutral Powers in Case of War on Land, and Convention (adopted 18 October 1907, entered into force 26 January 1910) . . . 53
Art 7 . . . 54
Convention (XIII) concerning the Rights and Duties of Neutral Powers in Naval War. The Hague (adopted 18 October 1907, entered into force 26 January 1910)
Art 1 . . . 55
Art 6 . . . 53
Covenant of the League of Nations (signed 28 June 1919, entered into force 10 January 1920)
Art 23(d) . . . 32–33
General Agreement on Tariffs and Trade (adopted 30 October 1947, entered into force 1 January 1948) 55 UNTS 187
Art 21 . . . 61–62
Geneva Convention for the Amelioration of the Condition of the Wounded and Sick in Armed Forces in the Field (adopted 12 August 1949, entered into force 21 October 1950) 75 UNTS 31 . . . 30
Art 1 . . . 55
Art 63 . . . 53

Protocol Additions to the Geneva Conventions of 12 August 1949, and Relating to the Protection of Victims of International Armed Conflicts (adopted 8 June 1977, entered into force 7 December 1979) 1125 UNTS 3
- Art 1 55

International Committee of the Red Cross, Commentary of 2016 on the First Geneva Convention of 12 August 1949 (2016) 162 55

International Convention for the Suppression of Acts of Nuclear Terrorism (adopted 13 April 2005, entered into force 7 July 2007) 2445 UNTS 89
- Art 2(4)(c) 105

International Convention for the Suppression of the Financing of Terrorism (adopted 9 December 1999, entered into force 10 April 2002) 2178 UNTS 197 58–59
- Art 2(1) 58–59
- Art 2(5)(a) 58–59
- Art 2(5)(c) 58–59

International Convention for the Suppression of Terrorist Bombings (adopted 15 December 1997, entered into force on 23 May 2001) 2149 UNTS 256 . . . . . 58–59, 104–5
- Art 2(3) 58–59
- Art 2(3)(c) 88–89, 107

International Covenant on Civil and Political Rights (adopted 16 December 1966, entered into force 23 March 1976) 999 UNTS 171 56

International Criminal Tribunal for the former Yugoslavia (ICTY) Statute
- Art 6 5
- Art 7(1) 71–72, 74

International Criminal Tribunal for ICTR Statute Rwanda (ICTR) Statute
- Art 5 5
- Art 6(1) 71–72, 74

Nuremberg Charter
- Art 6 75
- Art 10 75

Rome Statute of the International Criminal Court (adopted 17 July 1998, entered into force 1 July 2002) 2187 UNTS 105 . . . . . 1, 6, 13, 24, 30, 35, 40, 51–52, 58, 70, 105, 111, 133, 136–37, 139–40, 142–43, 144, 148–49, 152–53, 179, 180–81, 187–88, 193–94, 196, 197
- Art 6 48–49
- Art 7 48–49
- Art 8 48–49
- Art 13 99
- Art 13(b) 47, 99
- Art 15 . . . . . 25, 134
- Art 17 . . . . . 135, 137, 184
- Art 17(3) 48
- Art 20(3) 48–49
- Art 21 . . . . . 70, 72, 106–7
- Art 25 . . . . . 70, 71, 72, 88, 106–8, 137, 141–42, 184
- Art 25(1) 5, 130
- Art 25(3) 94, 139
- Art 25(3)(a) 77–78, 84
- Art 25(3)(c) 3, 16, 71, 72–73, 74–75, 77–78, 91–94, 139
- Art 25(3)(d) 3, 71, 72–73, 74, 75, 76, 77, 78, 80, 81, 84–85, 88–89, 92, 93–95, 101, 103, 104–5, 106–7, 139
- Art 25(3)(d)(i) 94, 95–96
- Art 25(3)(d)(ii) 3, 16, 17, 70, 71, 74–77, 78–79, 82–83, 84, 85–87, 89, 90, 91–92, 94, 95–97, 98, 99, 100, 101, 103, 106–8, 109, 138–39, 177, 196–97
- Art 28 . . . . . 71, 92, 109–10, 111
- Art 29 194
- Art 30 101
- Art 30(3) 101
- Art 53 . . . . . 134, 135, 185–86
- Art 53(1)(c) 185–86, 188
- Art 58 134
- Art 89(4) 48–49

Special Court for Sierra Leone (SCSL) Statute
- Art 6(1) 71–72, 74

Statute of the Special Tribunal for Lebanon 58

Vienna Convention on the Law of Treaties (adopted 23 May 1969, entered into force 27 January 1980) 1155 UNTS 331
Art 31(1) 88

UN SECURITY COUNCIL RESOLUTIONS

UNSC Res 181 (1963) UN Doc S/RES/181
para 3 41
UNSC Res 182 (1963) UN Doc S/RES/182
para 5 42
UNSC Res 282 (1970) UN Doc S/RES/282
Preamble 43
para 1(4)(b) 42
para 1(4)(c) 42
para 1(4)(d) 42
para 1(4)(e) 42
para 1(4)(f) 42
UNSC Res 418 (1977) UN Doc S/RES/418 43
Preamble 43
paras 2–4 42
UNSC Res 421 (1977) UN Doc S/RES/421 43
UNSC Res 558 (1984) UN Doc S/RES/558 42
UNSC Res 591 (1986) UN Doc S/RES/591
paras 1–2 42
para 3 42
para 6 42
para 10 42
para 11 42
UNSC Res 661 (1990) UN Doc S/RES/661 21–22
UNSC Res 713 (1991) UN Doc S/RES/713
para 6 .... 41, 44
UNSC Res 794 (1992) UN Doc S/RES/794 40
UNSC Res 827 (1993) UN Doc S/RES/827 47
UNSC Res 919 (1994) UN Doc S/RES/919 42
UNSC Res 929 (1994) UN Doc S/RES/929 40
UNSC Res 955 (1994) UN Doc S/RES/955 47
UNSC Res 997 (1995) UN Doc S/RES/997 168
UNSC Res 1078 (1996) UN Doc S/RES/1078 40
UNSC Res 1173 (1998) UN Doc S/RES/1173 168
UNSC Res 1267 (1999) UN Doc S/RES/1267 59
UNSC Res 1333 (2000) UN Doc S/RES/1333 59
UNSC Res 1373 (2001) UN Doc S/RES/1373 46–47
para 2(e) 59
UNSC Res 1493 (2003) UN Doc S/RES/1493 .... 166, 173–74
UNSC Res 1499 (2003) UN Doc S/RES/1499
para 6 173–74
UNSC Res 1533 (2004) UN Doc S/RES/1533 167
UNSC Res 1540 (2004) UN Doc S/RES/1540 46–47
UNSC Res 1593 (2005) UN Doc S/RES/1593 .... 47, 63–64
UNSC Res 1596 (2005) UN Doc S/RES/1596 167
UNSC Res 1636 (2005) UN Doc S/RES/1636
para 3 47
para 11 47
para 19 47
para 21 47
UNSC Res 1970 (2011) UN Doc S/RES/1970 47

UN REPORTS AND OTHER DOCUMENTS

OHCHR, 'Legally Binding Instrument to Regulate, in International Human Rights Law, the Activities of Transnational Corporations and other Business Enterprises' (16 July 2019) No UN Doc number <www.ohchr.org/EN/HRBodies/HRC/WGTransCorp/Session5/Pages/Session5.aspx> accessed 4 August 2024 57

OHCHR, 'Report of the Independent International Commission of Inquiry on the Syrian Arab Republic' (5 February 2015) UN Doc A/HRC/28/69 34–35
OHCHR, 'Report of the Mapping Exercise documenting the most serious violations of human rights and international humanitarian law committed within the territory of the Democratic Republic of the Congo between March 1993 and June 2003' (August 2010) <www.ohchr.org/EN/Countries/AfricaRegion/Pages/RDCProjetMapping.aspx> accessed 4 August 2024 162
OTP, 'Draft paper on some policy issues before the Office of the Prosecutor for discussion at the public hearing in The Hague on 17 and 18 June 2003' (18 June 2003) <www.legal-tools.org/doc/abb 9f7/> accessed 10 May 2020 .178–79
OTP, 'Paper on some policy issues before the Office of the Prosecutor' (5 September 2003) <www. legal-tools.org/doc/f53 870/> accessed 10 May 2020 . . . . .178–79, 190–91
Preamble. 178–79
OTP, 'Policy Paper on the Interests of Justice' (ICC Legal Tools Database, 1 September 2007) <www.legal- tools.org/doc/bb0 2e5/a6> accessed 4 August 2024 . . .186
UNGA, 'Draft Articles on the Responsibility of States for Internationally Wrongful Acts, Report of the ILC on the Work of its Fifty-third Session' (2001) UN Doc A/56/10 50
Art 16. 50–51
Art 21. 52–53
Art 25(4). 51
Art 41(1). 50–51
Art 41(2). 50–51
Art 41(2)[ii] 50–51
UNGA, 'Report of the Ad Hoc Committee established by UNGA Resolution 51/210 (17 December 1996)' (1997) UN Doc A/52/37 88–89
UNGA, 'Report of the Group of Governmental Experts established pursuant to General Assembly resolution 54/54 V' (15 December 1999). 165–66
UNGA, 'Report of the Group of Governmental Experts established pursuant to General Assembly resolution 60/81 to consider further steps to enhance international cooperation in preventing, combating and eradicating illicit brokering in small arms and light weapons' (30 August 2007) UN Doc A/62/163
para 8. 9–10
UNGA Res 55/255, 'Protocol against the Illicit Manufacturing of and Trafficking in Firearms, Their Parts and Components and Ammunition, supplementing the United Nations Convention against Transnational Organized Crime' (adopted 31 May 2001, entered into force on 3 July 2005) UN Doc A/RES/55/255. . . . . 33, 60, 188–89
UNGA, 'SADC Council Decisions, 13-14 August 1999: Prevention and Combating of Illicit Trafficking in Small Arms and Related Crimes' (21 October 1999) UN Doc A/54/488, S/1999/1082 .165
UNGA, 'United Nations Conference on the Illicit Trade in Small Arms and Light Weapons in All Its Aspects that took place on 9 to 20 July 2001' (2001) UN Doc A/CONF.192/15 (UN PoA). 6–7, 33, 60, 165–66, 188–89
UNHRC, 'General Comment No. 35: Article 9 (Liberty and security of person)' (16 December 2014) UN Doc CCPR/C/GC/36 56
UNHRC, 'General Comment No. 36: Article 6: right to life' (3 September 2019) UN Doc CCPR/C/GC/36 56
UNODC, 'Comparative Analysis of Global Instruments on Firearms and Other Conventional Arms: Synergies for Implementation'

(2016) <www.unodc.org/unodc/en/firearms-protocol/publications.html> accessed 4 August 2024... 60
UNSC, 'Addendum to the Final Report of the Panel of Experts on the Illegal Exploitation of Natural Resources and Other Forms of Wealth of the Democratic Republic of the Congo' (20 June 2003) UN Doc S/2002/1146.Add1..........173
UNSC, 'Addendum to the Report of the Panel of Experts on the Illegal Exploitation of Natural Resources and Other Forms of Wealth of the Democratic Republic of the Congo' (13 November 2001) UN Doc S/2001/1072
para 67..........................172
para 91..........................172
para 95..........................172
para 136..........................172
UNSC, 'Final report of the Group of Experts on the DRC submitted in accordance with paragraph 8 of Security Council resolution 1857 (2008)' (23 November 2009) UN Doc S/2009/603
para 344..........................194
UNSC, 'Final Report of the Panel of Experts on the Illegal Exploitation of Natural Resources and Other Forms of Wealth of the Democratic Republic of the Congo' (16 October 2002) UN Doc S/2002/1146 172
paras 29–31 172
UNSC, 'Final Report of the Panel of Experts on the Illegal Exploitation of Natural Resources and Other Forms of Wealth of the Democratic Republic of the Congo' (23 October 2003) UN Doc S/2003/1027 ..... 173–74, 179, 180
para 47........................ 173–74
UNSC, 'Interim report of the Group of Experts on the DRC submitted in accordance with paragraph 8 of Security Council resolution 1857 (2008)' (18 May 2009) UN Doc S/2009/253
paras 89–90 194
UNSC, 'Interim Report of the Panel of Experts on South Sudan Established Pursuant to Security Council Resolution 2206 (2015)' (21 August 2015) UN Doc S/2015/656...................28, 46
UNSC, 'Interim report of the United Nations Expert Panel on the Illegal Exploitation of Natural Resources and Other Forms of Wealth of the Democratic Republic of the Congo' (16 January 2001) UN Doc S/2001/49 170–71
UNSC, 'Interim report of the United Nations Expert Panel on the Illegal Exploitation of Natural Resources and Other Forms of Wealth of the Democratic Republic of the Congo' (22 May 2002) UN Doc S/2002/565.......... 170–71, 172
UNSC, 'Letter from the Secretary-General' (14 August 2000) UN Doc S/2000/796 170
UNSC, 'Report of the Panel of Experts appointed pursuant to Security Council resolution 1306 (2000), paragraph 19, in relation to Sierra Leone' (20 December 2000) UN Doc. S/2000/1195 ... 22–23
UNSC, 'Report of the Panel of Experts on the Illegal Exploitation of Natural Resources and Other Forms of Wealth of the Democratic Republic of the Congo' (12 April 2001) UN Doc S/2001/357......... 172
para 73....................... 171–72
para 74....................... 171–72
para 91....................... 171–72
para 215....................... 171–72
UNSC, 'Report of the Security Council Committee Established by Resolution 421 (1977) Concerning the Question of South Africa on Ways and Means of Making the Mandatory Arms Embargo Against South Africa More Effective' (19 September 1990) UN Doc S/14179............43
UNSC, 'Statement by the President of the Security Council' (2 June 2000) UN Doc S/PRST/2000/20 170–71

EUROPEAN UNION TREATIES AND DOCUMENTS

Common List of Equipment Covered by the Code of Conduct [2000] OJ C19 33–34
Convention Relating to Extradition between the Member states of the European Union [1996] OJ C313/11. 105
Art 3(4) 104–5, 107
Council Common Position 2002/829/CFSP of 21 October 2002 on the supply of certain equipment into the Democratic Republic of Congo [2002] OJ L285/1. 166
Council Common Position 2003/468/CFSP on the control of arms brokering [2003] OJ L156. 33–34
Council Common Position 2003/680/CFSP of 29 September 2003 [2003] OJ L249/64 167
Council Common Position 2008/944/CFSP of 8 December 2008 defining common rules governing control of exports of military technology and equipment [2008] OJ L335/99. 13
Art 2. 19
Art 2(2)(c) 108–9
Council Decision 2011/273/CFSP of 9 May 2011 concerning restrictive measures against Syria [2011] OJ L121/11
Art 1. 41
Art 2. 41
Art 3. 41
Council Regulation (EC) No 1727/2003 of 29 September 2003 concerning certain restrictive measures in respect of the Democratic Republic of Congo [2003] OJ L249/5 167
Council Regulation (EU) No 36/2012 of 18 January 2012 concerning restrictive measures in view of the situation in Syria and repealing Regulation (EU) No 442/2011 [2012] OJ L16/1 .41
Council Regulation (EU) No 442/2011 of 9 May 2011 concerning restrictive measures in view of the situation in Syria [2011] OJ L121/1
Annex 1. 41
Council Regulation (EU) No 509/2012 of 15 June 2012 amending Regulation (EU) No 36/2012 concerning restrictive measures in view of the situation in Syria [2012] OJ L156/10 41
Declaration (EC) 33/93 on Zaire (entered into force 7 April 1993) [1993] 166
Directive (EU) 2017/541 of the European Parliament and of the Council of 15 March 2017 on combating terrorism and replacing Council Framework Decision 2002/475/JHA and amending Council Decision 2005/671/JHA [2017] OJ L88
Art 8. 59
European Union Code of Conduct on Arms Exports [1998] Doc 8675/2/98 REV 2 33–34
Explanatory Report on the Convention relating to extradition between the Member states of the European Union [1997] OJ C191/13. . . . . .33–34, 104–5
Joint Action of 3 December 1998 adopted by the Council on the basis of Article K.3 of the Treaty on European Union, on money laundering, the identification, tracing, freezing, seizing and confiscation of instrumentalities and the proceeds from crime [1998] OJ L333 33–34

UNITED STATES LEGISLATION

Alien Tort Act. 120
Arms Export Control Act 22 USC
§ 2751 (2014). 61
§ 2773 164–65
Foreign Assistance Appropriation Act 164–65
Foreign Corrupt Practices Act 15 USC §78dd-1 (1977). 61
International Traffic in Arms Regulations 22 CFR §120, 126.7 (2014). 61
Model Penal Code
Art 2.06(3) 91

REGIONAL AGREEMENTS

Amendments to the Model Regulations for the Control of the International Movement of Firearms, their Parts and Components, and Ammunition: Broker Regulations (13 November 2003) Doc OEA/ Ser.L/XIV.2.34. 33–34
AU, African Common Position to the Review Conference on Progress Made in the Implementation of the UN Programme of Action to Prevent, Combat and Eradicate the Illicit Trade in Small Arms and Light Weapons in All Its Aspects (adopted 16 December 2005) 165
Declaration of Bogota: Inter-American Convention Against the Illicit Manufacturing of and Trafficking in Firearms, Ammunition, Explosives, and Other Related Materials (adopted 9 March 2004) Doc OEA/Ser.L/XXII.4. 33–34
Inter-American Convention Against the Illicit Manufacturing of and Trafficking in Firearms, Ammunition, Explosives, and Other Related Materials (adopted 14 November 1997, entered into force 1 July 1998) Doc A63 33–34
Inter-American Convention on Transparency in Conventional Weapons Acquisitions (adopted 6 July 1999) Doc A-64 33–34
Nairobi Declaration on the Problem of the Proliferation of Illicit Small Arms and Light Weapons in the Great Lakes Region and the Horn of Africa (signed 15 March 2000) 165
Nairobi Protocol for the Prevention, Control and Reduction of Small Arms and Light Weapons in the Great Lakes Region and the Horn of Africa (adopted 21 April 2004, entered into force 5 May 2005) 165
OAU, Bamako Declaration on an African Common Position on the Illicit Proliferation, Circulation and Trafficking of Small Arms and Light Weapons (adopted 1 December 2000) 165
OSCE Document on Stockpiles of Conventional Ammunition (19 November 2003) Doc FSC1/03 33–34
OSCE Handbook of Best Practices on Conventional Ammunition (25 October 2007) Doc FSC73/07. 33–34
OSCE Principles Governing Conventional Arms Transfers (adopted 25 November 1993) Doc FSC/3/96. 33–34
SADC, The Protocol on the Control of Firearms, Ammunition and Other Related Material in the Southern African Development Community Region (adopted 14 August 2001, entered into force 8 November 2004) 165
Wassenaar Arrangement on Export Controls for Conventional Arms and Dual-Goods and Technologies (adopted and entered into force 19 December 1995) 33–34

OTHER PRIMARY SOURCES

Assembly of States Parties, 'ASP 14th Session Resolution 1' (16 November 2015) ICC-ASP/14/Res.1. 115
Fatou Bensouda, 'Full Statement on external expert review and lessons drawn from the Kenya situation' (26 November 2019) <www.legal-tools.org/doc/32p2hy/> accessed 4 August 2024 115
Luis Moreno Ocampo, 'Report of the Prosecutor of the ICC' (Second Assembly of States Parties to the Rome Statute of the International Criminal Court, 8 September 2003) <www.legal-tools.org/doc/8873bd/> accessed 24 June 2020. . . . . .1, 177

Madeleine Albright, 'Statement by Secretary of State Madeleine Albright to the UN Security Council Ministerial on Small Arms' (New York, 24 September 1999) 164–65
OPCW, Third Report of the OPCW Fact-Finding Mission in Syria (18 December 2014) Doc S/1230/2014 34–35
US Executive Office of the President, 'Strategy to Combat Transnational Organized Crime: Addressing Converging Threats to National Security' (National Security Council, 25 July 2011) <https://obamawhitehouse.archives.gov/administration/eop/nsc/transnational-crime> accessed 4 August 2024 8
US State Department, Bureau of Intelligence, 'Arms Flows to Central Africa/Great Lakes Fact Sheet' (November 1999) <https://1997-2001.state.gov/global/arms/bureau_pm/fs_9911_armsflows.html> accessed 26 June 2020 164–65
US State Department, 'Section 655 Annual Report for Fiscal Year 1998' (30 June 1999). 164–65

Abbreviations

ADF	Allied Democratic Forces
ARSIWA	Articles on Responsibility of States for Internationally Wrongful Acts
ASECNA	Safety of Air Navigation in Africa and Madagascar
ASP	Assembly of States Parties
ATT	Arms Trade Treaty
AU	African Union
CAAT	Campaign Against the Arms Trade
CAR	Central African Republic
DRC	Democratic Republic of the Congo
EC	European Commission
ECCC	Extraordinary Chambers in the Courts of Cambodia
ECHR	European Convention on Human Rights
ECOWAS	The Economic Community of West African States
ECtHR	European Court of Human Rights
ESG	Environmental, Social and Governance
EU	European Union
ex-FAR	former Rwandan Armed Forces
FAC	Congolese Armed Forces
FARC	Revolutionary Armed Forces of Colombia
IACHR	Inter-American Convention on Human Rights
ICC	International Criminal Court
ICCPR	International Covenant on Civil and Political Rights
ICJ	International Court of Justice
ICRC	International Committee of the Red Cross
ICTR	International Criminal Tribunal for Rwanda
ICTY	International Criminal Tribunal for the former Yugoslavia
ILC	International Law Commission
IMF	International Monetary Fund
IMT	International Military Tribunal
ITAR	International Traffic in Arms Regulations
JCE	Joint Criminal Enterprise
MCW	Major Conventional Weapons
MONUC	United Nations Organization Mission in the Democratic Republic of the Congo
NATO	North Atlantic Treaty Organization
NGO	Non-Governmental Organization
OAS	Organization of American States
OAU	Organization of African Unity
OECD	Organization for Economic Cooperation and Development

OHCHR	Office of the United Nations High Commissioner for Human Rights
OPCW	Organization for the Prohibition of Chemical Weapons
OSCE	Organization for Security and Co-operation in Europe
OTP	Office of the Prosecutor of the International Criminal Court
PTC	Pre-Trial Chamber
RCD	Rassemblement congolais pour la démocratie
RPA	Rwandan Patriotic Army
SADC	Southern African Development Community
SALW	Small Arms and Light Weapons
SCSL	Special Court for Sierra Leone
SRI	Socially Responsible Investing
STL	Special Tribunal for Lebanon
UN	United Nations
UNDP	United Nations Development Programme
UNGA	United Nations General Assembly
UNHRC	United Nations Human Rights Committee
UNITA	União Nacional para a Independência Total de Angola
UN ITI	United Nations International Tracing Instrument
UNODA	United Nations Department for Disarmament Affairs
UNODC	United Nations Office of Drugs and Crime
UN PoA	United Nations Programme of Action on Small Arms and Light Weapons
UNSC	United Nations Security Council
UNTOC	United Nations Convention against Transnational Organized Crime
UNTS	United Nations Treaty Series
UPDF	Uganda People's Defence Forces
VCLT	Vienna Convention on the Law of Treaties
WCO	World Customs Organization
WTO	World Trade Organization
WWI	World War I
WWII	World War II
ZDF	Zimbabwe Defence Forces

1
Introduction

1.1 Introduction

'Those who (...) provide weapons could also be authors of the crimes'.
Luis Moreno Ocampo, former Prosecutor of
the International Criminal Court[1]

At the turn of the twenty-first century, the International Criminal Court (ICC) ushered in a new era for the investigation and prosecution of international crimes committed since 1 July 2002.[2] From the inception of the ICC, its first Prosecutor implicated the potential role of arms traders in war crimes and crimes against humanity. On 8 September 2003, prior to the opening of investigations in the Democratic Republic of Congo (DRC), Luis Moreno Ocampo had announced that arms traders were potential targets for prosecution. Those who provided weapons, he said, could be 'authors of the crimes', even if based in other countries.[3]

In doing so, the Prosecutor was not the first to recognize the position at international law—while the arms trade serves legitimate military and security purposes—individuals may be held criminally responsible for knowingly providing the means of commission of international crimes. The Prosecutor echoed the commitment of Justice Robert H Jackson at Nuremberg to investigate not only political and military suspects, but also those 'in the financial, industrial, and economic life of Germany who by all civilized standards are provable to be common criminals'.[4]

Likewise, the Prosecutor echoed those who had pointed to the role of arms export policies in atrocities in Rwanda,[5] Cambodia,[6] and Yemen,[7] those who argued

[1] Luis Moreno Ocampo, 'Report of the Prosecutor of the ICC Second Assembly of States Parties to the Rome Statute of the International Criminal Court (*ICC Legal Tools Database*, 8 September 2003) 4–5<www.legal-tools.org/doc/8873bd/> accessed 24 June 2020.

[2] Rome Statute of the International Criminal Court (adopted 17 July 1998, entered into force 1 July 2002) 2187 UNTS 105 ('Rome Statute').

[3] Ocampo (n 1) 4–5.

[4] Robert H Jackson, 'Justice Jackson's Report to President Truman on the Legal Basis for Trial of War Criminals' (1946) 19 Temple Law Quarterly 149.

[5] Stephen Goose and Frank Smyth, 'Arming Genocide in Rwanda' (1994) 73 Foreign Affairs 86, 91.

[6] John Ciorciari, 'China and the Pol Pot Regime' (2014) 14 Cold War History 215, 233, 235.

[7] Shavana Musa, 'The Saudi-Led Coalition in Yemen, Arms Exports and Human Rights: Prevention Is Better Than Cure' (2017) 22 Journal of Conflict and Security Law 433, 439.

The Arms Trade and International Criminal Law. Tomas Hamilton, Oxford University Press. © Tomas Hamilton 2025.
DOI: 10.1093/oso/9780192868671.003.0001

for UN Security Council arms embargoes to be imposed for allegations of international crimes,[8] and those who had advocated for the Arms Trade Treaty (ATT) to include provisions on international crimes and other serious human rights abuses.[9] And those who would subsequently conclude '[t]he trade in weapons is the most corrupt and unaccountable of all global trades'.[10]

More immediately, he echoed NGO and civil society advocacy that had publicized the findings of a UN Panel of Experts about the involvement of Rwanda and Uganda in arms transfers to non-state armed groups in the DRC.[11] And more broadly, the Prosecutor echoed the perspective of victims of atrocity around the world who recognized the harms they suffered were attributable not only to the soldier who pulled the trigger but to the arms dealer who profited from providing the weapons. In a world 'drowning in guns',[12] the Prosecutor echoed an increasing recognition of the structural—less visible—causes of systemic mass violence.

The Prosecutor's fanfare in the DRC Situation did not lead to arrest warrants or criminal charges against an arms trader at the ICC. In contrast to Jackson's approach at Nuremberg, which led to Post-World War II cases against individuals who armed the Nazi regime and provided Zyklon B gas used in concentration camps,[13] the ICC has never selected a case for the commercial supply of the physical means of commission of crimes.

This accountability gap forms the subject of the book. It examines the legal basis in international law for holding individuals responsible for supplying weapons to the perpetrators of genocide, war crimes, crimes against humanity, and aggression; the book looks at the unrealized potential of International Criminal Law to reinforce the existing system of arms embargoes, domestic arms export regulations, international agreements, and other subsidiary sources of transnational arms regulation. It then turns to focus on the institutional culture of the ICC to ask why, in practice, the legal basis for complicity in the Rome Statute has not led to prosecutions based on weapons supply.

[8] Raymond Paretzky, 'The United States Arms Embargo Against South Africa: An Analysis of the Laws, Regulations, and Loopholes' (1987) 12 Yale Journal of International Law 133.

[9] The Arms Trade Treaty (adopted 2 April 2013, entered into force 24 December 2014) 3013 UNTS, art 6. See Andrew Clapham, 'Article 6' in Andrew Clapham and others, *The Arms Trade Treaty: A Commentary* (OUP 2016) 204.

[10] Andrew Feinstein and Paul Holden, 'The Failure of Regulation of the Global Arms Trade as a Consequence of High-Level Conflicts in Interest' (2020) 27 Brown Journal of World Affairs 23.

[11] Human Rights Watch, 'Democratic Republic of Congo: The Curse of Gold' (Human Rights Watch, 2 June 2005) 25; Amnesty International, 'Democratic Republic of Congo: Arming the East' (Amnesty International, 4 July 2005).

[12] Harold Hongju Koh, 'A World Drowning in Guns' (2002) 71 Fordham Law Review, 2333.

[13] See Chapter 5.

1.2 Arms Traders as Accomplices

A central claim of this book is that some conduct in the arms trade is criminalized by the doctrines of accomplice liability in the Rome Statute, yet the scope of these doctrines is narrowed in practice by normative beliefs as to whether arms traders are rightful targets for prosecution. At the ICC, the legal basis in the Rome Statute to hold the arms trade to account is revealed as contingent on whether the Court's judges and lawyers believe that the aims and purposes of the Court include investigating and prosecuting arms traders. In building this claim, the book analyses the Rome Statute provisions on complicit assistance: aiding or abetting under Article 25(3)(c) and assisting under Article 25(3)(d). For reasons that will be explained, the book focuses on the latter provision, Article 25(3)(d), specifically on subsection (ii), which provides for the liability of an arms trader who 'contributes [in any other way] to the commission or attempted commission of [a crime] by a group of persons acting with a common purpose [...] in the knowledge of the intention of the group to commit the crime'.

A specific interpretation of Article 25(3)(d)(ii) of the Rome Statute is proposed in this book, which provides a legal basis for the complicity of some arms traders in both the lawful and illicit sectors of the global trade. The *ex post facto* accountability offered by International Criminal Law is thus shown to hold potential to complement the existing transnational system of Arms Trade Law (described in this book as 'Arms Trade Law') that is primarily directed at pre-emptive prevention.

The book then uses this doctrinal analysis as a springboard for an empirical study of the ICC's institutional culture, to better understand and explain why the ICC's complicity doctrines are not being fully enforced in practice, and to explore a case study of the Situation in the DRC. The potential of International Criminal Law is seen as particularly potent for small-scale arms brokers, transporters, and 'micro-traders' who have played an important role in funnelling weapon supplies into conflict zones, as seen in the Second Congo War, and for whom existing regulation is limited or ineffective.

The potential for accomplice liability of individuals working in the arms trade has existed for a long history in doctrine, yet there have been only limited instances of enforcement. Amongst the cases of international and internationalized jurisdictions heard by the post-World War II tribunals, the International Criminal Tribunal for the former Yugoslavia (ICTY), the International Criminal Tribunal for Rwanda (ICTR), the Special Court for Sierra Leone (SCSL), the Special Tribunal for Lebanon (STL), the Extraordinary Chambers in the Courts of Cambodia (ECCC), and the ICC, only a handful of cases involved charges of the commercial supply of items used to commit international crimes.

First, the industrialist Gustav Krupp was indicted by the International Military Tribunal at Nuremberg (IMT) for his role in Nazi Germany's major arms manufacturing corporation, Krupp AG, but he did not stand trial.[14] His son, Alfred Krupp, however, was tried by a US Military Tribunal in Nuremberg for his role in the corporation but was acquitted. His acquittal was based, inter alia, on a lack of knowledge of the intentions of the German government.[15]

Second, in a case involving the supply of prussic acid, in the form of the pesticide known as Zyklon B, used in the gas chambers of Auschwitz and other concentration camps, two agents of the German firm *Tesch and Stabenow* were convicted by a British Military Court at Hamburg in 1946 for war crimes, and sentenced to death by hanging.[16] According to the prosecution, the defendants had known that the gas was to be used for murder.[17]

Third, twenty-four senior employees of the IG Farben corporation were tried by a US Military Tribunal in Nuremberg in 1949 for their role in equipping the Nazi regime, also including the supply of toxic gas.[18] The managers of the company were acquitted on the charges relating to supplies to the concentration camps due to their lack of knowledge of the intended criminal use of the gas.

It is notable that, at the IMT and subsequent military tribunals, arms traders were prosecuted as amongst the types of perpetrators envisaged as part of international criminal justice. This view seems to have fallen away in the 1990s era of international accountability as there have been no further indictments of arms traders at the international criminal tribunals.[19] The cases of *Taylor* at the SCSL,[20] *Perišić* at the ICTY,[21] and *Katanga* at the ICC[22] included charges that relied on allegations that the accused had supplied weapons, but the defendants also had

14 See Volker Nerlich, 'Core Crimes and Transnational Business Corporations' (2010) 8 Journal of International Criminal Justice 895; Linde Bryk and Miriam Saage-Maaß, 'Individual Criminal Liability for Arms Exports under the ICC Statute: A Case Study of Arms Exports from Europe to Saudi-led Coalition Members Used in the War in Yemen' (2019) 17 Journal of International Criminal Justice 1116, 1119.

15 See *United States v Alfried Krupp and others*, 'Opinion and Judgment of Military Tribunal III' (31 July 1948) (1950) 9 *Law Reports of the Trials of War Criminals* 1327; Bryk and Saage-Maaß (n 14) 1120. The IMT might have tried Alfred Krupp had the judges not refused a motion for him to replace Gustav Krupp. See Christopher Burchard, 'Ancillary and Neutral Business Contributions to "Corporate-Political Core Crime": Initial Enquiries Concerning the Rome Statute' (2010) 8 Journal of International Criminal Justice 919, fn 2.

16 *Trial of Bruno Tesch and Two Others* (1–8 March 1946) (1947) 1 *Law Reports of Trials of War Criminals* 93. See Hans Vest, 'Business Leaders and the Modes of Individual Criminal Responsibility under International Law' (2010) 8 Journal of International Criminal Justice 864, fn 13. See Nerlich (n 14) 901.

17 *Trial of Bruno Tesch* (n 16) 100–01.

18 See *United States v Carl Krauch and others*, 'Opinion and Judgment of Military Tribunal VI' (30 July 1949) (1953) 13 *Law Reports of the Trials of War Criminals* 1081, 1167–71. See Florian Jeßberger, 'On the Origins of Individual Criminal Responsibility under International Law for Business Activity: IG Farben on Trial' (2010) 8 Journal of International Criminal Justice 783.

19 Burchard (n 15) 919.

20 *Prosecutor v Charles Ghankay Taylor* (Trial Judgment) SCSL-03-01-T (18 May 2012) paras 6909–6915.

21 *Prosecutor v Momčilo Perišić* (Appeals Judgment) IT-04-81-A (28 February 2013) para 49.

22 *United States v Krauch and others* (n 18) 1169.

military and political roles and these cases are distinct from the scenario of a disinterested commercial actor whose intention is only to profit from supplying weapons.[23] As discussed below, in cases such as these, the defendants' arms transfer conduct is often used as a source of evidence to prove a causal link for the defendants' liability as a principal perpetrator of an international crime. As such, transferring arms was not recognized as a criminally complicit contribution in itself, but was being used to establish a causal connection for the purposes of other charges.

At the national level, the Dutch cases of *Van Anraat* and *Kouwenhoven* analysed in Chapter 2 appear to be the only recent examples of arms traders charged for their complicity in international crimes. As Burchard comments, the 'vision' of Justice Robert H Jackson to target economic actors 'has yet to become a reality in modern international criminal justice, which to date has focused on political and military, but not business, figureheads'.[24]

These cases concern individuals, rather than the companies themselves. The Rome Statute does not at present provide for liability of the legal person of corporations that manufacture and distribute weapons, as set out in Article 25(1).[25] This is consistent with the Statutes of the ICTY and ICTR.[26] Most likely, the SCSL and ECCC could not have exercised jurisdiction beyond natural persons.[27] The STL found itself to have jurisdiction over legal persons in contempt proceedings and rendered the first 'unprecedented and potentially revolutionary'[28] conviction of a corporation under International Criminal Law.[29] Outside of a specific treaty framework, International Criminal Law can nonetheless impose obligations on corporations.[30] Despite its exclusion of corporate liability, nothing in the Rome Statute would prevent liability of natural persons who work as part of corporate or other organizational structures for their individual decision-making capacity in the arms trade.

[23] Nina Jørgensen, Charles Taylor Inc: Lessons from the Trial of a President, Businessman and Warlord' in Jørgensen (ed), *International Criminal Responsibility of War's Funders and Profiteers* (CUP 2020).

[24] Burchard (n 15) 920.

[25] Art 25(1) provides that 'the Court shall have jurisdiction over natural persons pursuant to this Statute'.

[26] ICTY Statute, art 6; ICTR Statute, art 5.

[27] Norman Farrell, 'Attributing Criminal Liability to Corporate Actors: Some Lessons from the International Tribunals' (2010) 8 Journal of International Criminal Justice 873, fn 5.

[28] Matthew Gillett, 'Testing the Limits of the Law against Those Who Test the Tribunal's Limits: Contempt Proceedings at the Special Tribunal for Lebanon' (2017) 15 Journal of International Criminal Justice 775, 784.

[29] *Prosecutor v Akhbar Beirut SAL and Ibrahim Al Amin* (Judgment) STL-14-06 F0262 (15 July 2016).

[30] Clapham (n 9) 902.

1.3 Unpacking the Global Arms Trade: Items, Actors, Conduct

In this book, 'international crime' and 'International Criminal Law' are defined in terms of the 'core crimes' of international law, or 'international crimes *sensu stricto*', corresponding to the Rome Statute and its Kampala amendment: genocide, crimes against humanity, war crimes, and the crime of aggression.[31] The definition of international crimes overlaps with serious violations of human rights.[32] International criminal law attributes responsibility for personal behaviour and, ultimately, the only question of interest to a criminal tribunal is whether the defendant can be convicted for what they did as an individual. Within the global arms trade and its plurality of *actors* transferring numerous types of *items*, which forms of individual *conduct* are of interest? Here are some brief comments on terminology, concept, and scope.

1.3.1 Types of 'Items'

International and domestic laws have established categories of arms, dual-use items, ammunition, and parts. Conventional weapons are defined in Article 2 of the ATT. They include what are often referred to as 'major' conventional weapons—battle tanks, armoured combat vehicles, large-calibre artillery systems, combat aircraft, attack helicopters, warships, and missiles and missile launchers.[33]

The category of Small Arms and Light Weapons (SALW) covers a vast range of items from pistols to large machine guns and portable mortars.[34] The defining characteristic of SALW is portability.[35] 'Small arms' have been defined by the United Nations Programme of Action on Small Arms and Light Weapons (UN PoA) as weapons designed for personal use, including revolvers and self-loading pistols, rifles, submachine guns, assault rifles, and light machine guns.[36] The UN PoA defined 'light weapons' as those designed for use by several persons serving as a crew, including heavy machine guns, certain types of grenade launchers, portable

[31] See Neil Boister and Robert J Currie (eds), *Routledge Handbook of Transnational Criminal Law* (Routledge 2014).

[32] The narrowing of this definition risks downgrading other serious human rights violations. Andrew Clapham, 'Human Rights and International Criminal Law' in William A Schabas (ed), *The Cambridge Companion to International Criminal Law* (CUP 2016) 11, 18.

[33] ATT, art 2(1).

[34] ATT, art 2(1)(h). Zeray Yihdego, *The Arms Trade and International Law* (Bloomsbury 2007) 8, 19; Asif Efrat, 'Toward Internationally Regulated Goods: Controlling the Trade in Small Arms and Light Weapons' (2010) 64 International Organization 97; Paul Holtom and Mark Bromley, 'The International Arms Trade' (2010) 40 Arms Control 8.

[35] Yihdego (n 34) 4.

[36] UNGA, 'United Nations Conference on the Illicit Trade in Small Arms and Light Weapons in All Its Aspects that took place on 9 to 20 July 2001' (2001) UN Doc A/CONF.192/15 (UN PoA).

anti-aircraft and anti-tank guns, and portable launchers of anti-aircraft missile systems.[37]

SALW are particularly prominent in armed conflict in the post-Cold War era, including the situations that have come before international criminal tribunals. The UN found that of 49 major conflicts in the 1990s, 47 were predominantly waged with small arms.[38] SALW have caused at least 300,000 deaths per year in armed conflict and 200,000 in homicides and suicides.[39] Figures of current circulation of SALW are difficult to establish, due to unrecorded transfers and unknown existing ownership levels, but Kalashnikov-pattern assault rifles are the most prevalent.[40] The predominance of SALW in today's conflict deaths is not reflected in the historical preoccupation with the risk of nuclear weapons in arms control on the risk to peace of non-conventional weapons, probably a legacy of the Cold War.[41] The importance of SALW in the perpetration of international crimes today highlights the important role of small-scale actors in the arms trade, who are often able to move very small quantities of SALW directly into the hands of perpetrators of international crimes.

Non-Conventional Weapons are prohibited under international law; there can be no lawful trade in chemical, biological, radiological, or nuclear technology.[42] Neither can there be any lawful trade in anti-personnel mines, non-detectable fragments, booby traps and other devices, blinding laser weapons, explosive remnants of war, and other types of prohibited weapons.[43]

As developed later in this book, complicit assistance can be based on the provision of arms, dual-use items, ammunition, constituent parts, *matériel*, munitions, or indeed any other type of object. Civilian goods, such as tarpaulins, fertilizers, pesticides, petrol and medical supplies, have everyday non-military uses, but they may nevertheless contribute to the commission of an international crime. The dependence of complicity on *actus reus* and *mens rea* means that the inherent nature of the weapon is prima facie irrelevant to liability, unlike in domestic arms export regulations. For the purposes of discussing complicity and the arms trade, it is necessary to keep an open mind about the types of items, including dual-use items, that may form the basis of complicit assistance. In essence, the legal definitional questions in arms control law about whether certain items qualify as 'an arm', a

[37] UN PoA.

[38] UNODA, 'Small Arms and Light Weapons' (*Conventional Arms Branch website*, May 2020) <http://disarmament.un.org:8080/cab/salw.html> accessed 4 August 2024.

[39] UNODA (n 38).

[40] Michael Klare, 'The Kalashnikov Age' (1999) 55 Bulletin of the Atomic Scientists 18.

[41] Feinstein (n 10).

[42] See David S Meyer, 'Framing National Security: Elite Public Discourse on Nuclear Weapons during the Cold War' (1995) 12 Political Communication 173; Nina Tannenwald, 'Stigmatizing the Bomb: Origins of the Nuclear Taboo' (2005) 29 International Security 5.

[43] See Convention on the Prohibition of the Development, Production, Stockpiling, and Use of Chemical Weapons and on their Destruction (adopted 13 January 1993, entered into force 29 April 1997) 1975 UNTS 45 (Chemical Weapons Convention) Protocols I, II, IV, and V.

'dual-use item', or a regular item that can be freely traded, are of limited importance to the issue of individual complicity, which are context dependent.

As such, when an individual transfers a shipment of agricultural machetes that they know is bound for a militia group that intends to use them to commit crimes against humanity, this transfer is relevant to the scope of this book, irrespective of whether the agricultural machetes are part of 'the arms trade' according to existing export regulations. Of course, this does not preclude the categories of arms control law from serving as evidentiary considerations; the prohibition of a certain weapon type under arms control laws may be an important factual indicator of *mens rea*.

1.3.2 'Actors' in the Arms Trade

The global transfer of weapons involves a complex web of actors of varying size, organizational complexity, and legality. They may contribute to international crimes in different ways, and are subject to varying degrees of regulation. Individuals may work in *arms manufacturing corporations*, as *state officials* who authorize transfers or may be involved in corrupt deals, as members of *transnational organized crime groups* that traffic weapons, and as small-scale *brokers, transporters, and 'micro-traders'* often responsible for the final stage of transfers at a local level to the site of commission of international crimes by the end users of the weapons.[44] The end users are, for the purposes of this book, the *perpetrators* of international crimes—they may be political officials, members of the national armed forces, or non-state actors.

In the 'lawful trade', the major *arms manufacturing corporations* produce new weapons and ammunition for domestic sale or foreign export. Some of their products eventually find their way into the hands of perpetrators of international crimes, either because the home state of manufacture is involved in crimes, or because national authorities fail to prevent the export of weapons to a foreign end user involved in crimes, or because illegal diversion takes place from a lawful end user such as a national armed force, police force, peacekeeping force, or private military and security companies.

[44] The picture of the global trade is completed by the *facilitators*: the accountants, attorneys, notaries, bankers, and real estate agents who are essential to the functioning of the trade. In addition to carrying out lawful work, some individuals enable the arms trade by facilitating corrupt transactions, creating shell corporations, opening offshore bank accounts, falsifying passports and other documents, bribing customs and other governmental authorities, maintaining safe house locations to conduct business, arranging weapons and ammunition storage, and creating front businesses for money laundering such as casinos. Their contributions are not the main subject of this book, yet their peripheral actions may be a basis for their complicity in international crimes. See US Executive Office of the President, 'Strategy to Combat Transnational Organized Crime: Addressing Converging Threats to National Security' (National Security Council, 25 July 2011) 8<https://obamawhitehouse.archives.gov/administration/eop/nsc/transnational-crime>accessed 4 August 2024.

According to figures of authorized transfers of small arms in 2016 as reported to the UN, the top exporters are the US, Italy, and Brazil accounting for 36 per cent of the global small arms trade, followed by Germany, Austria, South Korea, Croatia, the Czech Republic, Turkey, Russia, Israel, Belgium, and China.[45] The major arms corporations involve varying degrees of parastatal ownership. They are organizationally complex, involving tens of thousands of employees, and their turnovers play major roles in their domestic economies, and they are considered to operate in the 'lawful' or 'licit' arms trade, defined as 'those sales that conform to international law and the national laws of the countries involved in the transfer'.[46]

Weapons are also trafficked from post-conflict stockpiles (since the 1990s, often from former Soviet states) or sourced from the general proliferation of pre-used SALW and major conventional weapons in conflict zones. There is a risk, however, of scapegoating 'background proliferation' and stockpile leakage, to obscure the importance of new weapons produced in, and initially exported by, manufacturing states, which are diverted soon after. There is limited but increasing 'artisanal' or 'craft' production of SALW in some states.[47]

Transnational crime and organized criminal groups coordinate illicit arms trafficking. In the supply chain from source to perpetrator, large and powerful transnational organized crime groups play a widely recognized role, often involving designated terrorist organizations and networks associated with illegal drugs, human trafficking, and other transnational crimes. Smaller intermediaries—the arms brokers, transporters, and 'micro-traders' who transfer small quantities of weapons—play an under-recognized role at the local level, often at greater proximity to the site of atrocities.

'Brokers' are defined by the UN as 'a person or entity acting as an intermediary that brings together relevant parties and arranges or facilitates a potential transaction of small arms and light weapons in return for some form of benefit, whether financial or otherwise'.[48] 'Transporters' are agents participating in the trade by moving weapons by air, land, or sea, even if not directly involved in the sale transaction.[49] The 'micro-trade', sometimes referred to as the 'ant trade', is made up of sole individuals or very small businesses shipping small numbers of weapons that, while insignificant on their own, 'over time, result in the accumulation of large

[45] Michael Picard, Paul Holtom, and Fiona Mangan, 'Trade Update 2019: Transfers, Transparency, and South-east Asia Spotlight' (Small Arms Survey, December 2019) 20.

[46] Rachel Stohl and Suzette Grillot, *The International Arms Trade* (Polity 2009) 41.

[47] G Hays and NR Jenzen-Jones, 'Beyond State Control: Improvised and Craft-produced Small Arms and Light Weapons' (Small Arms Survey, November 2018).

[48] UNGA 'Report of the Group of Governmental Experts established pursuant to General Assembly resolution 60/81 to consider further steps to enhance international cooperation in preventing, combating and eradicating illicit brokering in small arms and light weapons' (30 August 2007) UN Doc A/62/163, para 8.

[49] See John Cartner and others, *The International Law of the Shipmaster* (Routledge 2013).

numbers of illicit weapons by unauthorized end users'.[50] This diverse category of small-scale intermediaries reappears throughout the book, as individuals who often operate in proximity to crime sites, who are poorly regulated by current arms controls, and who were important conduits for weapons from Rwanda, Uganda, and further afield in the Second Congo War, yet fell into a blind spot in the ICC's investigations in the DRC Situation.

A small number of international arms brokers has played a disproportionate role in the supply of weapons in recent armed conflict. The renowned Victor Bout recurs with impressive consistency in studies of the global arms trade.[51] Several authors have pointed to Bout's potential complicity in international crime—James G Stewart charts the activities of Bout in the context of an analysis of issues of pre-emptive causation in criminal law.[52] Bout is alleged to have transferred weapons to groups accused of atrocities in the DRC,[53] Libya, Afghanistan, Angola, Sierra Leone, Liberia, and Bosnia through a complex network of over fifty aircraft, several airline companies, and freight-forward companies.[54] At least some of these alleged transfers would be within ICC temporal jurisdiction having (at least in part) taken place since 1 July 2002 and prior to Bout's arrest in Thailand in 2008, as well as connecting to alleged criminal incidents in existing (open) ICC Situations. Arms brokers, transporters, and micro-traders often feature in the transfer of arms to perpetrators of international crimes. Much of their conduct is left largely untouched by Arms Trade Law. In addition, as intermediaries, these individuals will often be causally more proximate to the crimes, making it easier to establish their individual contribution to a criminal group.

1.3.3 'Arms Transfer Conduct'

The subject of International Criminal Law is the action and conduct of individuals. Hence in the arms trade context, we are interested in the acts and omissions of those who operate within the network of actors described above. 'Arms transfer conduct' may occur at any stage of the chain of supply, from the original source of weapons to the commission of atrocity, from manufacturing, selling, licensing, exporting, brokering, transporting across international borders, transporting

[50] Small Arms Survey, 'Illicit Trafficking' (Small Arms Survey, 2020) <www.smallarmssurvey.org/de/weapons-and-markets/transfers/illicit-trafficking.html> accessed 4 August 2024.

[51] Feinstein (n 10) 115, 124, 154, 155–57, 158–65, 416–18, 443, 450, 462–64, 505.

[52] James G Stewart, 'Overdetermined Atrocities' (2012) 10 Journal of International Criminal Justice 1189.

[53] Amnesty International (n 11).

[54] Peter Landesman, 'Arms and the Man' (*New York Times Magazine*, 17 August 2003); 'UN arms embargoes: an overview of the last ten years' Control Arms Campaign: Amnesty International, Oxfam International and International Action Network on Small Arms (16 March 2006) <https://www.amnesty.eu/wp-content/uploads/2018/10/06_03_16_UN_arms_embargoes.pdf> accessed 10 March 2023.

within states, to advertising,[55] transshipment, rental,[56] stockpile management, and ownership. Examples of 'arms transfer conduct' therefore include personal behaviours such as high-level decision-making in manufacturing corporations, risk assessment on behalf of state licensing authorities, communicating with recipients to ascertain the end-use of weapons, arranging the trafficking of weapons within a transnational organized crime group, or physically distributing weapons as a small-scale intermediary.

In social science models of the global arms trade, the 'basic dimensions' of any given transfer are defined by the type of arms, their market or trade value, the quantity, whether the activity is tied to the provision of follow-up services or training, the mode of payment, mode of production, including licensed production or co-production (often in more than one state), and finally the stage of delivery, including whether an arms transfer is completed or only agreed to.[57] It may involve a range of modes of payment from a pure grant or gift, to credits or loans, government-to-government cash, private industry-to-government cash, barter, and offsets.[58] The monetary value of a trade does not necessarily reflect its importance in contributing to a military objective, or to an international crime. For instance, low value exports from Germany and the US were pivotal in enabling Iraq to upgrade its Scud missiles in 1990.[59]

Individuals perform their conduct as part of the organizational constructs of the 'actors' described above, whose size and complexity is determinative of how readily the organizations' activities can be attributed to the individual's arms transfer conduct. Attributing responsibility to a government minister tasked with authorizing exports, or to a CEO of a major arms manufacturing corporation may involve complex structural attribution. The attribution of responsibility for small-scale brokers, transporters, and micro-traders is likely to be more straightforward—where individuals operate in their sole capacity, or where their personal conduct is closer to co-extensive with the small and less complex organizations in which they operate.

The analytic value of isolating 'arms transfer conduct' as the subject of the research in this book lies in showing the potential of criminal law, as distinct from existing arms regulation, and how the two can integrate and complement each other. The subject of analysis is the criminality of conduct in the arms trade, rather

[55] NR Jenzen-Jones and Ian McCollum, 'Web Trafficking: Analzying the Online Trade of Small Arms and Light Weapons in Libya' Working Paper 26 (2017) Small Arms Survey, Security Assessment in North Africa.

[56] Private enterprises increasingly offer weapon loaning services to circumvent regulations on sales. See Daniel M Salton, 'Starving the Dark Markets: International Injunctions as a Means to Curb Small Arms and Light Weapons Trafficking' (2013) 46 Connecticut Law Review 369.

[57] Edward J Laurance, *The International Arms Trade* (Lexington 1992) 20.

[58] Laurance (n 57) 17. Offsets reduce the amount of currency required and make it harder to establish that a trade took place.

[59] See Laurance (n 57) 20.

than its morality, there being 'no general dividing line between criminal and non-criminal conduct which corresponds to a distinction between immoral and moral conduct, or between seriously wrongful and other conduct'.[60] Furthermore, it is concerned with the criminality of conduct according to the doctrines of accomplice liability under International Criminal Law, and does not rely on the 'lawful' or 'illicit' arms trading from other areas of legal regulation of the arms trade to predetermine this analysis of criminality. The book recognizes that 'there is no straightforward moral or social test of whether conduct is criminal. The most reliable test is the formal one: is the conduct prohibited, on pain of conviction and sentence.'[61]

1.4 The Arms Trade in International Criminal Law Scholarship

The lack of prosecutions of complicit arms traders has been matched by a lacunae in the commentary on International Criminal Law. When this book was first conceived of in 2014, there was very limited. Until relatively recently, commentary about the arms trade has tended to overlook the relevance of complicity under International Criminal Law. While the ATT—the first multilateral binding treaty on the arms trade—predominates in discussion of controls on conventional weapons, it is surprising that the ATT's provisions on international crimes and serious human rights abuses have not prompted more attention to the relationship between export regulation and International Criminal Law. As 'arms control law' emerges as an epistemological field of scholarship, education, and legal expertise, to the extent it is concerned with international crimes, it concentrates on export regulation rather than complicity.

The lack of attention to complicity sits in the context of the economic and geostrategic importance of the arms trade to the major manufacturing states, particularly the permanent members of the UN Security Council. Even the very notion that the arms trade can be legally regulated remains divisive—described by one commentator as 'naïve' in light of the extent of corruption in the trade.[62] Existing studies tend to silo issues of arms regulation, overlooking potential synergies with International Criminal Law. A significant body of legal research concerns UN, EU, and unilateral arms embargoes,[63] focused on strengthening existing

[60] Andrew Ashworth and Jeremy Horder, *Principles of Criminal Law* (7th edn, OUP 2013).

[61] Ashworth and Horder (n 60) chs 1, 5.

[62] Bob Sullivan, 'Reformulating Bribery: A Legal Critique of the Bribery Act 2010' in Jeremy Horder and Peter Alldridge (eds), *Modern Bribery Law: Comparative Perspectives* (CUP 2013) 13, 15.

[63] eg Jennifer L Erickson, 'Punishing the Violators? Arms Embargoes and Economic Sanctions as Tools of Norm Enforcement' (2020) 46 Review of International Studies 96; Kathrin Kranz, 'European Union Arms Embargoes: The Relationship between Institutional Design and Norms' (2016) 29 Cambridge Review of International Affairs 970; Francesco Giumelli, *The Success of Sanctions*

enforcement[64] through improved end user documentation[65] or more targeted use of sanctions,[66] and the impact of sanctions on economic, social, and cultural rights.[67]

Meanwhile, the development and implementation of the ATT,[68] as well as the prominence in arms control of the EU Common Position,[69] generated a wealth of legal analysis centred on export regulation,[70] notably a comprehensive article-by-article commentary on the ATT by Clapham and others,[71] and Casey-Maslan's edited volume,[72] while Yihdego appears to have authored the only existing monograph devoted to the arms trade under international law.[73] Again, this work is not directed at the interactions of the ATT and the Rome Statute as two treaties that, in effect, both provide forms of regulation of the trade.

Comparative studies of national export controls have engaged with questions of criminal complicity to only a limited extent.[74] Research centres at the Small Arms Survey and the Stockholm International Peace Research Institute publish a wealth of research data,[75] as did the Geneva Academy's Weapons Law Encyclopaedia.[76] Iain Anthony edited a seminal volume in 1991.[77] Lustgarten has written perhaps

(Routledge 2019). See also Rosalyn Higgins and others, *Oppenheim's International Law: United Nations* (OUP 2018) 978; James Crawford, *Brownlie's Principles of Public International Law* (OUP 2019) 732.

[64] See Francesco Giumelli, *The Success of Sanctions* (Routledge 2019).

[65] Bjorn Hagelin, 'International Armament Embargoes and the Need for End-Use Documents' in Carina Staibano and Peter Wallensteen (eds), *International Sanctions: Between Wars and Words* (Routledge 2005).

[66] See Thomas J Biersteker, Sue E Eckert, and Marcos Tourinho (eds), *Targeted Sanctions* (CUP 2016); Tomas Hamilton, Natalie Lucas, Alex Prezanti, Megan Smith, and Amanda Strayer, 'Targeted Sanctions as a Pathway to Accountability: An Active Role for Civil Society?' (5 August 2024) Journal of International Criminal Justice.

[67] Andrew Clapham, 'Sanctions and Economic, Social and Cultural Rights' in Vera Gowlland-Debbas (ed), *United Nations Sanctions and International Law* (Kluwer 2001) 131.

[68] Arms Trade Treaty (adopted 2 April 2013, opened for signature 3 June 2013, entered into force 24 December 2014) 3012 UNTS. For a thorough recent analysis see Clare da Silva and Brian Wood (eds), *The Arms Trade Treaty: Weapons and International Law* (Intersentia 2021).

[69] Council Common Position 2008/944/CFSP of 8 December 2008 defining common rules governing control of exports of military technology and equipment [2008] OJ L335/99 (EU Common Position).

[70] eg Laurence Lustgarten, 'The Arms Trade Treaty: Achievements, Failings, Future' (2015) 64 ICLQ 569; Nina HB Jørgensen, 'State Responsibility for Aiding or Assisting International Crimes in the Context of the Arms Trade Treaty' (2014) 108 AJIL 722; Sam Perlo-Freeman, 'The ATT and War Profiteering: The Case of the UK' (2020) 12 Global Responsibility to Protect 178.

[71] Andrew Clapham and others, *The Arms Trade Treaty: A Commentary* (OUP 2016).

[72] Stuart Casey-Maslen (ed), Weapons Under International Human Rights Law (CUP 2014).

[73] Yihdego (n 34).

[74] See Erickson (n 63). eg Lucien J Dhooge, 'We Arm The World: The Implications of American Participation in the Global Armaments Trade' (1999) 16 Arizona Journal of International and Comparative Law 577.

[75] egSmall Arms Survey, 'Transfers' Small Arms Survey (2020) <www.smallarmssurvey.org/weapons-and-markets/transfers.html> accessed 4 August 2024; Sibylle Bauer and Mark Bromley, *The European Union Code of Conduct on Arms Exports: Improving the Annual Report* (SIPRI 2004).

[76] Weapons Law Encyclopaedia (*Weapons Law Encyclopaedia*, 2020) <www.weaponslaw.org> accessed 4 August 2024.

[77] Ian Anthony (ed), *Arms Export Regulations* (OUP 1991).

the most detailed comparative study of the export control regimes of eight major arms manufacturing states—the US, Russia, the UK, France, Germany, Sweden, China, and India.[78] Limited research has identified links between arms regulation and material support for terrorism.[79] A legal opinion from Sands, Clapham, and Ní Ghrálaigh on the matter of UK arms exports to Saudi Arabia for use in Yemen is an important document highlighting the potential for individual criminal responsibility.[80]

Outside legal scholarship, there is a larger body of multidisciplinary work analysing the arms trade as a social and political phenomenon.[81] Stavrianakis emphasizes the influence of postcolonialism and liberal militarism on UK arms export policy.[82] Erickson explores the responsiveness of embargoes and domestic export controls to human rights concerns.[83] Staibano and Wallensteen draw together work on the politicized use of sanctions, their effectiveness in achieving diplomatic goals, and their collateral cost for civilian populations.[84] Other research from international relations and political science is represented in Feinstein's study of the global arms trade[85] and Tan's edited volume.[86]

The lack of attention to International Criminal Law is attributable in part to the fact that, like international relations as a whole, arms trade studies have traditionally been focused on explaining the foreign policy behaviour of powerful states, rather than individual conduct.[87] Early social science models were concerned with broad patterns and trends in the global flow of weapons.[88] A 'systems approach' was

[78] Laurence Lustgarten, *Law and the Arms Trade: Weapons, Blood and Rules* (Bloomsbury 2020).

[79] See Ben Saul, 'The Legal Relationship between Terrorism and Transnational Crime' (2017) 17 International Criminal Law Review 417, 433–34.

[80] Philippe Sands, Andrew Clapham, and Blinne Ní Ghrálaigh, 'The Lawfulness of the Authorisation by the United Kingdom of Weapons and Related Items for Export to Saudi Arabia in the Context of Saudi Arabia's Military Intervention in Yemen' (*Saferworld*, 11 December 2015) 22 <www.saferworld.org.uk/downloads/pubdocs/legal-opinion-on-uk-arms-exports-to-saudi.pdf> accessed 4 August 2024.

[81] See Stohl and Grillot (n 46); Rodrigo Fracalossi de Moraes, 'Our Weapons, Our Problem: Arms Exports, Democracy and Civil Society in Brazil and the UK' (DPhil in International Relations, University of Oxford 2019); Siemon T Wezeman, 'The Global Arms Trade After the Cold War' in Andrew Tan (ed), *The Global Arms Trade: A Handbook* (Routledge 2014) 193; Richard A Bitzinger, 'Globalization revisit(ed)' in Andrew Tan (ed), *The Global Arms Trade: A Handbook* (Routledge 2014) 208.

[82] Anna Stavrianakis, 'When "Anxious Scrutiny" of Arms Exports Facilitates Humanitarian Disaster' (2018) 89 The Political Quarterly 92.

[83] Jennifer L Erickson, *Dangerous Trade: Conventional Arms Exports, Human Rights, and International Relations* (Columbia University Press 2015).

[84] eg Carina Staibano and Peter Wallensteen (eds), *International Sanctions: Between Wars and Words* (Routledge 2005).

[85] Andrew Feinstein, *The Shadow World: Inside the Global Arms Trade* (Macmillan 2011).

[86] Andrew Tan (ed), *The Global Arms Trade: A Handbook* (Routledge 2014).

[87] Stephanie G Neuman, *Military Assistance in Recent Wars: The Dominance of The Superpowers* (Praeger 1986).

[88] George Thayer, *The War Business: The International Trade in Armaments* (Weidenfield and Nicolson 1969); Stockholm International Peace Research Institute, *The Arms Trade with the Third World* (Pelican 1971); Keith Krause, *Arms and The State: Patterns of Military Production and Trade* (CUP 1995).

pioneered by Harkavy's 1975 study, modelling the trade as a system of 'actors', 'activities', and 'arms',[89] relying on political variables to understand state behaviour in terms of polarity, bloc ties, ideology, autarky, and alliance.[90] The systems approach predominated in subsequent studies.[91] In general, while the focus of international relations on state behaviour gave way in the early 1990s to greater concern for individual conduct,[92] studies of the arms trade have paid limited attention to criminal responsibility.

The doctrinal scholarship on complicity under international law has been well developed through monographs by Jackson,[93] Jain,[94] and Aksenova,[95] building on accounts of complicity in national systems of law, notably on Smith's seminal monograph,[96] and theoretical work by Gardner,[97] Kutz,[98] and Moore.[99] The growing interest in corporate accountability under International Criminal Law is seen in the work of Clapham,[100] Gallmetzer,[101] Nerlich,[102] Sluiter,[103] a recent volume edited by Jørgensen,[104] and numerous others.[105] The most notable treatment of arms trading as a specific form of complicity is probably Stewart's

[89] Robert E Harkavy, *The Arms Trade and International Systems* (Ballinger 1975).

[90] Harkavy (n 89) 4.

[91] See David J Louscher, *Marketing Security Assistance: New Perspectives on Arms Sales* (Free Press 1987); Edward J Laurance, *The International Arms Trade* (Lexington 1992) 12, 48, 205.

[92] Kalevi Jaakko Holsti, *International Politics: A Framework for Analysis* (Prentice-Hall Englewood Cliffs 1995).

[93] Miles Jackson, *Complicity in International Law* (OUP 2015).

[94] Neha Jain, *Perpetrators and Accessories in International Criminal Law: Individual Modes of Responsibility for Collective Crimes* (Bloomsbury 2014).

[95] Marina Aksenova, *Complicity in International Criminal Law* (Bloomsbury 2016).

[96] Keith JM Smith, *A Modern Treatise on the Law of Criminal Complicity* (Clarendon Press 1991).

[97] John Gardner, 'Complicity and Causality' (2007) 1 Criminal Law and Philosophy 127; John Gardner, 'Moore on Complicity and Causality' (2008) 156 University of Pennsylvania Law Review 432.

[98] Christopher Kutz, *Complicity: Ethics and Law for a Collective Age* (CUP 2007).

[99] Michael S Moore, *Causation and Responsibility: An Essay in Law, Morals, and Metaphysics* (OUP 2009).

[100] Andrew Clapham, 'Extending International Criminal Law Beyond the Individual to Corporations and Armed Opposition Groups' (2008) 6 Journal of International Criminal Justice 899; Andrew Clapham, 'Corporations and Criminal Complicity' in Gro Nystuen, Andreas Follesdal, and Ola Mestad (eds), *Human Rights, Corporate Complicity and Disinvestment* (CUP 2011) 222.

[101] Rienhold Gallmetzer, 'Prosecuting Persons Doing Business with Armed Groups in Conflict Areas: The Strategy of the Office of the Prosecutor of the International Criminal Court' (2010) 8 Journal of International Criminal Justice 947.

[102] Nerlich (n 14) 900–01.

[103] Göran Sluiter and Sean Shun Ming Yau, 'Aiding and Abetting and Causation in the Commission of International Crimes—The Cases of Dutch Businessmen van Anraat and Kouwenhoven' in Nina HB Jørgensen (ed), *The International Criminal Responsibility of War's Funders and Profiteers* (CUP 2020) 304.

[104] Nina HB Jørgensen (ed), *International Criminal Responsibility of War's Funders and Profiteers* (CUP 2020).

[105] eg Burchard (n 15) 919; Florian Jeßberger (n 18); Hans Vest, 'Business Leaders and the Modes of Individual Criminal Responsibility under International Law' (2010) 8 Journal of International Criminal Justice 864; See Menno T Kamminga and Saman Zia-Zarifi (eds), *Liability of Multinational Corporations under International Law* (Springer 2000); Alison Cronin, *Corporate Criminality and Liability for Fraud* (Routledge 2018).

sustained interest in weapons transfers, particularly on issues of causation and attribution within complex organizational structures.[106]

Finally, a limited number of papers have focused specifically on the role of the ICC in relation to the arms trade.[107] Like the work on the ATT, these papers are often siloed into focusing on International Criminal Law as a panacea to existing regulation, without seeing the potential for synergy and mutual reinforcement of arms controls and International Criminal Law. Moreover, these papers tend to focus on building, articulating, and advocating an activist argument that arms traders *ought* to be prosecuted by the ICC, rather than giving a descriptive account of the ICC's law and practice. Bryk, Saage-Maaß, and Aksenova, have written on the case for prosecuting European governmental officials and corporate officials at the ICC for their roles in arms supplies to Saudi Arabia used in war crimes in Yemen.[108] Finally, while existing work has tended to prioritize the Article 25(3)(c) mode of liability on aiding and abetting, this book argues that Article 25(3)(d)(ii) 'knowingly contributing to a group crime' would be of greater relevance in practice.

Van Sliedregt has argued that International Criminal Law is an area of doctrine that is overstudied, posing the risk of excessive theorization, specifically in relation to the modes of liability.[109] In van Sliedregt's account, this undue attention to the theoretical coherence of modes of liability is not only unhelpful to legal practice, it may even be hampered by it, for instance where disproportionate engagement with theories of liability conceived to deal with the Nazi bureaucracy and other highly organized entities has distracted from the need to capture the local reality of individual responsibility within militia groups in ICC Situations.[110] This perspective strongly informs the approach taken in this book: doctrinal analysis is the foundation of the work, while emphasizing the need to go further in assessing the

[106] See James G Stewart, 'Atrocity, Commerce and Accountability' (2010) 8 Journal of International Criminal Justice 314; James G Stewart, 'The Historical Importance of the Kouwenhoven Trial' (*Blog of James G Stewart*, 5 May 2017) <http://jamesgstewart.com/the-historical-importance-of-the-kouwenhoven-trial/> accessed 4 August 2024.

[107] Alexandra Boivin, 'Complicity and Beyond: International Law and the Transfer of Small Arms and Light Weapons' (2005) 87 International Review of the Red Cross 467, 484; Claudette Torbey, 'The Most Egregious Arms Broker: Prosecuting Arms Embargo Violators in the International Criminal Court' (2007) 25 Wisconsin International Law Journal 335; Tomas Hamilton, 'Regulating the Arms Trade: The Potential of International Criminal Law' (2015) International Crimes Database, Brief 17; Tomas Hamilton, 'Arms Transfer Complicity under Article 25(3)(d)(ii) of the Rome Statute' in Jørgensen (n 104); Leigh Rome, 'The Case for Prosecuting Arms Traffickers in the International Criminal Court' (2015) 36 Cardozo Law Review 1149; Bryk and Saage-Maaß (n 14) 1117.

[108] Bryk and Saage-Maaß (n 14); Marina Aksenova and Linde Bryk, 'Extraterritorial Obligations of Arms Exporting Corporations: New Communication to the ICC' (*Opinio Juris Blog*, 14 January 2020) <http://opiniojuris.org/2020/01/14/extraterritorial-obligations-of-arms-exporting-corporations-new-communication-to-the-icc/> accessed 4 August 2024.

[109] Elies Van Sliedregt, 'International Criminal Law: Over-studied and Underachieving?' (2016) 29 Leiden Journal of International Law 1, 7. See Elies Van Sliedregt, *Individual Criminal Responsibility in International Law* (OUP 2012).

[110] Van Sliedregt (n 109) 7–8.

practical application of the modes of liability to the working realities of the arms trade when it is connected to atrocity.

1.5 Overview of This Book

This book focuses on three under-examined questions about the arms trade and International Criminal Law: (1) To what extent does International Criminal Law criminalize the transfer of weapons and what distinguishes this from existing legal regulation of the arms trade? (2) How do International Criminal Law practitioners view the arms trade and what might this explain about the ICC's non-selection of cases involving commercial weapons transfers? (3) What does studying the arms trade tell us about how the legal doctrines of complicity are developing in the current practice of International Criminal Law?

After this Introduction, Chapter 2 examines the existing framework of national arms export regulation, at the international and national levels, and the extent to which it refers to standards on international crime. Chapter 3 completes the analysis of the current field of 'Arms Trade Law', demonstrating an accountability gap, and paving the way for International Criminal Law's potential to contribute to the existing assemblage of legal mechanisms. Chapters 4 and 5 develop the doctrinal argument that Article 25(3)(d)(ii) of the Rome Statute criminalizes a range of conduct in the arms trade, providing a legal basis for the ICC to hold complicit arms traders accountable. Turning to an empirical study, Chapter 6 looks at perceptions of the arms trade in the ICC's institutional culture, while Chapter 7 explores how this impacts whether the ICC selects a case against an arms trader. The case study of the Second Congo War in Chapter 8 shows some of the failings of the prevailing system of Arms Trade Law in the DRC between 1998 and 2003 and analyses the findings of a UN Panel of Experts that identified the role of arms brokers in initiating and perpetuating the commission of atrocities. Chapter 9 extends the case study to consider the ICC Situation in the DRC and suggests several blind spots in the Court's non-selection of arms trade cases.

The book concludes with a reflection on the place of International Criminal Law in regulating conduct that has traditionally been considered the realm of Transnational Criminal Law, drawing on the doctrinal, literature based, and empirical research of the preceding chapters. It identifies the contributions of the book to scholarly debate concerning political and realist constraints on the ICC, illuminating the prioritization of certain types of perpetrators in the aims and purposes of international criminal justice.

2
Complementing Export Regulation with Criminal Accountability

2.1 Introduction

When a shipment of weapons contributes to the commission of atrocities, national export regulation is the primary area of law that should have prevented the arms from reaching their destination. The cross-border transfer of conventional weapons and dual-use items is directly regulated by states, and coordinated transnationally by the Arms Trade Treaty (ATT), the EU Common Position, and other international conventions. As Chapter 3 finds, national export regulation is also subject to arms embargoes and a plurality of areas of 'Arms Trade Law' including the law of state responsibility, the *jus ad bellum*, the law of neutrality, counterterrorism law, international humanitarian law, human rights law, international economic law, cyber law, anti-corruption law, and transnational criminal law.

In the present chapter, the legal and practical limitations of arms export regulation are analysed in terms of their prohibitions, jurisdictional reach, and the protected interests at stake. These limitations highlight a potential role for International Criminal Law due to three distinctive strengths; it can hold actors individually responsible as accomplices, it has some degree of supranational jurisdiction, and it is underpinned by unique aspirational qualities to end impunity through accountability.

The analytic approach builds on Stahn's conceptualization of 'the scope of application of international criminal law', that is to say, the extent to which International Criminal Law has any appreciable impact on the activities of the world, defined in terms of the scope of conduct prohibited under its modes of liability, its jurisdiction, and the values or interests that it aspires to protect.[1] After considering national regulations (Section 2.2) and international agreements (Section 2.3), this chapter considers the interaction between International Criminal Law and national export regulations (Section 2.4) in terms of jurisdiction, complementarity, and defences.

[1] Carsten Stahn, *A Critical Introduction to International Criminal Law* (CUP 2019) 12.

The Arms Trade and International Criminal Law. Tomas Hamilton, Oxford University Press.
DOI: 10.1093/oso/9780192868671.003.0002

2.2 National Arms Export Regulations

In national legal systems, arms export regulations are the mechanism by which states determine to be permissible the cross-border transfers of weapons out of their jurisdictions. Building on research into national export regulations, the following sections analyse export regulations from the specific perspective of International Criminal Law, in order to understand how International Criminal Law could play a complementary role in the existing system of export regulation. This chapter builds on Lustgarten's detailed scholarly analysis of national arms export regulation, a comparative study of eight major arms manufacturing states—the US, Russia, the UK, France, Germany, Sweden, China, and India.[2]

2.2.1 National Export Criteria in Relation to International Crimes

National export criteria prohibit exports where there are unacceptable risks of items being used to commit international crimes. Notably, the two most significant international agreements on arms exports, the ATT and the EU Common Position, contain provisions on international criminal conduct. Article 2 of the EU Common Position requires an export licence to be refused where there is 'a clear risk' that arms 'might be used in the commission of serious violations of international humanitarian law'.[3] The ATT requires that a State Party must not transfer conventional arms, ammunition, parts, and components, where it has knowledge that the weapons will be used in the commission of war crimes or crimes against humanity, or where the State Party determines that there is an 'overriding risk' that the supplied arms will undermine peace and security or be used in the commission of war crimes or crimes against humanity.[4]

In relation to international crimes, national export regulations are pre-emptive in character (like arms embargoes). They provide a legal mechanism for states to stop transfers from leaving their territory, *ex ante*, in circumstances where the proposed transfer does not meet certain criteria. Even where these criteria incorporate standards relating to international crimes, export rules can only prevent items from reaching the perpetrators of international crimes, rather than providing any *ex post facto* accountability for those crimes. This is not to say that arms export regulations cannot be a basis for criminal punishment, but it is important to distinguish two

[2] Laurence Lustgarten, *Law and the Arms Trade: Weapons, Blood and Rules* (Bloomsbury 2020).

[3] Council Common Position 2008/944/CFSP of 8 December 2008 defining common rules governing control of exports of military technology and equipment [2008] OJ L335/99 (EU Common Position).

[4] ATT, arts 6 and 7. See Andrew Clapham 'Article 7' in Andrew Clapham and others, *The Arms Trade Treaty: A Commentary* (OUP 2016) 255.

types of criminality. Firstly, the criminal offence committed by the individuals involved in wrongfully transferring the items that arises from breaching arms export requirements (normally described as a customs, trafficking, or smuggling offence) and second, an international crime committed by the end recipient of the shipment (in which the supplier is complicit).

Export regulations suffer from a number of enforcement issues, including wide variance from state to state.[5] A breach of an export norms may be legally characterized—depending on the national jurisdiction—as a criminal offence, a regulatory offence (including strict liability offence with no *mens rea*), a civil tort, or another form of administrative infraction.[6] These are often the same enforcement measures used to punish breaches of the terms of Security Council or EU embargoes discussed above. There is a disparity between jurisdictions that impose harsh criminal penalties, for instance lengthy sentences of imprisonment for arms trafficking in Austria, the US, and South Africa,[7] versus those that may impose only an administrative fine.[8] In most jurisdictions, export authorizations are administered by regulatory bodies (often government departments) rather than judicial authorities.

Penal enforcement is quite rare. In cases when arms traffickers are punished under criminal law, it has almost never been in relation to the crimes of those to whom they sell weapons (eg atrocity crimes committed against victims in armed conflict zones). Instead, arms traffickers are prosecuted on charges relating to arms trafficking offences (eg for violating the state's custom laws).[9] The infamous arms broker and transporter Victor Bout[10] was, despite numerous allegations of his involvement in assisting international crimes,[11] eventually prosecuted for domestic terrorism offences.[12]

In reality, domestic export regulations have not succeeded in preventing weapons from reaching the perpetrators of international crimes around the globe.[13] Arms traders who knowingly supply weapons to perpetrators of atrocity do not face any credible threat that they will be punished for complicity in war crimes, crimes against humanity, or genocide, only for less serious offences that

[5] See Andrew Tan (ed), *The Global Arms Trade: A Handbook* (Routledge 2014).

[6] See Zeray Yihdego, *The Arms Trade and International Law* (Bloomsbury 2007) 111.

[7] Rachel Stohl and Suzette Grillot, *The International Arms Trade* (Polity 2009) 23. See Yihdego (n 6) 111.

[8] See Yihdego (n 6) 111.

[9] Andrew Feinstein and Paul Holden, 'Arms Trafficking' in Letizia Paoli (ed), *The Oxford Handbook of Organized Crime* (OUP 2014) 444.

[10] Feinstein and Holden (n 9) 115.

[11] See Leigh Rome, 'The Case for Prosecuting Arms Traffickers in the International Criminal Court' (2015) 36 Cardozo Law Review 1152.

[12] *United States v Victor Bout*, Trial Judgment, 2 November 2011, District Court for the Southern District of New York; *United States v Victor Bout*, Appeal Judgment, 27 September 2013, United States Court of Appeals for the Second Circuit, United States, 12-1487-cr, 3–4.

[13] See Annyssa Bellal, 'Arms Transfers and International Human Rights Law' in Stuart Casey-Maslen (ed), *Weapons Under International Human Rights Law* (CUP 2014) 448, 463.

involve different forms of criminality and protect different social interests. An important limitation of the existing system of national export regulations is therefore that it does not criminalize complicity in international crimes.

2.2.2 The Netherlands: Unlawful Exports as Complicity

The notable exception to the general lack of any enforcement of International Criminal Law against complicit arms traders comes from the Netherlands, the first national system to convict arms traders in domestic courts for their complicity in international crimes.[14] The two Dutch cases of *Van Anraat* and *Kouwenhoven* demonstrate how prosecutions for accomplice liability can complement the existing system of export regulation.

Frans van Anraat was convicted in 2005 in the District Court of The Hague for aiding and abetting the commission of offences under the War Crimes Act of the Netherlands by supplying chemicals that contributed to the commission of mustard gas attacks in Iraq and Iran between 1987 and 1998 under Saddam Hussein's regime.[15] The conviction was maintained by the Court of Appeal of the Hague in 2007 in a *de novo* trial[16] and left intact by the Supreme Court of the Netherlands in 2009.[17] The ECtHR declared an application from Van Anraat inadmissible in 2010.[18] The complicity of Van Anraat derived from his supplies of chemicals including thiodiglycol to the Republic of Iraq, as well as materials and advice for the manufacture of chemical weapons. The Dutch example shows the potential for similar cases of complicity in Saddam Hussein's crimes[19] to be brought in other EU jurisdictions.[20]

On 5 October 2003, the Dutch Prosecution Service had decided not to proceed against Van Anraat for violations of export regulations under the Import and Export Act,[21] even though, as the District Court later found, the accused

[14] See Marjolein Cupido, Mark J Hornman, and Wim Huisman, 'Lessons from the Netherlands on How to Address Remote Involvement' in Enneking L and others, *Accountability, International Business Operations and the Law: Providing Justice for Corporate Human Rights Violations in Global Value Chains* (Routledge 2019) ch 9.

[15] *Public Prosecutor v Frans Cornelis Adrianus van Anraat*, Judgment, District Court of The Hague (23 December 2005) ECLI:NL:RBSGR:2005:AU8685. He was acquitted of complicity in genocide. See Harmen G van der Wilt, 'Genocide, Complicity in Genocide and International v. Domestic Jurisdiction: Reflections on the van Anraat Case' (2006) 4 Journal of International Criminal Justice 239.

[16] *Public Prosecutor v Frans Cornelis Adrianus van Anraat*, Judgment, Court of Appeal of The Hague (9 May 2007) ECLI:NL:GHSGR:2007:BA4676 (official English translation).

[17] *Public Prosecutor v Frans Cornelis Adrianus van Anraat*, Judgment, Supreme Court of the Netherlands (30 June 2009) ECLI:NL:HR:2009:BG4822.

[18] *Van Anraat v The Netherlands*, Decision on Admissibility, App no 65389/09 (ECtHR, 6 July 2010).

[19] Harmen G van der Wilt, 'Genocide v War Crimes in The Van Anraat Appeal' (2008) 6 Journal of International Criminal Justice 557.

[20] See Michael J Kelly, '"Never Again"? German Chemical Corporation Complicity in the Kurdish Genocide' (2013) 31 Berkeley Journal of International Law 348.

[21] *Van Anraat*, District Court (n 15) para 5.1.

intentionally stated incorrect final destinations and false details of end usage on export documentation.[22] The conduct of Van Anraat in transferring chemicals preceded the Security Council arms embargo on Iraq in 1990, precluding charges on that basis.[23] The prosecution could, nonetheless, have opted to charge Van Anraat with domestic regulatory law breaches of the export restrictions on transferring certain chemicals to Iraq that had already been put in place at this time.[24] The novelty of the Dutch prosecution strategy here was to characterize Van Anraat's supplies as complicit assistance, rather than a breach of export rules.

The other Dutch case of arms transfer complicity for international crimes was against Augustinus Kouwenhoven.[25] The case concerned atrocities committed by former President of Liberia Charles Taylor and his armed forces in the period 2000 to May 2003.[26] The conviction was confirmed by the Supreme Court in 2018.[27] Unlike Van Anraat, the initial District Court conviction of Kouwenhoven in 2006 was not on the charges of complicity in international crimes laid before it, but for breaches of Dutch export regulations in the Sanctions Act.[28] Kouwenhoven was then acquitted by the Court of Appeal in 2008 of all charges.[29] In 2017, following the Supreme Court's quashing of the acquittal, the Court of Appeal convicted Kouwenhoven on a *de novo* retrial, this time for aiding and abetting war crimes as well as breaches of the Sanctions Act.[30] Kouwenhoven was thus convicted and sentenced to imprisonment for his complicity in international crimes. On 21 February 2020, however, a magistrate in South Africa denied the Netherlands' requests for Kouwenhoven's extradition on the basis of his Dutch nationality under the active personality principle, reportedly on the basis that the Dutch courts had not convicted Kouwenhoven from crimes committed in the Netherlands.[31]

It is notable that the Dutch prosecutions of *Van Anraat* and *Kouwenhoven* coincided with the interest of the International Criminal Court (ICC) in arms traders, as

[22] *Van Anraat*, District Court (n 15) para 11.3.

[23] UNSC Res 661 (1990) UN Doc S/RES/661.

[24] *Van Anraat*, Court of Appeal (n 16) para 11.

[25] See Göran Sluiter and Sean Yau, 'Aiding and Abetting and Causation in the Commission of International Crimes—The Cases of Dutch Businessmen van Anraat and Kouwenhoven' in Nina HB Jørgensen (ed), *The International Criminal Responsibility of War's Funders and Profiteers* (CUP 2020) 304.

[26] *Public Prosecutor v Guus Kouwenhoven* (Judgment) Supreme Court of the Netherlands (18 December 2018) ECLI:NL:HR:2018:2336, para 3.

[27] *Kouwenhoven*, Supreme Court Judgment (n 26).

[28] *Public Prosecutor v Guus Kouwenhoven* (Judgment) District Court of The Hague (7 June 2006) ECLI:NL:RBSGR:2006:AY5160.

[29] *Public Prosecutor v Guus Kouwenhoven* (Judgment) Court of Appeal of The Hague (10 March 2008) ECLI:NL:GHSGR:2008:BC6068, para 9.

[30] *Public Prosecutor v Guus Kouwenhoven* (Judgment) Court of Appeal of 's-Hertogenbosch (21 April 2017) ECLI:NL:GHSHE:2017:1760, English translation: ECLI:NL:GHSHE:2017:2650, L.2, see ss 1A in the further alternative, 2A in the further alternative, 3A in the further alternative, 4 and 5.

[31] Kaajal Ramjathan-Keogh and Andrew Feinstein, 'Why is South Africa providing a haven for an arms dealer convicted of war crimes?' (*Daily Maverick*, 18 March 2020) <www.dailymaverick.co.za/article/2020-03-18-why-is-south-africa-providing-a-haven-for-an-arms-dealer-convicted-of-war-crimes/#gsc.tab=0> accessed 22 June 2020.

reflected in Luis Moreno Ocampo's announcement on 8 September 2003 in the DRC investigations about 'those who provide weapons'.[32] At around the same time, the Dutch Prosecution Service was determining whether to proceed against Van Anraat.[33] Meanwhile, Kouwenhoven had previously been named by a UN Panel of Experts in 2000 as a member of Charles Taylor's 'inner circle' in Liberia responsible for arms transfers into Sierra Leone.[34] Kouwenhoven was named in the Panel report together with Victor Bout, perhaps the most infamous of arms dealers, and Leonard Minin.[35] Interestingly, Kouwenhoven had also been amongst the arms traders that the former SCSL Prosecutor indicated he was considering charging, as were Bout and Minin.[36]

The opening of the Dutch investigation in *Kouwenhoven* in the spring of 2004,[37] has been described by some commentators as a response to the UN Panel report and a Global Witness report dated March 2003.[38] But it also came on the heels of the Prosecutor's announcement in September 2003, and it may be that the Prosecutor's actions contributed to triggering the Dutch investigations. If true, even though Ocampo's fleeting attentiveness to arms transfers did not lead to charges at the ICC, the *Van Anraat* and *Kouwenhoven* cases could be regarded as an unrecognized success of the ICC in stimulating national enforcement of International Criminal Law through 'positive complementarity'.

2.2.3 The UK: Challenging the 'Lawful' Trade

The export regulations that relate to international crimes have been challenged in the UK through judicial review proceedings on the lawfulness of the British government's assessment of arms exports to Saudi Arabia for use in the conflict in Yemen. A significant legal development came in the 2017 decision of the Court of Appeal of England and Wales in *R (Campaign Against the Arms Trade) v Secretary of State for International Trade* that the UK government's assessment of arms exports to Saudi Arabia for use in the conflict in Yemen was unlawful.[39]

32 See Introduction.
33 *Van Anraat*, District Court (n 15) para 5.1.
34 UNSC, 'Report of the Panel of Experts appointed pursuant to Security Council resolution 1306 (2000), paragraph 19, in relation to Sierra Leone' (20 December 2000) UN Doc S/2000/1195, paras 215, 217.
35 UNSC Sierra Leone Report (n 34) paras 208–11, 217, 229–34.
36 Charles Chernor Jalloh, 'Special Court for Sierra Leone: Achieving Justice' (2011) 32 Michigan Journal of International Law 395, 424.
37 *Kouwenhoven*, Supreme Court Judgment (n 26), para 2.1.
38 Larissa van den Herik, 'The Difficulties of Exercising Extraterritorial Criminal Jurisdiction: The Acquittal of a Dutch Businessman for Crimes Committed in Liberia' (2009) 9 International Criminal Law Review 211, 211–12, citing Global Witness, 'The Usual Suspects. Liberia's Weapons and Mercenaries in Côte d'Ivoire and Sierra Leone. Why It's Still Possible, How it Works and How to Break the Trends' (Global Witness, March 2003). See *Kouwenhoven*, Supreme Court Judgment (n 26), para 2.1.
39 [2019] EWCA Civ 1020.

The judicial review litigation emerged from the initiatives of NGOs and civil society, notably the Campaign Against the Arms Trade (CAAT) to challenge the legality of UK arms exports to Saudi-led coalition members used in the War in Yemen.[40] A first step towards proceedings came in 2015 when Amnesty International, Saferworld, and Oxfam commissioned a legal opinion from Philippe Sands QC, Andrew Clapham, and Blinne Ní Ghrálaigh.[41] The challenge to the Secretary of State's grant of licences for the export of arms to the Kingdom of Saudi Arabia was dismissed at first instance by the Divisional Court in 2017.[42] On 20 June 2019, the Court of Appeal held in *R (Campaign Against the Arms Trade) v Secretary of State for International Trade* that the UK government assessed the 'clear risk' of international crimes irrationally, and therefore unlawfully.[43] After the proceedings were not heard by the UK's Supreme Court in 2020 as expected,[44] CAAT filed a renewed judicial review application and on 20 April 2021 was granted permission for its legal challenge to proceed to the High Court. On 6 June 2023, the High Court delivered a verdict dismissing the challenge to the resumption of exports and finding that the then Secretary of State for International Trade was not acting irrationally in their decision to license arms sales to the Saudi-led coalition.[45]

From the outset, the strategy of the NGOs was to seek judicial review of the UK government's failure to pre-emptively prevent exports to Saudi Arabia, rather than to focus on the individual accountability of British state and corporation officials for complicity in international crimes, for instance by seeking to trigger a private prosecution. The Rome Statute legal standards on war crimes were considered relevant and important to the UK's obligations under the ATT to assess its export authorizations.[46] However, since it was not within the scope of the judicial review proceedings to consider individual criminality, the UK litigation on Yemen has thus far emphasized only the preventative aspect of domestic export controls, rather than the accountability potential of International Criminal Law. A question implicitly raised by the expert opinion is whether, irrespective of the legality of a government's export authorization, the relevant state and corporate officials could be liable under International Criminal Law.

[40] Sam Perlo-Freeman, 'The ATT and War Profiteering: The Case of the UK' (2020) 12 Global Responsibility to Protect 178.

[41] Philippe Sands, Andrew Clapham, and Blinne Ní Ghrálaigh 'The Lawfulness of the Authorisation by the United Kingdom of Weapons and Related Items for Export to Saudi Arabia in the Context of Saudi Arabia's Military Intervention in Yemen' (*Saferworld*, 11 December 2015) <www.saferworld.org.uk/downloads/pubdocs/legal-opinion-on-uk-arms-exports-to-saudi.pdf> accessed 4 August 2024.

[42] [2017] EWHC 1726.

[43] See *Campaign Against the Arms Trade* (n 39).

[44] See also Admas Habteslasie, 'A Humanitarian Intervention? The Court of Appeal Decision in *CAAT v Secretary of State for Trade*' (2019) Judicial Review 169.

[45] Susanne Hansen, 'Exploiting and Constructing Legal Ambiguity. UK Arms Exports to Saudi Arabia during the War in Yemen' (2023) European Security 32(4) 607.

[46] Sands, Clapham, and Ní Ghrálaigh (n 41) paras 2.31–2.36.

In other words, regardless of the outcome of judicial review proceedings on the issue whether the UK government's export policy for Saudi Arabia is lawful under UK law, the question remains whether UK state officials, and corporate executives of the major British arms manufacturing corporations could be individually complicit under international law. The individual criminal responsibility of state officials and corporate executives for complicity in war crimes in Yemen is the issue taken up by an NGO complaint filed to the ICC under Article 15 of the Rome Statute.[47]

2.2.4 Export Regulations Are Constrained by Foreign Policy

The ineffectiveness of current regulation in stopping arms reaching atrocity situations underscores the potential of International Criminal Law. A primary criticism of national export regulations is that their effectiveness is constrained by the foreign policy concerns of the exporting state.[48] Arguably, the major arms manufacturing states have developed their national export controls, and participated in the development of international agreements including the ATT, in such a way as to ensure the protection of their economic, security, and strategic interests.[49]

The literature seeking to explain the aims and purposes of states in regulating exports identifies at least three sets of protected interests underlying the current system of national export regulation: (i) the needs of states to ensure they can trade freely on international markets, (ii) specific strategic and military interests to prevent exports to particular states (and in more recent time to particular non-state armed groups), and (iii) the more general security interests of states in response to threats to global peace and security, including by reducing arms proliferation.[50]

These interests differ from those at stake in the regulation of domestic gun ownership. For the US, as the only country in the world with extremely high levels of legal gun ownership amongst its citizens, there is a powerful economic interest for the government in ensuring sales of weapons to the domestic market. The interests of other countries in restricting weapons domestically centre on: (i) the protection of domestic security interests, (ii) the reduction of arms proliferation on the black market out of concern for terrorism and organized crime, and (iii) the prevention

[47] Linde Bryk and Miriam Saage-Maaß, 'Individual Criminal Liability for Arms Exports under the ICC Statute: A Case Study of Arms Exports from Europe to Saudi-led Coalition Members Used in the War in Yemen' (2019) 17 Journal of International Criminal Justice 1116, 1119.

[48] Anna Stavrianakis, 'Controlling Weapons Circulation in a Postcolonial Militarised World' (2019) 45 Review of International Studies 57.

[49] Michael Brzoska and Frederic S Pearson, *Arms and Warfare: Escalation, De-escalation, and Negotiation* (University of South Carolina Press 1998).

[50] See Barry Buzan and Eric Herring, *The Arms Dynamic in World Politics* (Lynne Rienner 1998); Anders Akerman and Anna Larsson Seim, 'The Global Arms Trade Network 1950–2007' (2014) 42 Journal of Comparative Economics 535.

of violent crime within their jurisdiction.[51] It is noticeable that the concerns for crime prevention and non-proliferation of small arms that are important for most governments in their domestic policy-making, do not seem to be as determinative of states' policies when exporting weapons extraterritorially.[52] As such, national export regulations may be structurally incapable of prioritizing the interests of foreign victims of international crimes, which fall far down the domestic political agenda when it comes to arms exports.

While scholars have identified 'a self-declared ethical turn' in domestic policy-making on arms exports, there is limited support for this in empirical studies, which do not show any significant shift towards more ethical arms export policies.[53] There has been an undeniable change in the rhetoric of major exporting states over the last half-century towards articulating their responsible arms policies. Platte and Leuffen's statistical analysis in 2016 found that German arms export decisions did not discriminate against human rights-violating and less- or non-democratic recipient countries.[54] Although there does not appear to have been a reduction in the export of weapons into conflicts where international crimes are committed, in the twelve years since the original concept for this book began in around 2012, irresponsible arms exports have gone from being a relatively fringe issue to a central human rights concern, for instance in conflicts in Yemen[55] and Israel/Gaza.[56]

Erickson conducted statistical analysis of the export practices of top supplier states from 1981 to 2010 for small arms and light weapons and major conventional weapons.[57] Erickson's study found that both before and after states' declarations of support for 'responsible' arms export initiatives, there was a lack of any significant reduction of exports in response to poor human rights performance of a recipient.[58] Commentators describe the increasing 'instrumentalization of arms export control policy in the service of economic and foreign policy goals',[59] and

[51] Douglas R Murray, 'Handguns, Gun Control Laws and Firearm Violence' (1975) 23 Social Problems 81, 81.

[52] Suzette R Grillot, 'Global Gun Control: Examining the Consequences of Competing International Norms (2011) 17 Global Governance 529, 532.

[53] Richard AI Johnson and Spencer L Willardson. 'Human Rights and Democratic Arms Transfers: Rhetoric versus Reality with Different Types of Major Weapon Systems' (2018) 62 International Studies Quarterly, 453; Richard Perkins and Eric Neumayer 'The Organized Hypocrisy of Ethical Foreign Policy: Human Rights, Democracy and Western Arms Sales' (2010) 41 Geoforum 247.

[54] Hendrik Platte and Dirk Leuffen, 'German Arms Exports: Between Normative Aspirations and Political Reality' (2016) 25 German Politics 561, 575.

[55] Bryk and Saage-Maaß (n 47).

[56] 'Arms exports to Israel must stop immediately' (*United Nations Human Rights*, 23 February 2024) <https://www.ohchr.org/en/press-releases/2024/02/arms-exports-israel-must-stop-immediately-un-experts> accessed 4 August 2024.

[57] Jennifer L Erickson, 'Punishing the Violators? Arms Embargoes and Economic Sanctions as Tools of Norm Enforcement' (2020) 46 Review of International Studies 142.

[58] Erickson (n 57) 142.

[59] Michael Bothe and Thilo Marauhn, 'The Arms Trade: Comparative Aspects of Law' (1993) 26 Revue Belge de Droit International 25.

claim that the relationship between some major arms manufacturers and governments to be 'ever-more symbiotic'.[60]

2.2.5 Limitations to Specified Types of Item

In comparison to International Criminal Law, national export regulations are structurally limited in their effectiveness due to their reliance on specified categories of arms, ammunition, *matériel*, and dual-use goods. Comparative studies of national export regulations show a great deal of variation in the categories of items in different jurisdictions,[61] including long-standing differences in how some countries traditionally define *matériel*, for instance to include cameras, bridge-building equipment, machinery and construction tools, or even blueprints and technical information, or industry knowledge.[62] The rise of digital technologies that may have dual uses (for instance: artificial intelligence for improving uranium enrichment), calls into question the sufficiency of existing regulation to regulate digital items, how the cross-border 'transfer' of digitally supplied electronic goods is regulated, and exacerbates concerns over effective enforcement of stated end users.[63]

Export controls are also limited by their reliance on end user certification.[64] Some states have recognized this limitation by imposing controls on re-exporting and monitoring requirements to ensure good receipt, to reduce diversion and transshipment.[65] It is also important to note that domestic export controls are limited to cross-border transfers, excluding transfers within the same jurisdiction, such as diversion from legitimate military and security forces, or UN peacekeeping forces.

A limitation of export regulation is therefore that it only applies to specific lists of items, while International Criminal Law can hold individuals responsible for supplying any sort of item, irrespective of whether it is covered by national export regulations. As an example, commercial drone components might be lawfully traded, yet used in alleged war crimes. Even if these items were permissible under the national regulations of the exporting state, this would not rule out international criminal liability. The assessment under International Criminal Law would be whether the drone components are supplied knowing that they will be used to

[60] Sam Perlo-Freeman, 'The United Kingdom Arms Industry in a Globalized World' in Andrew Tan (ed), *The Global Arms Trade: A Handbook* (Routledge 2014) 263.

[61] See Andrew Tan (ed), *The Global Arms Trade: A Handbook* (Routledge 2014).

[62] Bothe and Marauhn (n 59) 20, 27, 30.

[63] Roland Klein, Working Paper on 'International Law and Export Controls of Digital Dual-Use-Items', 29 November 2021, presentation at University of Amsterdam.

[64] See Tan (n 61).

[65] Karl M Meessen, *International Law of Export Control: Jurisdictional Issues* (Aspen Publishers 1992) 19.

commit atrocities. While national export regulations are limited by categorization of items, criminal law deals with *actus reus* and *mens rea*.

2.2.6 Ineffective Brokering Regulation

Export regulations are also limited in their effectiveness to address arms brokers. Despite being small scale and organizationally non-complex, these intermediaries can often be pivotal to the commission of international crimes. In South Sudan, for instance, the UN Special Panel found that small arms shipments were crucial to the SPLM/A in Opposition: the group had initially armed itself from defected sectors of the national armed forces, but as the conflict wore on it was unable to procure resupplies and ammunition, lacking access to official state-to-state transfers or a national arms industry.[66] The SPLM/A in Opposition therefore appeared to have relied on airdrops of ammunition from 'an external source'.[67] International Criminal Law has particular potential to address these sorts of small-scale but essential contributions, where there are few contributory sources of weapons and it is not necessarily the case that 'if this supplier had not sent the weapons, someone else would have'.

Brokers enable corporations and individuals to avoid regulation, since, by its nature, brokering is a business activity that can be easily relocated in order to take advantage of a more permissive regulatory environment in another state. Brokers are often shielded from liability by their residence in a third state, from where they coordinate trades between parties in other states, the arms never coming into the territory of the state where the broker resides. In this 'third state brokering', an individual reaches an agreement in jurisdiction A for weapons to be shipped from jurisdiction B via jurisdiction C to arrive in jurisdiction D. This creates a transnational enforcement problem wherein brokers are able to facilitate transfers between two states which would otherwise be in contravention of the exporting state's regulations.[68] In this way, the brokering activities are carried out from a third jurisdiction where controls on exporting are less stringent or inapplicable. While the extent of domestic brokering regulation varies from jurisdiction to jurisdiction, laws specifically addressed at brokering are weak in many states.[69]

[66] UNSC, 'Interim Report of the Panel of Experts on South Sudan Established Pursuant to Security Council Resolution 2206 (2015)' (21 August 2015) UN Doc S/2015/656, para 22.

[67] Conflict Armament Research, 'Weapons and Ammunition Airdropped to SPLA-iO Forces in South Sudan' (Conflict Armament Research, May 2015); Small Arms Survey, 'Small Arms Ammunition Documented at Bentiu Mosque' (Small Arms Survey, May 2014).

[68] Tomas Hamilton, 'Regulating the Arms Trade: The Potential of International Criminal Law' (2015) International Crimes Database, Brief 175.

[69] Rome (n 11) 1163. See also Elise Keppler, 'Comment, Preventing Human Rights Abuses by Regulating Arms Brokering: The US Brokering Amendment to the Arms Export Control Act' (2001) 19 Berkeley Journal of International Law 381, 387.

The problem is illustrated by the case of Leonard Minin, a well known associate of Charles Taylor.[70] Operating from Italian territory, Minin facilitated arms transfers from states in the Middle East to Liberia and Sierra Leone, in breach of Security Council embargoes.[71] Under Italian laws, the fact that the weapons were not exported from Italian territory led to Minin's acquittal.[72] As a counter-example, the British arms broker Gary Hyde was convicted under UK brokering laws that have developed in response to the third state brokering problem. Hyde arranged for the transfer of 40,000 AK-47 assault rifles, 30,000 rifles, 10,000 9mm pistols and 32 million rounds of ammunition, supposedly destined for the Nigerian police force. As in Minin's case, the defence for Hyde argued that export licence requirements did not apply to him since his activities were related to goods moving outside of the UK (from China to Nigeria), although he coordinated them from within the UK.[73] A lack of clarity in whether the UK's brokering regulations applied in such a situation led to Hyde's trial being suspended, but the Court of Appeal subsequently rejected his jurisdictional argument and Hyde was eventually convicted and sentenced to seven years' imprisonment.[74]

2.3 International Agreements on the Arms Trade

This section now turns to examine the limitations of the international treaties and conventions which coordinate national regulation of the arms trade, to further clarify the distinctive potential of International Criminal Law. Firstly, the ATT is drafted to prevent states from authorizing exports that contribute to international crimes, yet it does not require accountability for criminal complicity in those crimes. Secondly, a brief history of international agreements on the arms trade demonstrates how states have participated in these initiatives to protect their economic, security, and strategic interests, rather than the interests of victims of international crimes. An independent Prosecutor of the ICC, for example, may be able to address arms traders' complicity, where states would lack the motivation to do so.

[70] Feinstein (n 9).

[71] Feinstein (n 9).

[72] Matthew Schroeder, Dan Smith, and Rachel Stohl, *The Small Arms Trade: A Beginner's Guide* (Oneworld Publications 2012).

[73] Allan Urry, 'Jailed arms dealer sold guns to police and MoD' (*BBC News*, 15 January 2013) <www.bbc.co.uk/news/uk-20991545> accessed 22 June 2020; Paul Greenan, 'Jailed arms broker Gary Hyde's international deals' (*BBC News*, 5 December 2012) <www.bbc.com/news/uk-england-humber-20611401> accessed 22 June 2020.

[74] See Jamie Doward, 'How an illegal deal for 80,000 weapons led to the downfall of Britain's 'lord of war' (*The Guardian*, 2 December 2012) <www.theguardian.com/world/2012/dec/02/gary-hyde-illegal-arms-trader> accessed 22 June 2020.

2.3.1 The Arms Trade Treaty is Limited in Scope

When the ATT entered into force on 24 December 2014, there was no multilateral treaty with broad, arguably consensual,[75] membership of states aimed at regulating arms transfers on the basis of, inter alia, International Criminal Law standards including the risk of Rome Statute crimes.[76] Amongst international agreements on the arms trade, the ATT has the broadest membership of states, which, incidentally, is a similar group of states to those party to the Rome Statute.

The ATT has been widely criticized by academia and civil society as ineffective in achieving its original aims. Perlo-Freeman argues that countries who championed the ATT continue to supply arms in the face of clear evidence that they are being misused.[77] From a legal perspective, a significant limitation is '[t]he substantive obligations the treaty imposes are often drafted in an imprecise or ambiguous way'.[78] Several NGOs withdrew their involvement from the treaty negotiations as they developed.[79]

The ATT requires non-authorization of transfers based on unacceptable risks of international crimes.[80] The central provision concerning international crimes is Article 6(3), which provides that State Parties 'shall not authorize any transfer (…) if it has knowledge at the time of authorization that the arms or items would be used in the commission of genocide, crimes against humanity, grave breaches of the Geneva Conventions of 1949, attacks directed against civilian objects or civilians protected as such, or other war crimes as defined by international agreements to which it is a Party'.[81] In addition, Article 6(1) refers to non-authorization where a transfer would violate obligations under Security Council Chapter VII measures 'in particular arms embargoes'. Article 6(2) pertains to non-authorization if the transfer is contrary to other international agreements, in particular those relating to 'the transfer of, or illicit trafficking in, conventional arms'. Article 7 specifies that the relevant standard of assessment is one of 'overriding risk'.[82]

[75] See Dapo Akande, 'What Is the Meaning of 'Consensus' in International Decision Making?' (*EJIL: Talk!*, 8 April 2013) <www.ejiltalk.org/negotiations-on-arms-trade-treaty-fail-to-adopt-treaty-by-consensus-what-is-the-meaning-of-consensus-in-international-decision-making> accessed 4 August 2024.

[76] Sands, Clapham, and Ní Ghrálaigh (n 41) para 2.32 and 22.

[77] Perlo-Freeman (n 60) 178.

[78] Marlitt Brandes, 'All's Well That Ends Well, or Much Ado About Nothing: A Commentary on the Arms Trade Treaty' (2013) 5 Goettingen Journal of International Law 399, 428.

[79] See Philippa Webb, 'The Participation of Non-State Actors in the Multilateral Treaty Process' in Simon Chesterman, David M Malone, and Santiago Villalpando (eds), *The Oxford Handbook of UN Treaties* (OUP 2019).

[80] Andrew Clapham, 'Article 6' in Andrew Clapham and others, *The Arms Trade Treaty: A Commentary* (OUP 2016) 204.

[81] See Clapham (n 80) 18.

[82] See Andrew Clapham 'Article 7' in Andrew Clapham and others, *The Arms Trade Treaty: A Commentary* (OUP 2016) 255.

When it comes to criminal punishment, the ATT's obligations on states to take enforcement measures appear to be constructively ambiguous. Article 5(2) requires States Parties to establish 'national control systems' and Article 14 requires 'appropriate measures to enforce national laws and regulations'. The enforcement provisions of the Treaty do not specify that states must enforce individual breaches of the Article 6 and 7 prohibitions with criminal sanctions. This means that an arms trafficker who violates an export ban that has been imposed due to the 'overriding risk' of international crimes, as set out in Article 6(3), will not necessarily be punished criminally for the trafficking violation.

Additionally, the ATT seems ill equipped to adequately address the problem of third state brokering, where brokers take advantage of a more liberal jurisdiction to conduct their brokering activities. Brokering is a form of 'transfer' within the scope of the Treaty[83] and Article 10 requires states to 'take measures, pursuant to its national laws, to regulate brokering taking place under its jurisdiction'.[84] Article 10 suggests, but does not legally require, measures 'including requiring brokers to register or obtain written authorization before engaging in brokering'. It remains to be seen whether disparities in the implementation of the ATT in different states will leave havens for third state brokering through uneven implementation and a lack of extraterritorial application of brokering regulations.

Moreover, the object and purpose of the ATT is not to provide *ex post facto* accountability for international crimes. Article 1 of the ATT states: 'the object of this Treaty is to [...] Establish the highest possible common international standards for regulating or improving the regulation of the international trade in conventional arms; [and] [p]revent and eradicate the illicit trade in conventional arms and prevent their diversion.' The ATT is directed inter alia at states' pre-emptive prevention of export transfers that contribute to atrocities, which may be backed up by criminal enforcement for the export offence, but does not require *ex post facto* investigations and prosecutions for complicity in international crimes.

2.3.2 International Agreements and Accountability for Atrocity Victims

In considering the potential complementary role of International Criminal Law, it is important to recognize that international arms agreements have not been developed primarily to protect the interests of foreign victims of extraterritorial human rights violations. The central interests at stake in international agreements can be seen from their earliest origins in the Middle Ages, when European nations sought to protect their strategic and military interests through collective informal

83 ATT, art 2(2).
84 ATT, art 10.

agreements not to transfer weapons to the Turks.[85] The first regularized system for state-to-state transfers appeared in Europe in the sixteenth century.[86]

The Brussels Act of 1890 is emblematic of the origins of states' strategic development of arms agreements to protect the interests of weapons suppliers. Signed by colonial states, the leading arms manufacturers of the day, its stated objective was to abolish the African slave trade. The Act proclaimed its aims and purposes to 'efficiently [protect] the aboriginal population of Africa', and to 'secur[e] for that vast continent the benefits of peace and civilization'.[87] While the Brussels Act is often cited for the abolition of slavery, limited attention has been given to Articles 8 to 10 of the Act, which regulate the importation, sale, transportation, registration, marketing and licensing of arms and ammunition. Article 8 refers to 'the pernicious and preponderating part played by firearms in operations connected with the slave trade as well as internal wars between the native tribes'. Here, the primary concern of the signatories, rather than abolishing the slave trade, appears to have been the protection of their strategic interests in Africa by restricting weapons flows to territories that remained under their rule.[88] Meanwhile, the Brussels Act also allowed them to avoid unintended diversion of weapons to those who opposed their rule.[89]

International agreements were thus first developed by manufacturing states to achieve a balance between their economic interests in freely trading weapons overseas, their strategic and military interests in exerting control over the end-use of their armaments (whether by ensuring that weapons reached allies or restricting transfers to adversaries), and their broader collective security interests. Anthony describes how the prioritization of these strategic interests continued during World War I.[90] In 1919, the objective of the Covenant of the League of Nations was 'to promote international cooperation and to achieve international peace and security', noting the arms race that preceded the war, and 'entrust[ing] the League with the general supervision of the trade in arms and ammunition with the countries in which the control of this traffic is necessary in the common interest'.[91] This led, by the 1930s, to manufacturing states legislating the first domestic export controls,

[85] Stohl and Grillot (n 7) 139.

[86] Keith Krause, 'The Political Economy of the International Arms Transfer System: The Diffusion of Military Technique via Arms Transfers' (1990) 45 International Journal 687, 690.

[87] Convention Relative to the Slave Trade and Importation into Africa of Firearms, Ammunition, and Spiritous Liquors (adopted 2 July 1890, entered into force 31 August 1891) (Brussels Act) preamble.

[88] Robert E Harkavy, *The Arms Trade and International Systems* (Ballinger 1975) 213. See also Stohl and Grillot (n 7) 139.

[89] Neil Cooper, 'Race, Sovereignty, and Free Trade: Arms Trade Regulation and Humanitarian Arms Control in the Age of Empire' (2018) 3 Journal of Global Security Studies 444.

[90] Ian Anthony (ed), *Arms Export Regulations* (OUP 1991).

[91] Covenant of the League of Nations (signed 28 June 1919, entered into force 10 January 1920) art 23(d).

the United Kingdom in 1931, then Belgium, the US, Sweden, the Netherlands, and France in 1939.[92]

The historical development of agreements since the 1990s demonstrates the continued prioritization of individual and collective state interests over values of accountability for international crimes and other human rights violations. As Erickson puts it, '[t]he rare attempts to create conventional arms control in the twentieth century buckled under the weight of states' sovereignty, foreign policy, and economic interests'.[93] In July 2001, the UN Conference on Small Arms and Light Weapons (SALW) aimed to build international consensus on domestic arms trade standards and led to adoption of non-legally binding United Nations Programme of Action on Small Arms and Light Weapons (UN PoA).[94] The legally binding UN Firearms Protocol was adopted the same year[95] and the non-binding United Nations International Tracing Instrument (UN ITI) was adopted in 2005.[96] These international agreements referred to the importance of reducing arms proliferation in order to protect human rights, but did not require states to investigate and prosecute the involvement of arms suppliers in the most serious rights violations.

At the regional level, through the EU Common Position and other instruments, the EU has set standards for the non-authorization of exports, and provided guidance for domestic regulation and statements of best practice on exports[97] and brokering.[98] The 'clear risk' standard in the EU Common Position has been interpreted as equivalent to the prohibition in Article 7 of the ATT specifying that the relevant standard of assessment is one of 'overriding risk' of international crimes.[99] The Organization of American States (OAS) developed the *Inter-American Convention Against the Illicit Manufacturing of and Trafficking in Firearms, Ammunition, Explosives, and Other Related Materials* requiring states to establish

[92] Anthony (n 90) 9.

[93] Erickson (n 57) 5.

[94] UNGA, 'United Nations Conference on the Illicit Trade in Small Arms and Light Weapons in All Its Aspects that took place on 9 to 20 July 2001' (2001) UN Doc A/CONF.192/15 (UN PoA).

[95] UNGA Res 55/255, 'Protocol against the Illicit Manufacturing of and Trafficking in Firearms, Their Parts and Components and Ammunition, Supplementing the United Nations Convention against Transnational Organized Crime' (adopted 31 May 2001, entered into force on 3 July 2005) UN Doc A/RES/55/255 (UN Firearms Protocol).

[96] See Peter Batchelor and Glenn McDonald, 'Too Close for Comfort: An Analysis of the UN Tracing Negotiations' (UNIDIR *Disarmament Forum*, 2006).

[97] Sibylle Bauer and Mark Bromley, *The European Union Code of Conduct on Arms Exports: Improving the Annual Report* (SIPRI 2004) 4. See European Union Code of Conduct on Arms Exports [1998] Doc 8675/2/98 REV 2; Joint Action of 3 December 1998 adopted by the Council on the basis of Article K.3 of the Treaty on European Union, on money laundering, the identification, tracing, freezing, seizing and confiscation of instrumentalities and the proceeds from crime [1998] OJ L333; Common list of equipment covered by the Code of Conduct [2000] OJ C19.

[98] Common Position 2003/468/CFSP on the control of arms brokering [2003] OJ L156.

[99] See Andrew Clapham 'Article 7' in Andrew Clapham and others, *The Arms Trade Treaty: A Commentary* (OUP 2016) 255.

laws on the import, export, and tracing of arms, and to create enforcement mechanisms,[100] as well as several non-binding instruments.[101] The Wassenaar Group of states has developed a range of voluntary agreements since 1995.[102] Other agreements were developed by the Organization for Security and Co-operation in Europe (OSCE),[103] North Atlantic Treaty Organization (NATO),[104] and a range of sub-regional initiatives. Extensive regional initiatives in Africa on the arms trade were mostly non-binding in nature but arguably the most far-reaching in scope.

Arguably, the development of international arms agreements has often been overshadowed by the international community's focus on non-conventional weapons.[105] During the second half of the twentieth century, fears that the proliferation of nuclear or chemical weapons could be used to carry out massive atrocities in the West were foregrounded, and this may have pushed into the background the very real atrocities that were being exacerbated by global SALW proliferation. The nuclear threat pervaded international legal discourse throughout the Cold War era,[106] while the only instance of aggressive usage of nuclear weapons remains Hiroshima and Nagasaki in 1945.[107] In relation to chemical weapons, concerns about proliferation grew after they were used in WWI in almost all theatres of war,[108] in WWII in Asia and the European concentration camps, in Vietnam, Cambodia, and Laos in the 1960s[109] (in tactics that originated in British use of herbicides in Malaya in the 1950s),[110] in Iran and

[100] Inter-American Convention Against the Illicit Manufacturing of and Trafficking in Firearms, Ammunition, Explosives, and Other Related Materials (adopted 14 November 1997, entered into force 1 July 1998) Doc A63.

[101] Declaration of Bogota: Inter-American Convention Against the Illicit Manufacturing of and Trafficking in Firearms, Ammunition, Explosives, and Other Related Materials (adopted 9 March 2004) Doc OEA/Ser.L/XXII.4; Amendments to the Model Regulations for the Control of the International Movement of Firearms, their Parts and Components, and Ammunition: Broker Regulations (13 November 2003) Doc OEA/Ser.L/XIV.2.34; Inter-American Convention on Transparency in Conventional Weapons Acquisitions (adopted 6 July 1999) Doc A-64.

[102] Wassenaar Arrangement on Export Controls for Conventional Arms and Dual-Goods and Technologies (adopted and entered into force 19 December 1995).

[103] See OSCE Principles Governing Conventional Arms Transfers (adopted 25 November 1993) Doc FSC/3/96; OSCE Document on Stockpiles of Conventional Ammunition (19 November 2003) Doc FSC1/03; OSCE Handbook of Best Practices on Conventional Ammunition (25 October 2007) Doc FSC73/07.

[104] Owen Greene, 'Examining International Responses to Illicit Arms Trafficking' (2000) 33 Crime, Law and Social Change 151.

[105] Stohl and Grillot (n 7) 2, 7.

[106] See David S Meyer, 'Framing National Security: Elite Public Discourse on Nuclear Weapons during the Cold War' (1995) 12 Political Communication; Nina Tannenwald, 'Stigmatizing the Bomb: Origins of the Nuclear Taboo' (2005) 29 International Security 5.

[107] Richard A Falk, 'The Shimoda Case: A Legal Appraisal of the Atomic Attacks upon Hiroshima and Nagasaki' (1965) AJIL 759.

[108] Kim Coleman, *A History of Chemical Warfare* (Palgrave Macmillan 2005).

[109] Michael G Palmer, 'The Case of Agent Orange: International Perspectives and a Homage to Victims' (2007) 29 Contemporary Southeast Asia: A Journal of International and Strategic Affairs 172, 173, 175.

[110] David Zierler, *The Invention of Ecocide: Agent Orange, Vietnam, and the Scientists who Changed the Way we Think about the Environment* (University of Georgia Press 2011) 63.

Northern Iraq in the 1980s, by the Aum Shinrikyo group in Tokyo in 1995,[111] and more recently in Syria.[112]

There is potential for International Criminal Law to address chemical weapon supply, as in the *Van Anraat* case that concerned chemical precursors used to make mustard gas.[113]

In sum, there was a growth in international arms agreements in the late 1990s and early 2000s coinciding with the establishment of the ICC, at a time when values of international criminal responsibility were in their ascendency in human rights discourse. Yet the aspirations to end impunity and provide accountability for victims of atrocity were absent or overlooked. The development of arms agreements has thus been shaped primarily to protect states' individual and collective economic, security, and strategic interests, while committing states to pre-emptively review their arms exports rather than to investigate and prosecute the impact of exports afterwards.

2.4 Conclusion

The limitations of national export regulation demonstrate some of the potential complementary strengths that International Criminal Law could offer, by providing accountability in a select number of prosecutions of arms traders. The possibility of criminal complicity at the national level gives rise to another legal issue, arising from the fact that national regulation for export authorization exists in parallel to the criminal justice system. For instance, the standards in the ATT seek to ensure that State Parties do not export arms into the hands of perpetrators of international crimes, but at the same time, most of those states are also party to the Rome Statute, which entails State Parties commitment to prosecuting accomplices to crimes against humanity, genocide, war crimes, and aggression. This raises the important question of what happens when a state's determination pursuant to its ATT obligations results in a finding that the export is permissible, yet at the same time there are allegations of Rome Statute complicity. Can an arms trader be held criminally responsible for assisting an international crime when the exporting state has authorized the export as lawful?

As Ambos has identified, the legal value to be assigned to an export authorization by competent national authorities is unclear (Ambos considers this in the

111 Kyle B Olson, 'Aum Shinrikyo: Once and Future Threat?' (1999) 5 Emerging Infectious Diseases 513, 514.

112 OHCHR, 'Report of the Independent International Commission of Inquiry on the Syrian Arab Republic' (5 February 2015) UN Doc A/HRC/28/69, 43; OPCW, 'Third Report of the OPCW Fact-Finding Mission in Syria' (18 December 2014) Doc S/1230/2014.

113. Michael Crowley, 'International Legal Constraints upon the Weaponization of Toxic Chemicals' in Michael Crowley, Malcolm Dando, and Lihao Shang (eds), *Preventing Chemical Weapons: Arms Control and Disarmament as the Sciences Converge* (Royal Society of Chemistry 2018) 146, 151, 176.

context of allegations against major European arms manufacturers for complicity in crimes of Saudi Arabian coalition forces in Yemen).[114] Criminal liability could be considered to be relevant only in situations of 'illicit trafficking' where the arms export has been deemed unlawful by national licensing authorities (as was the case in the Dutch *Van Anraat* and *Kouwenhoven* cases). In this regard, it might be argued that the legality of a transfer under the national licensing scheme of the exporting state ousts international criminal liability, or that the export authorization by competent national authorities provides a substantive defence at trial to the criminal charges.

It would be wrong to assume that national licensing procedures obviate the need to assess criminal liability, as if a state's declaration that a private activity is lawful then absolves the actor of any potential responsibility under International Criminal Law. The authorization of a national export licence might at first glance seem to be equivalent to a defence to any criminal charges. In relation to the executives of major arms manufacturing corporations, as considered by Ambos,[115] does the fact that an export has been licensed by the competent regulatory authorities, vitiate per se the criminal *mens rea* of an individual who knowingly sells weapons in the awareness they will be used to perpetrate atrocities?

This can be explored through the hypothetical of an arms exporter who knows more than the competent national authorities about the risks of their weapons being used in atrocities. Ongoing business relationships with the purchasers of weapons may mean a supplier has a clear understanding of the use of the weapons. How could a corporation that has access to information about crimes that the regulatory authorities do not, which the corporation has not disclosed to the authorities in the assessment of the legality of the export, then plead a defence based on the existence of a national authorization when the corporation has actual knowledge that crimes would be committed with its weapons?

The foundational principle of International Criminal Law is that individuals may be held directly responsible under international law, in their personal capacity, and this includes responsibility for contributing to the commission of war crimes, crimes against humanity, genocide, and aggression. A licence to export weapons is a grant of permission to export, it does not require the exporter to do so, and it only indicates that the government is itself satisfied with the legality of the export.[116] The individual thus retains responsibility for their wrongful conduct and guilty mind.

In sum, the existing system of arms export regulation appears ineffective in fulfilling its goal of *preventing* weapons from being used in international crimes, and

114 Kai Ambos, 'Complicity in war crimes through (legal) arms supplies?' (*EJIL: Talk!*, 20 January 2020) <www.ejiltalk.org/complicity-in-war-crimes-through-legal-arms-supplies> accessed on 22 January 2020.

115 Ambos (n 114).

116 Ambos (n 114).

it was not explicitly designed to provide *accountability* for international crimes. The potential for International Criminal Law in relation to arms exports lies in bringing *ex post facto* investigations and prosecutions that enforce the legal rules on complicit participation in extraterritorial crimes, in a manner that complements the existing regulatory system.

3

'Arms Trade Law' and the Potential of International Justice

3.1 Introduction

As well as export regulation, the arms trade is subject to a plurality of other instruments and mechanisms of international and domestic law. Most importantly, arms embargoes and sanctions limit the flow of military assistance around the globe. In addition, the movement of weapons shipments is shaped by counter-terrorism laws, the law of state responsibility, international economic law, and several other subsidiary areas. These laws are 'subsidiary' in the sense that the stated subject of their regulation is not arms transfers per se; yet nonetheless, they hold the potential to indirectly impact arms transfers and contribute to shaping the decisions of those who supply weapons that may be used to commit atrocities.

There is currently no unified, accepted concept of a comprehensive body of 'Arms Trade Law' in international or transnational legal studies. Neither scholarship nor legal practice has pulled together the disparate forms of transnational legal authority that (directly or indirectly) affect the arms trade into a coherent legal taxonomy. The lack of existing concepts to describe a transnational 'Arms Trade Law' makes it necessary to engage with the pluralistic reality of global regulation, where 'legal pluralism' is defined as the situation in which 'two or more legal systems coexist in the same social field'.[1] Zumbensen refers to the 'complex, multi-layered and hybrid structure' of norms in contemporary society as a 'web of official and unofficial, "hard" and "soft" norms, that render a comparison of instruments and regulatory regimes much more challenging.'[2] Seeking an authentic description of how the commission of international crimes is regulated by the collective effect of 'Arms Trade Law' can be aided by mapping the landscape of transnational law from this broad perspective.

Following Chapter 2's analysis of export regulations, coordinated by international arms agreements, this chapter contextualizes the potential role of International Criminal Law, by analysing the sub-areas of Arms Trade Law and

[1] Sally Engle Merry, 'Legal Pluralism' (1988) 22 Law and Society Review 869, 870.

[2] Peer Zumbansen, 'Comparative, Global and Transnational Constitutionalism: The Emergence of a Transnational Legal-Pluralist Order' (2012) 1 Global Constitutionalism 16, 50–51.

The Arms Trade and International Criminal Law. Tomas Hamilton, Oxford University Press.
DOI: 10.1093/oso/9780192868671.003.0003

identifying potential synergies that could contribute to greater accountability for international crimes.

3.2 Arms Embargoes

In situations where international crimes are taking place, there is often a strong case for imposing an arms embargo. The legal basis for an embargo consists in non-permanent, temporally and geographically restricted agreements to sanction particular targets. In the UN, multilateral embargoes are imposed by Resolution of the Security Council, often in tandem with EU embargoes.[3] Several regional organizations have imposed multilateral embargoes, and certain states have imposed unilateral embargoes.[4]

The system of international, regional, and unilateral embargoes is subject to at least three limitations, which also serve to highlight the potential for integration with International Criminal Law. Firstly, in general embargoes are preventative and—at least in practice—they are not punitive. Even where accompanied by criminal enforcement, they do not provide *ex post facto* accountability for international crimes. Second, embargoes are contingent on the definitions of sanctioned categories of 'arms' and dual-use items. Third, their application is highly selective, such that, in practice, the embargo system fails to prevent weapons from flowing to many situations where international crimes are being committed.

3.2.1 Arms Embargoes Do Not Provide Criminal Accountability

The legal basis for the imposition of a UN embargo is Chapter VII of the UN Charter.[5] The Security Council may impose measures to maintain or restore international peace and security where it determines, pursuant to Article 39 of the Charter, the existence of a threat to peace or a breach of peace.[6] An embargo Resolution requires the concurring vote of the five Permanent Members of the Security Council.[7] Chapter VII embargoes are amongst the non-military (or 'non-forcible') measures the Security Council can take under Article 41 of the Charter

[3] See Kathrin Kranz, 'European Union Arms Embargoes: The Relationship between Institutional Design and Norms' (2016) 29 Cambridge Review of International Affairs 970.

[4] Jennifer L Erickson, 'Punishing the Violators? Arms Embargoes and Economic Sanctions as Tools of Norm Enforcement' (2020) 46 Review of International Studies 97, fn 35.

[5] Rosalyn Higgins and others, *Oppenheim's International Law: United Nations* (OUP 2018) 978.

[6] Charter of the United Nations (adopted 26 June 1945, entered into force 25 October 1945) 1 UNTS XVI, art 39 (UN Charter). See Alain Pellet and Alina Miron, 'Sanctions' in Rüdiger Wolfrum (ed), *Max Planck Encyclopedia of Public International Law* (OUP 2013).

[7] UN Charter, art 27.

(commonly referred to as 'sanctions').[8] Indeed, embargoes have been the most frequently used type of sanction and are often one of the first employed against violations of security norms, both on their own or as part of a broader sanctions package.[9]

The legal standard on which an Article 39 'threat to peace' is factually established has been described as 'mercurial'.[10] It is clear, however, from past Resolutions of the Security Council, inter alia those on Somalia, Rwanda, and Zaire, that the imminence of serious violations of human rights and humanitarian law is sufficient to trigger action under Chapter VII.[11] As such, it is also clear that the ongoing or imminent commission of international crimes is on its own a sufficient basis for the Security Council to impose an arms embargo. In essence, an 'unacceptable risk' that the embargo target intends to commit international crimes may amount to an Article 39 'threat to peace'. This means that in many of the situations in which arms traders may be potentially liable as accomplices to Rome Statute crimes, where it has been established that atrocities are being committed, there will also be a strong legal basis to impose a UN arms embargo.

Embargo enforcement does not usually lead to *ex post facto* accountability for international crimes. A Security Council Resolution normally requires all UN Member States to implement the embargo, including the incorporation of its terms into their national laws, as well as requiring compliance with Security Council cooperation requests, including requests for information and assistance, and cooperation with relevant fact-finding mechanisms such as UN Sanctions Committees and Panels of Experts.[12] However, Resolutions often do not specify the domestic measures through which states must provide enforcement for non-compliance.[13] Even where states provide for criminal enforcement of embargo breaches in their national laws, Resolutions do not usually contain specific requirements to undertake criminal investigations and prosecutions, and there is no supra-national body dedicated to UN embargo enforcement, with many states politically reluctant to advance in this regard.[14]

Even where there is a legal mechanism for enforcement in national courts, actual enforcement remains enormously rare. An empirical study by Stewart found that out of 502 alleged UN arms embargo violations documented by UN fact-finding bodies since 1993, only *one* led to legal accountability for sanctions

[8] Charter of the United Nations (adopted 26 June 1945, entered into force 25 October 1945) 1 UNTS XVI, art 41.

[9] Erickson (n 4) 104.

[10] James Crawford, *Brownlie's Principles of Public International Law* (OUP 2019) 734.

[11] UNSC Res 794 (1992) UN Doc S/RES/794; UNSC Res 929 (1994) UN Doc S/RES/929; UNSC Res 1078 (1996) UN Doc S/RES/1078.

[12] Carina Staibano, 'Trends in UN Sanctions' in Peter Wallensteen and Carina Staibano (eds), *International Sanctions: Between Words and Wars in the Global System* (Routledge 2005) 35.

[13] Erickson (n 4) 102–06.

[14] Katharine Orlovsky, 'International Criminal Law: Towards New Solutions in the Fight Against Illegal Arms Brokers' (2006) 29 Hasting International and Comparative Law Review 377.

violations.[15] From the perspective of International Criminal Law, whether or not arms embargoes are effective as pre-emptive sanctions, it is clear they do not lead to *ex post facto* criminal accountability where weapons have actually reached an embargoed recipient who then commits international crimes. Even in the vanishingly small number of cases where Security Council embargoes are enforced with criminal punishment, it must be emphasized that the conviction will normally be for one of the types of customs, smuggling, or administrative offence associated with breaching arms export regulations, not for complicity in the acts of atrocity carried out by the embargoed recipient. In other words, the enforcement system for arms embargoes, like export regulations, is intrinsically pre-emptive, designed to block transfers of weapons to undesirable end users, and embargoes do not provide *ex post facto* accountability for complicity.

3.2.2 Arms Embargoes Are Limited to Specific Categories of Item

The scope of application of arms embargoes is further limited by their applicability to specified categories of items. There is no fixed practice as to which types of weapons are prohibited, with each embargo tailored to circumstances on a case-by-case basis.[16] In 1963, the first Security Council embargo Resolution on South Africa referred loosely to the cessation of 'sale and shipment of arms, ammunition of all types and military vehicles'.[17] The UN embargo on Yugoslavia in 1991 covered 'weapons and military equipment',[18] while the EU's embargo of Syria in 2011 referred to 'the sale, supply, transfer or export of arms and related matériel of all types, including weapons and ammunition, military vehicles and equipment, paramilitary equipment and spare parts for the aforementioned, as well as equipment which might be used for internal repression'.[19] The EU subsequently made exceptions for arms and supplies destined for UN and other humanitarian bodies,[20] and later, the EU Council saw it necessary to provide specific detail about the categories of embargoed arms, including telecommunications monitoring and interception equipment and certain goods that might be used for the manufacture and maintenance of equipment, which might be used for internal repression.[21]

[15] See James G Stewart, 'The Historical Importance of the Kouwenhoven Trial' (*Blog of James G Stewart*, 5 May 2017) <http://jamesgstewart.com/the-historical-importance-of-the-kouwenhoven-trial/> accessed 4 August 2024.

[16] Orlovsky (n 14) 343, 348.

[17] UNSC Res 181 (1963) UN Doc S/RES/181, para 3.

[18] UNSC Res 713 (1991) UN Doc S/RES/713, para 6.

[19] Council Decision 2011/273/CFSP of 9 May 2011 concerning restrictive measures against Syria [2011] OJ L121/11, art 1; Council Regulation (EU) No 442/2011 of 9 May 2011 concerning restrictive measures in view of the situation in Syria [2011] OJ L121/1, Annex 1.

[20] Council Decision 2011/273/CFSP (n 19) arts 2 and 3.

[21] Council Regulation (EU) No 36/2012 of 18 January 2012 concerning restrictive measures in view of the situation in Syria and repealing Regulation (EU) No 442/2011 [2012] OJ L16/1; Council

The Security Council embargo of apartheid South Africa from 1963 to 1994 demonstrates the conceptual limitations of an embargo and the contingency of the UN arms embargo system, at the time, on the assessment of which types of items are deemed to be associated with the threat to peace. Over the course of three decades, the Security Council progressively expanded the categories of embargoed items.[22] In 1963, only a few months after the first loosely defined Resolution, the scope of the embargo was expanded in a second Resolution to cover 'equipment and materials for the manufacture and maintenance of arms and ammunition in South Africa'.[23] By 1970, the scope was further expanded to 'all vehicles and equipment for use of the armed forces and paramilitary organizations of South Africa', as well as spare parts.[24] The UN then called for the revocation of licences and military patents, prohibitions on investment or technical assistance for manufacturing, and military training and cooperation.[25]

In a 1977 watershed, the UN made the embargo legally binding on all states, and added specific reference to 'paramilitary police equipment'.[26] From 1984, the UN also encouraged the cessation of imports from South Africa of arms, ammunition, and military vehicles, and entry for display in international arms fairs and exhibitions.[27] Again in 1986, the Security Council significantly expanded the embargo to include spare parts and components.[28] Dual-use items were included where a state had 'reason to believe [the items were] destined for' South African state forces and were 'intended for military purposes', including aircraft, telecommunication equipment, computers, and four-wheel drive vehicles.[29] The 1986 Resolution also covered visits or exchanges involving technical support to military or police capabilities, and required states to take measures relating to supplies through third parties, thereby calling for greater consideration of the risks of diversion.[30] The Resolution requested states to implement the embargo into their national laws, including necessary monitoring mechanisms.[31]

The Security Council expanded the South Africa embargo over some thirty years, reflecting a realization that the effectiveness of Chapter VII measures required not only an assessment of the inherent characteristics of weapons, but close scrutiny of the context in which items were being used. The amendments were not

Regulation (EU) No 509/2012 of 15 June 2012 amending Regulation (EU) No 36/2012 concerning restrictive measures in view of the situation in Syria [2012] OJ L156/10.

22 See UNSC Res 919 (1994) UN Doc S/RES/919.
23 UNSC Res 182 (1963) UN Doc S/RES/182, para 5.
24 UNSC Res 282 (1970) UN Doc S/RES/282, para 1(4)(b), (c).
25 UNSC Res 282 (1970) UN Doc S/RES/282 para 1(4)(d), (e), (f).
26 UNSC Res 418 (1977) UN Doc S/RES/418, paras 2–4.
27 UNSC Res 558 (1984) UN Doc S/RES/558; UNSC Res 591 (1986) UN Doc S/RES/591, para 6.
28 UNSC Res 591 (1986) UN Doc S/RES/591, paras 1–2.
29 UNSC Res 591 (1986) UN Doc S/RES/591, para 3.
30 UNSC Res 591 (1986) UN Doc S/RES/591, paras 10, 11.
31 UNSC Res 591 (1986) UN Doc S/RES/591, paras 10, 11.

primarily a result of the worsening situation in South Africa but rather the realization that the preceding provisions have been ineffective.[32] The language of the early embargoes allowed too much interpretative latitude to states, particularly the omission of dual-use items which led to items reaching the military following importation under the guise of intended civilian usage.[33]

In a 1980 report, a Security Council Committee identified three key problems in the effectiveness of the 1977 Resolution: circumvention of the embargo, state compliance, and the 'phraseology' of the embargo.[34] The Committee referred to 'loopholes' arising from the broad wording of 'arms and related *matériel*' that enabled circumvention of the embargo.[35] This concern is reflected in the text of the 1970 and 1977 Resolutions.[36] Specifically in 1970, the Security Council was 'convinced [that the continuing situation in South Africa] was made possible by the continued acquisition of arms, military vehicles and other equipment and of spare parts for military equipment from a number of Member states and by local manufacture of arms and ammunition under licences granted by some Member states'.[37] Taken as a whole, the trajectory of the South African embargoes from 1963 to 1994 demonstrates the need for close scrutiny not only of the characteristics of supplied items but the context in which certain items may provide assistance to the embargoed recipient.

3.2.3 Arms Embargoes Are Used Selectively

Arms embargoes are not applied to all conflict scenarios, nor to all individuals within a conflict, nor at all stages in the development of a conflict. Embargoes come with geographical and temporal restrictions, often entailing that their scope of application is limited de facto to certain actors or to one side of a conflict. Even where embargoes are applied to an entire territory, the timing of an embargo and its subsequent removal or gradual relaxation may depend on political leveraging of sanctions in ways that are finely attuned to conflict mediation and transition processes.[38]

[32] Philip I Levy, 'Sanctions on South Africa: What Did They Do?' (1990) 89 The American Economic Review 415.

[33] André Wessels, 'The United Nations Arms Embargo Against South Africa, 1977–1994' (2010) 29 War and Society 137, 144; Deon Geldenhuys, *Isolated States: A Comparative Analysis* (CUP 1990).

[34] UNSC, 'Report of the Security Council Committee Established by Resolution 421 (1977) Concerning the Question of South Africa on Ways and Means of Making the Mandatory Arms Embargo Against South Africa More Effective' (19 September 1990) UN Doc S/14179.

[35] UNSC Res 418 (1977) UN Doc S/RES/418, 2. See UNSC Res 421 (1977) UN Doc S/RES/421.

[36] UNSC Res 282 (1970) UN Doc S/RES/282, preamble; UNSC Res 418 (1977) UN Doc S/RES/418, preamble.

[37] UNSC Res 282 (1970) UN Doc S/RES/282, preamble.

[38] Enrico Carisch, Loraine Rickard-Martin, and Shawna R Meister, *The Evolution of UN Sanctions: From a Tool of Warfare to a Tool of Peace, Security and Human Rights* (Springer 2017) 51–52.

Despite many years of initiatives to improve their efficiency, notably the Stockholm Process,[39] arms embargoes have been widely criticized for their contingency on political will, for their frequent enforcement failures that have not prevented the flow of weapons that are used in human rights abuses,[40] as well as for practical problems including unreliable end-user certification.[41] Criticisms of the Security Council's embargo practice pertain to broader weaknesses in its enforcement architecture, since, despite the UN presenting itself as a comprehensive public order system, it has 'at its heart [...] a broad collective discretion fettered by an unaccountable veto'.[42]

The selective use of embargoes appears to have increased in recent times. The early Article 41 practice of the Security Council imposed embargoes on the importation of arms to the entire territory of the state against which non-forcible measures were applied. The embargo of Yugoslavia in 1991 was construed in relatively broad terms, the Security Council requiring all Member States to 'immediately implement a general and complete embargo on all deliveries of weapons and military equipment to Yugoslavia'.[43] Since the 1990s, the scope of application of Security Council embargoes has narrowed, consistent with sanctions packages that have increasingly targeted particular individuals or groups,[44] often attributed to the growth in a perception of comprehensive sanctions as excessive and inhumane.[45] Changes to arms embargo practice are better understood, however, as reflecting the post-Cold War calibration of the UN sanctions system to fit 'the changing profiles of asymmetric opponents while at the same time taking heed of humanitarian concerns'.[46] This calibration was necessitated, primarily, by the rise of non-state armed groups in increasingly 'anarchic' armed conflict.[47]

The selectivity of embargoes is criticized as prioritizing the interests of powerful states.[48] In the non-embargo of Zimbabwe, China and Russia's objections trumped

[39] Carina Staibano, 'Trends in UN Sanctions' in Peter Wallensteen and Carina Staibano (eds), *International Sanctions: Between Words and Wars in the Global System* (Routledge 2005) 70.

[40] See Neil Cooper, 'What's the Point of Arms Transfer Controls?' (2006) 118 Contemporary Security Policy 27, 119–20.

[41] Bjorn Hagelin, 'International Armament Embargoes and the Need for End-Use Documents' in Carina Staibano and Peter Wallensteen (eds), *International Sanctions: Between Wars and Words* (Routledge 2005).

[42] Crawford (n 10) 732.

[43] UNSC Res 713 (1991) UN Doc S/RES/713, para 6.

[44] Staibano (n 39) 35. This was accompanied by a concomitant rise of mechanisms for challenging individual designations under targeted sanction measures. See Maya Lester and Brian Kennelly, 'Judicial Review of Sanctions Decisions: "The Wrong Point in the Wrong Court with the Wrong Defendant"?' (2013) 18 Judicial Review 206.

[45] Erickson (n 4) 101.

[46] Carisch, Rickard-Martin, and Meister (n 38) 51–52.

[47] See Andrew Clapham, *Human Rights Obligations of Non-State Actors* (OUP 2006) 13.

[48] See Philippa Webb and Christopher Michaelsen, 'Strengthening the Accountability of the UN Security Council' (2014) 19 Journal of Conflict and Security Law 385.

human rights concerns.[49] As the case study in this book discusses, the UN's embargo activity in response to the Second Congo War was 'too little, too late'. Whether or not the Security Council's use of embargoes to selectively 'take sides' in a conflict undermines the collective security rationale for Chapter VII of the UN Charter, the reality is that UN embargoes are imposed on only a narrow selection of the full range of actors who contribute to international crimes by providing weapons.

3.2.4 Integrating International Criminal Law and Arms Embargoes

In situations where international crimes are being committed, the criteria for activating the international system of arms embargo will often be met. As a consequence, there is potential for mutual reinforcement of arms embargoes and International Criminal Law—through legal and institutional integration of the two systems. When an individual arms trader is held responsible as an accomplice to international crimes, it will frequently be the case that such a prosecution will have the effect of reinforcing the same norms that are reflected in the arms embargo system.

The limitations of the existing arms embargo system—its lack of criminal accountability, its selectivity, and its contingency on sanctioning appropriate types of items—highlight the potential role that International Criminal Law could play. This can be discussed in three different scenarios: where no embargo applies to the perpetrators of international crimes, where an embargo applies but enforcement is weak or absent, and in the rarer case where there is already significant enforcement of an applicable embargo.

In the scenario where international crimes are being committed and no embargo has been imposed, such as the Second Congo War, or where the subjects of a narrowly construed embargo do not include the perpetrators of crimes, there is a role for criminal prosecution. International Criminal Law cannot immediately prevent the flow of weapons, but it can provide some measure of accountability. In particular, the International Criminal Court's (ICC) jurisdictional reach provides a basis to investigate and prosecute arms brokers, transporters, and micro-traders who are geographically proximate to the atrocities. While the choice of ICC Situations may be hamstrung by political constraints that are similar to those faced by the Security Council when imposing embargoes,[50] the Court nonetheless holds

[49] David B Kopel, Paul Gallant, and Joanne D Eisen, 'The Arms Trade Treaty: Zimbabwe, the Democratic Republic of the Congo, and the Prospects for Arms Embargoes on Human Rights Violators' (2010) 114 Penn State Law Review 101.

[50] Mark Kersten, 'A Fatal Attraction? The UN Security Council and the Relationship between R2P and the International Criminal Court' in Jeff Handmaker and Karin Arts (eds), *Mobilising International Law for 'Global Justice'* (CUP 2018) 142, 149.

a potential ability to investigate and prosecute cases involving complicit arms transfers that are not being dealt with by UN embargo.

In the second scenario, of weak or absent enforcement, International Criminal Law could provide reinforcement for the existing embargo system through *ex post facto* prosecutions. The ICC could interact, coordinate, and synchronize with the UN embargo system in a number of ways. Statements of the Office of the Prosecutor of the International Criminal Court (OTP) policy could refer to the investigation and prosecution of known embargo violators, cooperating with the Security Council, UN bodies, and national authorities, and highlighting embargo violators as amongst the priorities for case selection, offering a form of norm expression in itself. Even without opening new Situations, the OTP could look into known embargo violators in existing ICC Situations where evidence against arms traders has already been obtained in the course of investigations and placed onto case files.

There is potential for greater mutual cooperation between ICC investigations and UN fact-finding bodies set up by the Security Council pursuant to Article 41 of the UN Charter that permits the establishment of international commissions of inquiry to investigate allegations of international crimes.[51] The Security Council and fact-finding missions could ensure that where arms trafficking is regarded as an important factor in a situation of armed conflict or insecurity, attention is paid to the role of international criminal accountability. Mandates granted to fact-finding bodies could emphasize the need to attend to the arms trade. Indeed, as the case study on the Democratic Republic of the Congo (DRC) later in this book explores, UN fact-finding bodies have already begun to take an active role in identifying the criminally complicit role of economic actors in several Situations including the DRC, as well as Myanmar[52] and South Sudan.[53]

Security Council Resolutions could also encourage, or preferably require, UN Member States to take measures to hold accountable in their domestic courts any arms trader who breaches an embargo, including on the basis of complicity in international crimes where appropriate. The provisions in Security Council embargoes on national implementation could require Member States to introduce legislative measures to investigate and prosecute individuals who supply weapons in contravention of an arms embargo where there are allegations of their complicity in international crimes. There is legal precedent for using Chapter VII resolutions to mandate the passage of detailed domestic legislation, for instance the

[51] See Catherine Harwood, *The Roles and Functions of Atrocity-related United Nations Commissions of Inquiry in the International Legal Order: Navigating Between Principle and Pragmatism* (BRILL 2020) 40.

[52] See also Tomas Hamilton and Gabriele Caon, *Corporate Accountability for Atrocity Crimes in Myanmar: Business Complicity in the Investigations of the UN Fact-Finding Mission* (Chinese (Taiwan) Yearbook of International Law and Affairs, Brill Nijhoff 2023) 41.

[53] UNSC, 'Interim Report of the Panel of Experts on South Sudan Established Pursuant to Security Council Resolution 2206 (2015)' (21 August 2015) UN Doc S/2015/656.

counter-terrorism measures that the Security Council required following the events of 11 September 2001,[54] or in relation to measures regarding the non-proliferation of non-conventional weapons.[55]

When the Security Council refers a Situation of alleged international crimes to the ICC under Chapter VII of the UN Charter, as it did for Sudan and Libya,[56] the referral could stipulate that attention is given to the arms trade. A Security Council referral to the ICC is for a Situation and not a specific case, but it is inevitable that the referral, since it is based on an assessment that international crimes have been committed, implicitly invokes certain types of conduct, certain actors, and certain modes of liability. The terms of referral could identify the existence of relevant embargoes, emphasizing the Security Council's concern over the role of arms traders in contributing to alleged crimes within the Court's jurisdiction.[57]

Beyond specific ICC Situations and cases, the arms trade could be integrated into the Council's broader role in co-ordinating international criminal justice responses to atrocity. The 'threats to or breaches of the peace' that are the basis for Chapter VII embargoes are also grounds on which the Security Council can establish international criminal tribunals.[58] It did so for the ICTY[59] and the ICTR,[60] and a Chapter VII resolution initiated the establishment of the Special Tribunal for Lebanon (STL).[61] Furthermore, while the Security Council is the primary UN organ to initiate international criminal justice processes, there is potential for the General Assembly to play an enhanced role in bringing about international criminal accountability.[62]

3.2.5 Targeting 'Embargo Busters' Using International Criminal Law

In a third hypothetical scenario of International Criminal Law integration with the UN embargo system, a state may be taking measures against individual arms traffickers in the 'illicit' arms trade who are breaching an existing embargo.

54 UNSC Res 1373 (2001) UN Doc S/RES/1373. See Crawford (n 10) 738.

55 UNSC Res 1540 (2004) UN Doc S/RES/1540.

56 UNSC Res 1593 (2005) UN Doc S/RES/1593; UNSC Res 1970 (2011) UN Doc S/RES/1970.

57 Rome Statute (17 July 1998) 2187 UNTS 3, art 13(b). See Roger O'Keefe, *International Criminal Law* (OUP 2015) 549.

58 See *Prosecutor v Duško Tadić* (Decision) IT-94-1-A (2 October 1995) paras 28–30. See Higgins and others (n 5) 1284. See also UNSC Res 1636 (2005) UN Doc S/RES/1636, preambular paras 19, 21 and paras 3, 11.

59 UNSC Res 827 (1993) UN Doc S/RES/827.

60 UNSC Res 955 (1994) UN Doc S/RES/955.

61 See Nicolas Michel, 'The Creation of the Tribunal in its Context' in Amal Alamuddin, Nidal Nabil Jurdi, and David Tolbert (eds), *The Special Tribunal for Lebanon: Law and Practice* (OUP 2014) 27.

62 Michael Ramsden and Tomas Hamilton, 'Uniting Against Impunity: The UN General Assembly as a Catalyst for Action at the ICC' (2017) 66 International and Comparative Law Quarterly 893.

The state may even have convicted an individual for regulatory offences or for other infractions based on an embargo breach. But in such a scenario, the state will usually have taken no steps to enforce criminal law for the individual's complicity in international crimes.

It has been convincingly argued that an unintended consequence of arms embargoes is that they actually encourage a shift from lawful suppliers towards increased reliance on arms traffickers.[63] In addition, where embargoes are imposed, there is significant empirical evidence that arms imports systematically increase in neighbouring countries, providing new routes for supplies to bypass an embargo.[64] International Criminal Law could target the 'middlemen' who profit from the imposition of arms embargoes. This would reinforce the embargo system while providing some measure of accountability and deterrence for arms suppliers who 'bust' embargoes and facilitate atrocity.

In this third hypothetical scenario, could the ICC exercise jurisdiction under the complementarity standard in Article 17(3) of the Rome Statute?[65] Notwithstanding that the individual has been convicted for breaching the embargo on the basis of the same arms transfer that was the basis of a regulatory offence, could the ICC proceed to investigate and prosecute on the basis of accomplice liability? In its jurisprudence to date, the Court has applied a case-specific test of 'same person and substantially the same conduct' in relation to complementarity.[66] The discussion on the meaning of 'substantially the same conduct' has so far focused on the conduct of principals.[67] But in this third hypothetical scenario, the individual has been convicted by a national court as a principal perpetrator of a domestic regulatory offence, such as an offence of violating a UN or EU arms embargo, or a regular arms trafficking offence, leaving open the question of their secondary responsibility as an accomplice on the basis of attribution of responsibility for an international crime.

It could be argued that the domestic jurisdiction takes precedence since there has been a genuine prosecution for the conduct of exporting weapons. However, the wrongfulness of violating a regulatory rule is very different from that of

[63] Raymond Kuo and Jennifer Spindel, 'The Unintended Consequences of Arms Embargoes' 19(1) Foreign Policy Analysis (2023) 216–35.

[64] Vincenzo Bove and Tobias Böhmelt, 'Arms Imports in the Wake of Embargoes' (2021) 27(4) European Journal of International Relations 1114–35.

[65] See Mohamed M El Zeidy, 'The Principle of Complementarity: A New Machinery to Implement International Criminal Law' (2001) 23 Michigan Journal of International Law 869; Nicola Palmer, 'Tensions in Domestic and International Criminal Justice' (*OUPblog*, 29 June 2015) <https://blog.oup.com/2015/06/tensions-in-domestic-and-international-criminal-justice/> accessed 4 August 2024; Nicola Palmer, 'The Place of Consultation in the International Criminal Court's Approach to Complementarity and Cooperation' in Olympia Bekou and Daley Birkett (eds), *Cooperation and the International Criminal Court: Perspectives from Theory and Practice* (Brill Nijhoff 2016) 210.

[66] See Rod Rastan, 'What Is "Substantially the Same Conduct"? Unpacking the ICC's "First Limb" Complementarity Jurisprudence' (2017) 15 Journal of International Criminal Justice 1.

[67] Rastan (n 66) 3.

complicity in an international crime, and entails a different degree of punishment. The text of Article 20(3) of the Rome Statute refers to 'same conduct' in the following terms: '[n]o person who has been tried by another court for conduct also proscribed under article 6, 7 or 8 shall be tried by the Court with respect to the same conduct.' Indeed, the Statute's provisions on state cooperation in Article 89(4) contain explicit requirements in relation to concurrent action where the person sought is being proceeded against or has been sentenced for 'a crime different from that for which surrender to the Court is sought.' As Rastan clarifies, the Rome Statute thus distinguishes which cases form the subject of admissibility ('same person/same conduct') and which do not ('same person/different conduct').[68] The less serious criminality involved in investigations or prosecution of a breach of an arms embargo, a customs offence, or another arms trafficking offence would not prevent the ICC exercising its complementarity jurisdiction over the more serious allegation of complicity in an international crime. In this hypothetical scenario, the ICC could thus exercise jurisdiction over the same person for a case of complicit conduct in an international crime even where the individual had been convicted for their conduct in breaching an embargo.

This underlines the duality of the two sets of obligations under International Criminal Law and Arms Trade Law. Even where a jurisdictional state has met its relevant obligations to investigate a breach of an arms embargo, the state may nonetheless be regarded as unwilling or unable to investigate and prosecute the same individual for their complicity in an international crime.[69]

3.3 The Plurality of 'Arms Trade Law'

Existing literature tends to view arms trade regulation as the sole preserve of the three primary sources of Arms Trade Law—arms embargoes, arms export regulation, and international agreements. This chapter's research identifies at least twelve areas of Arms Trade Law that indirectly regulate arms transfer conduct, even though weapons are not the explicit subject of their regulation: the law of state responsibility, law on the use of force (*jus ad bellum*), the law of neutrality, international human rights law, international humanitarian law (*jus in bello*), counter-terrorism laws, tort liability, business and human rights, international economic law, cyber regulation, anti-corruption laws, as well as other areas of transnational criminal law that indirectly affect arms transfers (such as regulation of environmental and wildlife crime, human trafficking, illegal resource extraction, and drug

[68] Rastan (n 66) 7.

[69] See further Rod Rastan, 'Can the ICC Function Without State Compliance?' in Margaret M deGuzman and Valerie Oosterveld (eds), *The Elgar Companion to the International Criminal Court* (Edward Elgar 2020).

trafficking). When this transnational assemblage is viewed from the holistic perspective of 'Arms Trade Law', its limitations become clearer, as does the potential for International Criminal Law to contribute to it by punishing those who provide weapons that contribute to atrocity.

3.3.1 The Law of State Responsibility

Compared to many other industries, states play a particularly important role in the arms trade, due to the unusually close regulatory control that government authorities keep over arms exports and the scale of export subsidies. In some cases, arms manufacturing companies are fully state owned or parastatal. A state that supplies arms to another state that commits an internationally wrongful act may be liable under doctrines of complicity according to the customary law principles of state responsibility,[70] codified in the Draft Articles on the Responsibility of States for Internationally Wrongful Acts (ARSIWA).[71] The adoption of ARSIWA by the International Law Commission (ILC) in 2001, having being under consideration for forty-seven years, has been described as 'a radical leap forward in the morality of international law'.[72] Its ramifications for the arms trade,[73] and its interactions with individual responsibility, are complex and have not yet materialized in enforcement.[74]

Article 16 of ARSIWA requires (i) the provision of aid or assistance to a state that commits an internationally wrongful act; (ii) a nexus between the aid or assistance and the wrongful act; (iii) the assisting state possessing the necessary mental element; and (iv) the act being wrongful if committed by the assisting state itself.[75] Like the complicity of individuals under International Criminal Law, complicity under the principle of state responsibility is derivative,[76] meaning that responsibility is contingent on the principal liability of another state for a breach of

[70] See *Application of the Convention on the Prevention and Punishment of the Crime of Genocide (Bosnia and Herzegovina v Serbia and Montenegro)* (Judgment) [2007] ICJ Rep 43.

[71] UNGA, 'Draft Articles on the Responsibility of States for Internationally Wrongful Acts, Report of the ILC on the Work of its Fifty-third Session' (2001) UN Doc A/56/10; Vaughan Lowe, *International Law* (OUP 2007) 120.

[72] Vaughan Lowe, 'Responsibility for the Conduct of Other States' (2011) 4 Japanese Journal of International Law 12, 16; See Miles Jackson, *Complicity in International Law* (OUP 2015).

[73] Nina HB Jørgensen (ed), *International Criminal Responsibility of War's Funders and Profiteers* (CUP 2020) 722. See Silke Zwijsen, Machiko Kanetake, and Cedric Ryngaert, 'State Responsibility for Arms Transfers: The Law of State Responsibility and the Arms Trade Treaty' (2020) 1 Ars Aequi 151.

[74] David Caron, 'The ILC Arts on State Responsibility: The Paradoxical Relationship between Form and Authority' (2002) 96 AJIL 857.

[75] Articles 16, 41(1), and the first and second phrases of 41(2) of ARSIWA create four sets of obligations on states that are relevant to arms trading. Art 41(2)[ii] provides accomplice liability for 'rendering aid or assistance'.

[76] Helmut Philipp Aust, *Complicity and the Law of State Responsibility* (CUP 2011).

a primary rule of international law.[77] Where the injury is suffered by an individual or a corporation, the State of which they are nationals may bring an international claim on their behalf by 'exercising diplomatic protection'.[78]

There are other state obligations of potential relevance to arms supplies, for instance, Article 2(5) of the UN Charter prohibits states from assisting any other state against which the UN is taking preventive or enforcement action.[79] Moreover, the high levels of subsidization of arms exports[80] is a further route through which states may be providing support and services for arms transfers that assist international crimes, such as export credit agencies and official investment insurance or guarantee agencies.[81]

In practice, the threshold for establishing complicity under the law of state responsibility is high, whether one applies a knowledge standard of recklessness (or *dolus eventualis*) or virtual certainty (or *dolus indirectus*).[82] The potential for enforcement of state complicity before the ICJ brings with it the potential for individual responsibility and state responsibility to be considered by different courts in relation to the same factual scenarios.[83] In the Rome Statute, there is a definite separation between individual and state responsibility and Article 25(4) underscores that 'no provision in [the] Statute relating to individual criminal responsibility shall affect the responsibility of States under international criminal law'. The international law of state responsibility is therefore closely linked to the criminal responsibility of state officials,[84] yet only the latter form of responsibility provides individual accountability.

3.3.2 Law on the Use of Force

Under this area of law (*jus ad bellum*), the provision of weapons may constitute a violation of the prohibition on the use of force. Article 2 of the UN Charter provides: '[a]ll members shall refrain in their international relations from the threat or the use of force against the territorial integrity or political independence of any state, or in any other manner inconsistent with the purposes of the United Nations'.

[77] See James Crawford, *The International Law Commission's Articles on State Responsibility: Introduction, Text and Commentaries* (CUP 2002).

[78] See Vaughan Lowe, *International Law* (OUP 2007) 120.

[79] Crawford (n 77).

[80] Paul W Thurner and others, 'Network Interdependencies and the Evolution of the International Arms Trade' (2019) 63 Journal of Conflict Resolution 1736, 1738.

[81] See Philippa Webb and Rosana Garciandia, 'State Responsibility for Modern Slavery: Uncovering and Bridging the Gap' (2019) 68 ICLQ 539, 560.

[82] See Kevin Heller and Lena Trabucco, 'The Legality of Weapons Transfers to Ukraine Under International Law' (2022) Journal of International Humanitarian Legal Studies *13*(2) 251–74, 271.

[83] See Philippa Webb, 'Scenarios of Jurisdictional Overlap among International Courts' (2006) 19 Revue québécoise de droit international 277.

[84] On ARSIWA's interaction with International Criminal Law, see Jackson (n 72).

The prohibition of the use of force is the conceptual foundation for the Rome Statute crime of aggression, which is defined more narrowly.[85]

Article 51 of the UN Charter provides: 'Nothing in the present Charter shall impair the inherent right of individual or collective self-defense if an armed attack occurs against a Member of the United Nations.' In the ICJ case of *Nicaragua*, the Court held that the US 'arming and training' of the *contras* in a non-international armed conflict constituted a violation of the Article 2 prohibition of the use of force against Nicaragua.[86] The principle of a state's non-intervention in the internal affairs of another state may create obligations on states not to supply weapons to non-state armed groups on the territory of another state. The ICJ held that the supply of weapons constituted a 'clear breach' of this principle.[87]

The ICJ's reasoning in *Nicaragua* would almost certainly apply to an international armed conflict where State A provides lethal military assistance to State B for military use against State C. The application of the ICJ's reasoning in *Nicaragua* would mean that State A's actions are a use of force against State C. It has been argued that the applicability of the *Nicaragua* reasoning depends on the recipient State B being 'engaged in hostilities against' State C.[88] There remains some doubt however, whether the existence of hostilities would mean per se that any weapons provided to a State B would constitute a use of force under Article 2. It may be necessary to show, not only that weapons have been provided, but that the weapons are specifically directed at State B's use against State C (rather than for other reasons consistent with the recipient State B's lawful military and security needs).

In other words, applying the *Nicaragua* reasoning would probably mean there is no violation on the prohibition of the use of force under Article 2(4) unless the provision of weapons is linked to specific military use against another state. Moreover, even where the supply of weapons would constitute a 'use of force', if State A is providing the weapons or other support to State B on the basis of rights to collective self-defence, the use of force will not be unlawful. As stated in Article 21 of ARSIWA, '[t]he wrongfulness of an act of a State is precluded if the act constitutes a lawful measure of self-defence taken in conformity with the Charter of the United Nations'. It would therefore be a lawful use of force under Article 2 to provide another state with weapons to defend itself. Nonetheless, according to the ICJ's *Nuclear Weapons* Advisory Opinion, such support must comply with the

[85] Kevin Heller, 'Who Is Afraid of the Crime of Aggression?' (2021) Journal of International Criminal Justice 19(4) 999.

[86] *Military and Paramilitary Activities in and against Nicaragua (Nicaragua v United States of America)* (Merits) [1986] ICJ Rep 14 ('*Nicaragua* case') paras 228–29.

[87] *Nicaragua* case (n 86) para 242.

[88] Michael Schmitt, 'Providing Arms and Materiel to Ukraine: Neutrality, Co-Belligerency, and the Use of Force' (*Articles of War*, 7 March 2022) https://lieber.westpoint.edu/ ukraine-neutrality-co-belligerency-use-of-force/ cited by Heller and Trabucco (n 82) 254.

requirements of necessity and proportionality.[89] In sum, the *jus ad bellum* renders certain arms supplies unlawful, yet the limitation of this area of law is that its prohibitions do not speak to whether weapons are used to commit war crimes.

3.3.3 The Law of Neutrality

The law of neutrality applies to states where there is a situation of international armed conflict and a 'generalized state of hostilities' between two or more other states.[90] A state that is considered legally to have 'neutral' status is not party to the conflict and the core duty of a neutral state is to refrain from providing militarily means to the warring parties, the belligerents, in an international armed conflict.[91] The Hague Conventions of 1907, which prohibited neutral states 'from providing belligerents with war-ships, ammunition, or war material of any kind whatever',[92] and the Geneva Conventions,[93] are sources of the law of neutrality, while the ICJ has confirmed its customary international law status in the *Advisory Opinion on the Legality of the Threat or Use of Nuclear Weapons* in 1996.[94]

The types of activities that could violate the law of neutrality, meaning that a state loses its neutral status and becomes a belligerent party to the international armed conflict, are those that constitute support that is 'capable of influencing the outcome' of the conflict.[95] These activities certainty include the provision of weapons and other lethal military support, and may also include non-lethal material support, as well as intelligence sharing, providing military advisers, and similar backing for a belligerent state.[96] It probably does not include any actions taken by a state in relation to its nationals travelling to fight for or against a belligerent state.[97] The law of neutrality should not be confused with the similar but unrelated question of whether a state supplying weapons can be considered a co-belligerent under international humanitarian law.[98]

[89] *Legality of the Threat or Use of Nuclear Weapons* (Advisory Opinion) [1996] ICJ Rep (226) ('*Nuclear Weapons* Advisory Opinion') 41.

[90] Georgios Petrochilos, 'The Relevance of the Concepts of War and Armed Conflict to the Law of Neutrality' (1998) 31 Vanderbilt Transnational Law Journal 575, 605.

[91] Paul Seger, 'The Law of Neutrality' in Andrew Clapham and Paola Gaeta (eds), *The Oxford Handbook of International Law in Armed Conflict* (OUP 2014) 248.

[92] Convention (V) Respecting the Rights and Duties of Neutral Powers in Case of War on Land, and Convention (adopted 18 October 1907, entered into force 26 January 1910) ('Hague Convention V'); Convention (XIII) concerning the Rights and Duties of Neutral Powers in Naval War. The Hague (adopted 18 October 1907, entered into force 26 January 1910), Article 6.

[93] Geneva Convention for the Amelioration of the Condition of the Wounded and Sick in Armed Forces in the Field of August 12, 1949 (entered into force 21 October 1950) 75 UNTS 31, Article 63.

[94] *Nuclear Weapons* Advisory Opinion (n 89) 41, 88.

[95] Seger (n 91).

[96] Heller and Trabucco (n 82) 258–59.

[97] Heller and Trabucco (n 82) 259.

[98] Heller and Trabucco (n 82) 264–65.

There are at least two points of connection between the law of neutrality and the prevention of international crimes through the regulation of arms transfers. As Heller and Trabucco argue in relation to the Ukraine conflict, it is unclear whether the law of neutrality imposes obligations on a neutral state to prevent a private corporation under its jurisdiction from exporting arms to a belligerent state.[99] It would appear from the text of Article 7 of Hague Convention V that, even where a neutral state is prohibited from providing arms itself, it is not obligated to 'prevent the export or transport, on behalf of one or other of the belligerents, of arms, munitions of war, or, in general, of anything which can be of use to an army or a fleet'.[100] There is legal uncertainty on this point, however, and it is arguable that customary international law extends the law of neutrality to private entities.[101] As well as major arms manufacturing corporations, operating in the so-called 'lawful' trade, it could also be argued that the law of neutrality applies to a state's obligations to take measures to prevent illicit arms trafficking within its jurisdiction from supporting a belligerent. A state that allows 'third-state brokers' to operate on its territory, as discussed in Chapter 2—individuals who export weapons that support a belligerent state—would then lose its neutral status under the law of neutrality.

Secondly, while International Criminal Law exists independently of the law of neutrality, it is clear that a neutral state which provides arms used by a belligerent state in the commission of international crimes against another belligerent would lose 'neutral' status. The effect of losing neutral status is that it permits the belligerent to take counter-measures against the offending state.[102] However, the law of neutrality has also been considered as becoming 'qualified' in the face of aggression that violates the *jus ad bellum*.[103] According to this view (the status of which is unclear under customary international law), 'qualified neutrality' allows neutral states to discriminate in favour of the victim of aggression. This means the state can support the victim state while retaining neutral status and fully conforming with their duty of impartiality.[104] A finding that a state or its officials are complicit in a belligerent's atrocities, through supplying weapons, would almost certainly mean the supplier state loses its neutral status. But under the 'qualified neutrality' view, a state could remain neutral when supplying weapons to fight off an aggressor, and the commission of atrocities by the recipient state would not appear to affect the supplier's neutral status under this area of law.

[99] Heller and Trabucco (n 82) 259.

[100] Hague Convention V, Article 7.

[101] Heller and Trabucco (n 82) 260.

[102] Pearce Clancy, 'Neutral Arms Transfers and the Russian Invasion of Ukraine' (2023) ICLQ 72(2) 527–43, 528.

[103] Heller and Trabucco (n 82) 260.

[104] Clancy (n 102) 543.

3.3.4 International Humanitarian Law

The provision of weapons into situations of armed conflict gives rise to concerns for legality under international humanitarian law, violations of which may also constitute international crimes. States are under duties to respect and ensure respect for international humanitarian law, reflected in Common Article 1 of the Geneva Conventions[105] and Article 1 of the First Additional Protocol.[106]

Common Article 1 of the Geneva Conventions is generally interpreted as conferring a responsibility on third-party states not involved in an armed conflict not to encourage a party to an armed conflict to violate international humanitarian law, nor to take action that would assist in such violation.[107] The authoritative commentary of the International Committee of the Red Cross (ICRC) interprets the Common Article 1 obligations as creating a negative obligation on states in the specific context of arms transfers, as follows: weapons should not be supplied in situations where there is 'an expectation, based on facts or knowledge of past patterns, that such weapons would be used to violate the [Geneva] Conventions'.[108] This implies that the recipient will need to have a poor record of repeated and systematic violations of international humanitarian law and that isolated incidents will not be enough to bar an export.

The ICRC claims that Common Article 1 should be interpreted to contain not only the negative obligation to refrain based on knowledge that weapons 'would be used' in violations, but also a positive obligation on states to influence a Party to a conflict to respect the Geneva Conventions.[109] According to this positive obligation, a state is prohibited from providing another state with weapons when there is 'a foreseeable risk' that those weapons will be used in violations.[110]

International humanitarian law provides a clear basis for refusing to transfer weapons based on an assessment of the likelihood that international crimes will be committed with the weapons. The standard of Common Article 1's negative obligation ('weapons would be used') is likely to prohibit fewer arms transfers than the lower threshold of its positive obligation ('foreseeable risk that weapons will be used'). The positive obligation, if it exists in Common Article 1, probably approximates the threshold of the EU export standard analysed in Chapter 2 ('clear risk that weapons might be used').

[105] Verity Robson, 'The Common Approach to Article 1: The Scope of Each State's Obligation to Ensure Respect for the Geneva Conventions' (2020) Journal of Conflict and Security Law 25(1) 101–15.

[106] Protocol Additions to the Geneva Conventions of 12 August 1949, and Relating to the Protection of Victims of International Armed Conflicts (adopted 8 June 1977, entered into force 7 December 1979) 1125 UNTS 3.

[107] Marko Milanovic, 'Intelligence Sharing in Multinational Military Operations and Complicity under International Law' (2021) 97 International Law Studies 1269, 1325.

[108] International Committee of the Red Cross, Commentary of 2016 on the First Geneva Convention of 12 August 1949 (2016) 162.

[109] Milanovic (n 107) 1338.

[110] Milanovic (n 107) 1338.

3.3.5 International Human Rights Law

The rights protected under the ICCPR,[111] ECHR,[112] and other human rights instruments require states to adequately regulate arms transfers to prevent transfers that facilitate violations. For instance, the United Nations Human Rights Committee (UNHRC) stated in 2014 that 'States parties [should] protect their populations [against] the risks posed by excessive availability of firearms'[113] and in 2019 that 'States parties engaged in the deployment, use, sale or purchase of existing weapons and in the study, development, acquisition or adoption of weapons, and means or methods of warfare, must always consider their impact on the right to life.'[114]

The substantive requirements of international human rights law provide the basis for tortious claims in many jurisdictions, which could extend to the sales of weapons used in serious violations of human rights.[115] In the US, claims under universal civil jurisdiction have been brought under the Alien Tort Statute. US proceedings were brought against the *Chiquita* corporation for transferring weapons to a Columbian paramilitary group.[116] Corporate liability for torts in violation of the law of nations under the Alien Tort Statute has been developed in the Supreme Court cases of *Kiobel* and *Jesner* and the *Nestle* and *Cargill* cases.[117]

An evolving set of non-binding standards on business and human rights deem corporations socially irresponsible if they transfer arms that facilitate atrocity. Compacts such as the *OECD Guidelines for Multinational Enterprises*,[118] constitute benchmarks for what is considered acceptable within the 'ordinary course of business' for certain business communities. They are non-criminal in nature, yet they could form the basis for assessing an individual's knowledge that they are supplying weapons to a recipient that would not be considered acceptable by prevailing business standards. The UN Panels of Experts have invoked non-binding business and human rights standards as benchmarks of corporate behaviour, as Chapter 7 finds in the Second Congo War.

[111] International Covenant on Civil and Political Rights (adopted 16 December 1966, entered into force 23 March 1976) 999 UNTS 171.

[112] Convention for the Protection of Human Rights and Fundamental Freedoms (adopted 4 November 1950, entered into force 3 September 1953) 213 UNTS 222.

[113] UNHRC, 'General Comment No. 35: Article 9 (Liberty and security of person)' (16 December 2014) UN Doc CCPR/C/GC/36, para 9.

[114] UNHRC, 'General Comment No. 36: Article 6: right to life' (3 September 2019) UN Doc CCPR/C/GC/36, para 65.

[115] See Stuart Casey-Maslen (ed), *Weapons Under International Human Rights Law* (CUP 2014).

[116] Caleb Wheeler, 'Re-examining Corporate Liability at the International Criminal Court through the Lens of the Art 15 Communication against Chiquita Brands International' (2018) 19 Melbourne Journal of International Law 369.

[117] See Russell Hopkins, 'What Next for the Alien Tort Statute?' (*Corporate War Crimes Blog*, 30 March 2020) <https://corporatewarcrimes.com/2020/03/30/what-next-for-the-alien-tort-statute> accessed 4 August 2024.

[118] *OECD Guidelines for Multinational Enterprises* (OECD 2011).

Binding legal obligations on business and human rights may emerge in future: notable in this respect is the EU corporate due diligence legislation passed in May 2024,[119] the French *loi de vigilance*, Dutch corporate due diligence legislation, and the Draft Treaty of the UN Human Rights Council Working Group.[120] A treaty of this nature could expand the obligations on states to take measures to ensure that corporations within their jurisdiction refrain from knowingly transferring arms for use in the commission of an international crime.[121] However, it is possible that binding due diligence standards may provide 'carve-outs' for certain industries including the arms trade, which would effectively leave the arms trade to be regulated by existing standards, such as in the ATT and EU Common Position.[122]

Standards for socially responsible financial investment are another source of indirect regulation of arms transfer conduct. Criteria such as the Principles for Responsible Investment usually exclude arms companies[123] There is a long history of arms sales being amongst the most frequent negative social screens for ethical investment,[124] which likely dates back to the refusal of the Quakers and Methodists to invest in the arms trade.[125] There is also the question of the theoretical possibility of an individual shareholder's liability for microscopic contributions to an international crime by holding shares in an arms manufacturing corporation.[126] As Clapham notes, since at least the early 2000s, the sovereign wealth funds of some states have committed to screening out, and divesting from, corporations where there is an unacceptable risk of contributing to corporate complicity in violations of international law.[127] Socially Responsible Investing (SRI) and Environmental, Social and Governance (ESG) investment increasingly influences business actor behaviour and there is potential here for further integration with UN fact-finding and other international crimes investigations. Standards for divestment could be increasingly tied to reports of arms companies knowingly contributing to

[119] Human Rights Watch, 'New EU Law on Corporate Value Chains' 24 May 2024 <https://www.hrw.org/news/2024/05/24/questions-and-answers-new-eu-law-corporate-value-chains> accessed 4 August 2024.

[120] Human Rights Watch (n 119); OHCHR, 'Legally Binding Instrument to Regulate, in International Human Rights Law, the Activities of Transnational Corporations and other Business Enterprises' (16 July 2019) No UN Doc number <www.ohchr.org/EN/HRBodies/HRC/WGTransCorp/Session5/Pages/Session5.aspx> accessed 4 August 2024.

[121] See Stéfanie Khoury and David Whyte, 'Sidelining Corporate Human Rights Violations: The Failure of the OECD's Regulatory Consensus' (2019) 18 Journal of Human Rights 363.

[122] León Castellanos-Jankiewicz and Melanie Schneider, 'Including the Arms Sector in the EU Corporate Due Diligence Directive' (19 May 2023) *Verfassungsblog* <https://verfassungsblog.de/including-the-arms-sector-in-the-eu-corporate-due-diligence-directive> accessed 4 August 2024.

[123] See Principles for Responsible Investment (2020) <www.unpri.org> accessed 4 August 2024.

[124] Silvana Signori, 'Socially Responsible Investors: Exploring Motivations and Ethical Intensity' in Leire San-Jose, José Luis Retolaza, and Luc van Liedekerke (eds), *Handbook on Ethics in Finance* (Springer 2020) 1, 4, 15.

[125] Philippe Gillet and Julie Salaber-Ayton, 'The Recent Development and Performance of Ethical Investments' in Othmar M Lehner (ed), *Routledge Handbook of Social and Sustainable Finance* (Routledge 2017) 2.

[126] Christopher Kutz, *Complicity: Ethics and Law for a Collective Age* (CUP 2007) 209.

[127] Clapham (n 47).

international crimes, even in situations such as Yemen where the arms exporting state considers the exports to be lawful.[128]

3.3.6 Counter-Terrorism Law

Counter-terrorism laws are an important area in which states are increasingly criminalizing the conduct of those who conspire to provide material support to terrorist organizations. These laws have an indirect effect on the arms trade by criminalizing transfers to certain designated groups and individuals. Arms regulation thus occurs indirectly through the mechanisms by which states seek to protect their security interests by preventing terrorism.

Terrorism is not generally characterized as an international crime at international criminal tribunals,[129] with the exception of the STL.[130] The international crimes in the Rome Statute do not include terrorism[131] and the Preparatory Committees in drafting the Rome Statute explicitly rejected the proposed to include several 'transnational crimes'.[132] Counter-terrorism laws prohibit certain arms transfers that are linked to terrorism, and often this same conduct can be legally characterizable as complicity in an international crime.[133] For instance, the actions of a trafficker who provides weapons to a designated terrorist organization such as ISIL, which is engaged in committing international crimes, can be legally characterized in terms of complicity in international crimes and complicity in terrorist offences. It is therefore relevant to consider the extent to which the ongoing and rapid expansion of counter-terrorism treaty law, domestic criminal laws, and terrorism-related Security Council sanctions, are increasing the breadth of prohibited arms transfer conduct.

The eighteen UN 'sectoral conventions' on terrorism have required states to prohibit and punish an increasingly broad range of complicit conduct in recent

[128] See Duncan Macintyre and others, 'Letter: Divestment for Health: Consider the Arms Industry' (28 February 2020) 368 BMJ 765.

[129] Alejandro Chehtman, 'Terrorism and the Conceptual Divide Between International and Transnational Criminal Law' in Harmen Van Der Wilt and Christophe Paulussen (eds), *Legal Responses to Transnational and International Crimes: Towards an Integrative Approach?* (Edward Elgar 2017) 15. See Ben Saul, *Defining Terrorism in International Law* (OUP 2010).

[130] See Philippa Webb, 'Individual Criminal Responsibility' in Amal Alamuddin, Nidal Nabil Jurdi, and David Tolbert (eds), *The Special Tribunal for Lebanon: Law and Practice* (OUP 2014) 88, 90.

[131] The Statute of the Special Tribunal for Lebanon accords terrorism a special status within the subject matter jurisdiction of the tribunal. See *Prosecutor v Ayyash and others* (Decision) STL-11-01/1 F0010 (16 February 2011).

[132] Douglas Guilfoyle, 'Transnational Crimes' in Kevin Heller and others (eds), *The Oxford Handbook of International Criminal Law* (OUP 2020) 791.

[133] Mark Drumbl, 'Victimhood in Our Neighborhood: Terrorist Crime, Taliban Guilt, and the Aysmmetries of the International Legal Order' (2002) 1 North Carolina Law Review 81; Bill Wiley and Nina Jørgensen, 'Linking Economic Actors to the Core International Crimes of the Syrian Regime' in Jørgensen (n 73) 93.

years.[134] The Financing Terrorism Convention criminalizes financiers who know that their funds will be used to support terrorist activities[135] while the Terrorism Bombing Convention criminalizes the supply of materials used in a terrorist bombing.[136]

UN Security Council sanctions have prohibited all forms of support for designated terrorist organizations, such as in Resolution 1267 requiring UN Member States to take measures to ensure that no financial resources are made available to Al-Qaida or the Taliban.[137] Similarly, EU directives have broadened the criminalization of arms transfer conduct that is considered to be connected to terrorism, for instance the criminal prohibition on 'receiving instruction on the making or use of explosives, firearms or other weapons or noxious or hazardous substances, or on other specific methods or techniques, for the purpose of committing, or contributing to the commission of terrorist offences'.[138]

Meanwhile, some national legal systems are increasingly adopting inchoate terrorism offences to sanction conduct prior to and irrespective of the commission of any harm, thereby expanding the scope of criminal liability in systems that traditionally would not punish mere preparatory acts.[139] The US is arguably the site of the most dramatic recent expansion of domestic criminal laws in pre-emptive counter-terrorism offences, exemplified by the *Holder v Humanitarian Law Project* case.[140]

Counter-terrorism laws are thus expanding criminal liability to cover supplies of arms to recipients who do not carry out envisaged crimes, or even attempt to carry them out, and this expansion extends to the criminalization of assistance in acts that may also be characterized as international crimes. The transnational assemblage of Arms Trade Law encompasses counter-terrorism laws, which may criminalize the same arms transfer conduct as International Criminal Law. The important difference is that counter-terrorism prosecutions serve to protect national security interests, rather than providing accountability for victims under International Criminal Law.

[134] Erling Husabø and Ingvild Bruce, *Fighting Terrorism Through Multilevel Criminal Legislation* (Brill 2009).

[135] International Convention for the Suppression of the Financing of Terrorism (adopted 9 December 1999, entered into force 10 April 2002) 2178 UNTS 197, Arts 2(1), 2(5)(a), and 2(5)(c).

[136] International Convention for The Suppression of Terrorist Bombings (adopted 15 December 1997, entered into force on 23 May 2001) 2149 UNTS 256, art 2(3).

[137] UNSC Res 1267 (1999) UN Doc S/RES/1267. See also UNSC Res 1333 (2000) UN Doc S/RES/1333; UNSC Res 1373 (2001) UN Doc S/RES/1373, para 2(e).

[138] Directive (EU) 2017/541 of the European Parliament and of the Council of 15 March 2017 on combating terrorism and replacing Council Framework Decision 2002/475/JHA and amending Council Decision 2005/671/JHA [2017] OJ L88, art 8.

[139] Ben Saul, 'Terrorism in International and Transnational Criminal Law' (2015) Sydney Law School Research Paper 14.

[140] *Holder v Humanitarian Law Project* [2010] 561 US 1.

3.3.7 Other Subsidiary Areas of Arms Trade Law

Several other areas of law have some indirect effect on arms transfers that support international crimes. Firstly, under Transnational Criminal Law, there are widely acknowledged links between the arms trade and several forms of transnational criminality[141] including human trafficking, illegal resource extraction, drug trafficking,[142] and environmental and wildlife crime.[143] Indeed, arms trafficking is frequently so bound-up with other types of transnational crimes, for example where weapons are sold to fund drug trafficking, that it makes little sense to distinguish it as a separate area of activity of an organized criminal group.[144] Effective regulation of other areas of transnational crimes therefore indirectly impact how arms trafficking is controlled.

In the field of Transnational Criminal Law, the United Nations Office of Drugs and Crime (UNODC) plays an important role in coordinating UN initiatives on the arms trade including supporting transnational regulation of the trade through the implementation of the international agreements on firearms and conventional weapons, namely the United Nations Convention against Transnational Organized Crime (UNTOC), the Firearms Protocol, United Nations Programme of Action on Small Arms and Light Weapons (UN PoA), United Nations International Tracing Instrument (UN ITI), and Arms Trade Treaty (ATT). Yet the policies and publications of the UNODC focus on transnational regulation and have not to date recognized the potential synchronicity of UN initiatives with International Criminal Law.[145] There is potential for synergy and reinforcement between arms trade regulation and other forms of regulation of transnational crime. As Chapter 7 finds, the UN recognized the interconnectedness of resource extraction and arms transfers in the Panel of Experts on Resource Exploitation in the DRC.

Cyber laws are also relevant in that the regulation of arms transfer conduct in the supply of cyber weapons or 'digital arms' exists through international and domestic instruments.[146] Regulation remains under-developed and there is little

[141] Zeray Yihdego, *The Arms Trade and International Law* (Bloomsbury 2007) 19.

[142] Neil Boister, *An Introduction to Transnational Criminal Law* (2nd edn, OUP 2018) 212; Dee Cook, Martin Roberts, and Jason Lowther, 'The International Wildlife Trade and Organised Crime: A Review of the Evidence and the Role of the UK' (World Wide Fund for Nature 2002).

[143] See Mariya Polner and Daniel Moell, 'Interagency Collaboration and Combating Wildlife Crime' in Grant Pink and Rob White (eds), *Environmental Crime and Collaborative State Intervention* (Palgrave Studies in Green Criminology 2016) 59.

[144] See Peter Reuter and Davin O'Regan, 'Smuggling Wildlife in the Americas: Scale, Methods, and Links to Other Organised Crimes' (2017) 18 Global Crime 77, 78, 83.

[145] See UNODC, 'Comparative Analysis of Global Instruments on Firearms and Other Conventional Arms: Synergies for Implementation' (2016) <www.unodc.org/unodc/en/firearms-protocol/publications.html> accessed 4 August 2024.

[146] Mischa Hansel, Max Mutschler, and Marcel Dickow, 'Taming Cyber Warfare: Lessons from Preventive Arms Control' (2018) 3 Journal of Cyber Policy 44.

control of the sale of cyber weapons—in some respects the development and sale of cyber weapons cannot be regulated in the same way as conventional weapons.[147] There has been little discussion of the extent to which International Criminal Law may provide accomplice liability for supply of cyber weapons for complicity in an international crime, yet the potential of cyber weapons for use in international crimes is becoming increasingly concrete. In 2017, WannaCry ransomware was reported to have infected over 200,000 computers in more than 150 countries and directly affected health facilities, costing at least £5.9 million to the National Health Service in the UK alone.[148]

Anti-corruption laws are a final area of regulation that indirectly but significantly impacts arms transfers that assist international crimes. Allegations of corruption in the arms trade are rife. The effectiveness of anti-corruption legislation, such as the Bribery Act in the UK, has an indirect but highly significant potential to regulate the flow of weapons to perpetrators of international crimes.[149] Domestic export regulations are often integrated with provisions from anti-bribery legislation.[150] In the US for instance, violations of the Foreign Corrupt Practices Act are written into The Arms Export Control Act and the International Traffic in Arms Regulations (ITAR) as grounds for the suspension, revocation, amendment, or denial of an arms export licence.[151] Again, it is impossible to describe the global regulatory environment of the arms trade without viewing anti-corruption laws as an important component of Arms Trade Law.

Last but not least, international economic law affects the arms trade. The arms trade is indirectly regulated by changes to international trade agreements, policies of the World Trade Organization (WTO) and International Monetary Fund (IMF), and international investment law. Importantly, the arms trade is one of the few remaining areas of international trade that is subject to export subsidies,[152] due to a WTO policy exemption for 'essential security interests' recorded in the General Agreement on Tariffs and Trade (GATT).[153] In addition, the practical effectiveness of enforcement of arms export regulation depends on how customs rules and transport regulations are administered by the World Customs Organization (WCO) and international bodies such as the International Civil Aviation Organization and

[147] Henry Prunckun, 'The Rule of Law: Controlling Cyber Weapons' in Henry Prunckun (ed), *Cyber Weaponry: Issues and Implications of Digital Arms* (Springer 2018) 87.

[148] Shayer Ghafur and others, 'A Retrospective Impact Analysis of the WannaCry Cyberattack on the NHS' (2019) 2 Nature Partner Journals: Digital Medicine 98.

[149] Bob Sullivan, 'Reformulating Bribery: A Legal Critique of the Bribery Act 2010' in Jeremy Horder and Peter Alldridge (eds), *Modern Bribery Law: Comparative Perspectives* (CUP 2013) 13, 15.

[150] See Sullivan (n 149).

[151] Foreign Corrupt Practices Act 15 USC §78dd-1 (1977); Arms Export Control Act 22 USC §2751 (2014); International Traffic in Arms Regulations 22 CFR §120, 126.7 (2014).

[152] María del Carmen García-Alonso and Paul Levine, 'Arms Export Controls, Subsidies and the WTO Exemption' (2005) 52 Scottish Journal of Political Economy 305.

[153] The General Agreement on Tariffs and Trade (adopted 30 October 1947, entered into force 1 January 1948) 55 UNTS 187, art 21.

the Agency for the Safety of Air Navigation in Africa and Madagascar (ASECNA). As well as being essential to the enforcement of Arms Trade Law, regulation by customs and transportation bodies is itself increasingly providing direct regulation of areas outside technical customs regulation.[154] A joined-up view of the interactions of international economic law with arms transfers can provide a picture of the full extent of Arms Trade Law.

3.4 A Potential Role for International Criminal Law?

The analysis of the preceding two chapters has shown the range of areas of a putative 'Arms Trade Law' that could have some direct or indirect legal effect on the behaviour of an arms trader involved in supplying weapons for use in atrocity. Since these areas deal with cross-boundary supplies of weapons, would a so-called field of Arms Trade Law be simply another field of 'Transnational Criminal Law'? According to Boister, Transnational Criminal Law is 'the indirect suppression by international law through domestic penal law of criminal activities that have actual or potential trans-boundary effects'.[155] By this definition, the concept of Transnational Criminal Law is too narrow to contain the various sub-areas of Arms Trade Law. Security Council arms embargoes do not impose positive international law obligations on states to punish breaches through domestic penal law and domestic export regulations do not rely exclusively on penal laws.

A growing body of literature uses 'Transnational Criminal Law' to define international crime in opposition to transnational crime.[156] Yet this distinction is increasingly challenged[157] and the plurality of Arms Trade Law blurs the distinction between the two. The conceptual blurring of Transnational Criminal Law and International Criminal Law is explored in Chapters 6 and 7, in considering whether the arms trade is perceived to be a legitimate subject of International Criminal Law (or rather is viewed through the lens of transnational criminality).

[154] Christine Kaufmann, 'World Customs Organization' in Frauke Lachenmann and Rüdiger Wolfrum (eds), *International Economic Law: The Max Planck Encyclopedia of Public International Law* (OUP 2015) 904, para 19.

[155] Neil Boister, *An Introduction to Transnational Criminal Law* (1st edn, OUP 2012).

[156] David Luban, Julie R O'Sullivan, and David P Stewart, *International and Transnational Criminal Law* (Aspen 2010); Neil Boister, 'Transnational Criminal Law?' (2003) 14 EJIL 953.

[157] Prabha Kotiswaran and Nicola Palmer, 'Rethinking the 'International Law of Crime': Provocations From Transnational Legal Studies' (2015) 6 Transnational Legal Theory 55; Douglas Guilfoyle, 'Transnational Crimes' in Kevin Heller and others (eds), The Oxford Handbook of International Criminal Law (OUP 2020).

3.4.1 Limitations of Existing Arms Trade Law

An effective role for International Criminal Law vis-à-vis the arms trade lies in addressing gaps and weaknesses in Arms Trade Law, particularly where the values of individual accountability can be brought to bear. Three limitations of Arms Trade Law illustrate this potential: its scope, jurisdictional aspects, and protected interests.

Firstly, in terms of scope, Arms Trade Law is mostly pre-emptive; it creates a system with the potential to prevent weapons from assisting atrocity, but provides only limited *ex post facto* accountability (for instance in counter-terrorism prosecutions for material assistance, or in customs offences). It never offers accountability for complicity in international crime. Arms Trade Law is unable to provide a legal response to the scenario where an arms transfer is authorized by a state's competent authorities on the grounds that it does not pose a sufficient risk of being used in an international crime, but it is shown subsequently that in fact the arms transfer contributed to the commission of an international crime. As discussed above, International Criminal Law is uniquely positioned to provide such *ex post facto* accountability. The scope of Transnational Criminal Law is limited by territory—the de facto effectiveness of export controls varies across jurisdictions and does not apply to certain items or types of activity, while the selectivity of arms embargoes means that many scenarios are left unembargoed. International Criminal Law does not distinguish between specific categories of weapon type, is prima facie applicable to intra-state transfers where there is no cross-border element, is not dependent on end-user certificates, and it applies to a range of assistive conduct, such as brokering and transportation.

Second, Arms Trade Law relies on national enforcement, with no international forum having jurisdiction to prosecute transnational crimes of arms trafficking or other customs offences, and the UN embargo system lacks any permanent enforcement mechanism. By contrast, the supranational nature of International Criminal Law has potential to address a range of scenarios. The ICC has a broad jurisdictional reach that has been described as '*potentially* worldwide jurisdiction [that] will be fully realized only after all states become parties to its Statute'.[158] The realization of the ICC's idealized aspiration of global membership is a distant prospect, yet the Court already has jurisdiction over a large number of situations and may address any situation in the event of a referral by the Security Council under Chapter VII of the UN Charter.[159] Of increasing importance, complicity in international crimes can also be applied in prosecutions

[158] Robert Cryer and others, *An Introduction to International Criminal Law and Procedure* (3rd edn, CUP 2014) 166.

[159] UNSC Res 1593 (2005) UN Doc S/RES/1593.

under the principles of universal jurisdiction, in theory enabling national courts to exercise jurisdiction over complicit arms transfers for crimes occurring anywhere in the world.

Third, the protected interests and politicization of Arms Trade Law provide another area of weakness, whereas the ICC has at least some degree of supranational political independence and impartiality. In practice, the scope of application of Arms Trade Law is limited by the underlying protected interests that shape how it has developed and how it is applied. As discussed above, the development of Arms Trade Law is not driven primarily by the accountability interests of victims of international crimes. States have been more concerned with preventing the supply of their manufactured weapons from reaching potential enemies. Although the interests that International Criminal Law claims to be constituted by are contested, it is broadly agreed that International Criminal Law is characterized by supranational, cosmopolitan, and normatively infused aspirations.[160] As Stahn comments, an equally important characteristic of International Criminal Law is that it is typified by 'a certain gap between normative ambition and reality'.[161] And is important to recall that, when asserting that actors such as arms traders can be held responsible as accomplices directly under international law, International Criminal Law does so even though it lacks any single source of sovereign power.[162] Ultimately though, International Criminal Law remains an area of great potential to challenge state sovereignty, including over the most irresponsible arms exports, since 'its essence and normative order transcends the authority of individual states'.[163]

A further distinctive potential of International Criminal Law vis-à-vis the limitations of existing arms trade law lies in providing not only symbolic recognition of the criminality involved in profiting from atrocity, but to open up routes to monetary reparations on the basis of the harm of international crime (which do not attach to a conviction for a breach of an export regulation). The fact that the *Van Anraat* case led to reparations for Kurdish victims is an under-recognized feature of the case.[164] At the ICC, for instance, there is significant potential for victims reparations through the Trust Fund for Victims that may not be available in other proceedings.[165]

160 Kevin Heller and others (eds) *The Oxford Handbook of International Criminal Law* (OUP 2020) 7.

161 Carsten Stahn, *A Critical Introduction to International Criminal Law* (CUP 2019) 113.

162 Quincy Wright, 'The Scope of International Criminal Law: A Conceptual Framework' (1975) 15 Virginia Journal of International Law 561.

163 Stahn (n 161) 8.

164 Tomas Hamilton and Göran Sluiter, 'Principles of Reparations at the International Criminal Court: Assessing Alternative Approaches' (2022) 25 Max Planck Yearbook of United Nations Law 272.

165 Hamilton and Sluiter (n 164).

3.4.2 Complicity in the 'Lawful' and 'Illicit' Arms Trade

An implication of International Criminal Law's potential role in tackling irresponsible arm transfers is that it poses a conceptual challenge to the boundary between the so-called 'lawful' and 'illicit' areas of the arms trade. The current system of Arms Trade Law reinforces this boundary: while government authorities regulate the major arms manufacturing corporations in the 'lawful' trade, customs authorities and the regular criminal justice system regulate the 'illicit' trade of transnational criminality carried out by organized crime groups and arms brokers, transporters, and micro-traders.

Importantly, the distinction between the lawful and illicit trade silos different areas of activity into different legal mechanisms and it is not clear whether the same legal standards are being applied in both. As the UK judicial review proceedings discussed in the previous chapter demonstrate, the regulated 'lawful' trade is subject to authorization by administrative export authorities. This stands in contrast to the cases of *Kouwenhoven* and *Van Anraat*, which were investigated by the Dutch prosecution service as suspects already operating in the 'illicit' trade. The challenge posed by International Criminal Law is its assertion that all individuals, whether arms traffickers engaged in illicit trading, or the heads of major arms manufacturing corporations operating in the lawful trade, should be held to the same international standards of criminal complicity when it comes to assisting atrocities.

3.4.3 Expressing the Seriousness of Complicity

There is a final, more fundamental value at stake in the accountability gap of Arms Trade Law, which underpins the potential of International Criminal Law. At present, even in the rare situations where an arms trafficker is prosecuted for export offences or an embargo breach, such a prosecution will not express the seriousness of the primary offence carried out with the weapons. When this offence is an international crime, the lack of recognition of the criminality involved is a major accountability gap. It follows that holding an arms trader complicit under International Criminal Law, rather than sanctioning them for breaching an arms export regulation, elevates the seriousness of their offending recognized by the conviction, and brings with it a powerful symbolic expression of the wrongfulness of profiting from atrocity.

This is one answer to the valid question of what is the added value of an ICC conviction. An ICC prosecution offers not only accountability—as a complement to the preventative character of Arms Trade Law—but also a powerful expression of the direct links between the individual actions of arms traders and the perpetration of atrocity. Ultimately this would reinforce the core aim of the ICC to end impunity. As Anderson and Pildes argue, expressivist assessments of the ICC's activities should not be construed as goals in themselves,[166] rather, expressivism allows us to see the ways in which an ICC case could complement the existing Arms Trade Law system by better meeting established goals of retribution, deterrence, and restoration.[167] These goals remain opaque in International Criminal Law and an expressivist perspective can help to clarify them.

Following Anderson and Pildes' understanding of expressivism, the heightened symbolic value of an arms trade conviction may offer a powerful symbol that contributes to the deterrent effect of International Criminal Law. On the one hand, Van der Wilt has argued that corporate prosecutions would have heightened deterrence effects on 'calculating businessmen' who conduct a more rational cost-benefit analysis, than on the 'average perpetrator of international crimes' who may be imbued with ideological fervour or forced by circumstances to participate in crime.[168] On the other hand, Payne and Pereira have pointed to cases such as the British Military Court conviction of *Tesch*, which is analysed elsewhere in this book, commenting that the case 'could have, or maybe should have, changed business behaviour. But it did not.'[169]

In this regard, Van der Wilt's observations about the heightened deterrence value of such prosecutions is supported by the increasing attention of corporations to business and human rights standards, accompanied by corporate behavioural change in response to reputational risks of serious stigma associated with complicity in atrocities.[170] While the empirical basis for deterrent effects of international criminal prosecutions remains limited, and the concrete impact of symbolic prosecutions on corporate behavioural change is unproven and normatively unclear, there are good reasons to believe that International Criminal Law has particular communicative value. The unprecedented expression of an international arms trade prosecution would bring an unprecedented level of attention to the issue of corporate accountability, communicating the wrongfulness of complicity to the business community and to a wider public.

[166] Elizabeth S Anderson and Richard H Pildes, 'Expressive Theories of Law: A General Restatement' (2000) 148 University of Pennsylvania Law Review 1503, 1513–15.

[167] Anderson and Pildes (n 166).

[168] Harmen van der Wilt, 'Genocide v War Crimes in The Van Anraat Appeal' (2008) 6 Journal of International Criminal Justice 557, 567.

[169] Leigh A Payne and Gabriel Pereira, 'Corporate Complicity in Dictatorships' (*Oxford University Saïd Business School website*, 2014) <https://ora.ox.ac.uk/objects/uuid:fae61c56-9b8d-4f82-b731-283330bc051e/files/m2e5a9886323844ff0f901ebb3b04fc99> accessed 15 October 2024.

[170] See Nadia Bernaz, 'Conceptualizing Corporate Accountability in International Law: Models for a Business and Human Rights Treaty' (2021) 22 Human Rights Review 45.

3.4.4 Context and Content in an Expressive Prosecution

An arms trade case focusing on individual complicity could thus add the weight of international criminal accountability to the existing system of Arms Trade Law. Yet, as Palmer emphasizes, the content of expressivism should not be restricted to well-worn beliefs in the value of universal condemnation of international crimes. In the context of Rwandan extradition proceedings, Palmer argues that the expressivist 'turn' in the international criminal justice literature has often lacked the nuances of context and content.[171]

For valuable communicative effects of criminal law, context is needed, such that the expressivist work being done by a conviction depends on which court is involved and what is its audience. Meanwhile, the content of an expressivist conviction depends on the message that is expected to be communicated through the criminal proceedings—how would a judgment of an ICC arms trade case be drafted and what modalities exist for publicly communicating it? The context and content of expressivism should therefore be understood as contingent on the criminal justice system involved, and the message that is expressed through the criminal trial; as Palmer highlights, these values cannot be assumed to be fixed.[172]

Expressivist readings of the value of an ICC arms trade prosecution must therefore pay attention to the plurality of different forms of expression in a given case, taking into account the multiple audiences to whom messages are directed. An ICC case based on arms transfer complicity could send messages, firstly, to the 'lawful' trade, communicating to decision-making individuals in major arms manufacturing corporations that government authorization will not shield them against supranational individual complicity. It would communicate to a public audience that actors in the so-called 'lawful' trade are sometimes involved in international crimes. Alternatively, the messages could be directed at actors in the 'illicit' trade, to signal that lacunae in the enforcement of existing Arms Trade Law (weak and ineffective sanctions, export regulations, and jurisdictional shortcomings) may be filled by the ICC. In this way, bringing the arms trade into the picture of accountability for international crimes demonstrates the different expressive functions a case could perform. International Criminal Law holds the potential to express international condemnation in ways that Arms Trade Law cannot offer alone.

[171] Nicola Palmer, 'International Criminal Law and Border Control: The Expressive Role of the Deportation and Extradition of Genocide Suspects to Rwanda' (2020) Leiden Journal of International Law 1.

[172] Palmer (n 171).

3.5 Conclusion

The preceding analysis looked at an accountability gap in the primary and subsidiary areas of Arms Trade Law, with a view to identifying a potential role for International Criminal Law, specifically how it can complement this transnational assemblage. The field of Arms Trade Law is mostly preventative in character, relying on domestic export regulation coordinated by the ATT and EU Common Position and arms embargoes. Arms Trade Law often fails to prevent the ready availability of weapons in atrocity scenarios. International Criminal Law is not well-placed to remedy those weaknesses, but it does hold potential to address the accountability gap that exists in relation to *ex post facto* prosecutions for complicity in international crimes.

A distinguishing feature of International Criminal Law is its aspirational, cosmopolitan, and normatively infused vision of supranational justice, based on protecting the interests of victims. As Mégret observes, 'international criminal law, as the project to replace or at least compete with the ordinary functioning of a state-based legal order based on coexistence by a cosmopolitan system based on individual responsibility, is paradigmatically in tension with international law'.[173] It seeks to do something different to Arms Trade Law, which, as the analysis of the last two chapters has shown, is characterized by its state-centric nature that emphasizes sovereignty, foreign strategic and military interests, international free trade, and global peace and security.

The aspirational qualities of International Criminal Law are a potential strength, but they also risk encouraging the view of individual accountability as a cure-all panacea. Its globalist aspirations to unite the diversity of humanity against common threats risks self-undermining, and reducing the available forms of justice.[174] It would be a mistake to view prosecutions of complicit individuals as a sole solution to the ineffectiveness of Arms Trade Law, or as a substitute for other efforts to strengthen export regulations and embargoes. Furthermore, it would be futile to ignore the powerful state interests that create enforcement asymmetries in international justice,[175] and the real constraints this imposes on the likelihood of prosecutions of state officials or heads of corporations in major arms manufacturing states.

The challenge of thinking critically about the role of International Criminal Law is therefore to strike a balance, between the need to maintain the unfulfilled aspirations of international criminal justice, including the ICC and other forums

[173] Frédéric Mégret, 'International Criminal Justice as a Juridical Field' (2016) 13 Champ pénal 1.

[174] Sarah Nouwen and Wouter Werner, 'Monopolizing Global Justice: International Criminal Law as Challenge to Human Diversity' (2015) 13 Journal of International Criminal Justice 157.

[175] Sergey Vasiliev, 'Watershed Moment or Same Old? Ukraine and the Future of International Criminal Justice' (2022) 20 Journal of International Criminal Justice 893.

to fulfil their mandates by playing a useful role in expressing the wrongfulness of selling weapons to perpetrators of atrocity. On the other hand, it is necessary to adopt a perspective of sufficient humility to recognize the limited impact that International Criminal Law is able to have on the reality of global arms proliferation and the availability of weapons in atrocity situations.

With this in mind, there appears to be a particular potential for the ICC to regulate small-scale arms brokers, transporters, and micro-traders—the intermediaries who funnel weapons into conflict zones—such as those who feature in the case study on the DRC later in this book. These actors are often poorly regulated under existing Arms Trade Law and are not always protected by powerful states interests. As demonstrated by the ICC Prosecutor's statement on 'those who provide weapons', and the Dutch precedents in *Kouwenhoven* and *Van Anraat* demonstrate, there can sometimes be prosecutorial willingness to take on such cases.

4
The *Actus Reus* of a Complicit Arms Transfer

4.1 Introduction

International Criminal Law provides for individuals' direct responsibility under international law for conduct contributing to an international crime, including when individuals provide assistance or aid.[1] The doctrines of accomplice liability reflect the nature of International Criminal Law as a hybrid body of law derived from a combination of national criminal law and public international law. Although customary International Criminal Law was well developed before the entry into force of the Rome Statute on 1 July 2002, the International Criminal Court's (ICC) substantive and procedural law has come to occupy a central place in supranational criminal law. Even while it is not definitive of the field, the Rome Statute takes centre stage here and for the subsequent chapters on ICC's institutional culture and the case study chapters on the DRC.

The complicity provisions of the Rome Statute have caused uncertainty and confusion over their scope of application, and much has already been written in academic scholarship about the modes of liability. This chapter argues for a specific interpretation of accomplice liability under Article 25(3)(d)(ii) of the Rome Statute, in accordance with the sources of applicable law in Article 21 of the Statute and in light of the drafting history of its *travaux préparatoires*.[2] The chapter builds on Chapter 3's arguments about the potential of International Criminal Law to complement existing Arms Trade Law, by focusing in on the exact parameters of accomplice liability under the Rome Statute, to see which areas of the arms trade would likely be criminalized by applying Article 25. It also builds on the author's argument that the *mens rea* for complicity at the ICC is not the 'purpose' standard of aiding and abetting, as is often believed, but 'knowledge' under Article 25(3)(d)(ii).[3]

[1] See Gerhard Werle and Florian Jessberger, *Principles of International Criminal Law* (OUP 2014) 31; Robert Cryer and others, *An Introduction to International Criminal Law and Procedure* (3rd edn, CUP 2014).

[2] Gilbert Bitti, 'Article 21 and the Hierarchy of Sources of Law before the ICC' in Carsten Stahn (ed), *The Law and Practice of the International Criminal Court* (OUP 2015) 427.

[3] Tomas Hamilton, 'An arms trade case at the International Criminal Court: Would the Article 25(3)(c) "purpose" requirement really matter?' (*Rethinking SLIC*, 23 September 2021) <https://rethinkingslic.org/blog/criminal-law/93-an-arms-trade-case-at-the-international-criminal-court-would-the-article-25-3-c-purpose-requirement-really-matter> accessed 4 August 2024.

The Arms Trade and International Criminal Law. Tomas Hamilton, Oxford University Press.
DOI: 10.1093/oso/9780192868671.003.0004

Chapters 4 and 5 discuss specific issues of interpretation of *actus reus* and *mens rea*. If the interpretation of Article 25 proposed in this book is followed by the ICC, it would provide a legal basis for the accomplice liability of a disinterested commercial arms trader who is neither part of, nor shares the intentions of, a group that commits a crime pursuant to a common purpose. The arms trader would have to provide weapons that do, in fact, make a significant contribution to the commission of crimes. The arms trader would need to know that the weapons they supply will, in the ordinary course of events, contribute to a specific international crime, and they must be aware of all the essential elements of that crime. On this basis, the mode of liability in Article 25(3)(d)(ii) is an appropriate label for arms traders who 'knowingly contribute to a group crime'.

4.2 Complicit Assistance in the Rome Statute

Articles 25 and 28 of the Rome Statute define the modes of liability, within which Articles 25(3)(c) and (d) contain the provisions on complicit assistance. Aiding or abetting under Article 25(3)(c) is the first potential avenue for the liability of an arms trader. Under this provision, a person shall be criminally responsible and liable for punishment for a crime within the jurisdiction of the Court if that person:

> [f]or the purpose of facilitating the commission of [a crime], aids, abets or otherwise assists in its commission or its attempted commission, including providing the means for its commission.

'Contributing in any other way' under Article 25(3)(d) is the second potential avenue for liability. The full text of Article 25(3)(d) provides that a person shall be criminally responsible and liable for punishment for a crime within the jurisdiction of the Court if that person:

> [i]n any other way contributes to the commission or attempted commission of such a crime by a group of persons acting with a common purpose. Such contribution shall be intentional and shall either:
> (i) Be made with the aim of furthering the criminal activity or criminal purpose of the group, where such activity or purpose involves the commission of a crime within the jurisdiction of the Court; or
> (ii) Be made in the knowledge of the intention of the group to commit the crime.

At the ad hoc tribunals, complicit assistance was found in the provisions on aiding and abetting in Article 7(1) of the International Criminal Tribunal for the former Yugoslavia (ICTY) Statute, Article 6(1) of the International Criminal Tribunal for

Rwanda (ICTR) Statute, and Article 6(1) of the Special Court for Sierra Leone (SCSL) Statute, all of which provided for responsibility inter alia of a person 'who aided and abetted in the planning, preparation or execution' of an international crime.

4.3 Preliminary Remarks on Interpretation

Before discussing the requirements of the Rome Statute in further depth, it is necessary to say something about what is expected in terms of the interpretation and application of this provision. As much as it may be desirable to speak of 'settled jurisprudence', 'established practice', or 'a consistent approach' at the ICC, this cannot be plausibly claimed to exist for many substantive and procedural legal issues at this stage in the Court's history. This is especially so for accomplice liability given the Court's limited jurisprudential output with regard to Articles 25(3)(c) and (d).

ICC benches are not bound by the common law principle of *stare decisis*[4] and the Court's jurisprudence may be many years or decades away from being able to talk credibly of a *jurisprudence constante* based on a substantial number of cases, heard by a substantial number of judges from different legal traditions, and addressing a substantial range of fact patterns, that develop a well-established usage of legal concepts.[5] In interpreting the Rome Statute, special care must be taken to attribute due weight to isolated judicial decisions.[6] Importantly, very little jurisprudence on complicity has been subject to Appeals Chamber scrutiny. In addition, a lack of international or domestic case law on different fact patterns of complicit arms transfers made it difficult to predict how liability under Article 25 of the Rome Statute would be applied by ICC judges and lawyers. As Posner observes, the responses of international courts to the limited fraction of fact patterns to have come before them may not be the most accurate guide to future judicial decisions.[7]

Beyond the basic elements of Articles 25(3)(c) and (d), then, the extent of accomplice liability over arms transfers cannot be considered 'certain' in the legal sense. Increasing legal certainty is desirable, not least since it contributes to the deterrent effects of the Court's work by enhancing and clarifying the social threat

[4] Article 21 of the Rome Statute provides that '[t]he Court may apply principles and rules of law as interpreted in its previous decisions'.

[5] See Robert Henry, '*Jurisprudence Constante* and *Stare Decisis* Contrasted' (1929) 15 American Bar Association Journal 11.

[6] Volker Nerlich, 'The Status of ICTY and ICTR Precedent in Proceedings before the ICC' in Carsten Stahn and Göran Sluiter (eds), *The Emerging Practice of the International Criminal Court* (Brill 2009) 314.

[7] Richard A Posner, *How Judges Think* (Harvard University Press 2010).

of its investigations and prosecutions, including through national prosecutions under the principle of complementarity.[8] Legal certainty may be particularly significant to the arms trade due to the proposed rational attitude of commercial actors, discussed in Chapter 3, in deciding whether to take actions that may render them liable for international crimes.[9] The prospect that an arms transfer will attract not only a degree of moral opprobrium but also criminal responsibility may enhance the Court's potential deterrent effect,[10] but a credible threat of investigation and prosecution relies partly on the Court's liability regime being predictable to those involved in arms transfers.

Before going further into the Rome Statute provision, it is also important to distinguish, at a conceptual level, two broad categories of complicity. The focus in this book is on complicit *assistance*. But supplying weapons may also *encourage* the commission of crimes. The willingness of a contributor to sell a gun to a perpetrator may embolden them to commit the crime, for instance where the perpetrator is aware that the seller knows of their intentions.[11] This makes it unfortunate that the finding of the *Katanga* trial bench in relation to encouragement chose the following examples: '[the contribution under Article 25(3)(d)] may be connected to either the material elements of the crimes (it may then, for instance, take the form of provision of resources such as weapons) or to their subjective elements (it may involve encouragement)'.[12]

An individual's conduct may be able to exert a particularly encouraging effect in scenarios where they are the only source of weapons, rather than one of many providers. An arms broker involved in illicit trafficking, who—exceptionally—agrees to provide the weapons, when others are unable or unwilling to violate an embargo or export regulations, may have an enhanced individual effect on the recipient's actions. Encouragement could be particularly relevant in the prosecution's selection of charges in cases where it is difficult to obtain evidence to establish a material link between the supply of weapons and the perpetrator's use thereof. Often, arms supplies may be legally characterized as physical assistance or mental encouragement, and from an evidentiary perspective, the latter may sometimes be easier to prove.

[8] Hyeran Jo and Beth Simmons 'Can the International Criminal Court Deter Atrocity?' (2017) 71 International Organization 419.

[9] Raymond Paternoster and Sally Simpson, 'Sanction Threats and Appeals to Morality: Testing a Rational Choice Model of Corporate Crime' (1996) 30 Law and Society Review 549.

[10] Rienhold Gallmetzer, 'Prosecuting Persons Doing Business with Armed Groups in Conflict Areas: The Strategy of the Office of the Prosecutor of the International Criminal Court' (2010) 8 Journal of International Criminal Justice 956.

[11] Recognized by the UK Supreme Court in the joint criminal enterprise case of *R v Jogee* [2016] UKSC 8 para 10.

[12] *Prosecutor v Germaine Katanga* (Trial Judgment) ICC-01/04-01/07-3436 (7 March 2014), para 1635. See also *Prosecutor v Callixte Mbarushimana* (Confirmation Decision) ICC-01/04-01/10 (16 December 2011) para 267.

4.4 The Quiet Primacy of Article 25(3)(d)(ii) of the Rome Statute

Complicit assistance in the Rome Statute is found in both subsections (c) and (d) of Article 25(3). In seeking to elucidate the outer limits of the ICC's net of liability for complicit assistance—for the purposes of the subsequent chapters on ICC practice—it is necessary to determine which of these Rome Statute provisions provides the least onerous legal requirements for complicit assistance. In practice, a Prosecutor in an ICC arms trade case is likely to bring charges under the 'easiest' mode of liability (despite concerns of appropriate labelling, discussed below).

The analysis in this chapter identifies Article 25(3) subsection (d)(ii) as the most expansive and least onerous mode of liability for complicit assistance. This entails that the provision that often receives most attention when discussing complicit assistance—Article 25(3)(c) on those who 'aids, abets or otherwise assists in [the commission of a crime] or its attempted commission, including providing the means for its commission'—is not determinative of the outer limits of complicit assistance in the Rome Statute.

In terms of *actus reus* of Article 25(3)(c), the ICC jurisprudence has held that it 'does not require the meeting of any specific threshold'.[13] This departs from the ad hoc tribunals' requirement of a specific threshold of 'substantial' effect on the principal crime. It was held in relation to complicit assistance at the ICTY, ICTR, and SCSL that the common wording of the provisions on aiding and abetting in Article 7(1) of the ICTY Statute, Article 6(1) of the ICTR Statute, and Article 6(1) of the SCSL Statute required judicial interpretation as to the threshold required of the assistance. The *Tadić* Appeals Chamber held in 1999 that aiding and abetting requires the assistive conduct to have a 'substantial' effect on the commission of the crime.[14] The 'substantial' threshold was understood in the ICTY jurisprudence as meaning assistance that is more than *de minimis*. Although in evidentiary terms it may be challenging to quantify this requirement, the smallest contribution of 'no specific threshold' for the *actus reus* of Article 25(3)(c) is lower than at the ad hoc tribunals 'substantial effect'.

As to the *mens rea* of Article 25(3)(c), there is an elevated mental requirement of 'purpose', which corresponds with the lower material requirements of *actus reus* under Article 25(3)(c). The text of the provision—'[f]or the purpose of facilitating the commission of [a crime]'—has caused much consternation in commentary on the ICC. Although it has often been regarded as having profound implications for complicit assistance at the ICC, much of this consternation reflects an incorrect reading of the Statute. The existence of the lower *mens rea* requirements of Article

13 *Prosecutor v Bemba et al* (Trial Judgment) ICC-01/05-01/13-1989-Red (19 October 2016) para 93; *Prosecutor v Bemba et al* (Appeal Judgment) ICC-01/05-01/13-2275-Red) para 1327.

14 ICTY *Tadić* Appeals Judgment, 15 July 1999, para 229.

25(3)(d)(ii) render the aiding or abetting provisions of little practical relevance, since a prosecution for complicit assistance will never stand or fall on the basis of 'purpose'; the Prosecutor will bring charges under the 'easier' mode of liability. This issue returns in Chapter 5 on *mens rea.*

Due to lower *mens rea* requirements—which a Prosecutor is unlikely to ignore when making charging decisions—this book focuses on Article 25(3)(d)(ii) as the most relevant mode of liability for complicit arms transfers. Although prima facie the concepts of 'aiding and abetting' and 'providing the means of commission' found in Article 25(3)(c) of the Rome Statute are descriptively enticing, they would be of less relevance to an ICC arms trade case.[15]

4.5 Basic Requirements of Article 25(3)(d)(ii)

There is a startling variety of proposed interpretations of Article 25(3)(d), projecting onto the text of the Rome Statute similar-sounding modes of liability from previous tribunals; conspiracy (as per Article 6 of the Nuremberg Charter), membership of a criminal group or organization (as per Article 10 of the Nuremberg Charter), and liability by conspiracy or joint criminal enterprise (as developed in the jurisprudence of the ICTY and ICTR).[16] Several commentators note that Article 25(3)(d) was a negotiated compromise between States Parties that wished to include a conspiracy doctrine of liability in the Statute and those who did not.[17] Some commentators believe that the contradictions in the text of Article 25(3)(d) are so serious that it should be altogether rewritten through statutory amendment.[18]

The Court's jurisprudence has not acquiesced in the face of admitted interpretive difficulties in the text. Chambers have been relatively consistent in pronouncing that Article 25(3)(d) has the following basic elements:[19]

[15] For the author's fuller analysis of this issue see Hamilton (n 3).

[16] See Robert Cryer, *Prosecuting International Crimes: Selectivity and the International Criminal Law Regime* (CUP 2005) 315.

[17] Gerhard Werle, 'Individual Criminal Responsibility in Article 25 of the ICC Statute' (2007) 5 Journal of International Criminal Justice 970. See Johannes Block, *Reconciling Responsibility with Reality: A Comparative Analysis of Modes of Active Leadership Liability in International Criminal Law* (Springer 2023).

[18] Jens Ohlin, 'Joint Criminal Confusion' (2009) 12 New Criminal Law Review 408, 417.

[19] *Mbarushimana* (Confirmation Decision) (n 12) paras 268–289; *Prosecutor v Germaine Katanga* (Trial Judgment) ICC-01/04-01/07-3436 (7 March 2014) para 1620; *Prosecutor v Laurent Gbagbo* (Confirmation Decision) ICC-02/11-01/11-656 (12 June 2014) para 252; *Prosecutor v Bosco Ntaganda* (Confirmation Decision) ICC-01/04-02/06-309 (9 June 2014) para 158; *Prosecutor v William Samoei Ruto and Joshua Arap Sang* (Confirmation Decision) ICC-01/09-01/11-373 (23 January 2012) para 351; *Prosecutor v Uhuru Muigai Kenyatta* (Summons Decision) ICC-01/09-02/11-1 (8 March 2011) para 47; *Prosecutor v Ahmad Al Faqi Al Mahdi* (Confirmation Decision) ICC-01/12-01/15-84 (24 March 2016) para 27; *Prosecutor v Dominic Ongwen* (Confirmation Decision) ICC-02/04-01/15-422 (23 March 2016) para 44.

1. A crime within the jurisdiction of the Court was attempted or committed;
2. The crime was committed or attempted by a group of persons acting with a common purpose;
3. The accused contributed to the commission or attempted commission of the crime in 'any other way';[20]
4. The contribution was intentional;[21] and
5. The contribution was made either:
   (i) with the aim of furthering the criminal activity or criminal purpose of the group;[22] or
   (ii) in the knowledge of the intention of the group to commit the crime.

The first three basic elements define the *actus reus* of Article 25(3)(d). Of these, the first and second elements are relatively unproblematic in terms of the liability of the arms trader—they establish the conditions for the primary perpetration of the crime from which the accomplice liability of the arms trader is derived. The third basic element requires a contribution and the nature of this contribution is of central importance, raising several issues about the connection between the accomplice's conduct and the perpetration of the crime—ie the causal nexus. The following sections analyse three *actus reus* issues as to whether a trader's contribution would be sufficient to attribute wrongdoing to them under Article 25(3)(d)(ii):

(i) Whether the arms transfer is 'significant' (ie the degree of contribution required), including whether the arms transfer must be per se unlawful

[20] *Mbarushimana* (Confirmation Decision) (n 12) paras 268–289; *Prosecutor v Germaine Katanga* (Trial Judgment) ICC-01/04-01/07-3436 (7 March 2014) para 1620; *Prosecutor v Laurent Gbagbo* (Confirmation Decision) ICC-02/11-01/11-656 (12 June 2014) para 252; *Prosecutor v Bosco Ntaganda* (Confirmation Decision) ICC-01/04-02/06-309 (9 June 2014) para 158; *Prosecutor v William Samoei Ruto and Joshua Arap Sang* (Confirmation Decision) ICC-01/09-01/11-373 (23 January 2012) para 351; *Prosecutor v Uhuru Muigai Kenyatta* (Summons Decision) ICC-01/09-02/11-1 (8 March 2011) para 47; *Al Mahdi* (Confirmation Decision) (n 19) para 27; *Ongwen* (Confirmation Decision) (n 19) para 44.

[21] The contributor must '(i) mean to engage in the relevant conduct that allegedly contributes to the crime and (ii) be at least aware that his or her conduct contributes to the activities of the group of persons'. *Mbarushimana* (Confirmation Decision) (n 12) para 288; *Katanga* (Trial Judgment) (n 19) para 1639. Arguably, this wording is preferable to a more recent formulation in *Al Mahdi* and *Ongwen* that: 'With respect to the relevant mental element, this form of responsibility requires that the person meant to contribute to the commission of the crimes.' See *Al Mahdi* (Confirmation Decision) (n 19) 27; *Ongwen* (Confirmation Decision) (n 19) para 44.

[22] This element does not require that the accused satisfy the mental elements of the charged crimes. *Mbarushimana* (Confirmation Decision) (n 12) para 289. The difference between subsections (i) and (ii) 'seems to be that the second standard requires the prosecution to prove that the person knew the specific crime the group intended to commit, whereas the first standard requires it to prove only that the person intended to further the group's general criminal activity'. Kevin Heller, 'The Rome Statute in Comparative Perspective' in Kevin Heller and Markus Dubber (eds), *The Handbook of Comparative Criminal Law* (Stanford Law Books 2010) 26.

('neutral' contributions) and whether the group's activities must be unlawful (specific direction).
(ii) Whether the arms transfer must cause the crime (causal remoteness) and multiple causes and fungibility (overdetermination and pre-emption).
(iii) Whether the defendant's contribution needs to be made from outside of the group (common purpose).

As developed below, although these issues are treated foremost as matters of *actus reus*, disentangling them from the assessment of *mens rea* is not always straightforward.

4.6 'Significant' Arms Transfers (Degree of Contribution)

What degree of contribution is considered legally 'significant' enough to warrant criminal responsibility? Does an arms shipment need to be a particular quantity or type of weapons to trigger liability? In determining the extent of International Criminal Law's potential to regulate the arms trade, several facts about the arms trade are salient: the individual conduct involved is often performed at geographical and structural distance away from the perpetration of the crimes; a shipment of weapons may be one amongst many similar shipments; the supply of weapons may be fungible ie easily interchanged; only a small percentage of the arms supplied may be used in criminal activity, the rest may be for lawful usage; and the weapons may be distributed amongst many perpetrators, only some of whom perpetrate crimes. These factual features raise questions as to the degree of legal 'contribution' required under Article 25(3)(d).

The *chapeau* of Article 25(3)(d) reads 'in any other way contributes' or '*toutes autres contributions*'. This is clear enough on its face: it covers all arms transfer contributions that are not addressed by Articles 25(3)(a) through (c).[23] As noted above, this renders the material requirement less onerous than aiding and abetting under Article 25(3)(c). It is also less onerous than the SCSL's requirement that 'provision and facilitation of the supply of arms and ammunition [have] a *substantial effect* on the commission of crimes charged'.[24] There appears to be no qualifying criterion to delimit the requirement of '*any* other' contribution. However, the *Mbarushimana* Confirmation Decision imposed a quantitative threshold that the contribution be at least 'significant' out of concerns for the imposition of liability on 'bakers',

[23] *Ruto and Sang* (Confirmation Decision) (n 19) para 354; *Mbarushimana* (Confirmation Decision) (n 12) para 278.

[24] *Taylor* (Trial Judgment) (n 20) para 6913; *Prosecutor v Charles Ghankay Taylor* (Appeals Judgment) SCSL-03-01-A-1389 (26 September 2013) para 390.

'grocers', and other categories of individuals who the Pre-Trial Chamber (PTC) described as making 'infinitesimal' contributions to crimes.[25]

Aside from the plain wording of Article 25(3)(d) and the lack of support in the *travaux préparatoires*, the PTC's concerns were unfounded. At a superficial and phenomenological level, the supply of weapons may look very different to the activities of baking bread or selling vegetables, which the PTC considered it necessary to protect as so-called 'lawful' activities. However, it is a counterintuitive aspect of accomplice liability that neither the nature nor the size of a contribution is per se determinative of its unlawfulness. As Smith explains in his singular treatise on secondary liability, a remarkable feature of any system of complicity rules is the vastness of the range of conducts and attitudes that it covers.[26] Whereas principal liability is categorically distinguished by the type of crime in question (murder, rape, theft, etc), complicity is not per se defined by a particular category of conduct. Thus, at the level of attribution of responsibility, the lawfulness of a large shipment of missiles is not distinguished from providing crates of ammunition, nor from giving food to troops or baking bread for them. These phenomenologically differentiated contributions are not distinguished on the sole basis of intrinsic qualities. Whether they are criminal depends on the *actus reus* and *mens rea* of the mode of accomplice liability in question.

The *Mbarushimana* conception of infinitesimal contributions fails to differentiate between the degree and the nature of a contribution.[27] Article 25(3)(d)(ii) does not render any category of individual conduct prima facie criminal, including arms transfer conduct that may be considered illicit under other international and domestic regulations. Neither is any category of conduct per se innocent, since any form of contributory activity (sale of consumer commodities, provision of financial services, logistical assistance, legal advice etc) may be criminalized provided that the necessary elements including causal linkage and *mens rea* exist. A hardware store may innocently sell a thousand pocket knives, yet the sale of a single knife may attract criminal liability when a customer explicitly states he intends to use it for murder.

The nature of the required contribution under Article 25(3)(d)(ii) also raises questions over the lawfulness of the arms transfer and the lawfulness of the group's activities. The former is often referred to as the problem of neutral contributions, while the latter relates to so-called 'specific direction. Is it relevant whether the assistance itself is per se unlawful? If an individual provides a shipment of food does that differ per se—when it comes to criminal *complicity*—from the shipment of a prohibited chemical weapon. This question arises particularly in the context of

[25] *Mbarushimana* (Confirmation Decision) (n 12) para 283.

[26] Keith JM Smith, *A Modern Treatise on the Law of Criminal Complicity* (Clarendon Press 1991) 142.

[27] Alejandro Kiss, 'La contribución en la comisión de un crimen por un grupo de personas en la jurisprudencia de la Corte Penal Internacional' (2013) 2 InDret 1, 19.

whether individuals be held responsible when the items they supply are 'neutral' in the sense of everyday lawful activities, such as making bread etc which may be transformed into a criminal context when the bread is baked knowing that it will support troops who are carrying out massacres. There is no need for the conduct of the arms trader to be intrinsically criminal. What matters is that the conduct results, factually, in the assistance of the criminal act, as recognized by the Appeals Chamber of the SCSL.[28]

Can individuals be held responsible when the perpetrators to whom they supply weapons are engaged in lawful and unlawful activities? This issue appears particularly relevant to the supply of dual-use items, but it is important to underscore that in principle any type of item, good, or service could be the basis for complicit assistance. The concern over incriminating bread bakers is illusory—any form of activity can be a basis for criminal contribution and liability will only be incurred when there is sufficient *actus reus* and *mens rea*. However, different forms of activity are regulated differently under other areas of law, raising the conflict of laws issue discussed in Chapter 2. In sum, an illicit arms transfer prohibited under Arms Trade Law will not necessarily be the basis for complicity in international criminal liability. Likewise, as argued in previous chapters, neither will a determination that the transfer is lawful under export requirements rule out accomplice liability.

In terms of whether the arms can be transferred to a group with criminal and non-criminal activities, this raises the so-called 'specific direction' issue. Weapons are mostly supplied to organizations or regular armed forces that have legitimate military and security needs. The specific direction issue arises where the recipient of weapons is involved not only in these lawful activities but also in the unlawful commission of international crimes. Some defendants have asserted that the prosecution must prove that the accused 'specifically directed' their assistance to the organization's criminal activities—ie proof they provided general assistance to the organization is not enough. This is particularly relevant in the context of the 'lawful' trade when a major arms manufacturing corporation supplies an armed force with weapons that are mostly for lawful usage, but some of the supplied weapons are used to carry out atrocities. 'Specific direction' has often been treated as an *actus reus* issue, however, the analysis here returns to consider it in the context of *mens rea* below.

The indifference of criminal law's *actus reus* requirements to the type of weapon, dual-use item, or service being supplied, suggest a resolution to the concerns of the *Mbarushimana* bench for so-called 'infinitesimal' contributions. This resolution lies in the concept of causal remoteness, which has received only limited articulation in the Court's jurisprudence. Remoteness is the law's recognition that, while

[28] *Taylor* (Appeals Judgment) (n 24) para 395.

there is nothing intrinsically lawful about conduct such as baking bread or selling groceries, these activities are usually too remote, causally, to form a basis for liability. In English criminal law, for example, an individual who supplies petrol to the driver of an unroadworthy vehicle is not considered liable for the road traffic offence.[29] The underlying rationale is not that supplying petrol is inherently a non-criminal activity, nor that the contribution of supplying petrol falls below a particular quantitative threshold. Instead, without excluding that the supply of petrol may be causally linked in an absolute sense to the offence (the so-called 'but for' test of direct causation that requires factual causation wherein the contribution was sine qua non such that in its absence the crime could not have occurred in the way that it did[30]), the supply of petrol is not deemed sufficiently proximate, in the legal causal sense, to attribute responsibility.[31] As Kiss emphasizes, the problem with the *Mbarushimana* conception of infinitesimal contributions is that it overlooks normative considerations that emphasize value judgment, failing to attend closely to criminal law notions of causation.[32]

The ICC Confirmation Decisions in *Al Mahdi* and *Ongwen* subsequently took the view that it is unnecessary for the contribution under Article 25(3)(d) to be 'significant' or reach a certain minimum degree.[33] Recognizing the problems of a quantitative threshold, these views have, in effect, retained but reinterpreted the 'significance' requirement by recognizing that the interpretation of the term 'significant' as 'more than *de minimis*' or 'not negligible' does nothing to clarify the test of 'any other contribution'.[34] As a UK Supreme Court opinion held in a different legal and factual context:

> this court should avoid attempting to explain the word 'significant.' It would be a gloss; attention might then turn to the meaning of the gloss and, albeit with the best of intentions, the courts might find in due course that they had travelled far from the word itself.[35]

Even after recognizing these limits, judges may wish to retain the 'significance' standard, if only to emphasize that the standard is not one of 'substantial contribution', and is therefore distinct from the customary law standard for the *actus reus* of aiding or abetting.

29 Smith (n 26) 150–51.
30 Herbert LA Hart and Tony Honoré, *Causation in the Law* (OUP 1985) 110.
31 Smith (n 26) 150–51.
32 Kiss (n 27) 19.
33 *Al Mahdi* (Confirmation Decision) (n 19) para 27; *Ongwen* (Confirmation Decision) (n 19) para 44.
34 'significant', *Stroud's Judicial Dictionary* (9th edn, Sweet and Maxwell 2018).
35 *Re B (A Child)* [2013] UKSC 33, para 26.

4.7 Causal Relationship with the Arms Transfer

A central interpretive issue for Article 25(3)(d) is whether 'contributing to the commission or attempted commission' of the crime means something different to 'contributing to the crime itself'. This issue has ramifications for arms transfer conduct that usually takes place at a spatial, temporal, and organizational distance from the direct perpetrators who carry out the crimes. There will often be little or no evidence that a particular gun or piece of ammunition was used in the perpetration of a specific incident of violence.

Aiding and abetting under customary international law does not require a direct causal link between the action of an accomplice and the ultimate harm. The *Furundžija* Trial Chamber at the ICTY elaborated on the effect of assistance, holding that the acts of the accomplice need not 'bear a causal relationship to, or be a *conditio sine qua non* for, those of the principal'.[36] Given the central importance of causation in international criminal law theory, international criminal tribunals including the ICC have given surprisingly little attention to causation in practice.[37]

The contribution and its causal relationship to the commission or attempted commission of a crime is also connected to the jurisprudence on the 'significant' threshold discussed above. The *Katanga* Trial Chamber's interpretation of the 'significance' requirement in Article 25(3)(d) came closer to recognizing the concept of remoteness by focusing on the causal nexus between the contribution and the commission of the crime. Although the Trial Chamber did not reject the *Mbarushimana* 'significance' requirement in name, it held that the contribution 'will be considered *significant* where it *had a bearing on* the occurrence of the crime and/or the manner of its commission'.[38] A contribution that is too causally remote would therefore be one that cannot be said to have 'had a bearing on' the commission of the crime. The reasoning of the *Katanga* trial judgment tended towards the concept of remoteness:

> in international criminal law the prime focus of investigations and prosecutions is those who, whilst physically, structurally or causally remote from the physical perpetrators of the crimes, indirectly committed them or facilitated their commission by virtue of the position they held, however remote.[39]

[36] *Prosecutor v Anto Furundžija* (Trial Judgment) IT-95-17/1-T (10 December 1998) para 223.

[37] James G Stewart, 'Atrocity, Commerce and Accountability' (2010) 8 Journal of International Criminal Justice 314.

[38] *Katanga* (Trial Judgment) (n 19) paras 1632–1633. The Trial Chamber left some ambiguity with the contingent finding: 'the Chamber wishes to lay stress on a contribution which *may* influence the commission of the crime' (emphasis added).

[39] *Katanga* (Trial Judgment) (n 19) para 1636 (emphasis added).

Yet the Chamber did not elaborate on its view, and in the absence of reasoning, the Chamber appears to conflate or confuse the factual concepts of physical proximity and organizational hierarchy with the legal concept of causation.

The explanation of causation in doctrines of complicity is a deeply contested area of law and varies between jurisdictions.[40] Accounts of complicity require causation of accomplices, as in Gardner's account where, ultimately, causation is about 'making a difference to what happens in the world'.[41] These accounts address recurring factual situations where legal causation provides a limiting factor on factual causation. Accounts of causeless complicity, as advanced by Kutz, lack such a limiting feature.[42] While asserting that not all complicit contributions are causal, this question does not provide a means for delimiting the factually over-determined causes of an international crime.

The concept of remoteness drawn from criminal law in common law systems is a useful and pragmatic means of limiting the excessive reach of simple 'but for' factual causation in complicity. It excludes conduct that is 'too remote, too trivial or too accidental to have a just bearing on the doer's liability'.[43] Legal remoteness thus recognizes the reality that there is a level of judicial discretion in determining whether an arms transfer is sufficiently important, causally, to attract liability. As Moore describes it, 'the simple idea behind such a remoteness test is that causation is a scalar relation—a more or less sort of thing, not an all-or-nothing sort of thing'.[44] Given the range of doctrinal approaches of causation, it is highly probable that ICC determinations of causality will remain vague and open to judicial discretion. Since this entails assumptions, beliefs, and commitments about what type of contribution is 'too remote' from the crime, the culturally imagined views of practitioners about who these sufficiently proximate causal actors are, is highly important. Chapter 6 returns to these imagined perpetrator types.

How would a causation requirement in Article 25(3)(d)(ii) apply to the conduct of an arms trader? The trial judgment in *Katanga* found that causation may involve an impact on dual parameters, the 'occurrence of the crime', or the 'manner of its commission'.[45] In this regard, we can consider a hypothetical scenario where an individual supplies a state with weapons used by its army to unlawfully relocate a population of a certain ethnic group. The armed forces may have access to sufficient weaponry such that the supplier's conduct has no bearing on whether the crimes are going to occur. The supply of weapons is thus immaterial to whether

[40] Miles Jackson, *Complicity in International Law* (OUP 2015) 42.

[41] John Gardner, 'Complicity and Causality' (2007) 1 Criminal Law and Philosophy 132, 136–41; John Gardner, 'Moore on Complicity and Causality' (2008) 156 University of Pennsylvania Law Review 432.

[42] Christopher Kutz, 'Causeless Complicity' (2007) 1 Criminal Law and Philosophy 289.

[43] Glanville Williams, 'Finis for Novus Actus' (1989) 48 CLJ 391, 414.

[44] Michael S Moore, *Causation and Responsibility: An Essay in Law, Morals, and Metaphysics* (OUP 2009) 102.

[45] *Katanga* (Trial Judgment) (n 19) paras 1632–1633.

the force element of the crime is made out, since the army was able to relocate the population even without the additional supplies. However, the hypothetical scenario might posit that the shipment of weapons is proven to have increased the *degree of force* used in the relocation, or alternatively, that the type of weapon used altered the *manner in which the force is exercised*. The shipment would now be considered sufficiently proximate, in the causal sense.[46]

Remoteness[47] is also a useful response to Stewart's problem that 'those who make imperceptibly small contributions to joint harm are still responsible for that harm when operating in collective constructs'.[48] Stewart asserts that it may be desirable to do away entirely with quantitative material requirements for complicity. However, 'significance', read into the terms of Article 25(3)(d)(ii) as merely an indicator of a 'more than *de minimis*' contribution, would account for the possibility of individuals being responsible for imperceptibly small contributions, subject to the criterion of remoteness as a delimitation on the individual's responsibility in order to avoid excessive reach or absurd results. The assessment of remoteness would depend on judicial discretion and ultimately, the benefits of adopting a causation requirement may be practical: if ICC judges were to interpret and apply a causation requirement in Article 25(3)(d)(ii), they would benefit from a wealth of case precedent from different jurisdictions as well as scholarly writing on remoteness in criminal law that would enhance the doctrinal coherence of their jurisprudence.[49]

4.8 Remoteness as a Useful Juridical Concept

The concept of causal remoteness in complicity can accommodate more or less direct contributions to the principal wrong.[50] For arms transfers characterized as assistance, there is already a relatively increased level of causation involved since the weapon directly increases the ability to do harm.[51] By contrast, cases of encouragement involve more indirect causation of the end result.[52] However, ultimately the accomplices contribution can only be indirectly causal, according to Gardner: 'The relationship we have to our own actions is direct: we answer for

[46] Likewise, even where there are multiple shipments of arms from different contributors, a mixture of which is used in the commission of a mass atrocity, in many factual scenarios each contributor's shipment of weapons will nonetheless have an independent effect on the factual contours of the manner of commission of crimes by impacting the scale of the violence, the number of victims, the nature of the injuries etc.

[47] See generally, Moore (n 44).

[48] Stewart (n 37) 1216.

[49] Christopher Burchard, 'Ancillary and Neutral Business Contributions to "Corporate–Political Core Crime": Initial Enquiries Concerning the Rome Statute' (2010) 8 Journal of International Criminal Justice 923.

[50] Jackson, *Complicity in International Law* (n 40) 43.

[51] Jackson, *Complicity in International Law* (n 40) 43.

[52] Jackson, *Complicity in International Law* (n 40) 43.

them as such. The relationship we have to the actions of others is indirect: we answer for them only inasmuch as, by our own actions, we contribute to them.'[53] As Gardner asserts, the distinction between directness and indirectness are built into the structure of rational agency.[54]

According to the Court's current jurisprudence, while complicity under Article 25(3)(d)(ii) requires causation, it would not be necessary to show that an arms trader's personal behaviour had directly caused each legal element of the crime carried out by the direct perpetrator of the crime.[55] The requirement for some form of causal nexus does not necessitate a direct relationship between the conduct of the contributing individual and each element of the crime. It appears that Chambers have envisaged an indirect causal connection to the crime's commission, although the jurisprudence has not expounded on the distinction between direct and indirect causation in this context.[56] Chambers have sometimes overlooked the distinction between the group's activities in committing the crime and the crime itself, by referring to 'contributing to commission' in their reasoning whilst making their findings with respect to a contribution to the crime itself,[57] or vice versa, using the terms interchangeably.[58]

The lack of a direct causal nexus makes sense if we accept that the definition of 'commission' in Article 25(3)(d) must include commission by a group of co-perpetrators under Article 25(3)(a) whose individual responsibility results from the collective combination of their causal contributions. The *Lubanga* Trial Chamber explained that co-perpetration is a doctrine of mutual attribution:

> [It is not necessary that] the contribution of the accused, taken alone, caused the crime; rather, the responsibility of the co-perpetrators for the crimes resulting from the execution of the common plan arises from mutual attribution, based on the joint agreement or common plan.[59]

It also stands to reason that the 'common purpose group' in Article 25(3)(d) may commit the crime through the mutual attribution of their respective acts. The accomplice's conduct, in assisting the group by providing weapons, indirectly causes the crime, and cannot be required to be directly causal in the same way as the group members' collective perpetration of the crime.[60] The implications for the

[53] Gardner, 'Complicity and Causality' (n 41) 18.

[54] Gardner, 'Moore' (n 41) 441.

[55] *Katanga* (Trial Judgment) (n 19) para 1635; *Mbarushimana* (Confirmation Decision) (n 12) paras 284–285.

[56] See Hart and Honoré (n 30).

[57] *Mbarushimana* (Confirmation Decision) (n 12) paras 283, 285.

[58] *Ruto and Sang* (Confirmation Decision) (n 19) paras 351, 353.

[59] *Prosecutor v Thomas Lubanga Dyilo* (Trial Judgment) ICC-01/04-01/06-2842 (14 March 2012) para 994.

[60] Kiss (n 27) 9–10.

arms trade are particularly important when the fungible nature of weapons and ammunition is considered, an issue that concerned the Appeals Chamber of the SCSL in *Taylor* in applying its complicity provisions.[61]

It is often difficult to establish that a particular gun, item of weaponry, or piece of ammunition was actually used to carry out a particular criminal incident, and that therefore, the individual's conduct was a direct cause of the criminal outcome. Unlike in domestic criminal justice systems where forensic firearm examination and DNA evidence is commonplace in cases of violent crime, international criminal tribunals often deal with unstable conflict environments and frequently lack evidence to identify the use of a particular gun or piece of ammunition, although advances in bullet tracing technologies and associated initiatives are changing this.[62] Even where such evidence exists, an arms supplier may argue the impossibility of establishing that their weapons were used in specific criminal incidents, that another dealer would have stepped in to provide the weapons had they not done so, or that their piece of weaponry or ammunition was interchangeable with any other available piece. As Stewart has pointed out, the criminal complicity of arms transfers is an interesting case for considering whether causal over-determination is problematic, since very often the arms supplier could be immediately substituted for another individual who would act in the same manner.[63]

4.9 The Significance of a Particular Shipment

It is significant that the ICC's jurisprudence to date would not require proof of a direct causal nexus, made out by evidence of the use of a particular weapon or piece of ammunition in a particular incident, and has instead required a contribution 'to the commission or attempted commission of the crime'.[64] Liability is established on the basis of the assistive nature of the arms transfer in the carrying out of the group's activities in the perpetration of 'the crime' as legally characterized in the charges (eg a crime against humanity of murder, rape, pillaging), irrespective of whether it is demonstrated that a particular gun was used to carry out any one particular incident of violence amongst those that comprise the crime. The fungible nature of arms supplies does not therefore appear as a per se ouster of liability under Article 25(3)(d)(ii). In these cases where arms transfers were involved, often the arms trading is not per se the subject of the criminality in the case. It is not so

[61] *Taylor* (Appeals Judgment) (n 24) para 391.
[62] See Conflict Armament Research, 'Weapon Supplies into South Sudan's Civil War: Regional Re-Transfers and International Intermediaries' (Conflict Armament Research, November 2018).
[63] Stewart (n 37) 1189–218, 1209.
[64] *Katanga* (Trial Judgment) (n 19) para 1635; *Mbarushimana* (Confirmation Decision) (n 12) paras 284–285; See *Prosecutor v Laurent Gbagbo and Charles Blé Goudé* (Transcript) ICC-02/11-01/15-T-223-ENG (3 October 2018) 35.

much the distribution of arms that is of concern but rather the use of evidence of the distribution of arms to established a connection between the accused and the actual commission of the violence.

When legally characterizing a shipment of weapons as a causal contribution. First, there is the situation where arms transfer conduct contributes to the commission of crimes whose harm is not a result of victims being shot. Also in *Katanga*, the Defence argued that the arms transfer conduct of the accused was relevant only to crimes 'involving bullets':

> Even if the Chamber finds that there is sufficient evidence that Katanga distributed weapons that were used to kill civilians in Bogoro, he can still not be held liable for any of the allegations of rape and sexual slavery. Nor can he be held liable for pillage, destruction or the use of child soldiers. The Prosecutor must prove that he made a direct contribution to the crimes. In the event that the Chamber finds that Katanga's alleged role in the distribution of weapons constituted a direct contribution to the crimes committed by a group of persons acting with a common purpose, this cannot extend to any crimes which did not involve bullets.[65]

Even if, contrary to current ICC jurisprudence, a 'direct contribution to the crime' was required, Katanga's submission that arms cannot assist the commission of crimes of rape, sexual slavery, pillage, destruction, or the use of child soldiers is erroneous. The mere presence of weapons may contribute to the commission of crimes, for instance in producing a 'coercive environment' that is taken advantage of to perpetrate rape.[66] Moreover, while a range of crimes other than the crime against humanity of murder or the war crime of murder may occur as a direct result of shooting bullets (extermination, genocide, causing serious injury, and so on), there are numerous conventional weapons such as explosives or mortars that do not 'involve bullets.' The Chamber in any case rejected the argument. This shows that evidence of the distribution of arms was being used to establish a connection between the accused and the actual commission of the violence.

In these existing cases, where arms transfers were undertaken by military and political actors, Article 25(3)(d)(ii) could have been used to emphasize the activity of transferring arms as a form of criminality in its own right. Instead, in the cases to date, arms transfers were used as an evidentiary vehicle to support other charges, perhaps because those charges were perceived by the Office of the Prosecutor of the International Criminal Court (OTP) to be more important. As Chapter 6

[65] *Prosecutor v Germaine Katanga* (Defence Filing) ICC-01/04-01/07-3369 (15 April 2013) para 88.
[66] See *Bemba* (Trial Judgment) (n 13) para 102 (iii).

shows, such perceptions about the arms trade could be seen amongst ICC judges and lawyers.

The nature of the contribution of a shipment of arms may be misconstrued due to a lack of knowledge and understanding about how the arms trade operates. Wilson's work on the role of expert evidence in international criminal proceedings shows the potential for judges to benefit from expert evidence on the arms trade.[67] Indeed, expert evidence on weapons and ballistics was called in ICTY cases, Wilson finding that judges were relatively receptive to expertise on such material–object science,[68] with weapons and ballistics expert evidence having more impact on ICTY judgments than any other category of expert.[69] Social science data could assist judges' assessment of the nature of an arms transfer contribution to an international crime.

Firstly, numerous NGO reports and social science studies provide data on background levels of arms proliferation.[70] Expert or documentary evidence of this nature could provide context when assessing the impact of a shipment of weapons or ammunition on the commission of crimes. Put simply, in a scenario where no ammunition is available locally, a single shipment could be particularly instrumental in enabling a specific criminal incident. In the Second Congo War study in Chapter 7, for instance, the availability of AK-47s was found to be the prime limiting factor on some of the violence. Similarly, expert evidence could be adduced to show the diversity of different sources of a certain type of weaponry, or lack thereof, and its market availability or the difficulties of supplying it in certain conditions. Evidence of this nature would go towards demonstrating the 'significance' of the contribution.

Secondly, judges may be particularly receptive to expert evidence that shows a particular supplied weapon was used in a particular crime. One ICTY judge in Wilson's study valued expert evidence to such an extent that he considered that 'common human experience hardly counts when it comes to ballistics'.[71] Expert witness testimony may be particularly relevant to proving that a particular weapon was used in a specific criminal incident. Although such 'specific use' is not per se a requirement of Article 25(3)(d)(ii), it may support the proposition that the arms supplier made a contribution to the commission of the crime. In particular, developments in bullet tracing technology may assist investigators in obtaining evidence that a particular piece of ammunition, provided by a particular supplier, was used in a particular incident.

[67] Richard Wilson, 'Expert Evidence on Trial: Social Researchers in the International Criminal Courtroom' (2016) 43 American Ethnologist 730.

[68] Wilson, *Expert Evidence* (n 67) 732.

[69] Wilson, *Expert Evidence* (n 67) 734.

[70] Wilson, *Expert Evidence* (n 67) 732.

[71] Wilson, *Expert Evidence* (n 67) 741.

4.10 Transferring Arms from Outside the Group of Perpetrators

Article 25(3)(d) requires that an individual contributes to a crime committed or attempted by 'a group of persons acting with a common purpose'. Some commentators have argued that Article 25(3)(d) was never intended to apply to persons who are also members of the common purpose group and that the contributor must be a non-member.[72] Their position is supported by a good faith reading of Article 25(3)(d) in accordance with the ordinary meaning of its terms,[73] which sees two distinct subjects—the 'person', who contributes, and the 'group', whose members share a common purpose.[74] On that basis, Article 25(3)(d) was aimed primarily at encapsulating the conduct of non-group members, such as arms traders, who make an external contribution of assistance to the group.

Chambers have nonetheless found the provision applicable to members of the group,[75] and most academic commentators concur, in some cases asserting that Article 25(3)(d) was intended primarily for group members and that the interpretive issue is whether to extend the provision to non-group individuals.[76] Crucially however, as Ambos concludes when reading Article 25 as a whole, 'the rationale of the provision [is] to extend punishability to contributions from outside the group since these may otherwise remain exempt from punishment'.[77]

A further indicator that the drafters of Article 25(3)(d) did not envisage a form of liability that would be used primarily for group members is the fact that a distinct mental requirement was stipulated in subsection (i). As a member of the Article 25(3)(d) 'group', the person is amongst those who act with the common purpose and there is no need to assess whether they acted 'with the aim of furthering the criminal activity or criminal purpose of the group'. In other words, the mental state in subsection (i) would be subsumed by the individual's shared intentions with the common purpose group specified in the *chapeau* of the provision.

Looking to the origins of the text, Article 25(3)(d) is known to have been drawn from international conventions that were intended primarily to criminalize ancillary, non-member contributors to terrorist and organized crime groups. The text is nearly identical to Article 2(3)(c) of the International Convention for the Suppression of Terrorist Bombings. Indeed, many commentators have agreed that

72 Antonio Cassese, *International Criminal Law* (2nd edn, OUP 2008) 213.

73 Vienna Convention on the Law of Treaties (adopted 23 May 1969, entered into force 27 January 1980) 1155 UNTS 331, art 31(1).

74 See *Katanga* (Defence Filing) (n 65) para 115. *Prosecutor v Germaine Katanga* (Defence Filing) ICC-01/04-01/07-3369 (15 April 2013) para 115.

75 *Mbarushimana* (Confirmation Decision) (n 12) para 275; *Katanga* (Trial Judgment) (n 19) para 1631.

76 Kai Ambos, 'Comments on Article 25' in Kai Ambos and Otto Triffterer (eds), *Commentary on the Rome Statute of the International Criminal Court* (Hart 2016) 1013.

77 Ambos (n 76) 1013.

the Statute provision was 'taken directly from' the Convention.[78] Saland, a negotiator at Rome, recalled that 'we were helped by the successful negotiation in 1997 of [the Convention], which had been adopted by consensus. [...] it was easy to reach agreement to incorporate, with slight modifications, the text from that Convention which we now find in paragraph 3(d) of Article 25.'[79] The academic commentary has not recognized that specific individuals with prominent roles in the Rome negotiations, namely Ambassador Kirsch and former ICC President Fernández de Gurmendi, were both involved in drafting the Bombing Convention.[80] It stands to reason that the views of Judge Fernández in the *Mbarushimana* opinion discussed above, about the nature of Article 25(3)(d), were informed by an understanding of its origins and context.[81]

In sum, it is not necessary that the contributor is a member of the group and does not need to share the common purpose of the group's members. In fact, this provision was intended primarily for non-group members. 'Common purpose liability' is therefore a misnomer for Article 25(3)(d). The question of group membership is a mixed *actus reus* and *mens rea* issue. Whether or not the individual is a member of the group is determinative of the nature of their contribution for *actus reus*. But this issue is particularly important because a requirement for common purpose would dramatically increase the requirements of *mens rea* under this provision.

4.11 Conclusion

There is scope for diverging interpretations of Article 25(3)(d)(ii) amongst the ICC judges, leaving ambiguity as to how the provision would be applied in an arms trade case. The limited ICC jurisprudence on Article 25(3)(d)(ii) has not ruled on all its elements, nor applied it to commercial conduct, and the existing passages of jurisprudence on Article 25(3)(d) have considered only a narrow range of factual scenarios, especially when one considers the broad variety of complicit conduct that may constitute 'any other contribution'. Article 25(3)(d)(ii) has not been applied to a sufficiently broad range of fact patterns, across multiple cases, before a sufficient number of judicial benches to constitute a truly constant line of case law that could be relied upon to predict the boundaries of liability. Moreover, despite shortcomings, the text of the provision is unlikely to be amended by the Assembly of States Parties.

[78] Cryer (n 16) 315; Ambos (n 76) 595–96.

[79] Per Saland, 'International Criminal Law Principles' in Roy Lee (ed), *The International Criminal Court: The Making of the Rome Statute* (Martinus Nijhoff 1999) 189, 199.

[80] UNGA, 'Report of the Ad Hoc Committee established by UNGA Resolution 51/210 (17 December 1996)' (1997) UN Doc A/52/37.

[81] *Prosecutor v Callixte Mbarushimana* (Judgment) regarding the normative and causal links to assess the *actus reus* of contribution: ICC-01/04-01/10-514 (30 May 2012) 30–34.

The lack of legal certainty limits the ability of those working in the arms trade to predict the permissible boundaries of non-criminal commercial conduct. It also renders the law of limited utility to decision makers in the ICC and domestic criminal justice systems. A reasonable degree of certainty for making commercial decisions is only likely to be realized through an ICC case involving arms transfer conduct, especially since the Court has not developed any mechanism analogous to the International Court of Justice's issuance of advisory opinions, nor has the majority of ICC judges tended to give *obiter dicta* views on hypothetical matters. In sum, this chapter has analysed three important areas of interpretation in Article 25(3)(d)(ii) relating to the degree of contribution, the causal relationship between the arms transfer and the crime, and the issue of group membership. Together with the next chapter, this proposes a specific interpretation of the Rome Statute complicity provisions.

5

The *Mens Rea* of a Complicit Arms Transfer

5.1 Introduction

The centrality of *mens rea* in establishing the complicity of a weapons supplier was summed up in an English case as follows:

> If one man deliberately sells to another a gun to be used for murdering a third, he may be indifferent whether the third man lives or dies and interested only in the cash profit to be made out of the sale, but he can still be an aider and abettor.[1]

This chapter begins by recalling the mental requirements of accomplice liability in the Rome Statute, before advancing a specific interpretation of the requirements of 'contributing to a group crime' under Article 25(3)(d)(ii).

5.2 Article 25(3)(c) Aiding or Abetting

Article 25(3)(c) of the Statute is a potential avenue for the liability of an arms trader who '[f]or the purpose of facilitating the commission of [a crime], aids, abets or otherwise assists in its commission or its attempted commission, including providing the means for its commission'. The '[f]or the purpose of' language appears to derive from Article 2.06(3) of the US Model Penal Code that requires an accomplice to have acted 'with the purpose of facilitating the perpetrator's conduct'. As discussed in Chapter 4, it is this requirement that makes Article 25(3)(d)(ii) the most relevant mode of liability when it comes to complicit arms transfers.[2]

It has often been said that a plain reading of the requirement that the assistor must act '[f]or the purpose of facilitating a crime' involves a volitional element of *mens rea* that most disinterested commercial activity will not satisfy.[3] Specifically, it has been noted that the purposive requirement in Article 25(3)(c) 'will certainly

[1] *National Coal Board v Gamble* (1959) 1 QB 11 (QB) 23 (Devlin J).

[2] Analysed in Tomas Hamilton, 'An arms trade case at the International Criminal Court: Would the Article 25(3)(c) "purpose" requirement really matter?', Rethinking SLIC, 23 September 2021 <https://rethinkingslic.org/blog/criminal-law/93-an-arms-trade-case-at-the-international-criminal-court-would-the-article-25-3-c-purpose-requirement-really-matter> accessed 4 August 2024.

[3] Robert Cryer and others, *An Introduction to International Criminal Law and Procedure* (2nd edn, CUP 2010) 377.

The Arms Trade and International Criminal Law. Tomas Hamilton, Oxford University Press. © Tomas Hamilton 2025.
DOI: 10.1093/oso/9780192868671.003.0005

make prosecuting those who sell arms or other war matériel which is used for international crimes difficult to prosecute'.[4] This limitation for prosecutions under Article 25(3)(c) does not, however, reduce the overall prospects of conviction at the International Criminal Court (ICC), due to the existence of Article 25(3)(d)(ii). In this regard, the PTC held in the *Mbarushimana* Confirmation Decision:

> [U]nlike the jurisprudence of the *ad hoc* tribunals, Article 25(3)(c) of the Statute requires that the person act with the purpose to facilitate the crime; *knowledge is not enough for responsibility under this Article.* Unless the requisite superior-subordinate relationship exists to charge responsibility under Article 28 of the Statute, 25(3)(d) liability is the only other way a person can be held criminally responsible for acting merely with knowledge of the criminal intentions of others.[5]

The Trial Chamber in *Bemba and others* took a different view, holding that the purposive language of Article 25(3)(c) affects *mens rea* vis-à-vis the aider or abettor's own actions and does not concern the *mens rea* of the principal's crime:

> [for the purpose of facilitating] introduces a higher subjective mental element and means that *the accessory must have lent his or her assistance with the aim of facilitating the offence.* It is not sufficient that the accessory merely knows that his or her conduct will assist the principal perpetrator in the commission of the offence. Mindful of the twofold intent of the accessory (viz. firstly, the principal offence and, secondly, the accessory's own conduct), the Chamber clarifies that this elevated subjective standard relates to the accessory's facilitation, *not the principal offence.*[6]

The view of the Trial Chamber in *Bemba and others* thus departed from a literal reading of the Statute, as upheld by the Confirmation of Charges Decision in the same case, which found that the contribution must be 'made with the purpose of facilitating such commission [of the offence]'.[7] The view of the Trial Chamber was not endorsed by the Appeals Chamber, which did not take the opportunity to clarify this legal issue, or perhaps saw no need to do so.[8] In addition, the Trial Chamber's view does not find agreement in the Confirmation of Charges Decision in *Blé Goudé* that under Article 25(3)(c) the accused must 'intend [...]

[4] Cryer (n 3).

[5] *Prosecutor v Callixte Mbarushimana* (Confirmation Decision) ICC-01/04-01/10 (16 December 2011) para 274 (emphasis added).

[6] *Prosecutor v Jean-Pierre Bemba Gombo and others* (Trial Judgment) ICC-01/05-01/13-1989 (19 October 2016) para 97.

[7] *Prosecutor v Jean-Pierre Bemba Gombo and others* (Confirmation Decision) ICC-01/05-01/13-749 (15 November 2014) para 35.

[8] *Prosecutor v Jean-Pierre Bemba Gombo and others* (Appeals Judgment) ICC-01/05-01/13-2275 (8 March 2018) para 21.

to facilitate the commission of the crime',[9] a position that was quoted by the subsequent Confirmation Decisions in *Ongwen* and in *Al Mahdi* (both of which also cited the *Bemba and others* Confirmation Decision). The dominant view amongst ICC judges to date has thus been to reaffirm a literal interpretation of the terms of the Statute.[10] This makes sense when the relatively elevated *mens rea* of 'purpose' is read together with the relatively decreased *actus reus*, which does not require a 'substantial contribution' to the crime as was required for aiding and abetting at the ad hoc tribunals.

Without entering further into the active debate surrounding Article 25(3)(c)'s *mens rea*, this chapter notes, as Scheffer has emphasized in the context of the American courts' interpretation of the Rome Statute, that Article 25(3)(c) was not drafted to reflect customary international law and requires further ICC judicial interpretation before it can be regarded as legally certain.[11] At the same time, according to Van Sliedregt and Popova, the purposive language cannot be teleologically 'interpreted away, into non-existence'.[12] At the very least then, it is difficult to deny that the *mens rea* of Article 25(3)(c) imposes a 'specific subjective requirement stricter than mere knowledge'.[13]

The *mens rea* of Article 25(3)(c) is therefore more stringent than that of Article 25(3)(d), even if the *Bemba and others* Trial Chamber interpretation of Article 25(3)(c) is accepted. This holds even if the *actus reus* of Article 25(3)(d) is interpreted as extending to 'any other contributions' not covered by other modes of liability, meaning that by definition it extends to acts that fall below the threshold required by the *actus reus* for aiding and abetting.[14] Article 25(3)(d) of the Rome Statute therefore appears to be of greater relevance to the outer boundaries of accomplice liability for commercial arms transfers and in particular for arms brokers, whose polyvalent business arrangements with different clients mean that they are less likely to share the criminal intentions of a particular client, whilst at the same

[9] *Prosecutor v Charles Blé Goudé* (Confirmation Decision) ICC-02/11-02/11-186 (12 December 2014) paras 167 and 170.

[10] *Prosecutor v Dominic Ongwen* (Confirmation Decision) ICC-02/04-01/15-422 (23 March 2016) fn 24; *Prosecutor v Ahmad Al Faqi Al Mahdi* (Confirmation Decision) ICC-01/12-01/15-84 (24 March 2016) fn 15.

[11] David Scheffer, '*Amicus Curiae* Brief in Support of the Issuance of a Writ of Certiorari) Presbyterian Church of Sudan, and others v Talisman Energy, Inc. (Supreme Court of the United States, 9 May 2010) 5, 7<http://hrp.law.harvard.edu/wp-content/uploads/2013/07/talisman-amicus-final-filed-4-30-10.pdf> accessed 4 August 2024.

[12] Elies van Sliedregt and Alex Popova, 'Interpreting "for the Purpose of Facilitating" in Art 25(3)(c)?' (*Blog of James G Stewart*, 22 December 2014) <http://jamesgstewart.com/interpreting-for-the-purpose-of-facilitating-in-Article-253c/> accessed 4 August 2024.

[13] Kai Ambos, 'Comments on Article 25' in Kai Ambos and Otto Triffterer (eds), *Commentary on the Rome Statute of the International Criminal Court* (Hart 2016) 1009.

[14] See Kai Ambos, 'The ICC and Common Purpose: What Contribution is Required Under Article 25(3)(d)?' in Carsten Stahn (ed), *The Law and Practice of the International Criminal Court* (OUP 2015) 595, 595–96; Alejandro Kiss, 'La contribución en la comisión de un crimen por un grupo de personas en la jurisprudencia de la Corte Penal Internacional' (2013) 2 InDret 1, 2.

time their greater proximity to end users often gives them greater knowledge of the use of the weapons than manufacturers.

This view about the primacy of Article 25(3)(d) diverges from the focus of much existing scholarship on ICC corporate complicity, which has often overlooked the unique features of Article 25(3), perhaps due to seeing the ICC through the lens of a particular domestic jurisdiction, a lens of existing human rights litigation, or of customary international law standards. In any event, the Rome Statute is a *sui generis* legal system in which the Statute has primacy over customary definitions of aiding and abetting.[15]

5.3 Contributing to a Group Crime under Article 25(3)(d)

As a reminder, the full text of Article 25(3)(d) provides that a person shall be criminally responsible and liable for punishment for a crime within the jurisdiction of the Court if that person:

> (d) In any other way contributes to the commission or attempted commission of such a crime by a group of persons acting with a common purpose. Such contribution shall be intentional and shall either:
> (i) Be made with the aim of furthering the criminal activity or criminal purpose of the group, where such activity or purpose involves the commission of a crime within the jurisdiction of the Court; or
> (ii) Be made in the knowledge of the intention of the group to commit the crime.

The distinctiveness of the mental states in Article 25(3)(d)(i) and (ii) suggests that each should be interpreted as a discrete mode of liability, in the sense that the two subsections describe fundamentally different states of mind in which the Article 25(3)(d) contribution was made. A commercial arms trader may be liable for 'knowingly contributing' to an international crime without having 'intentionally furthered' the crime. The difference between the two *mens rea* is significant, and as Jackson emphasizes, an accurate distinguishing of the perpetrator's role should be recorded in international tribunal judgments, since 'a properly differentiated model of responsibility accurately labels participants in the attribution of responsibility and conveys to the wider public the general nature of their wrongdoing'.[16]

[15] In *Van Anraat,* the Dutch Court of Appeal appeared to differentiate the 'aider or abettor' under international law from the Dutch legal framework for accessorial assistance. *Public Prosecutor v Frans Cornelis Adrianus van Anraat,* Judgment, Court of Appeal of The Hague (9 May 2007) ECLI:NL:GHSGR:2007:BA4676 (official English translation), paras 2, 12.4, 13.

[16] Miles Jackson, 'The Attribution of Responsibility and Modes of Liability in International Criminal Law' (2016) 29 Leiden Journal of International Law 879, 890. See contra James G Stewart, 'The

Some scholars have asserted that subsection (i) is unnecessary and redundant since it is subsumed by subsection (ii).[17] However, while it is true that subsection (i) requires a higher *degree* of mental commitment ('intentionally furthering'), the subsection (ii) requirement carries a greater *specificity* of mental awareness (the knowledge under this subsection must relate to 'the crime'). There are common situations in which an individual supports a group with the aim of furthering its criminal activity or criminal purpose whilst remaining ignorant of a specific crime that the group intends to commit. In such a situation, (i) is not subsumed by (ii). A donor who enthusiastically funds a designated terrorist group with the fervent desire of achieving a long-term political aim may nonetheless be unaware of specific details of the group's plan to carry out a particular terrorist attack. The donor may be liable under (i) even when not liable under (ii).

The absence of any volitive *mens rea* requirement in subsection (ii) increases its relevance to commercial arms transfers.[18] Only rarely will it be possible to prove that a commercially minded actor harbours the aim to further the criminal activity or criminal purpose of a group that would satisfy the requirement of subsection (i). This is not a question of personal *motive*, which is generally irrelevant to criminal liability, but rather a practical observation that in commercial cases there will rarely be evidence of anything other than the supplier's pecuniary interest in making a sale.

5.4 Specificity of Knowledge: 'Essential Matters'

The *mens rea* requirement that the contribution is 'made in the knowledge of the intention of the group to commit the crime' remains open to interpretation. The limited jurisprudence on Article 25(3)(d)(ii) has held that 'the accused must be aware that the intention existed when engaging in the conduct which constituted his or her contribution'.[19] While this mode of liability allows for relatively low thresholds for the 'significant' contribution and *mens rea* of knowledge, this corresponds to an elevated degree of specificity as to awareness of the principal crime.

In interpreting what 'knowledge of the crime' entails, it may be useful to consider the dual parameters of *specificity* and *degree*, which Smith argues are a general distinguishing feature of all doctrines of complicity.[20] Compared to Article 25(3)

Strangely Familiar History of the Unitary Theory of Perpetration' in Bruce Ackerman and others (eds), *Visions of Justice, Essays in Honor of Professor Mirjan Damaška* (Duncker and Humblot 2016) 31.

[17] Jens Ohlin, 'Joint Criminal Confusion' (2009) 12 New Criminal Law Review 417.

[18] See Sarah Finnin, 'Elements of Accessorial Modes of Liability: Article 25(3)(b) and (c) of The Rome Statute of The International Criminal Court' (2012) 61 ICLQ 325.

[19] *Prosecutor v Germaine Katanga* (Trial Judgment) ICC-01/04-01/07-3436 (7 March 2014), para 1641.

[20] Keith JM Smith, *A Modern Treatise on the Law of Criminal Complicity* (Clarendon Press 1991) 141.

(d)(i), the *mens rea* of Article 25(3)(d)(ii) requires a greater *degree* of mental commitment to the group, but a lesser *specificity* with respect to the group's criminality. Likewise, while subsection (i) requires intent ('with the aim of furthering') as to a generalized range of possible criminality described in terms of the group's criminal activity or purpose, subsection (ii) lowers the mental requirement to simple knowledge while requiring a more specific knowledge 'of the crime'.

The required specificity of the accomplice's knowledge is a significant doctrinal issue for any system of rules of complicity.[21] At one extreme, the requirement may be drawn in very general terms, concerning a range of unlawful purposes where the contributor's knowledge need not distinguish a particular offence. Alternatively, a rule of complicity may require a more specific awareness of the type of crime (violent, sexual, commercial etc). However, in any legal system, mere knowledge of a broad category of criminality is unlikely to be sufficient as a *mens rea* of accomplice liability, as per the reasoning in the English case of *Bullock*: 'if an accused lends a man a revolver believing that it may be used to commit *a crime of violence* but with nothing specific in mind, it may not be enough'.[22]

The rule of complicity might be drawn with greater mental specificity, requiring the accused's awareness of the legal characterization of a certain crime (murder, rape, fraud, etc) but nothing more precise. Under this test, an individual 'X' who agrees to fly a plane loaded with AK-47s, for instance, to another individual 'Y', with the general awareness that Y is a broker known to supply non-State armed groups with dubious records of committing war crimes or crimes against humanity of murder and torture might be considered to be sufficiently aware of the nature of a range of crimes that the group intends to commit.

Alternatively, a rule of complicity might require even greater specificity of knowledge relating to the attendant circumstances surrounding the crime and the precise manner of its commission (awareness of the location, timing, identity of intended victims and direct perpetrators, *modus operandi*, etc). Such a requirement would be satisfied, for example, in a scenario where an individual 'A' provides explosives to 'B' in the specific awareness of B's plan to detonate a motorcycle bomb the following morning in order to kill a particular named individual.

The *Katanga* Trial Chamber affirmed that for Article 25(3)(d)(ii), knowledge of a general criminal intention is insufficient and knowledge of the intention to commit the crime must be established.[23] The bench held that the contributor must know of the group's intention to commit 'each of the crimes forming part of the common purpose',[24] which should be understood as meaning that in relation to

[21] Miles Jackson, *Complicity in International Law* (OUP 2015) 50.
[22] *Bullock* (1955) 38 Criminal Appeal Reports 151, 153 (emphasis added).
[23] *Katanga* (Trial Judgment) (n 19) para 1642.
[24] *Katanga* (Trial Judgment) (n 19) para 1642, 'prouver [...] que l'accusé savait que le groupe avait l'intention de commettre chacun des crimes qui faisaient partie du dessein commun'.

each criminal charge it must be shown that the accused knew of the common purpose of the group to commit 'the charged crime' in question.[25]

As mentioned above, while Katanga was found guilty of international crimes on the basis of Article 25(3)(d)(ii), and while his conduct included distributing weapons,[26] the Trial Chamber did not recognize this 'arms transfer conduct' as a form of complicit criminality in its own right. The *Katanga* finding does not exclude contributions made in the awareness of a range of potential crimes that are expected to occur based on what is known of the group's intentions at the time of the transfer, even where the group eventually succeeds in attempting or carrying out only one or more of those crimes. It might be thought that expanding specificity to include contemplation of a range of offences is inconsistent with complicity's fundamental derivative nature.[27] If the contributor's liability is essentially dependent on the commission of the principal's crime, how can it be that they are potentially liable for a range of crimes when the principal in fact only commits one of them? As Smith explains, this apparent theoretical difficulty has been accommodated by the English courts on the basis that the contributor's culpability is founded on them taking certain actions that they know will expose them to being connected to a crime ie the assumption of risk,[28] an approach that is consistent with that taken by the Trial Chamber is *Katanga*.

The ICC's jurisprudence has not yet discussed the specificity of knowledge in any depth, beyond rehearsing the statutory wording of 'the crime'. Given the lack of provision in the Statute, it may be useful to consider customary standards for specificity of complicit knowledge.[29] The ICC might adopt an 'essential matters' test, similar to the test applied at the International Criminal Tribunal for the former Yugoslavia (ICTY) for aiders and abettors, which may provide a useful limiting criterion for Chambers in applying Article 25(3)(d)(ii). The consistent position in ICTY case law is that it is unnecessary for an accomplice to know the 'precise crime' intended or committed by the perpetrator,[30] instead the applicable standard was an awareness that 'one of a number of crimes' would probably be committed.[31] The ICTY Trial Chamber held in *Furundžija*:

> [I]t is not necessary that the aider and abettor should know the precise crime that was intended and which in the event was committed. If he is aware that one of a number of crimes will probably be committed, and one of those crimes is in

[25] See contra *Prosecutor v Laurent Gbagbo and Charles Blé Goudé* (Defence Filing) ICC-02/11-01/15-1198 (28 September 2018) para 507.

[26] *Katanga* (Trial Judgment) (n 19) paras 642–651.

[27] Smith (n 20) 194.

[28] Smith (n 20) 194.

[29] Rome Statute, art 21.

[30] *Prosecutor v Tihomir Blaškić* (Appeals Judgment) IT-95-14-A (29 July 2014) para 50.

[31] *Prosecutor v Pavle Strugar* (Trial Judgment) IT-01-42-T (31 Jan 2005) para 350. Nina HB Jørgensen (ed), *International Criminal Responsibility of War's Funders and Profiteers* (CUP 2020).

> fact committed, he has intended to facilitate the commission of that crime, and is guilty as an aider and abettor.[32]

An analogous test of 'essential matters' exists in modern English case law, as recalled in *Johnson v Youden*: 'Before a person can be convicted of aiding and abetting the commission of an offence he must at least know the essential matters which constitute that offence.'[33] In the context of Article 25(3)(d)(ii), it should be understood that 'essential matters' would refer to the contributor's knowledge of the basic factual contours of the crime with which they are charged, rather than necessarily having knowledge of the legal elements of a particular form of criminality.

Applying an 'essential matters' criterion to Article 25(3)(d)(ii) would capture a range of arms transfer conduct. In Burchard's view, it is a fair generalization to say that commercial suppliers will not usually be aware of a specific impending crime, even if they know of broader criminal purposes.[34] However, the commercial setting in which arms transfers take place is a key variable that limits the generalizability of Burchard's observation. A financial institution that operates electronically and from a location geographically remote from the commission of crimes has a different claim to ignorance of specific crimes when compared to an arms broker who has an immediate awareness of the conflict in which they are doing business, for instance by personally flying the plane and hand delivering the weapons to the direct perpetrators of crimes. Crucially, although at the level of attribution of responsibility, weapons are no different per se from food, factually speaking, the act of supplying armaments carries with it the knowledge of the intrinsic capacity of weapons to facilitate violence and this will often make it harder to claim ignorance of impending crimes.

5.5 Sources of Knowledge: Awareness of a UN Embargo or Fact-Finding

In a putative ICC case involving arms transfer conduct, the relevant considerations for the Court's determination of 'essential matters' could be to some extent elaborated to provide judicial guidance for this specific type of conduct. For example, the existence of a relevant Chapter VII arms embargo, or the publicly known placement of the arms transfer recipient on a Security Council sanctions list, could be taken as factually relevant to the assessment of a supplier's constructive knowledge that the recipient would use the weapons to commit a particular type of crime.

32 *Prosecutor v Anto Furundžija* (Trial Judgment) IT-95-17/1-T (10 December 1998) para 246.

33 *Johnson v Youden* (1950) 1 KB 544 (KB) 546.

34 Christopher Burchard, 'Ancillary and Neutral Business Contributions to "Corporate–Political Core Crime": Initial Enquiries Concerning the Rome Statute' (2010) 8 Journal of International Criminal Justice 944.

The existence of a Security Council embargo will often mean there is potential for cases of 'knowing assistance' since, as Chapter 5 argues, under the knowledge standard for complicity under Article 25(3)(d)(ii) of the Rome Statute, an embargo may be indicative of an arms trader's actual or constructive knowledge that an embargoed recipient of weapons intended to commit international crimes. Expert evidence about the operation of an arms traders' business and the public availability of information about embargoed recipients can contribute to demonstrating a defendant's complicit *mens rea*. A publicly known UN or EU arms embargo would make the intentions of an embargoed recipient even clearer than in cases such as *Van Anraat* discussed below, where it was shown that the defendant knew the criminal intentions of the Saddam Hussein regime even before a UN embargo was in place. In *Van Anraat*, a trading partner of the defendant gave evidence about his understanding of the uses of supplied chemical substances in poison gas, their firm's supply chain, the availability of information to the defendant about the intended crimes in Iraq,[35] and the defendant's deliberate concealment of the final destination of the weapons.[36] As Richard Wilson found in the context of incitement to genocide,[37] qualitative expert evidence of a similar nature could be an important source of authority for judicial decision-making in the international criminal tribunals.[38]

A Security Council referral is made pursuant to Article 13 of the Rome Statute, and this invokes a legal standard (the Council's assessment of a threat to peace under Article 39 of the UN Charter) that is equivalent to that required for the Security Council's imposition of arms embargoes.[39] An ICC Situation referred by the Security Council may involve perpetrators of international crimes who are concurrently subject to an embargo. In this scenario, the Resolution that imposes the embargo, as well as the Resolution referring the Situation to the ICC, may both be founded on the same or similar Article 39 grounds.

The non-binding standards of business and human rights referred to in Chapter 3 could also be relevant for assessing criminal *mens rea*, by providing indicators as to whether an individual knew that a particular transfer of arms was unacceptable by the prevailing acceptable practices of the day. Additionally, due diligence legislative developments or initiatives such as the Draft Treaty of the UN Human Rights Council Working Group could refer to International Criminal Law standards in their provisions and make provision for information sharing or investigative cooperation with the ICC.

35 See *Public Prosecutor v Frans Cornelis Adrianus van Anraat*, Judgment, Court of Appeal of The Hague (9 May 2007) ECLI:NL:GHSGR:2007:BA4676 (official English translation) para 11.10.

36 *Van Anraat*, Court of Appeal Judgment (n 35) paras 11.11–12.

37 Richard A Wilson, *Incitement on Trial: Prosecuting International Speech Crimes* (CUP 2017).

38 Wilson, *Expert Evidence* (n 57). See Nicola Palmer and Felix Kroner, 'Anthropology, Transitional Justice and Criminal Law' (2019) 13 International Journal of Transitional Justice 398, 400.

39 Rome Statute (17 July 1998) 2187 UNTS 3, art 13(b).

In the Dutch case of *Kouwenhoven,* the Court of Appeal held that the defendant must have been aware that weapons and ammunition would be used due to, inter alia, the fact that his transfers contravened UN Resolutions on arms and ammunition.[40] The finding that Kouwenhoven had constructive knowledge of the crimes was based on a range of other information available to him, including his relationship with Charles Taylor, dealings with the Liberian armed forces, his 'use of RTC Camp Bomi Wood as a collection and distribution site for [...] arms and ammunition', and his conduct, based primarily on a letter he wrote discussing the deals.[41]

The existence of a Security Council Resolution is unlikely to be a sufficient basis from which to extrapolate that a contributor knew particular crimes would occur, since embargoes are generally imposed on entire states on the basis of broad Chapter VII concerns. However, certain embargoes are imposed in relation to geographically, temporally, and thematically specific human rights violations where sanctions are targeted at certain individuals. In such cases, when the existence of a Security Council embargo is combined with an awareness of other publicly known mechanisms such as a recipient's placement on the US Specially Designated Nationals list, ICC judges might find a sufficient factual basis on which to conclude that an arms trader must have known of the essential matters of the crimes to be committed by the embargoed recipient.

5.6 Degree of Knowledge: 'Occurrence in the Ordinary Course of Events'

Alongside the issue of the specific facts known to the contributor, the second parameter of *mens rea* under Article 25(3)(d)(ii) is to what degree of certainty the contributor must know that the group intends that the facts will materialize. Otherwise put, this is the question of the quanta of knowledge, the extent, the probability, the likelihood, or the level of certainty in the contributor's mind as to what the group intends to happen in the future. Without such a threshold, 'knowledge' is a shallow concept for practical purposes. As Smith notes, there is greater complexity in doctrines of complicity than in principal liability, since complicity requires an assessment of the degree of the accomplice's knowledge as to the principal's intentions. While the latter is concerned with the principal's own knowledge of what they wish to do, the former requires an assessment of what one individual knows about another's knowledge.[42]

[40] *Public Prosecutor v Guus Kouwenhoven* (Judgment) Court of Appeal of The Hague (10 March 2008) ECLI:NL:GHSGR:2008:BC6068, s L2.1.

[41] *Kouwenhoven*, Court of Appeal Judgment (n 40) s L2.1.

[42] Smith (n 20) 162.

The issue of the degree of knowledge in Article 25(3)(d) raises the judicial and scholarly debate over whether specific direction is an element of aiding and abetting under customary international law, and has caused much confusion,[43] including whether the requirement relates to *actus reus* or *mens rea*. The so-called 'specific direction' debate is of limited relevance in the Rome Statute context, yet some of the same concerns that fuelled the proposal of a specific direction requirement have been raised in the Rome Statute context in relation to 'generic [contributions made] with simple knowledge of the existence of a group acting with a common purpose'.[44] These concerns appear to be ameliorated at the ICC by interpreting complicity in terms of the *specificity* and *degree* of knowledge required. In situations where an arms supplier provides assistance that could be used for lawful and unlawful activities, it will be a question of whether they have sufficiently specific and sufficiently certain awareness of the group's unlawful intentions. In this regard, Jackson has pointed to a gordian solution to the so-called 'specific direction' issue by highlighting the potential of defences of justification to provide for 'lawful complicity'.[45]

The default definition of the degree of knowledge in the Rome Statute under Article 30(3) is either to be aware that *a circumstance exists* or alternatively, to be aware that *a consequence will occur in the ordinary course of events*. Since the contributor's knowledge under Article 25(3)(d)(ii) relates to an intention, rather than to criminal consequences, the plausible reading of Article 30 in relation to the accomplice's knowledge of the principal's *mens rea* is that the group's intention is a 'circumstance' within the meaning of Article 30(3) and the contributor must therefore be aware of the existence of the group's intention. Accordingly, the Trial Chamber in *Katanga* found that the contributor must know that the group 'means to cause [the criminal consequence of the crime] or is aware that it will occur in the ordinary course of events'.[46] The Chamber found that the contributor's knowledge should be inferred from relevant facts and circumstances.[47] The assessment of those facts and circumstances will overlap to a significant extent with the assessment of remoteness discussed above, since there will often be a strong correlation between the degree of an individual's familiarity with an impending crime and the individual's causal proximity to its commission.

In relation to the accomplice's awareness of the likelihood of the crime occurring, the knowledge that the crime 'will occur in the ordinary course of events' inevitably implies an assessment of the probability or risk that an incident is going to take place. Arguably, there is something distinctive about selling weapons that

[43] Carsten Stahn, *A Critical Introduction to International Criminal Law* (CUP 2019) 114–16.

[44] *Katanga* (Trial Judgment) (n 19) Minority Opinion of Judge Christine Van den Wyngaert, para 287.

[45] Miles Jackson, 'Virtuous Accomplices in International Criminal Law' (2019) 68 ICLQ 817.

[46] *Katanga* (Trial Judgment) (n 19) paras 774–777, 1641.

[47] *Katanga* (Trial Judgment) (n 19) para 1642.

often increases the risk that violence will follow, when compared to other forms of assistance. The English case of *NCB v Gamble* chose the example of an arms supplier to describe knowledge in terms of a lack of purpose or an 'indifference' as to the principal's criminal intentions:

> Evidence of an intent in the crime or of an express purpose to assist it will greatly strengthen the case for the prosecution. But an indifference to the result of the crime does not of itself negative abetting. If one man deliberately sells to another a gun to be used for murdering a third he may be indifferent about whether the third man lives or dies and interested only in the cash profit to be made out of the sale, but he can still be an aider and abettor. To hold otherwise would be to negative the rule that mens rea is a matter of intent only and does not depend on desire or motive.[48]

The sale of a gun is a carefully chosen illustration of blameworthy complicit knowledge since the disinterested accomplice cannot avoid the awareness that the gun may help kill the third man. This distinctive factual example was also chosen by the UK Supreme Court in its reasoning in the important case of *Jogee*, to typify the situation where an accomplice lacks the positive intent that a particular offence will be committed and where, at the time the contribution is made, 'it remains uncertain what [the perpetrator] will do.'[49] All other things being equal, 'what the perpetrator may do' is inherently more certain when you hand them a gun, as opposed to providing them with finance or food. In the case of finance or food, it will often be less clear whether an accomplice's lack of direct intent as to the principal offence negates *mens rea*.[50] The sale of a gun holds an inherent potential for violence, thereby increasing the risk assented to by the seller upon making the sale.

As mentioned above, there are practical limitations to the conceivable degree of an accomplice's knowledge of the group's intentions, since, as Smith observes, 'an accessory cannot "know" something yet to occur' when it relates to the intentions of another, in the same way that the principal can know their own intentions.[51] In situations of mass atrocity, this is exacerbated by the complexity of international crimes, when they are perpetrated collectively with physical and structural distance separating the contributor from the point of commission. For instance, in *Kouwenhoven*, the Court of Appeal found that the defendant must have been aware that 'in the ordinary cause of events weapons and ammunition would be used' to commit atrocity.[52] But only a weak analogy can be made between, on the one hand,

48 Although there is English jurisprudence to the contrary, this standard was largely reaffirmed in subsequent cases. See *R v Bryce* [2004] EWCA Crim 1231.

49 *R v Jogee* [2016] UKSC 8 para 10.

50 Andrew Simester and others, *Criminal Law: Theory and Doctrine* (6th edn, Hart 2016) 232.

51 Smith (n 20) 181.

52 *Kouwenhoven*, Court of Appeal Judgment (n 40) s L2.1.

an international crime and on the other, a violent crime under domestic law where, for instance, the accomplice A hands the perpetrator B a knife while standing next to an anticipated victim C. The assessment of probability is central to criminal law standards of complicit knowledge, essentially describing different gradations of mental acceptance of risk. Even the standard of 'occurrence in the ordinary course of events' simply describes a degree of risk.

The Rome negotiations rejected a recklessness standard and this is as reflected in Article 30. However, in the practical application of Article 25(3)(d)(ii) the differences between 'knowledge' and 'recklessness' may be difficult to distinguish in scenarios of complicity.[53] This practical and evidentiary issue (how to apply *mens rea* to the defendant's knowledge of intentions that are not their own) is particular to Article 25(3)(d)(ii), since it is the only knowledge-based form of complicity in the Statute.

According to Smith, common law systems of law treat the standard of 'virtual certainty' and 'recklessness' as being quantitative points on a spectrum, which ranges from the accomplice being certain through to the accomplice seeing a remote possibility.[54] In this light, a difficulty with interpreting the required degree of knowledge under Article 25(3)(d)(ii) is not so much a formalistic question of how best to describe or name the appropriate standards of 'knowing the intention of the group', but rather, how best to understand the level of acceptable risk to which the contributor may assent when making an arms transfer, and how best to apply this notion of acceptable risk to evidence in concrete cases.

In the Court's current interpretation of the degree of knowledge under Article 25(3)(d)(ii), an arms supplier must know that the crime 'will occur in the ordinary course of events', requiring a factual assessment of the contributor's awareness of the risk that the group intends to use the weapons to commit the crime. This raises the possibility of unknowing assistance under Article 25(3)(d). For instance, an arms transporter may claim to have unwittingly shipped a cargo of weapons by air, sea, or land without realizing that the plane, vessel, or vehicle contains weapons. This scenario occurs in drug trafficking cases where captains of ocean-going vessels may be held strictly liable for shipments found on board the vessel even in the absence of evidence of the captain's knowledge of the presence of the drugs. Under Article 25(3)(d)(ii), such an individual in this scenario would have neither the requisite knowledge of the group's intentions, nor the requisite intentionality as to the contribution itself. Evidence of larger-scale patterns of distribution may show repeated transfers undermining the transporters' claimed ignorance.[55]

[53] Smith (n 20) 181.
[54] Smith (n 20) 182–83.
[55] See John Cartner and others, *The International Law of the Shipmaster* (Routledge 2013) 187.

5.7 Aligning with Arms Trade Law: A Risk-based Approach

The assessment of 'occurrence in the ordinary course of events' to prove knowledge under Article 25(3)(d)(ii), will need to be based on assessments of the factual possibilities and risks known to the supplier. This evidentiary question could be informed by the acceptable levels of risks identified in Arms Trade Law in Chapters 2 and 3 in domestic licensing regimes for arms exports, the international obligations in the Arms Trade Treaty (ATT), the potential for state complicity on the basis of arms supplies, the standards of Security Council and EU arms embargoes, international and national prohibitions on material assistance to terrorism, as well as non-binding commercial standards in the arms trade.[56] These standards offer decision makers a wealth of factual criterion when interpreting and applying the acceptable level of risk.

The use of social science data in international criminal proceedings, as discussed in Wilson's work, has great potential relevance for the judicial assessment of *mens rea* in an arms trade case.[57] Judges could benefit from expert evidence on (i) the internal working of the business including decision-making and information-sharing processes within a corporate organizational structure, whether a large corporation or an individual broker, (ii) operational aspects of the arms trade, the common flows of weapons into a situation, and the range of supplies available to the perpetrators in a particular incident, and (iii) weapons experts who could evidence as to the weapons used in a conflict and explain tracing issues.

In the *Van Anraat* case, the fact evidence of a business associate of the defendant related to the usual operating procedures of the company, the fact that in the usual course of business, the defendant would have been aware of the national and international prohibitions on shipping the chemicals in question to Iraq, as well as the specific administrative moves that could be taken to circumvent these prohibitions and comply with export regulations and end-user documentation requirements. The perceived complexity of arms trade cases, found in Chapters 6 and 7, could be ameliorated by expert social science evidence on these issues.

5.8 Appropriate Labelling of Arms Transfer Complicity

Although it is widely recognized that Article 25(3)(d) was based on the Terrorist Bombing Convention, it is curious that neither the jurisprudence nor the existing academic commentary on the ICC has mentioned that Article 25(3)(d) finds near-identical wording in Article 3(4) of the EU Extradition Convention.[58]

[56] See Chapter 2.

[57] Wilson, *Expert Evidence* (n 57).

[58] Convention Relating to Extradition between the Member States of the European Union (adopted 27 September 1996) OJ C313/11.

The Explanatory Report to the EU Extradition Convention indicates that the wording of the text was originally envisioned as an alternative mode of liability, which could be chosen by Member States by way of treaty reservation, to avoid doctrines of criminal association or conspiracy in relation to terrorist offences, offences related to organized crime including drug-trafficking and violent offences. The Explanatory Report refers to contributions 'ancillary in nature, (mere material preparation; logistic support to the movement or harbouring of persons and similar conduct)', stating explicitly that 'the person contributing to the commission of the offence [need not be] a "member" of the group'.[59]

Furthermore, it has also not been noted in the jurisprudence or commentary that near-identical wording was subsequently adopted in Article 2(4)(c) of the Nuclear Terrorism Convention of 2005, again with the aim of criminalizing external non-group assistive contributions.[60] The relatively free movement of text, from the EU Extradition Convention, to the Terrorist Bombing Convention, then to the Rome Statute (in a manner that Saland described as 'easy'), and subsequently onwards to the Nuclear Terrorism Convention, represents a surprising fluidity of legal transplant.[61] That the provision could be transplanted between treaties on transnational crime and the leading international crimes treaty conflicts with some of the dominant doxa of the field of 'Transnational Criminal Law', defining in terms of treaty crimes under what Guilfoyle describes as 'the sources book' of Transnational Criminal Law.[62] This sharing of doctrinal sources might unsettle some of the views of ICC judges and lawyers in Chapter 6 that saw international crimes as a hermetically sealed category that does not interact with the less serious category of transnational criminality, to which arms trading was perceived to belong.

Article 25(3)(d) seems to have been most readily envisaged as a form of liability for the ancillary contributions of non-group individuals who contribute to the commission of a crime by a group.[63] Contrary to this, the practice of the ICC Prosecutor has so far been to deploy Article 25(3)(d) primarily in relation to group members, such as militia leaders, whose contributions might have been more fairly labelled as co-perpetrators,[64] perhaps reflecting a tendency to use the 'residual' Article 25(3)(d) to charge individuals who would be phenomenologically considered to be central actors in military or political hierarchical structures.

[59] Explanatory Report on the Convention relating to extradition between the Member States of the European Union [1997] OJ C191/13.

[60] International Convention for the Suppression of Acts of Nuclear Terrorism (adopted 13 April 2005, entered into force 7 July 2007) 2445 UNTS 89.

[61] On transplants see James G Stewart and Asad Kiyani, 'The Ahistoricism of Legal Pluralism in International Criminal Law' (2017) 65 The American Journal of Comparative Law 393.

[62] Douglas Guilfoyle, 'Transnational Crimes' in Kevin Heller and others (eds), The Oxford Handbook of International Criminal Law (OUP 2020) 800.

[63] See Marina Aksenova, 'The Modes of Liability at the ICC: The Labels that Don't Always Stick' (2015) 15 International Criminal Law Review 629.

[64] *Katanga* (Trial Judgment) (n 19).

The Prosecutor has seemed to suggest that Article 25(3)(d) is intended primarily for group members, and only secondarily for external contributors. In oral argument in the *Gbagbo and Blé Goudé* half-time hearing, the Prosecutor reasoned that '[t]o confine application of Article 25(3)(d) to outsiders to the group who contribute to the commission of crimes would unduly circumscribe its reach, in contravention of a plain reading of the provision'.[65] Without explaining this 'plain reading', the Prosecutor cited *Mbarushimana* jurisprudence that simply notes that the provision does not specify whether it applies to group members or outsiders.[66] This suggests that, rather than aiming for appropriate labelling in its charges, the Office of the Prosecutor of the International Criminal Court (OTP) has adopted an instrumental approach to the modes of liability, wherein crimes are undercharged, in order to make the complicity requirements easier to satisfy, an approach which some judicial chambers have upheld.

Irrespective of whether there is any legal barrier to charging a suspect under a range of modes of liability that reflects their conduct, there is a threat to the Court's legitimacy if Article 25(3)(d) becomes a routine 'backdoor' to convict senior high-level perpetrators.[67] Meanwhile, arms suppliers who do not share the common purposes of the group and knowingly provide external assistance to the group are the archetypal 'non-group' contributors that were envisaged by the drafters of Article 25(3)(d) of the Rome Statute.

The potential of complicity in International Criminal Law is also to ensure the law better labels the relevant conduct, by more accurately reflecting the individual's wrongdoing than a domestic law regulatory breach. The conduct of an arms trader sanctioned administratively for breaching customs regulations may be poorly labelled when that same conduct renders them responsible for an international crime. However, it is fundamental to any criminal law system that individual wrongdoing is accurately described.[68] This is not only a matter of the criminal law's expressive, communicative, truth-telling, or declaratory functions, but of fairness to the defendant.[69] Furthermore, the degree of culpability of an arms trader convicted for a breach of an export regulation and the severity of the sentence imposed, even where the arms export was prohibited on the basis of the risk of an international crime, will frequently be of a lesser seriousness than if they had been convicted for the international crime itself.

Many interpretations of Article 25(3)(d) have viewed it as a form of 'common purpose liability' that would entail a *mens rea* akin to doctrines of joint criminal

65 *Prosecutor v Laurent Gbagbo and Charles Blé Goudé* (Prosecution Filing) ICC-02/11-01/15-1207-Anx1 (8 November 2018) para 1979.

66 *Mbarushimana* (Confirmation Decision) (n 5) para 275.

67 See Douglas Guilfoyle, 'Responsibility for Collective Atrocities: Fair Labelling and Approaches to Commission in International Criminal Law' (2011) 64 CLP 255.

68 Glanville Williams, 'Convictions and Fair Labelling' (1983) 42 CLJ 85.

69 Andrew Ashworth and Jeremy Horder, *Principles of Criminal Law* (7th edn, OUP 2013) 79.

enterprise. This is erroneous, since *liability* through this provision attaches to the individual making the assistive contribution, not the group acting with a 'common purpose' which they assist. Under subsection 25(3)(d)(ii) such liability can accrue to an individual who does not share the common purpose of the group. Under subsection (ii) the defendant need only know of the group's intentions. It is therefore not only a misnomer to refer to Article 25(3)(d) as 'common purpose liability', it labels this mode of liability with expressly the opposite connotation to a plain reading of its provisions.

5.9 Conclusion

Based on the specific interpretation proposed in these last two chapters, a broad range of arms transfer conduct is potentially criminalized by the mode of liability in Article 25(3)(d)(ii) of the Rome Statute. Exactly how far this range extends will depend on the interpretation and application of the *actus reus* and *mens rea*. Notwithstanding some interpretive difficulties, perhaps due to the fact 'the overall structure of Article 25 was incompletely theorized by its drafters and was the product of negotiated compromises and drafting by committee',[70] a coherent reading of Article 25(3)(d)(ii), based on the Article 21 sources of applicable law, and its place in the Court's framework for liability, leads to the following interpretation.

First, even though commercial arms traders will not usually be members of the 'common purpose group', this is not a requirement of complicity under Article 25(3)(d)(ii). Not only does Article 25(3)(d)(ii) apply to non-group members, it was in fact those individuals who appear to have been primarily envisaged by the drafters of the Rome Statute when they followed the wording of Article 2(3)(c) of the Terrorist Bombing Convention 1997 and Article 3(4) of the EU Extradition Convention 1996, both of which were treaty provisions aimed at curtailing the activities of the external actors who assist terrorists and organized crime, rather than the terrorists and criminal gangs themselves (who were addressed by other modes of liability). Article 25(3)(d)(ii) is thus eminently, or even primarily, suitable for external actors such as arms traders.

In terms of labelling criminal conduct, 'knowingly contributing to a group crime' is an appropriate label for complicit responsibility based on arms transfers. The Prosecutor and Pre-Trial Chambers would be respecting the intentions of the drafters of Article 25(3)(d)(ii) by bringing and confirming charges against economic actors, whose relatively peripheral form of participation in crimes is completely represented by this residual label. Demanding that the modes

[70] Ohlin (n 17) 417.

of liability be used to fairly represent the conduct of the accused is not inconsistent with arguments about the legal correctness and utility of a 'hierarchical reading' of Article 25.[71] Appropriate labelling does not require fixed and mutually exclusive categories, and without going as far as to invent a strict taxonomy of liability, different modes can nonetheless be associated with certain forms of participation.

Second, Article 25(3)(d)(ii) requires a contribution that is significant in the sense that there is a tangible causal connection *to the commission or attempted commission* of the crime. This may include a nexus with the manner of commission of the crime but no direct causal connection to the crime itself is necessary, hence the fungible and interchangeable nature of arms is not in itself a barrier to liability. Furthermore, although the contribution may in theory be infinitesimally small, a threshold is provided by the requirement of remoteness, meaning that the contribution must be sufficiently proximate in the causal sense. In determining causation, it is, therefore, unnecessary to show that a particular weapon or piece of ammunition was used in a particular incident of violence. Furthermore, causation may be present even where the crimes do not involve firing a weapon, for instance where crimes of sexual and gender-based violence are based on an element of force due to the threatening presence of weaponry. Additionally, the causal link may be to the mental elements of crimes, as in the situation where the supply of guns encourages a perpetrator.

Third, an arms trader will not be liable under Article 25(3)(d)(ii) unless they know enough specific information about the intended usage of the weapons, such that they can be said to be aware of the *essential matters* of the impending crime. In other words, they must know what the crime's basic factual contours are going to be. In addition, it must be proved that they believed that *in the ordinary course of events*, the group's intention to commit the crime would be realized, a test based on a prediction as to the likely future usage of the weapons. As such, this chapter has argued that the standard will be satisfied where the arms trader takes on an unacceptably high degree of risk that the end-user group intends to commit the charged crime.

The criminal standard would be higher than the regulatory standard on which a export authorization is refused at the national level. The necessary *mens rea* for a criminal prosecution based on complicity would be higher, than, for instance the standard in UK law derived from Article 2 criterion (2)(c) of the EU Common Position, requiring non-authorization where there is 'a clear risk' that arms 'might be used in the commission of serious violations of international humanitarian law'

[71] *Ruto and Sang* (Confirmation Decision) (n 19) para 354. The Chamber did not explain the legal basis for reading Article 25 as a 'hierarchy'. See Elies van Sliedregt, 'International Criminal Law: Over-studied and Underachieving?' (2016) 29 Leiden Journal of International Law 8–9.

or the standard in Article 7(3) of the ATT requiring an 'overriding risk' standard for export denial.[72]

Interpreted and applied in this manner, liability under Article 25(3)(d)(ii) criminalizes the conduct of an individual who transfers arms to a group of which they are not a member and to whose aims and intentions they are utterly indifferent. Even where only a relatively small quantity of arms is supplied, for example, relative to the total amount of weaponry used in a large-scale attack, liability may exist for the provider where there is a non-remote causal impact on the commission or attempted commission of the crimes. Evidence that a shipment of weapons affected the manner of commission of a crime would be sufficient. Furthermore, it would be unnecessary to tender evidence identifying the very same weapons from the shipment that were fired or otherwise used in a particular criminal incident.

The lack of a causal requirement between the supply and the specific criminal act would mean the sale of a shipment of ammunition to a militia group contributing to increasing the scale of an assault on a village could satisfy liability under Article 25(3)(d)(ii). In relation to a crime against humanity of murder, for example, a lack of evidence that a specific killing was carried out using one of the vendor's bullets would not necessarily bar liability. An arms broker could be responsible if they trade weapons in a scenario where they do not know exactly which criminal incident will follow (in terms of timing, location etc), but they are in a position of awareness of the elements of a specific crime that will follow, for instance a war crime of rape. Often then, liability could be imposed under this provision where there is an egregious and widely known situation of attacks against civilians or violations of humanitarian law, creating a scenario where a trader knows, by accepting an unacceptable level of risk, that selling weapons is going to contribute to the occurrence of more crimes of that specific type. The presence of widespread reports of previous atrocities, or an arms embargo, would be relevant indicia of the supplier's constructive knowledge.

The last two chapters have argued in favour of a specific interpretation of Article 25(3)(d)(ii) that demonstrates that the Rome Statute could be used to prosecute commercial arms traders. In a suitable ICC situation, an investigation into arms transfers could take place in synergy with cases against other actors. The ICC Prosecutor might identify arms transfers as a subject of thematic prosecution in their policy documents. the Prosecutor might then choose a relatively simple commercial arms trade case against a 'small fish' broker, probably involving low-volume shipments of small arms and light weapons and ammunition.

Indeed, it is not unlikely that the OTP has in its possession, or is aware of, evidence against arms traffickers or sole-trading arms brokers arising from its previous

[72] See Andrew Clapham 'Article 7' in Andrew Clapham and others, *The Arms Trade Treaty: A Commentary* (OUP 2016) 255.

investigations. The arms transfer conduct of these individuals would be eminently suited to the label of Article 25(3)(d)(ii) 'knowingly contributing to a group crime'. In interpreting and applying the 'residual' mode of liability in this way, the potential of International Criminal Law to support and reinforce the existing assemblage of Arms Trade Law identified in Chapter 3 becomes clear. In addition, it shows how Arms Trade Law, rather than leaving International Criminal Law cases as stand-alone events, could interact with International Criminal Law in various ways—both by providing legal tests and criteria to inform judicial development of the complicity standards, and in offering factual evidence when establishing the elements of complicity, in particular the accused's knowledge.

6
Observing ICC Legal Culture on the Arms Trade

6.1 Introduction

So far, this book has set out the proposition that the Rome Statute provides a legal basis for the accomplice liability of arms traders that remains largely unfulfilled in practice. Next, it looks at how the International Criminal Court's (ICC) legal professionals view the arms trade —changing methodological direction to examine the Court's legal culture. Based on participant observation and interviews with judges and lawyers, this chapter argues that there are consistent patterns in how the arms trade is construed in the ICC's legal culture, which in turn shape whether certain types of defendants are likely to be prioritized for investigation and prosecution. If we wish to fully understand how Article 25(3)(d)(ii) of the Rome Statute is applied in practice, and why no arms trade case has been forthcoming as yet, a doctrinal analysis appears insufficient. We cannot ignore the influence of individual's assumptions, beliefs, and commitments on the work of the Court.

By looking beyond 'law in the books', Section 6.2 explains the essential concept of 'legal culture' and its analytic value vis-à-vis the interpretation and application of the Rome Statute. In Sections 6.3 and 6.4, a close analysis of empirical data delineates two 'frames' through which the arms trade and its regulation is often perceived. Through Frame 1, the arms trade is widely seen as appropriately regulated by Arms Trade Law (and not by International Criminal Law). Practitioners were often reluctant to accept that the ICC could hold an arms trader accountable as an accomplice, and it was not viewed as 'regulator' of the trade. In Frame 2, the practitioners perceived a number of intractable, pragmatic constraints, which they believed would preclude arms trade cases from being selected for prosecution. The empirical findings in this chapter pre-empt the discussion of Chapter 7 as to how the scope of the accomplice modes of liability at the ICC is being narrowed in practice through the unstated, motivating values held by legal actors.

6.2 The Concept of 'Legal Culture'

To engage with the analysis that follows, one needs to accept as a starting point that doctrinal analysis may be insufficient to entirely explain legal outcomes in the

The Arms Trade and International Criminal Law. Tomas Hamilton, Oxford University Press. © Tomas Hamilton 2025.
DOI: 10.1093/oso/9780192868671.003.0006

real world. As Rosen puts it, whereas law 'has often been seen as a relatively autonomous domain', in reality, 'cultural concepts deeply inform the evaluation of issues and the shape of a judge's decision'.[1] The notion that culture is a determinant factor in legal decision-making is at once contested, by legal scholars closer to the positivist tradition, and irrefutable, to many social science scholars.[2] To the cultural anthropologist, all human activity is performative and the law is simply another component of human sociality.[3] Geertz would say that 'law, rather than a mere technical add-on to a morally (or immorally) finished society, is, along of course with a whole range of other cultural realities from the symbolics of faith to the means of production, an active part of it'.[4] From this perspective, cultural features of the ICC's work are constitutive of, and give meaning to, its legal proceedings.[5] According to this view, the application of International Criminal Law to arms traders can only be fully understood by looking at how the legal cultures of international justice institutions shapes their practice.[6]

Many scholars have commented on the shift towards more empirical methods in legal scholarship,[7] and specifically in the fields of criminal law,[8] international law, and international criminal law.[9] Innovative empirical research has questioned existing legal scholarship, for instance, how sources of law are relied upon,[10] or how judges go about solving legal problems in practical reality.[11] Studies of judicial decision-making[12] have developed descriptive theories about how judges make their decisions.[13] While bringing the empirical foundations of social science

[1] Lawrence Rosen, *The Anthropology of Justice: Law as culture in Islamic Society* (CUP 1989) i.

[2] Jeremy Webber, 'Culture, Legal Culture, and Legal Reasoning: A Comment on Nelken' (2004) 1 Australian Journal of Legal Philosophy 29, 34.

[3] Paul W Kahn, *The Cultural Study of Law: Reconstructing Legal Scholarship* (2nd edn, University of Chicago Press 1999) 36; Wendy James, *The Ceremonial Animal: A New Portrait of Anthropology* (OUP 2005) 6.

[4] Clifford Geertz, *Local Knowledge: Further Essays In Interpretive Anthropology* (Fontana Press 1988) 218.

[5] David Nelken, 'Using The Concept of Legal Culture' (2004) 29 Australian Journal of Legal Philosophy 1, 1 (emphasis added).

[6] Phil Clark, *Distant Justice: The Impact of the International Criminal Court on African Politics* (CUP 2018); Sarah Nouwen, *Complementarity in the Line of Fire: The Catalysing Effect of the International Criminal Court in Uganda and Sudan* (CUP 2013); Nicola Palmer, *Courts in Conflict: Interpreting the Layers of Justice in Post-Genocide Rwanda* (OUP 2015); Richard A Wilson, *Incitement on Trial: Prosecuting International Speech Crimes* (CUP 2017).

[7] Michael Heise, 'Past, Present, and Future of Empirical Legal Scholarship: Judicial Decision Making and the New Empiricism' (2002) The University of Illinois Law Review 819.

[8] Robert Weisberg, 'Empirical Criminal Law Scholarship and the Shift to Institutions' (2013) 65 Stanford Law Review 1371.

[9] Leslie Vinjamuri and Jack Snyder, 'Advocacy and Scholarship in the Study of International War Crime Tribunals and Transitional Justice' (2004) 7 Annual Review of Political Science 345.

[10] Louis J Sirico and Jeffrey B Margulies 'Citing of Law Reviews by the Supreme Court: An Empirical Study' (1986) 34 UCLA Law Review 131.

[11] Peter J Van Koppen and Jan Ten Kate 'Individual Differences in Judicial Behavior: Personal Characteristics and Private Law Decision-Making' (1984) Law and Society Review 225.

[12] Gregory C Sisk, Michael Heise, and Andrew P Morriss, 'Charting the Influences on the Judicial Mind: An Empirical Study of Judicial Reasoning' (1998) 73 New York University Law Review 1377,

[13] Philippa Webb, *International Judicial Integration and Fragmentation* (OUP 2013).

methodology to the law, this literature is often criticized for failing to appreciate the source-based arguments of doctrinal analysis or being unable to address questions of legal practice: 'social sciences literature on judicial behaviour has been generally uninterested in the role of legal argument'.[14] These tensions were central to the methodological decision to conduct research to blend doctrinal approaches with empirical data and the author's practical insight from working in international criminal tribunals.

A growing body of empirical research on international criminal justice has examined how International Criminal Law is applied in practice. Empirical research by Clark, Nouwen, Palmer, Wilson, Kersten, Kelsall, Lohne, Christensen, and others has examined the working methods used by international justice practitioners, how they perceive their roles, and what they understand to be the limitations and possibilities of the law.[15] Such approaches have been deployed in the context of international criminal tribunals to combine doctrinal analysis of International Criminal Law with empirical research.[16] The approaches build on studies in transitional justice,[17] the anthropology of international institutions,[18] and the well-established conceptual frameworks of criminology in national justice systems, redeployed in an international context.[19] In-depth empirical research with communities affected by atrocity is still surprisingly limited in the field of International Criminal Law. Although claims are often made on behalf of victims, only a small number of scholars have carried out substantial ethnographic fieldwork in situation countries dedicated to exploring the effects of the Court's activities.[20] Notably, within the existing work

[14] Richard L Revesz, 'A Defense of Empirical Legal Scholarship' (2002) The University of Chicago Law Review 169, 178.

[15] Clark, *Distant Justice* (n 6); Nouwen (n 6); Palmer (n 6); Wilson, *Incitement on Trial* (n 6); Mark Kersten, *Justice in Conflict: The Effects of the International Criminal Court's Interventions on Ending Wars and Building Peace* (OUP 2016); Tim Kelsall, *Culture under Cross-Examination: International Justice and the Special Court for Sierra Leone* (CUP 2009); Kjersti Lohne, *Advocates of Humanity: Human Rights NGOs in International Criminal Justice* (OUP 2019); Mikkel J Christensen, 'The Creation of an Ad Hoc Elite and the Value of International Criminal Law Expertise on a Global Market' in Kevin Heller and others (eds), *The Oxford Handbook of International Criminal Law* (OUP 2020) 89.

[16] Phil Clark, *The Gacaca Courts, Post-Genocide Justice and Reconciliation in Rwanda: Justice Without Lawyers* (CUP 2010); Clark , *Distant Justice* (n 6); Kersten (n 15); Palmer (n 6); Nouwen (n 6); Richard A Wilson, *Writing History in International Criminal Trials* (CUP 2011); Wilson, *Incitement on Trial* (n 6); Kelsall (n 15); Lohne (n 15); Christensen (n 15) 89; Mikkel J Christensen, 'The Symbolic Economy of International Criminal Justice: Shaping the Discourse of a New Field of Law' in Joanna Nicholson (ed), *Strengthening the Validity of International Criminal Tribunals* (Brill 2018). See Nancy A Combs, *Fact-Finding without Facts: The Uncertain Evidentiary Foundations of International Criminal Convictions* (CUP 2010).

[17] eg Kieran McEvoy and Lorna McGregor (eds), *Transitional Justice from Below: Grassroots Activism and the Struggle for Change* (Bloomsbury 2008).

[18] eg Ronald Niezen and Maria Sapignoli (eds), *Palaces of Hope: The Anthropology of Global Organizations* (CUP 2017); Wilson RA (ed), *Human Rights, Culture and Context* (Pluto 1997).

[19] See David Garland, *Punishment and Modern Society: A Study in Social Theory* (Clarendon Press 1991).

[20] See Tomas Hamilton, 'Situating 'Law' as 'Culture' in Scholarly Discourse on the International Criminal Court' (2022) 18 International Journal of Law in Context 517.

on 'legal culture' and the ICC, most studies have been concerned with the cultural exegesis of the communities that are subject to the ICC's investigations, rather than the legal culture of the Court itself.[21] Although International Criminal Law is an area of law with much overlap of practitioners and academics,[22] there has been limited long-term participant observation within the ICC as an institution to date.[23]

6.2.1 Interpreting 'ICC Legal Culture'

The content of 'legal culture' has been variously described in terms of shared assumptions, beliefs, commitments, attitudes, narratives, symbols, morals, concepts, discourses, practical experiences, habits, professional intuitions, values, mentalities, non-rational commitments, sensibilities, consciousness, and sentiments.[24] Garland refers to a 'more-or-less bounded, more-or-less unified (…) set of customs, habits, values and beliefs'.[25] Meierhenrich defines the cultural practice of ICC judges and lawyers in terms of 'recurrent and meaningful work activities—social or material—that are performed in a regularized fashion and that have a bearing, whether large or small, on the operation of the ICC'.[26] This definition reflects anthropology's broad concern with the way in which actions are given meaning through individuals' shared understandings of the cultural significance of behaviour.[27]

This chapter refers to the 'assumptions, beliefs, and commitments' of ICC judges and lawyers as a descriptive indicator of the Court's institutional culture. It builds on Palmer's work, which draws on Garland's interpretive account of penal systems,[28] which described the International Criminal Tribunal for Rwanda (ICTR) legal culture as comprised of 'the collection of concepts, practical experience and professional intuitions that give meaning to the actions of [ICTR] judges and lawyers'.[29] It is further inspired by Wilson's account of the 'internal procedures and organizational culture' of international criminal tribunals, in which he pays

[21] cf Julie Fraser and Brianne McGonigle Leyh (eds), *Intersections of Law and Culture at the International Criminal Court* (Edward Elgar Publishing 2020).

[22] Christensen (n 15).

[23] See Julien Seroussi, 'How Do International Lawyers Handle Facts? The Role of Folk Sociological Theories at the International Criminal Court' (2018) 69 The British Journal of Sociology 962.

[24] See David Nelken, 'Comparative Legal Research and Legal Culture: Facts, Approaches, and Values' (2016) 12 Annual Review of Law and Social Science 45, 56.

[25] Garland (n 19) 423.

[26] Jens Meierhenrich, 'The Practices of the International Criminal Court' (2013) 1 Law and Contemporary Problems i–x, i.

[27] Tim Ingold, *Companion Encyclopedia of Anthropology: Humanity, Culture, and Social Life* (Routledge 1994) 329.

[28] Garland (n 19).

[29] Palmer (n 6) 54.

attention to the 'invisible assumptions and procedures' to analyse what judges and lawyers 'actually do'.[30]

To speak of an ICC 'legal culture' might be understood as requiring a 'shared community'.[31] It is probably not possible to discern a shared community across all the organs of the ICC—in judicial chambers, prosecution, defence, victims, and so on. Values and beliefs within the ICC are highly contested with different organs having their own 'cultures'—judges in Chambers, judicial staff, the Office of the Prosecutor of the International Criminal Court (OTP), or the legal culture of individual teams within those organs, or of cross-cutting groups constituted by shared cultures based on nationality, background, type of legal training, and so on. The concept of an ICC-wide legal culture is thus challenged by the different roles of actors within the Court, with judges and lawyers each 'occup[ying] a particular position in the antagonistic arena of the international courtroom' based on the strategic outcomes each legal actor is mandated to pursue in the trial.[32]

Given this inevitable plurality, perhaps it is not useful to speak of a coherent 'ICC legal culture', yet to some extent its judges and lawyers may share assumptions, beliefs, and commitment due to their common frames of reference and shared understanding of the very concept of international criminal justice. There may be some orthodoxies that the Court's institutional units have in common, constituting a distinct enough 'community' to sustain an empirically discernible legal culture. As Webber puts it: 'institutional boundaries are often used as rough approximations for cultural boundaries. Institutions, by structuring interaction, tend to generate cultures moulded to their contours.'[33] Indeed, the notion of an institution-wide culture has been actively developed by the Court, in the form of a 'One Court Policy' that actively seeks to inculcate shared values amongst the individual judges and lawyers of the Court.[34]

The book therefore views the 'assumptions, beliefs, and commitments' of ICC judges and lawyers as reflective of an institutional legal culture, which is only one of many different ways of describing the Court. In Garland's discussion of legal culture, there is a delineation of 'different social wholes, each of which is understood as a distinctive "culture"' that can help us to understand more broadly the place of a court as a social process.[35] Similarly, in this book, 'ICC legal culture' is viewed as one of a plurality of descriptive and explanatory frameworks for representing the Court's activities.

[30] Wilson, *Incitement on Trial* (n 6) 12.
[31] Kelsall (n 15).
[32] Wilson, *Expert Evidence* (n 57) 731.
[33] Webber (n 2) 32.
[34] eg Fatou Bensouda, 'Full Statement on external expert review and lessons drawn from the Kenya situation' (*ICC Legal Tools Database*, 26 November 2019) para 8 <www.legal-tools.org/doc/32p2hy/> accessed 4 August 2024; Assembly of States Parties, 'ASP 14th Session Resolution 1' (16 November 2015) ICC-ASP/14/Res 1, paras 5(a), 12.
[35] See Garland (n 19) 423.

6.2.2 Beyond 'Law versus Politics'

A dominant paradigm in International Criminal Law scholarship views ICC practice in terms of a dialectic between law and politics. This commentary tends to portray the Court as an actor struggling to negotiate between the ideals of a legalistic justice and the constraints of political reality. It views the Court's activities as constituted, on the one hand by its legal foundations and the doctrines applied by the Court,[36] and on the other hand, the influence of political dynamics.[37] These political instrumentalization critiques are of course well founded, yet their over-emphasis may also constrain analysis of the Court and obscure alternative explanations.

In this 'law versus politics' paradigm, there is a risk of over-emphasizing intentionality, active decision-making, and the agency of the Court, and falling into a binary between deliberate political compromise and the dictates of law. This paradigm tends to exclude or downplay the role of cultural features of the Court's practice that are not driven by political imperative nor motivated by adherence to the law. As Nouwen has recognized, these accounts are framed in terms of constraints extending from the clash of law and politics, while overlooking cultural features that are visible in the Court's social practice.[38]

This is not to deny that law and politics are primary explanations and justifications, nor that culture may be expressed and encapsulated in legal and political argument. Clark has provided one of the most nuanced accounts of the ICC's politicization, depicting the institution as caught in a struggle to balance contending legal and political concerns in the African Situations it investigates.[39] Clark shows how this tension serves ultimately to distance the Court from the realities of the African communities that it directly affects.[40] Culture, however, has a life of its own. Some aspects of the ICC's practice may be best explained by non-political aspects of the institution which nonetheless pull the Court away from its legal mandate: for instance, the professional identities and career paths of individual legal practitioners seen in Christensen's work,[41] or the institutional culture described in other studies of the OTP.[42]

[36] eg Andrew Novak, *The International Criminal Court: An Introduction* (Springer 2015) 104.

[37] eg David Bosco, *Rough Justice: The International Criminal Court in a World of Power Politics* (OUP 2013).

[38] See Sarah Nouwen, 'The Importance of Frames: The Diverging Conflict Analyses of the United Nations and the African Union' (2013) 107 Proceedings of the American Society of International Law 330.

[39] Phil Clark, 'Law, Politics and Pragmatism: The ICC and Case Selection in the Democratic Republic of Congo and Uganda' in Nicholas Waddell and Phil Clark (ed), *Courting Conflict: Justice, Peace and the ICC in Africa* (Royal African Society 2008).

[40] Clark, *Distant Justice* (n 6).

[41] See Christensen (n 15); Mikkel J Christensen and Astrid Kjeldgaard-Pedersen, 'Competing Perceptions of Hybrid Justice: International v National in the Extraordinary Chambers of the Courts of Cambodia' (2018) 18 International Criminal Law Review 127; Christensen (n 15).

[42] Kai Ambos and Ignaz Stegmiller, 'Prosecuting International Crimes at the International Criminal Court: Is there a Coherent and Comprehensive Prosecution Strategy?' (2013) 59 Crime, Law and Social

6.2.3 Identifying Legal Culture at the ICC

The rest of this chapter explores how legal practitioners at the ICC view the arms trade. It draws on scholarship on the Court's law and culture, the author's participant observation from working at the ICC, and thirty-two semi-structured interviews with ICC judges and lawyers conducted in 2015 and 2016. The interviewees comprised twelve judges, twelve judiciary and presidency legal staff, five legal staff from the OTP, and three defence lawyers.[43] In seeking to describe the perceptions of ICC judges and lawyers about the arms trade, the interview-based research was structured around the following nine themes.[44]

1. Whether international criminal tribunals are appropriate fora for prosecuting arms traders, such as traffickers, brokers, transporters, and company directors.
2. The issue of liability under International Criminal Law for the legal person of an arms trading corporation.
3. Possible explanations for the small number of cases concerning the arms trade, in particular the absence of such cases before the ICC.
4. The likelihood that an arms trader will be prosecuted before an international tribunal.
5. The practical limitations to bringing an arms trader case before a tribunal such as the ICC.
6. The following statement: 'Some people were tried [at Nuremberg] who should not have been—they were a bunch of eager selfish big businessmen like you would find in any country.'[45]
7. The modes of liability most relevant to an arms trader prosecution at the ICC.
8. The level of knowledge required to convict an arms trader who supplies weapons to the principal perpetrator of an international crime.

Change 415; Jens Meierhenrich, 'The Evolution of the Office of the Prosecutor at the International Criminal Court: Insights from Institutional Theory' in Martha Minow, Cora C True-Frost, and Alex Whiting (eds), *The First Global Prosecutor: Promise and Constraints. Law, Meaning, and Violence* (University of Michigan Press 2015) 97.

[43] The majority of practitioners wished to remain anonymous—revealing the identities of the minority would risk identifying others by process of elimination. The interviews had a duration of between approximately thirty and ninety-five minutes and a mean average of approximately fifty minutes. Interviewees were assigned reference codes to assist the data analysis and to enable each practitioner to be referred to by category. Judges are J1 to J12, Judiciary legal staff JS1 to JS12, OTP lawyers P1 to P5; Defence lawyers D1 to D3, and three miscellaneous others, M1 to M3, were two journalists and an arms-trade campaigner who were interviewed while trialling the research method. Four interviews were conducted in French, the remainder in English.

[44] Pierre Bourdieu and others, *The Weight of the World: Social Suffering in Contemporary Society* (Polity 1999).

[45] Judge Morris, US Supreme Court Justice who sat on the Nuremberg trial that acquitted directors of *IG Farben* corporation for arming the Nazi regime (stated after his retirement).

9. The causal links between the supply of weapons and the international crime required to convict an arms trader.

The data from interviews and participant observation were intended to provide some empirical insight into the assumptions, beliefs, and commitments of ICC judges and lawyers about the arms trade.[46] The aim of drawing on this method of examining an area of law was to generate practical insights into not only the ICC's work, but also how practitioners perceived their work.[47] This sought to address some of the limitations of desk-based research described by Meierhenrich:

> the ratio of field research to desk research in the study of international law, in which both [international law] and [international relations] scholars have arguably been rather too content with observing international adjudication from afar, [has] predictable consequences for the depth and subtlety of resultant observations.[48]

Analysing and reflecting on the empirical data revealed some common patterns, from which two predominating 'frames' emerged—ways in which the arms trade and its regulation was perceived in the institutional culture of the Court. Drawing on interpretive approaches to qualitative data, these two frames seek to describe and explain not only what the Court is doing, but also what the Court's practitioners think they are doing.

6.3 Frame 1: Obscuring the Arms Trade through an Arms Trade Law Lens

The first predominant frame to emerge from the research data was that ICC judges and lawyers tended to see the arms trade through a lens of transnational Arms Trade Law, instead of seeing the potential for individual criminal responsibility under International Criminal Law. The judges and lawyers often rejected the proposition that arms traders could be prosecuted, with little explanation, appearing to view the trade through a preconceived lens that obscured careful consideration of accomplice liability under International Criminal Law.

[46] Meierhenrich (n 26) i.

[47] Palmer (n 6) 53–54.

[48] Jens Meierhenrich, 'The Practice of International Law: A Theoretical Analysis' (2014) 76 Law and Contemporary Problems 1, 5.

6.3.1 The ICC is Not a 'Regulator' of the Arms Trade

The majority of ICC judges and lawyers believed that regulation of the arms trade was not an appropriate activity for the ICC.[49] One member of judicial staff stated succinctly and without further explanation:

> The arms trade is already regulated and I do not see this kind of prosecution will appear at the ICC.[50]

This answer and others like it suggested that practitioners were prima facie excluding arms trade from the scope of application of International Criminal Law. A member of judicial staff stated that the arms trade would 'never be the central focus of international criminal law' without providing any rationale, and without explaining why, even if their assertion was true, the arms trade could not be one amongst a range of different actors prosecuted under International Criminal Law.[51]

Some responses showed practitioners' awareness of the existence of other institutions, mechanisms, or instruments for regulating the arms trade although they did not specifically identify them:

> We are unlikely to have prosecutions [...] already there are bodies for dealing with arms trade and terrorism.[52]

The judge did not describe what these bodies were, but believed, however, when asked in a follow-up question, that these bodies had limited effectiveness in prevention and enforcement.[53] Nonetheless, for this judge the existence of these 'other bodies for dealing with the arms trade' was sufficient reason that the ICC need not consider arms trade cases.

A significant majority of the interviewees, twenty of the thirty-two judges and lawyers, gave answers that expressed significant disagreement with the statement that 'international criminal tribunals are appropriate fora for prosecuting arms traders, such as traffickers, brokers, transporters, and company directors'.[54] Implicit in the answers of these twenty interviewees was a view that arms transfer

[49] Interviews with practitioners P1, P2, J1, J2, J4, J5, J6, J7, J9, J10, J11, J12, JS2, JS3, JS5, JS6. JS7, JS8, JS9, JS10, JS11, M2, D1, and D2 (twenty-four of thirty-two interviewees).

[50] Interview with practitioner JS9.

[51] Interview with practitioner JS6.

[52] Interview with practitioner J4.

[53] Interview with practitioner J4.

[54] Interviews with practitioners P1, J2, J4, J5, J6, J8, J9, J10, J11, JS2, JS3, JS4, JS6. JS8, JS9, JS10, JS11, M2, D1, and D2.

conduct was better regulated by other, unspecified institutions, authorities, or organizations, and that this rendered international criminal tribunals such as the ICC inappropriate fora for prosecution, so the ICC was unable to contribute to better regulation of the arms trade. The very use of the term 'regulation' provoked responses that the purpose of the ICC was not to 'regulate' activity or conduct.[55] ICC judges and lawyers seemed uncomfortable with the notion that the Rome Statute system could play a role in regulating economic activities associated with the structural causes of mass violence.

6.3.2 The Arms Trade is 'Already Regulated'

As mentioned above, some practitioners appeared reluctant to consider the potential role of the Court in regulating the arms trade since they believed the arms trade was 'already regulated' by domestic export controls, arms embargoes, the ATT, or other areas of Arms Trade Law. They saw the existence of these other areas of law as negating the need for International Criminal Law accountability.[56]

Two practitioners referred to the importance of the United Nations Office of Drugs and Crime (UNODC).[57] One interviewee emphasized UNODC's role in coordinating transnational and national responses to illicit arms trafficking.[58] Another interviewee stated: 'transnational crimes like arms dealing are within the competence of international bodies including the existing jurisdiction of UNODC'.[59] This view of ICC jurisdiction as mutually exclusive with the UNODC's mandate was not based on an understanding of UNODC's powers or function. Another interviewee referred to the US Alien Tort Act as a more appropriate means to 'secur[e] greater accountability for business wrongs at the international level'.[60] Again, this view lacked further explanation.

Seven of the thirty-two ICC judges and lawyers noted that 'special domestic courts' and 'hybrid' tribunals, with subject matter jurisdiction to prosecute international arms trafficking crimes, would be more appropriate fora to address arms transfer conduct than the ICC.[61] Three of these interviewees suggested the invention of a specialist institution with the sole aim of addressing 'arms trafficking' or 'the arms trade'.[62] It was striking that the relatively innovative and ambitious

55 Interviews with practitioners J2, J8, JS2, JS11, and M2.

56 Interviews with practitioners P1, P2, J1, J2, J4, J5, J6, J7, J9, J10, J11, J12, JS2, JS3, JS5, JS6. JS7, JS8, JS9, JS10, JS11, M2, D1, and D2.

57 Interviews with practitioners J4 and JS5.

58 Interview with practitioner J4.

59 Interview with practitioner JS5.

60 Interview with practitioner JS7.

61 Interviews with practitioners P2, J4, J6, J8, JS2, JS6, and JS10.

62 Interviews with practitioners P2, J8, and JS6.

proposition of constituting a new tribunal or mechanism for arms trading was seen as reasonable and acceptable, while the notion of addressing the arms trade at the ICC was less accepted.

Most interviewees were unfamiliar with arms trade regulation. As a notable exception, one member of judicial staff gave a detailed description of arms embargoes, the role of domestic courts, the different forms of accomplice liability, and the Preparatory Committee discussions about the expansion of the ICC's subject matter jurisdiction to cover human trafficking and narcotics.[63] This practitioner recognized the potential role for International Criminal Law. Interestingly, however, this was construed as principal liability in relation to so-called 'treaty crimes', and the practitioner did not consider the potential for accomplice liability. Unlike the majority of practitioners who tended not to support their views about the arms trade with legal reasoning, this practitioner linked the inappropriateness of the ICC as a forum for arms transfer regulation to the establishment of the Court and its aims and purposes as expressed through its *travaux preparatoires*.[64] The practitioner went on to say that:

> this does not mean, in any way, for practical purposes, that there could not be a call to revise the subject matter jurisdiction of the ICC, given that this is a permanent international criminal court, a permanent international institution, unlike others.[65]

The interviewee's view was consistent with seven interviewees who referred to internationalized jurisdictions as more appropriate than the ICC.[66]

Many of these opinions viewed the issue through an 'Arms Trade Law lens', which recognized that arms traffickers could be convicted as principal perpetrators under domestic laws, but did not see the potential for International Criminal Law to impose liability on accomplices. A total of six of the ICC judges and lawyers specifically stated that international criminal tribunals or the ICC were not the appropriate fora for arms transfer conduct—for the reason that arms trading did not itself constitute *the principal conduct* of an international crime.[67] The views of these practitioners suggested a professional intuition that overlooked the argument in Chapters 4 to 5 that the transfer of weapons may be characterized as complicity in an international crime.

63 Interview with practitioner JS11.
64 Interview with practitioner JS11.
65 Interview with practitioner JS11.
66 Interviews with practitioners P2, J4, J6, J8, JS2, JS6, and JS10.
67 Interviews with practitioners P2, J5, J10, JS2, JS6. and JS10.

6.3.3 The ICC 'Must Defer to National Authorities'

A total of twelve of the interviewed ICC judges and lawyers emphasized that national jurisdictions were better placed to deal with arms trading.[68] These views appeared largely based on a 'professional intuition', lacking reasoning or explicit legal justification. Without referencing the principle of complementarity, the interviewees considered that arms transfer conduct fell under the remit of domestic courts rather than the ICC:

> It is the national courts who prevent arms trafficking and these are matters for states to determine whether their national authorities can prevent the guns from being sold abroad and it is like this with the gun licensing.[69]

If the Court was perceived as categorically different to national jurisdictions, it was on grounds that were normative, rather than legal. None of the practitioners who gave answers about national jurisdictions being more appropriate, gave any legal analysis of the relevant forms of domestic regulation that they had in mind.[70] One judge said the ICC 'must defer to national authorities' and said it would be impossible for the Court to prosecute individuals *ex post facto* where an arms transfer has been pre-emptively authorized by national authorities.[71] Another judge stated that 'usually the country itself will be in the best position to counter illegal arms dealers'.[72] Views were not justified by reference to the principle of complementarity but by an intuitive assumption that national courts were best placed to deal with arms trading. This recalls Meierhenrich's observations about the importance of professional intuitions in legal decision-making, describing the need for 'taking seriously the everyday life of international law'.[73] These comments again dismissed arms traders on a prima facie basis and did not consider the possibility that arms exports that are permitted under national laws could still potentially lead to unlawful complicity in an international crime.

Only three practitioners mentioned the potential for states' national prosecuting authorities to cooperate with the ICC on arms trade issues. One practitioner mentioned the announcement about arms traders of the first Prosecutor in the Democratic Republic of the Congo (DRC) Situation on 8 September 2003.[74] They said this could have had a positive effect on Dutch prosecutors taking actions that eventually led to domestic prosecutions in the *Van Anraat* and *Kouwenhoven*

68 Interviews with practitioners P2, J1, J4, J5, J10, JS2, JS5, JS6. JS9, JS10, D1, and D2.
69 Interview with practitioner JS6.
70 Interviews with practitioners P2, J1, J4, J5, J10, JS2, JS5, JS6. JS9, JS10, D1, and D2.
71 Interview with practitioner J10.
72 Interview with practitioner J4.
73 Meierhenrich (n 26) iv.
74 Interview with practitioner P1.

cases.[75,76] Another interviewee said that evidence of arms trafficking could be uncovered incidentally in ICC investigations and shared with other organizations.[77] These answers were the exception to the rule in that they recognized the potential for regulating arms transfer conduct through International Criminal Law and some of the potential for exchange and interaction with existing Arms Trade Law.

6.3.4 Delineating Frame 1: International Criminal Law's Role Seen as Distinct from Arms Trade Law

In the patterns identified in Frame 1, ICC judges and lawyers did not see the Court as a legal mechanism to address the arms trade. They believed this role was already performed by other international and national bodies. The interviews and observations indicated a particular view of the potential of international criminal justice. One judge said, 'this stretches it too broadly; the ICC was set up for particular crimes'.[78] This view appeared to prima facie exclude business activity without reference to a legal rule or principle.

While comfortable with the Court prosecuting military and political leaders, practitioners were instinctively reluctant to consider its role in addressing the arms trade, a more structural cause of mass violence. This recalled Garland's work on domestic criminal justice systems, the institutional frameworks of modern penology are described as narrowing our perceptions of punishment.[79] Many of the interviewed ICC judges and lawyers were prima facie excluding arms trading from the (narrow) collection of activities that they believed the Court should be investigating.

In recent years, several commentators have begun to argue that the ICC may need to view its role in the world with greater humility. The sense that the ICC may be driven by uncalibrated aspirations, or misconstrued ambitions about its own place in the world, has led to calls for greater 'modesty' in the Court's work,[80] 'humility' in its approach to the law,[81] while noting that the virtues of humility, modesty, and sensitivity are fundamental to the Court's investigations.[82] This humility has appeared to be deployed in a selective manner.[83] The tension between the ICC practitioners' belief in the Court's mission to combat impunity, and the

[75] Interview with practitioner P1.
[76] Interview with practitioner JS8.
[77] Interview with practitioner JS8.
[78] Interview with practitioner J4.
[79] Garland (n 19) 1.
[80] Sara Kendall and Sarah Nouwen, 'Speaking of Legacy: Toward an Ethos of Modesty at the International Criminal Tribunal for Rwanda' (2016) 110 AJIL 212.
[81] Kieran McEvoy, 'Beyond Legalism: Towards a Thicker Understanding of Transitional Justice' (2007) 34 Journal of Law and Society 411.
[82] Jamie Gaskarth, 'The Virtues in International Society' (2012) 18 European Journal of International Relations 431, 446–47.
[83] Nicola Palmer and Tomas Hamilton, 'Legal Humility and Perceptions of Power in International Criminal Justice' (2022) 23(3) International Criminal Law Review 1–27.

suggestion of a more humble role in regulating the structural causes of mass violence, is consistent with Kennedy's description of the contradictions inherent in institutions that seek to impose new legal orders (such as the ICC).[84] The success of these institutions depends fundamentally on their personnel internalizing the aggrandized aspirations of the project. But the imperative to internalize ambitious aspirations like 'ending impunity' creates internal dissonance when, inevitably, the practitioners realize the illusory or intangible quality this lends to their everyday work. Kennedy describes this as follows:

> On the one hand, it seems reasonable to propose reforms to global institutions like the Security Council or the World Trade Organization as if they were central to global order. On the other, it also seems obvious such institutions are not that central—things are more plural and open and confusing than that. This oscillation is repeated in countless settings. People propose institutional reforms, norms and regulations from environmental law to human rights, corporate social responsibility, or international criminal law, as if a lever to move the world had been identified, while remaining intensely aware that this is more aspiration than reality. This doubled sensibility—at once earnest and jaded, committed and cynical—is also a mark of disenchanted expertise.[85]

The aspects of ICC legal culture seen in Frame 1 may have reflected an unease with accepting the Court's potential role in addressing the arms trade, as a more structural causes of mass violence. While the ICC judges and lawyers tended to view their work as ending impunity ('*as if a lever to move the world had been identified*'), their instincts told them that the arms trade was not part of that endeavour and they should not consider roles for the court that were too ambitious. The Court's work was thus seen as a *sui generis* legal project that did not overlap with existing Arms Trade Law.

6.4 Frame 2: Excluding the Arms Trade Due to Pragmatic Constraints

In the second of the predominant frames to emerge from the empirical research, ICC judges and lawyers believed that the investigation and prosecution of arms traders would not be feasible due to various pragmatic constraints. Often, practitioners did not explain why these constraints made arms trade cases more difficult than other types of ICC case, or explain which types of 'arms traders' they

[84] David Kennedy, *A World of Struggle: How Power, Law, and Expertise Shape Global Political Economy* (Princeton University Press 2018) 15.
[85] Kennedy (n 84) 15.

had in mind. These perceptions coalesced around three areas of pragmatic constraint: dangerous security risks, difficulties in obtaining evidence, and the complexity of large business structures.

6.4.1 Arms Traders Pose Dangerous Security Risks to the Court

Several members of judicial staff regarded arms traders as a particularly dangerous type of target for the Court. This concern was expressed in terms of the security risks not only for investigators in the field, but also for judges and ICC staff at the seat of the Court in The Hague.[86] One judge expressed a strong view that security risks were the 'first and foremost' practical limitation to an arms trader case.[87] It was striking that the judge considered that the risk to judges of engaging in a case of this nature would be prohibitively high, noting: 'even without the court taking cases against businesspeople, there are risks to judges'.[88] Another judge stated that there would be the 'constant possible danger from organised crime networks'.[89] This concern was stated in the absolute and unqualified terms of 'a danger' and was not compared in relative terms to other threats that the Court might face. The judge stated that the organized crime networks responsible for arms trading were involved in 'drugs trafficking and people trafficking', that these groups were highly organized, and 'can be dangerous, even in The Hague'.[90] These were not expressed as minor concerns, suggesting a high level of genuine anxiety about serious risks. This judge also commented that there were potential security risks 'especially' for investigators located in the Situation countries.[91]

This interview data suggested that strategic aspects of the ICC's case selection is shaped by a type of political consideration that has received relatively limited attention in the 'law versus politics' literature on the ICC. It appeared that the power of states, non-state armed groups and individuals was perceived as posing 'dangerous' risks to the Court's personnel. It was notable that the perception of power held by 'organised crime networks' was singled out but was not compared with prominent examples of the Court investigating other undeniably powerful individuals, including sitting Heads of State. For instance, the prosecution of the President of Kenya resulted in charges being withdrawn due to evidentiary concerns and the Kenyan Government's non-cooperation.[92]

[86] Eight of the thirty-two interviewed ICC judges and lawyers. Interview with practitioners J1, J2, J4, J8, JS6, JS11, D1, and D3.
[87] Interview with practitioner J1.
[88] Interview with practitioner J1.
[89] Interview with practitioner J4.
[90] Interview with practitioner J4.
[91] Interview with practitioner J4.
[92] *Prosecutor v Uhuru Muigai Kenyatta* (Notice) ICC-01/09-02/11-983 (5 December 2014).

Coupled with this, the security risks raised by practitioners were not described with much specificity: there was little indication of what types of individuals posed a danger or what tangible form the danger might take. These observations can help better understand that, firstly, these views were based on a generalized and uninterrogated image of the dangers of 'organised crime networks' that may not be representative of reality. The views thus appeared to be more spontaneous than strategic.

Second, these answers relied on a narrow view of the range and variety of actors involved in the arms trade. The ICC judges and lawyers appeared to envisage a certain type of powerful 'arms trader' suspect, such as the head of a major arms manufacturing corporation or a member of a transnational organized crime group. Yet they did not seem to consider that some arms trade actors, for instance brokers like Kouwenhoven and Van Anraat discussed in previous chapters,[93] may not have held the same degree of power that they feared.

Third, the interviewees did not refer to whether the dangerous risks they had in mind were faced by other criminal courts and investigatory bodies. There was no discussion of why the perceived danger would be any different for domestic judges, or why the perceived danger should be a reason not to pursue these cases and to leave their adjudication to domestic judges, or not to act where those domestic states were unable or unwilling to investigate and prosecute in relation to the same person and substantially the same conduct.

A variety of actors are involved in the arms trade who perform different contributory roles in the stages from manufacture to the shipment and eventual supply of weapons into the hands of a direct perpetrator of an international crime. Many of these individuals, such as sole trading arms brokers, do not have the power to cause the security risks envisaged in the practitioner interviews, or at least would pose no greater security risk than other suspects against whom the ICC has issued arrest warrants.

6.4.2 Obtaining Evidence Would Be Exceptionally Challenging

The second set of pragmatic constraints, expressed by twenty-two of the thirty-two judges and lawyers, concerned the availability of evidence.[94] These constraints developed into a recurrent theme throughout the interviews. Even amongst the ten remaining practitioners who did not mention these constraints by their own accord, six who were asked follow-up questions responded positively that obtaining

[93] Harmen van der Wilt, 'Genocide v War Crimes in The Van Anraat Appeal' (2008) 6 Journal of International Criminal Justice.

[94] Interviews with practitioners P2, P3, P4, P5, J3, J4, J7, J8, J10, J11, J12, JS1, JS2, JS4, JS5, JS8, JS9, JS11, M2, D1, D2, and D3.

evidence would be particularly difficult for arms trade cases.[95] On this point, therefore, there was near unanimous support amongst the interviewed practitioners.

Again, most of these interviewees did not explain why these complexities were unique to arms trading cases, rather than common to all ICC investigations. Nor were the evidentiary challenges of obtaining evidence for the ICC held up in comparison with the same difficulties facing other national or international fact-finding or prosecutorial authorities. Several exceptions to this included one judge who pointed out the deficits of evidence associated with transnational crime, including arms trading, stating adamantly that the lack of evidence would make an arms trading case impossible.[96] The judge identified powerful groups, not for reasons of danger, but for their organizational ability to deflect investigations:

> the ICC [is not] equipped to investigate cases with transnational criminals [belonging] to very sophisticated groups that are part of organised crime networks [...] they would be too organized.[97]

This particular understanding of transnational crime seemed to lump together arms trading with other forms of transnational crime, and perhaps suggested a lack of sensitivity to the range of different activities in the arms trade beyond the 'very sophisticated groups' and 'organised crime networks' referred to by the judge. As discussed in the Introduction to this book and Chapter 3, the role of micro-traders in the arms trade is generally under-recognized, and constant low-level flows of weapons across porous borders that take place in an atmosphere of impunity often takes place quite openly, with little attempt to conceal activity or to avoid producing an identifiable paper trail. It is often possible for a broker to arrange a trade using third-party states where the lack of export restrictions make the transfer legally permissible with little need for subterfuge.

It is unclear why practitioners perceived arms traders as organizationally too complex to investigate, especially when compared to other cases. Arms trader cases can undoubtedly bring their own complexities—the *Van Anraat* investigations were complicated by the twenty-year lapse of time, challenges to international co-operation for collecting and assessing evidence, difficulties of conducting defence investigations to ensure equality of arms, and the need for the court to hear fact and expert witnesses on relevant matters of international and domestic politics, manufacture of weaponry, and international business relations.[98] But the ICC judges and lawyers did not give a rationale as to why cases such as *Van Anraat* would be overall more complex than other ICC investigations into complex crimes.

95 Interviews with practitioners J5, J9, JS3, JS7, and JS10.
96 Interview with practitioner J4.
97 Interview with practitioner J4.
98 Van der Wilt (n 93) 558.

Obtaining evidence was often perceived as less problematic for national jurisdictions than for the ICC. The judge who stated 'usually the country itself will be in the best position to counter illegal arms dealers' also commented that amongst the reasons the ICC must defer to national authorities were 'the problems of finding evidence and [obtaining] suspects' in arms trade cases.[99] This last comment was notable in that it explicitly identified a view that was implicit in many practitioners' answers, namely that national jurisdictions would find it easier to investigate arms traders, locate evidence, and obtain suspects. However, this did not explain why the Court should not select such cases where domestic authorities were unwilling or unable to investigate and prosecute.

In another interview, one of the lawyers discussed prosecuting military and political figures where arms transfers were amongst a range of charges,[100] for instance where charges relating to arms transfers were brought due to difficulties in charging the other crimes. The Office of the Prosecutor of the International Criminal Court (OTP) lawyer pointed out that such individuals might conceal their primary activities but that arms transfers might be easier to prosecute:

> prosecutorial authorities are opportunistic [...] where a prosecutorial authority has identified an individual on the basis that they strongly suspect he has reprehensible conduct, if it is not possible to prosecute him for a serious crime, they are more likely to prosecute him for something, even if it is for relatively minor criminal conduct.[101]

The lawyer gave the example of the US prosecution of Al Capone, who, known to authorities for his involvement in serious organized crime and violent crimes, was ultimately convicted for tax evasion.[102] The lawyer believed that arms transfer charges would be relevant in scenarios were there was insufficient evidence to charge the individual with 'more seriously involvement' for other offences.[103] In this view, unlawful arms supplies would be most appropriately charged as a 'substitute' charge that enables a prosecution to proceed when there is a lack of evidence for other charges.

6.4.3 Arms Trade Investigations Involve Complex Business Structures

Six of the thirty-two interviewed ICC judges and lawyers were concerned that the complexity of business structures would be an important challenge for arms trade

99 Interview with practitioner J4.
100 Interview with practitioner P4.
101 Interview with practitioner P4.
102 Interview with practitioner P4.
103 Interview with practitioner P4.

cases.[104] They appeared to view the arm trade narrowly, seeing only the large and complex business structures of major arms manufacturing corporations. The view that arms cases would prima facie involve more complex and difficult attribution of responsibility within hierarchical structures than other ICC cases against senior figures in political and military institutions was not explained or justified. One member of judicial staff said that for a criminal law response:

> you would always have to get the people [...] within companies, rather than the company itself [...] [to do that] [...] of course you need to build a whole new system of individual criminal responsibility and accountability for actions and so on, and it's going to be hugely complicated.[105]

The member of judicial staff appeared to have in mind a very specific notion of the form of company that would be involved in an arms transfer conduct case. The certainty of the view that arms trader prosecutions would require substantial changes to the ICC's legal system was notable.

Although the interviewee discussed the liability of individuals within a company and appeared to recognize the Rome Statute's bar to liability for the corporate legal person, there was nonetheless a focus on the problem of proving the knowledge of the corporation itself. When asked about who could be prosecuted within a company, the response was that: 'to do that you would have to redesign... there is a huge problem of accountability—when does the company know?'.[106] Another member of judicial staff referred to individuals being protected by the so-called 'corporate veil' as a potential 'pragmatic challenge to such cases'.[107] In another interview, a member of judicial staff expressed similar views, giving the example of a 'CEO running the daily business' of a company who may not know about what actions its subordinate workers are taking to set up a deal, or what actions the owner of the business is taking, such that the CEO might be wrongly held liable when they did not in fact have knowledge of the deal or 'proper control'.[108] The member of judicial staff said that this situation 'all just makes it all very blurry and murky, it is just, very difficult'.[109]

These interviewees perceived major challenges of attributing the knowledge of the corporation to an individual corporate director, but appeared unaware of the potential for arms trade cases that were not against major arms manufacturing corporations, such as those with smaller, less complex business structures. The immediate rejection of the idea that the ICC was equipped to tackle corporate business structures was striking.

104 Interviews with practitioners JS2, JS5, JS9, and P3.
105 Interview with practitioner JS9.
106 Interview with practitioner JS9.
107 Interview with practitioner JS6.
108 Interview with practitioner JS5.
109 Interview with practitioner JS5.

Another perceived pragmatic constraint was that arms trade cases were inherently more costly than other cases brought by the ICC. One interviewee explicitly articulated the concern that international criminal tribunals may have avoided investigating arms traders on the basis that their funding did not extend to those sorts of cases.[110] A member of judicial staff considered that 'the Court's funding situation would not extend to arms traders'.[111] This again begged the question, why were arms traders seen as more costly to prosecute than other cases including against powerful, sitting Heads of State? This comparison was not undertaken nor any explanation given.

Another form of exclusion of arms trade cases stemmed from a lack of clarity over international criminal liability for business actors. The exclusion of corporate liability under Article 25(1) of the Rome Statute was widely recognized by the ICC judges and lawyers, yet the possibilities for accountability of corporate officers may not have been fully recognized. None of the ICC judges and lawyers expressed the view that International Criminal Law was applicable to the corporate legal person, yet they frequently raised weakly articulated concerns over legal barriers to the individual accountability of corporate officers. Two individuals suggested that there was a growing trend in domestic jurisdictions to criminally prosecute the legal person of the corporation, and that this could in future lead to, or encourage, the development of liability at the international level.[112]

6.4.4 Delineating Frame 2: Arms Trade Cases Not Seen as Pragmatic

In the common patterns identified in Frame 2, the ICC judges and lawyers often saw pragmatic constraints on the Court's investigation and prosecution of arms trade cases, without explaining or justifying why such cases would differ from other perpetrator types, nor comparing the ICC's challenges with the ability of domestic judicial authorities to tackle the same constraints of dangerous risks, obtaining evidence, and the complexity of large business structures.

When asked, sixteen of twenty-three practitioners recognized weaknesses in the enforcement of Arms Trade Law.[113] Yet none of these practitioners suggested that other areas of arms regulation would face the same pragmatic constraints that they believed the ICC would encounter.[114] Three practitioners believed that there was no need for the ICC to regulate arms trading because 'illicit trading' was

[110] Interview with practitioner M2.
[111] Interview with practitioner JS10.
[112] Interviews with practitioners J6 and JS7.
[113] Interviews with practitioners P1, P2, J1, J5, J6, J7, J9, J10, J11, JS2, JS3, JS5, JS7, JS8, JS9, JS10, JS11, M2, and D1.
[114] Interviews with practitioners P1, P2, J1, J6, J7, J9, J10, J11, JS2, JS3, JS7, JS8, JS9, JS11, M2, and D1.

sufficiently dealt with outside of the Court. The judge's answer that 'the arms trade is regulated already' was a clear example.[115]

When pressed about how they perceived that the arms trade was already regulated, it almost always became clear that practitioners identified some weaknesses in or limitations to Arms Trade Law, including difficulties of enforcement. Yet, the interviewees generally remained confident that other forms of regulation were the most appropriate way of regulating the arms trade and that this role was not appropriate for the ICC. Taken together, this attitude suggested a degree of 'ICC exceptionalism', which regarded the ICC as somehow not comparable as a body tasked with criminal law enforcement to other regulatory bodies.

Although a small number of interviewees did make the point that the most likely challenges to an arms trader prosecution would be similar to any other ICC case, those interviewees were the exception to the prevailing view.[116] Instead, pragmatic constraints were identified as specific to arms trading; centring around the idea that the Court had practical strengths and weakness and that overall the Court was not practically equipped to deal with arms traders, whether in terms of ensuring the security of its activities, obtaining evidence and arresting suspects, or dealing with the particularities of arms trading corporate structures. The way in which these constraints were often identified, but rarely justified or explained, can be described as a 'professional intuition' that arms trade cases were 'just not right' for the Court and this was loosely justified by referring to pragmatic constraints.

6.5 Conclusion

The empirical observations in this chapter suggest an ICC legal culture with blind spots over the potential to select ICC cases against arms traders. In Frame 1, ICC judges and lawyers saw the arms trade primarily through the lens of Arms Trade Law rather than International Criminal Law accountability. The arms trade was viewed as 'already regulated'. Arms traders were not imagined as appropriate targets for ICC prosecutions, perhaps reflecting aspirations for the ICC to do something more than addressing the more structural cause of mass violence.

Emerging from the interview data was an impression that ICC judges and lawyers often saw an imagined arms trader, part of either a major arms manufacturing corporation or a powerful transnational organized crime network, neither of which were believed to be appropriate targets for ICC case selection. The potential of the ICC to prosecute small-scale brokers, transport agents, and micro-traders was obscured from view.

[115] Interviews with practitioners J5, JS5, and JS10.
[116] Interviews with practitioners P3, JS2, JS6, JS10, and D2.

In Frame 2, ICC judges and lawyers saw specific pragmatic constraints that they intuitively believed would prevent the ICC from investigating. Arms trade cases were considered too difficult due to issues of security, financial cost, obtaining evidence, and the challenges of large business structures. Crucially, there was limited explanation as to why these constraints were specific and unique to arms traders. The Court was often described as exceptional in facing investigatory challenges, and comparisons were not made with the other forms of arms regulation that may have faced the same challenges.

In sum, Frames 1 and 2 have sought to describe some of the perceptions about arms transfers that predominate in the ICC's institutional key. A key aspect of the empirical data from the interviews and participant observation is not only that ICC judges and lawyers were generally reluctant to consider the idea of arms trade prosecutions, but what is distinctive is that their reluctance often seemed to be intuitive or impulsive, rather than based on specific legal argument, or a practical concern uniquely pertaining to the arms trade.

7
Imagining the Arms Trade in ICC Case Selection

7.1 Introduction

Is the lack of an International Criminal Court (ICC) arms trade case easily explained by legal reasons? The empirical observations of the previous chapter suggest the arms trade was consistently framed as an inappropriate target for the ICC, but on unclear legal grounds. This chapter turns to consider how the cultural assumptions, beliefs, and commitments of ICC judges and lawyers may influence which cases are selected for investigation and prosecution. The decision-making of the Office of the Prosecutor (OTP) may be contingent on cultural notions about which types of perpetrators should be prosecuted and which should not. If priority is given to particular types of perpetrators (ie senior military and political leaders) who are believed to be the archetypal 'classic' defendants to international crimes charges, the OTP may be deprioritizing the prosecution of other types of actor (such as arms traders) who represent more structural causes of violence. The effect is that the full breadth of conduct criminalized by the Rome Statute's doctrines of complicity will not be reflected in the ICC's practice.

Section 7.2 assesses the legal framework for case selection in the Rome Statute, highlighting the indeterminacy of the rules, which leave decision-making dependent on prosecutorial policy and discretion. There are no legal criteria to determine that only senior military and political leaders should be prosecuted, or that other actors representing the more structural causes of violence should not be prosecuted. This legal indeterminacy means that decisions about the types of cases to prioritize are more open to (cultural) construction through OTP policy. It returns to the empirical research with ICC judges and lawyers to consider the (limited) role of legal reasoning in practitioners' perceptions of the arms trade. Section 7.3 suggests that the highly legalistic nature of the ICC's institutional culture makes it more difficult for practitioners to accept when their views are not based on law. It concludes with a reflection on existing scholarship as to how the practice of international criminal justice constructs meaning, and what this says about the narrowing of the types of actors considered for prosecution by the ICC.

The Arms Trade and International Criminal Law. Tomas Hamilton, Oxford University Press.
DOI: 10.1093/oso/9780192868671.003.0007

7.2 The Indeterminacy of Rules on ICC Case Selection

Within the confines of an ICC Situation, the selection of cases is largely a question of OTP policy. Firstly, the legal framework for case selection does not impose a legal obligation on the prosecutor to focus only on high-ranking political and military leaders, although currently prevailing practice and policy calls for this.[1] Secondly, nothing in the ICC legal framework for case selection excludes economic actors such as arms traders per se. Thirdly, the lack of legal parameters for case selection leaves significant discretion in the hands of the Prosecutor to choose who will be sought for arrest or summonsed to appear pursuant to Article 58 of the Rome Statute. Taken together, these are indications of indeterminacy in the legal rules for ICC case selection, which leaves greater scope for assumptions and beliefs to influence which cases are ultimately selected.

7.2.1 Case Selection

The criteria for case selection are distinct from those that lead to an investigation into an ICC Situation.[2] With respect to the selection of *Situations* for investigation, the OTP and Pre-Trial Chamber (PTC) play 'gatekeeper' functions.[3] Where a referral from the UN Security Council or a State Party has taken place, the Prosecutor has discretion to refuse to proceed with a Situation, and a Situation that has not been referred to the Court by the UN Security Council or a State Party may nonetheless be selected by the Prosecutor opening an investigation *proprio motu*. In either scenario, the PTC holds the power to overturn the Prosecutor's selection or refusal of a Situation, pursuant to Articles 15 or 53, respectively.

Even at the stage of opening investigations into a new Situation, the Prosecutor will inevitably have in mind potential defendants, a de facto feature of how case selection operates in practice, which the PTCs have recognized.[4] Likewise, when the Security Council or a State Party refers a Situation to the Court, it is inevitable that particular individuals, or at least groups of individuals, are envisaged before the referral is made. As the investigation progresses, the parameters of a Situation will inevitably focus on particular suspects, even though it is only at the stage of proceedings to issue an arrest warrant or summons that specific suspect(s) and mode(s) of liability are settled upon.

[1] Ward Ferdinandusse and Alex Whiting, 'Prosecute Little Fish at the ICC' (2021) 19 Journal of International Criminal Justice 759.

[2] As Rastan points out, the distinction is often misrepresented in commentary on the ICC: Rod Rastan, 'What Is a "Case" for the Purpose of the Rome Statute?' (2008) 19 Criminal Law Forum 435.

[3] See William Schabas, 'Selecting Situations and Cases' in Carsten Stahn (ed), *The Law and Practice of the International Criminal Court* (OUP 2014) 368.

[4] *Situation in the Republic of Kenya* (Authorization Decision) ICC-01/09-19-Corr (31 March 2010) para 50.

The PTC is empowered to accept or refuse an application from the Prosecutor for an arrest warrant or summons to appear. Although the issue of selectivity is sometimes described as a prosecution issue, more familiar to understandings of the role of an independent prosecuting authority in common law systems of law, the PTC has a significant oversight role at this stage of ICC proceedings. Arguably, in cases to date there have been only limited instances of judges exercising their full powers to shape the Situations and cases brought before the Court.[5]

Several provisions are relevant. Article 53 of the Rome Statute provides that the Prosecutor shall initiate an investigation unless there is no reasonable basis to proceed with the investigation, taking into consideration whether a Rome Statute crime is committed, whether the case is admissible under Article 17, and the interests of justice (taking into account the gravity of the crime and the interests of victims).

7.2.2 OTP Policy and Regulation 33

Regulation 33 of the Regulations of the Office of the Prosecutor (OTP Regulations), entitled 'selection of cases within a Situation' transform, in effect, the Article 53 considerations into parameters to determine case selection. Regulation 33 states that the Prosecutor's approach to selecting cases based on 'the most serious crimes committed within the Situation' taking into account 'jurisdiction, admissibility (including gravity), as well as the interests of justice'. It is important to recognize that the OTP Regulations are temporary internal policy 'to govern the operation of the Office', meaning that Regulation 33 has no binding legal value and may be amended by the Prosecutor with immediate effect.[6] It is therefore necessary to understand Regulation 33 as a matter of policy that can be changed, for example by a new Prosecutor.

Accordingly, while setting exclusionary criteria for case selection (that the Prosecutor should consider whether a case is outside of jurisdiction, inadmissible, or contrary to the notion of 'interests of justice'), Regulation 33 provides no guidance as to how a Prosecutor should prioritize different individuals in practice. Within a Situation, although it is clear that selection should be based on 'the most serious crimes', there may be numerous suspects with equal responsibility for the same crime, but with very different roles.

The OTP Regulations have been criticized as lacking specificity, particularly in Regulation 33 mentioned above, and for lacking the legitimate support of the ASP.[7]

[5] See Margaret deGuzman, 'Choosing to Prosecute: Expressive Selection at the International Criminal Court' (2012) 33 Michigan Journal of International Law 265, fn 32.

[6] Internal Rule 9; OTP Regulation, Regulations 1(2) and 3.

[7] Dapo Akande, 'Is There Still a Need for Guidelines for the Exercise of ICC Prosecutorial Discretion?' (*EJIL: Talk!*, 28 October 2009) <www.ejiltalk.org/is-there-still-a-need-for-guidelines-for-the-exercise-of-icc-prosecutorial-discretion/> accessed 4 August 2024.

Several critical perspectives have sought to propose criteria to better structure the Prosecutor's exercise of discretion.[8] The existing explanations of ICC case selection are most convincing when they do not offer an abstract, decontextualized explanation of the Prosecutor's behaviour as a simple exercise of applying the law; indeed the interviews with ICC judges and lawyers in this chapter show that case selection can only be convincingly understood with reference to 'extra-legal' features including the ICC's culture.

The Prosecutor's policy papers and public statements are, like the OTP Regulations, subject to change over time, may be reactive to the short-term policy goals of the Prosecutor, and are likely to vary with the arrival of each new Prosecutor for a nine-year term. The justiciable restrictions on case selection are thus highly indeterminate. As Akande comments, '[i]t is universally recognised that the ICC Statute confers significant discretion on the ICC Prosecutor with respect to decisions as to which Situations to investigate and what charges to bring against whom.'[9] William Schabas observes that 'the [P]rosecutor has a very free hand', and that Regulation 33 is 'utterly laconic'.[10] Even the criterion of gravity 'provides the prosecutor with a seemingly objective but ultimately an extraordinarily subjective standard'.[11]

The lack of determinate legal rules means that ICC case selection decisions rely on a broad prosecutorial and judicial discretion. The link between indeterminacy of legal rules and enhanced exercise of discretion is supported by studies of decision-making in national criminal justice systems.[12] Within this legal framework, the policy discussions that take place within the OTP can therefore come to play an important role in case selection. In turn, the cultural beliefs of key individuals within the OTP can play a more influential role than if there were more criteria for case selection. In other words, such conditions mean that the assumptions, beliefs, and commitments identified in Chapter 6 can play an enhanced role in determining who ICC prosecutes.

7.2.3 Legal Reasoning for Not Selecting Arms Trade Cases

In the empirical observations of Chapter 6, ICC judges and lawyers were often reluctant to accept the Court's potential role in prosecuting arms traders and, notably, their reasons for this were not well articulated through law. Most practitioners

[8] Philippa Webb, 'The ICC Prosecutor's Discretion Not to Proceed in the "Interests of Justice"' (2005) 50 Criminal Law Quarterly 305, 346; Allison Marston Danner, 'Enhancing the Legitimacy and Accountability of Prosecutorial Discretion at the International Criminal Court' (2003) 97 AJIL 510.

[9] Akande (n 7).

[10] Schabas (n 3) 377.

[11] Schabas (n 3) 380.

[12] Loraine Gelsthorpe and Nicola Padfield, *Exercising Discretion: Decision-Making in the Criminal Justice System and Beyond* (Willan 2003).

did not reject the idea of arms trade prosecutions on the grounds that the scope of the Rome Statute modes of liability did not extend to arms traders, nor on the basis of the legal provisions relating to case selection. To the contrary, the assumptions, beliefs, and commitments expressed by these interviewees often had an intuitive character.

This was seen in Frame 1 where the arms trade was viewed as the subject of existing regulation and therefore an inappropriate focus for International Criminal Law accountability. Yet remarkably, considering that the interviewees were all legal practitioners, there was only limited argument that the Rome Statute did not criminalize arms transfer conduct under Article 25 of the Rome Statute. In this way, ICC judges and lawyers prima facie excluded arms trading from view without addressing questions of liability. Similarly, despite a belief that the ICC must defer to national authorities on the legality of arms transfer conduct, there was little consideration of the principle of complementarity under Article 17 of the Rome Statute and little recognition that International Criminal Law liability coexists with, and is not precluded by, Arms Trade Law.

In Frame 2, ICC judges and lawyers saw specific practical constraints that they intuitively believed would prevent the ICC from investigating arms trade cases. Again, it was remarkable that these extra-legal perceptions about security risks and obtaining evidence, and quasi-legal concerns over the attribution of responsibility within major arms manufacturing companies, dominated the centre frame of their thinking rather than questions of legal liability.

7.2.4 Weakly Articulated Legal Grounds

There was some discussion of law. Several interviewees pointed to the legal difficulties of proving *mens rea*, but these difficulties were mostly described in general terms and were not the primary rationale for excluding arms trade cases.[13] Several practitioners, who had not raised *mens rea*, were prompted about this issue and all of them considered that it a significant issue.[14] Often the *mens rea* rule or standard was not specified, nor linked to Rome Statue liability requirements, and practitioners referred generally to the challenges of making a link with criminal purposes in economic crimes. One interviewee stated that:

> [A]lthough there is a great deal of evidence in tribunals pointing to economic actors [there is] [...] [however] as with any other transnational economic actor

[13] Twenty-three of the thirty-two practitioners interviewed expressed concerns about the intent or knowledge of economic actors. Interviews with practitioners P1, P2, P4, J2, J3, J4, J6, J7, J8, J9, J11, J12, JS1, JS3, JS4, JS5, JS7, JS8, JS10, M2, D1, D2, and D3.

[14] Interviews with practitioners P3, P5, J10, JS6, and JS9.

> who engages in criminal activities by economic means [the problem that] oftentimes the link will not suffice to construe a link [...] as in an aiding and abetting scenario.[15]

A member of judicial chambers raised the criminal law distinction between *mens rea* and motive, stating that for the imposition of criminal liability, 'in general, if you have the required level of intent, then your motive doesn't matter'.[16] In general there was little discussion of the *actus reus* and *mens rea* issues discussed in Chapters 5 and 6.

When asked about *mens rea*, approximately one-third of the interviewed practitioners cited evidentiary challenges of investigating commercial arms traders who could deny knowledge of the final use of their products.[17] On the other hand, another one-third of the interviewees aligned with the view that 'the most serious human rights'[18] and 'international crimes'[19] are usually widely known, and are reported by publicly accessible news sources.[20] One practitioner said *mens rea* would be undeniable in situations where ongoing and repeated abuses are being carried out, such that 'public opprobrium has developed'.[21] This second group of practitioners were implicitly identifying information that could be a basis for constructive knowledge to satisfy the *mens rea* requirement of Article 25(3)(d)(ii) of knowledge of the essential matters of an international crime, as argued in Chapter 5, that would incriminate arms traders who were indifferent to the crime and lacked any purposive intent.

Actus reus came up even less frequently during the interviewees than *mens rea*.[22] One interviewee said: 'for prosecutors, arms trading is a very difficult crime. It is not a simple task to link the sale of weapons to the committing of a crime'.[23] When asked if this 'link' was to do with the knowledge of an arms trader about a transfer, they responded: '[n]ot necessarily. I think the major issue is not the knowledge [requirement]. In the arms industry, weapons may be sold to despotic regimes, but the weapons cannot always be said to have been responsible for everything that a regime does'.[24] What was interesting about these interviews (leaving aside the

[15] Interview with practitioner M2.

[16] Interview with practitioner JS4.

[17] Ten of the thirty-two ICC judges and lawyers highlighted evidentiary difficulties. Interviews with practitioners P2, J6, J9, J11, JS3, JS7, JS10, D1, D2, and D3.

[18] Interview with practitioner JS5.

[19] Interview with practitioner J3.

[20] Nine of the thirty-two ICC judges and lawyers made this point. Interviews with practitioners P1, J3, J4, J7, J8, J11, JS5, JS8, and M2.

[21] Interview with practitioner M2.

[22] Only seven of the ICC judges and lawyers identified issues associated with the *actus reus*. Interviews with practitioners P2, P5, J1, J8, J12, JS4, and JS11. A further five ICC judges and lawyers did so after prompting. Interviews with practitioners J3, J7, JS2, JS5, and JS10.

[23] Interview with practitioner JS2.

[24] Interview with practitioner JS2.

practitioners views on the substantive legal issues) was that the ICC judges and lawyers sometimes mentioned *actus reus*, yet did not discuss it with reference to the Rome Statute provisions.

Consistent with Chapter 4's argument that the importance of Article 25(3)(d)(ii) has been under-recognized in the commentary on economic actors, when ICC judges and lawyers were asked about the most relevant modes of liability, the majority of interviewees identified only Article 25(3)(c) of the Rome Statute.[25] Interviewees saw the connection between the arms trade and 'aiding and abetting' but overlooked the residual mode of liability for 'any other contribution'. Only one practitioner mentioned the legal distinction between the two sub-provisions of Article 25(3)(d)(i) and (ii).[26] The majority of practitioners did not comment on the issues of interpretation in Article 25(3) that were raised earlier in this book.

Two notable comments on Article 25(3)(d) were from a judge and a member of judicial staff who both commented on the intent requirement of accomplice liability in Article 25(3)(c), and said that it was included in the Rome Statute for policy reasons by states who were particularly concerned with the possibility that this mode of liability might allow for liability, specifically that would impinge on their arms export arrangements.[27] Notable as an exception, one member of judicial staff stated:

> [it was] Article 25(3)(d) [that] changed the picture for economic actors [...] it is the only [one], the last possibility that can be used [...] on the arms trade, on everything that is not in the commission of crimes, but around the commission of crimes [...] it is the only provision that allows you to prosecute those who are outside of the criminal circle.[28]

It was unclear whether this practitioner's reference to 'the criminal circle' was meant in a legal or phenomenological sense. Clearly, if criminal liability was established for the 'outside' individuals the practitioner had in mind, they would be viewed by the law as 'inside' the so-called 'circle of criminality'. This appeared to reflect a persistent idea in ICC legal culture that, even if there was a legal basis for the liability of these individuals, their behaviour was somehow qualitatively different to criminal conduct of 'the criminal circle', of the 'true criminals' that the ICC intended to deal with.

In sum, when ICC judges and lawyers rejected the suggestion of prosecuting arms traders at the ICC, they rarely invoked the law. Occasionally, they would refer to issues of *mens rea*, and to a lesser extent *actus reus*. But doctrinal arguments

25 Twenty-six of the thirty-two ICC judges and lawyers. Interviews with practitioners P2, P3, P4, J1, J2, J3, J4, J5, J7, J8, J10, J11, J12, JS2, JS3, JS4, JS5, JS6. JS7, JS8, JS10, JS11, M2, D1, D2, and D3.

26 Interview with practitioner JS7.

27 Interviews with practitioners J10 and JS1.

28 Interview with practitioner JS1 (author's translation from French original).

about the Rome Statute were clearly not the predominant reason that interviewees were reluctant to accept the idea of arms trade cases.

7.3 Legalism in ICC Case Selection

The ICC is a judicial institution with a legalistic culture, so it is perhaps counterintuitive that the judges and lawyers in Chapter 6 appeared to express views that were weakly articulated with legal grounds. It was surprising that, rather than making claims that arms traders did not fall within the legal rules, most practitioners gave more intuitive answers to the effect that economic actors were simply not the right type of defendants to be prosecuted. Paradoxically, an institutional culture of legalism may make it more difficult for practitioners to be aware of the ways in which their views on the arms trade were not based primarily on the Rome Statute, and were influenced by cultural assumptions, beliefs, and commitments. The following section explores how legalism can exacerbate blind spots when forms of argumentation become decoupled from law.

7.3.1 Concepts of 'Legalism'

In legal scholarship, 'legalism' has been described as the lawyer's primary means of comprehending their practice, or as Pirie puts it, as 'a way of thinking and acting; it is what could be said to be distinctive about legal, as compared to other schemes of meaning'.[29] From Pirie's perspective, we might consider legalism as a mindset of ICC judges and lawyers that imagines legal meaning as detached from cultural and pragmatic considerations, through which ICC judges and lawyers interpret their practice as devoid of any extra-legal influence, thereby explicitly or implicitly ignoring the possibility that culture might shape their actions in legal processes and decision-making.

For Shklar, the detached quality of legalistic thought means that practitioners perceive of law as 'out there', upholding the idea that law is a 'discrete entity, discernibly different from morals and politics'.[30] When ICC judges and lawyers discussed the arms trade, their exclusionary rationales tended to express views of decision-making as if it were taking place in a legal vacuum. The interaction of law with decision-making is, in Shklar's terms, imagined as isolated and hermitically sealed from other (cultural) influences that were imagined as extra-legal, outside of law. The impermeable nature of legalism, as described by Shklar, leads to an internal conflict for practitioners. On the one hand, the apparent lack of doctrinal

29 Fernanda Pirie, *The Anthropology of Law* (OUP 2013) 131.
30 Judith N Shklar, *Legalism: Law, Morals, and Political Trials* (Harvard University Press 1964) 9.

reasons amongst ICC judges and lawyers for excluding arms trade cases, would be difficult to internally reconcile with their reluctance, on the other hand, to accept the validity of arms trade cases.

Like any 'ism', 'legalism' refers to a relative rather than binary concept. Shklar emphasizes that varying degrees of legalism exist within the culture of ostensibly legalistic institutions such as courts,[31] and that legalism can be strong or weak, varying in 'the extent to which it finds institutional organization'.[32] The empirical research points to a tension between the strongly legalistic character of the ICC as a judicial institution, and the weak non-legal logic by which arms trade cases were generally excluded prima facie from consideration. This understanding of ICC practice recalls Posner depiction of legalism:

> Global legalism is not a doctrine or theory. It is akin to an attitude or posture—a set of beliefs about how the world works, one that, in various forms, dominates the thinking of academic international lawyers, as well as practicing international lawyers.[33]

The increasing dominance of legalism, according to McEvoy, is a major trend in post-conflict accountability and the field of transitional justice.[34] As the scholarship on legalistic responses to atrocity has developed, so too has awareness grown of the tensions between different forms of intervention and their impact.[35] When ICC judges and lawyers imagined the arms trade, it may have been difficult for them to express that their views were based on anything other than legal reasoning, reflecting Scheele's description of the nature of legalism as '[e]xplicit rules and their attendant categories [that] have a certain compelling logic'.[36] This 'compelling logic' may mean that practitioners who work within a highly legalistic institutional culture such as the ICC insist that their work is being carried out in accordance with legalistic rationales, without perhaps realizing the role that cultural perception may play in their work.

The highly legalistic character of the ICC's institutional culture may have made it more challenging for the Court's judges and lawyers to realize that the doctrines of complicity in Article 25 were actually of marginal significance in their reasons for rejecting the notion of arms trade prosecutions. The dominance of legalism

[31] Shklar (n 30) 117.

[32] Shklar (n 30) 117.

[33] Eric Posner, *The Perils of Global Legalism* (University of Chicago Press 2009) 16.

[34] Kieran McEvoy, 'Beyond Legalism: Towards a Thicker Understanding of Transitional Justice' (2007) 34 Journal of Law and Society.

[35] Nicola Palmer, Briony Jones, and Julia Viebach, 'Ways of Knowing Atrocity: A Methodological Enquiry into the Formulation, Implementation, and Assessment of Transitional Justice' (2015) 30 Canadian Journal of Law and Society 173, 180.

[36] Judith Scheele, 'In Praise of Disorder: Breaking the Rules in Northern Chad' in Paul Dresch and Judith Scheele (eds), *Legalism: Rules and Categories* (OUP 2015) 153.

cannot erase the role that cultural perception played in ICC judges and lawyers' views about the arms trade, but it can obscure from view the interpretive frameworks through which those views were constructed.

7.3.2 Legalism versus Aspiration in ICC Case Selection

In the empirical work of Chapter 6, the central aspirations of ICC judges and lawyers seemed to be to fight impunity through the prosecution of senior military and political figures, but not arms traders. At the same time, their legal objections to the idea of prosecuting arms traders were mostly unvoiced or weakly articulated. This can be described in terms of a conflict between the legalistic and aspirational aspects of the ICC's institution culture. On the one hand, a legalistic view of ICC case selection provides weak grounds for excluding arms traders. On the other hand, the aspirations of practitioners did not include selecting cases against this type of perpetrator.

The idealism that drives international criminal justice has been described by D'Aspremont in terms of a tendency towards 'expansionism', characterized by a fundamental belief in the ability of international criminal justice to progressively end mass violence through retribution and deterrence.[37] This account of international criminal justice places 'expansionist' aspirations at the centre of the ICC's culture of fighting against impunity. In the empirical research with judges and lawyers, D'Aspremont's expansionism appeared to be contingent on specific beliefs about the types of actors who were imagined to be at the centre of the 'fight against impunity'. It is not only that the ICC's institution culture reflects ambitious goals to end impunity, but also that these aspirations are specifically limited to a particular understanding about what 'ending impunity' might involve and who needs to be prosecuted in order to reach that goal.

In the legalistic institutional environment of the ICC, the notion that the 'fight against impunity' is culturally constructed would not sit easily with legalistic values. The empirical research suggested a conflict in the views of ICC judges and lawyers between, on the one hand, their aspirational beliefs about who the Court should investigate and prosecute, and on the other hand, their commitment to the Court's legal mandate. In general, the ICC judges and lawyers avoided commenting on the issue of arms traders' liability under the Rome Statute, perhaps because doing so would have forced them to accept that their reluctance was not based on doctrine but on their particular vision of how to end impunity, posing a challenge to their

[37] Jean D'Aspremont, 'The Two Cultures of International Criminal Law' in Kevin Heller and others (eds), *The Oxford Handbook of International Criminal Law* (OUP 2020) 400, 405, 422. See also David S Koller, 'The Faith of the International Criminal Lawyer' (2007) 40 New York University Journal of International Law and Politics 1019.

credo of legalism. Perhaps because arms traders were not central to their prevailing assumptions about the Court's mission, the ICC judges and lawyers avoided confronting the non-legalistic rationales on which their views were based.

One of the interviewed judges described themselves three times during the interview as a 'legalist', stating 'well, I am a legalist judge'.[38] Other interviewees were at pains to emphasize the legalistic qualities of the Court, the 'independence of the Court in proceeding with investigations' and its 'impartial decisions'.[39] The apparent need to emphasize legalism was suggestive of the internal conflicts that must exist within practitioners who have been trained to believe in legal process, who are required to operate in an institutional reality with limitations and challenges. As Krever argues, in international criminal trials the pressures generated by criticism of a court's politicization and cultural contingency often lead to the creation of a diametric and over-simplified portrayals of a court, which in turn encourages a purified ideal of legalism.[40] A strong belief in legalism would obscure the much more culturally contingent motivations for rejecting the idea of an arms trade case.

7.3.3 Cognitive Dissonance: Legalism versus Aspiration

The conflict between legalism and aspiration could be understood in terms of a cognitive dissonance experienced by ICC judges and lawyers at the level of individual psychology. Nouwen draws on cognitive dissonance theory to describe the conflicts between idealism and reality faced by international criminal justice activists.[41] Citing De Waal's research on humanitarian workers,[42] Nouwen identifies the interpretive processes through which activists, as they make contact with the realities of practice, experience the disparity between the idealism that motivated their original commitment to the field of international criminal justice, and the inherently compromised actuality of working in the field. Nouwen argues that this results in a 'tragedy' that arises from 'a mismatch between a universal idealism and a reality of horrific constraint'.[43] A similar view can be taken of the perceptions of the ICC judges and lawyers—idealistically the practitioners

[38] Interview with practitioner J11.

[39] Interviews with practitioners J6, JS2.

[40] Tor Krever, 'Unveiling (and Veiling) Politics in International Criminal Trials' in Christine Schwöbel-Patel, *Critical Approaches to International Criminal Law: An Introduction* (Routledge 2014) 117, 125. Krever says that this encourages a polarizing of views of international criminal proceedings as either 'a show trial' or 'a fair trial'.

[41] Alex De Waal, 'The Humanitarians' Tragedy: Escapable and Inescapable Cruelties' (2010) 34 Disasters 130.

[42] De Waal (n 41) 130.

[43] Sarah Nouwen, 'Justifying Justice' in James Crawford and Martti Koskenniemi (eds), *The Cambridge Companion to International Law* (CUP 2012) 337.

aspired to prosecute dictators and architects of mass murder, while from a legal perspective they could not see a good legal reason for excluding arms trade cases from consideration.

The theory of cognitive dissonance was developed by Festinger, a social psychologist who argued that individuals have an inner drive to seek harmony and avoid disharmony.[44] Faced with disharmony, individuals try to 'rationalize away' the internal dissonance.[45] In Nouwen's research, the tragedy for international criminal justice practitioners manifested at a personal level as a cognitive dissonance between their emotional investment in international criminal justice, and the reality of its application. Nouwen found that 'the prevailing coping strategy [in response to cognitive dissonance] is that of argumentative defence. Rational arguments are put forward to reason the observed dissonance away.'[46]

Nouwen writes in the context of the tautologies of international intervention in Sudan and the so-called 'justice versus peace' dilemma. Practitioners in Nouwen's study respond to this dilemma by putting forward rational arguments that decouple the discussion of peace from that of justice, thereby 'sidestepping' a tension that would have challenged the credo of international criminal justice.[47] The practitioners imagined justice as having its own, isolated ends, leaving the coherence of the justice narrative intact while avoiding the difficult questions about the pragmatic compromises of peace. In a similar way, ICC judges and lawyers appeared to sidestep the dissonance between their beliefs about what international criminal justice was supposed to be doing (not prosecuting arms traders), and the scope of application of international criminal law (the Rome Statute provisions on accomplice liability do in fact extend to arms traders).

This 'sidestepping' recalls a central precept of Festinger's theory: responses to cognitive dissonance are characterized by the psychological development of a powerful motivation to maintain cognitive consistency, leading to maladaptive behaviour.[48] At the ICC, rather than addressing the uncomfortable conflict between their aspirations for the Court and their commitment to legalism, ICC judges and lawyers gave answers such as 'the arms trade is already regulated' or 'this is simply not what the Court was intended to do' in an apparent coping strategy. A cognitive dissonance, generated by the highly legalistic institutional culture of the Court, would have made it harder for practitioners to simply accept that the Rome Statute provides for the accomplice liability of a wide range of economic actors, that they lacked legal grounds not to take those cases seriously, and that culturally

[44] Leon Festinger *A Theory of Cognitive Dissonance* (Stanford University Press 1957).

[45] Festinger (n 44). See Leon Festinger (ed), *Conflict, Decision, and Dissonance* (Stanford University Press 1964).

[46] Nouwen (n 43) 338.

[47] Nouwen (n 43) 338.

[48] Saul Kassin, Steven Fein, Hazel Rose Markus (eds), *Social Psychology* (9th edn, Cengage 2014) 236. Festinger (n 44).

constructed beliefs about the arms trade were instrumental to their belief that the ICC should not pursue these cases.

In the book which precipitated the development of cognitive dissonance theory, Festinger describes a covert participant observation study of an American religious group— 'the *Seekers*'—whose members believed the earth was to be imminently destroyed by a flood, closely followed by the arrival of UFOs to rescue true believers.[49] The study examined the beliefs of the group's members, in particular their reactions after 21 December 1954, the prophesized date of the flood.[50] After the non-occurrence of the flood and alien visitation, the members of the *Seekers* suffered what Festinger described as an 'anxiety', which he attributed to the internal conflict generated when their beliefs were challenged by reality. The majority of the *Seekers* continued to follow their leaders, who had made the timely revelation that the flood was averted by the members' devotion to the cult. Rather than negating their prior beliefs, Festinger found that most individuals developed new rational explanations for the change in circumstances to protect and maintain their self-esteem.[51] Festinger further observed that members with a greater commitment to the *Seekers* (a number had made personal and professional sacrifices to join the group), were less likely to overturn their faith in the group after the non-occurrence of the flood. By contrast, fringe members were more likely to acknowledge that they had been foolish to believe in the flood in the first place.

The theory of cognitive dissonance illuminates the way in which practitioners mediate the internal conflict between their aspirational beliefs in international criminal justice and their disappointment in its practical realities by adopting coping strategies of 'argumentative defence'.[52] It may be that the ICC judges and lawyers experienced an analogous cognitive dissonance, when their aspirations for the ICC to prosecute certain types of actor, did not fit with their legal assessment of the accomplice liability of arms traders.[53]

7.3.4 Constructing Case Selection Decisions through ICC Legal Culture

The aspects of ICC legal culture discussed in this chapter and the previous chapter are not just a description of how ICC judges and lawyers think about their work. These assumptions, beliefs, and commitments are also constitutive of how they make decisions and perform their roles. This understanding of interpretive

[49] Leon Festinger, Henry Riecken, and Stanley Schachter, *When Prophecy Fails: A Social and Psychological Study of a Modern Group that Predicted the Destruction of the World* (Harper 1956).
[50] Festinger (n 49).
[51] Festinger (n 49).
[52] Nouwen (n 43) 338.
[53] Nouwen (n 43) 338.

practices can be illuminated from the different theoretical perspectives of Taylor's social imaginaries, Bourdieu's *habitus*, and Fish's interpretive communities.

Taylor's philosophical work has provided the notion of the 'social imaginary' as a means to better understand modernity.[54] Rather than looking to the role of culture in terms of 'ideas' and 'institutions', Taylor posits the social imaginary as 'what enables, through making sense of, the practices of a society'.[55] The notion of social imaginaries has been deployed to describe the concept of the rule of law,[56] how virtual technologies mediate combat and decision-making,[57] and how the ICC's intervention in Uganda reimagined the conflict's cultural and political parameters.[58] The 'social imaginary' has been deployed in studies aimed at understanding the construction of shared imaginaries of 'global justice' in world society,[59] and how political ideologies manifested in the shared imaginary that emerged with the rise of globalization.[60] It develops Geertz's conception of law as a 'species of social imagination'[61] wherein 'legal reasoning is one of the most significant ways in which people try to make explicit sense of their world, and it is itself partially constitutive of that world'.[62] The notion of social imaginaries enables a better understanding of how a shared sense of the ICC's aspirations is engendered and sustained in the belief systems of individual judges and practitioners.

We might also conceive of the interpretive processes of ICC judges and lawyers that excluded arms transfers in terms of Bourdieu's notion of '*habitus*', which, rather than focusing on the agency of practitioners in actively imagining the Court's aspirations in a certain way, refers to the way in which practitioners habitually carry out their practices and inherit cultural actions and assumptions that they absorb without necessarily questioning or becoming aware of them.[63] Taking seriously the unintended consequences of habitual legal practices, therefore, means recognizing that the ICC's social functioning cannot be understood through explanations that over-emphasize the intentionality of practitioners. As Meierhenrich notes, an

[54] Charles Taylor, *Modern Social Imaginaries* (Duke University Press 2004) 2.

[55] Taylor (n 54) 2.

[56] Christopher May, 'The Rule of Law as a Social Imaginary' in Christopher May (ed), *The Rule of Law: The Common Sense of Global Politics* (Elgar 2014) 11.

[57] Neil Whitehead and Sverker Finnström (eds), *Virtual War and Magical Death: Technologies and Imaginaries for Terror and Killing* (Duke University Press 2013) 2.

[58] Sverker Finnström, 'Today He Is No More: Magic, Intervention, and Global War in Uganda' in Whitehead and Finnström (n 57) 122.

[59] Claudius Messner, 'Observing Victims: Global Insecurities and the Systemic Imagination of Justice in World Society' in Ronnie Lippens (ed), *Imaginary Boundaries of Justice Social and Legal Justice across Disciplines* (Hart 2004).

[60] Manfred Steger, *The Rise of the Global Imaginary: Political Ideologies from the French Revolution to the Global War on Terror* (OUP 2008) 11.

[61] Clifford Geertz, 'Local Knowledge: Fact and Law in Comparative Perspective' in Clifford Geertz, *Local Knowledge: Further Essays in Interpretive Anthropology* (Basic Books 1983) 184.

[62] Chris Fuller, 'Legal Anthropology: Legal Pluralism and Legal Thought' (1994) 10 Anthropology Today 9, 11.

[63] Pierre Bourdieu and others, *The Weight of the World: Social Suffering in Contemporary Society* (Polity 1999) 625.

accurate description of ICC practice cannot avoid recognizing that whatever individuals may believe or proclaim that they are doing, in reality they lack 'the capacity to fully determine their own behavior'.[64]

We could also view the assumptions, beliefs, and commitments of the ICC judges and lawyers in terms of an 'interpretive community'. According to Fish, assumptions (such as the assumption that the ICC does not prosecute arms traders) are highly subjective, only taking on meaning through being shared and reinforced by whoever belongs to the same interpretive community. This narrows the diversity of beliefs within the same interpretive community.[65] The interviews with ICC judges and lawyers suggested an interpretive community that holds shared views about the Court's central aspiration to end impunity that are mutually reinforcing. In this view, the status quo exclusion of arms traders would be strengthened within the interpretive community of the ICC.

These theoretical approaches help to describe and explain how ICC's legal culture involves interpretive processes that ultimately have some bearing on the Court's decision-making processes. The empirical research with ICC judges and lawyers provides a 'thicker' understanding of how ICC judges and lawyers assessed whether it would be meaningful for the Court to pursue arms traders. As in Palmer's account of the International Criminal Tribunal for Rwanda (ICTR), the ways in which the ICC judges and lawyers ascribe meaning to the Court's actions reflect broader aspects of its institutional legal culture.[66] While they often feel compelled to rationalize their experience of working at the Court in legalistic terms (even where a legal rationale was not clear), in reality, as Palmer found at the ICTR, the way in which legal decision-making took place meant that the 'ideas, reasoning, practical experience, and institutional wisdom that allow[ed] the judges and lawyers to infuse the court's social actions with meaning'.[67]

7.3.5 ICC Legal Culture in the Narrowing of Actors Considered in Case Selection

The empirical research with ICC judges and lawyers pointed towards an aspiration to 'end impunity' through retribution against, and deterrence of, a narrow selection of the full range of actors who contribute to international crimes (as

[64] Jens Meierhenrich, 'The Practice of International Law: A Theoretical Analysis' (2014) 76 Law and Contemporary Problems 19.

[65] Stanley Fish, *Is There a Text in This Class?: The Authority of Interpretive Communities* (Harvard University Press 1982) 11.

[66] Nicola Palmer, *Courts in Conflict: Interpreting the Layers of Justice in Post-Genocide Rwanda* (OUP 2015) 73.

[67] Palmer (n 35) 69.

determined by the Rome Statute doctrines of liability). This narrow selection of actors prioritized military and political leaders as the most familiar targets of international criminal prosecution, and deprioritized actors in the arms trade who are involved in more structural causes of mass violence.

Hoover has criticized contemporary global understandings of moral agency, according to which the ICC reflects 'emerging understandings of responsibility in world politics [that] have been too focused on the actions of individuals, leading to the neglect of structural causes of mass violence and more indirect lines of responsibility revealed by attending to the wider social context'.[68] Part of Hoover's trouble with international tribunals' assignment of moral agency is to do with who is being held up as immoral. He points to the cases selected by the Special Court for Sierra Leone (SCSL), including Charles Taylor, while noting that other prosecutions would have better represented the structural causes of the conflict[69] (as the subsequent Dutch prosecution of arms dealer Kouwenhoven eventually did).

Hoover emphasizes that 'collective violence and mass suffering never have simple causes or single lines of accountability' and he recognizes the possibility of assigning moral blame to a wider range of actors including corporate actors.[70] Similarly, Hoover refers to Moreno Ocampo's 'denunciation' of Joseph Kony in the Uganda situation as a 'moral monster', commenting that: '[t]he danger of constructing criminal identities in terms of irrational evil or otherwise exceptional forms of agency is that the identities of 'good' and 'bad' are insulated from contestation and the social conditions and power relations that enable them are naturalized'.[71] The empirical research in Chapter 6 supports Hoover's critique insofar as, if we treat the commercial supply of weapons as part of the 'structural causes of mass violence', the ICC's legal culture appears to neglect this particular cause, being overly focused on the roles of familiar cases against 'bad' military and political figures.

As a matter of law, however, the ICC modes of liability do have the capacity to address some of the 'structural causes of mass violence and more indirect lines of responsibility revealed by attending to the wider social context'. Hoover's critique of the ICC is not about the potential of the Rome Statute to address these structural causes; his critique is better understood as a comment on the Court's current practice, which is failing to attend to structural causes that it could address.[72]

The assumptions, beliefs, and commitments of the interviewed ICC judges and lawyers were consistent with Hoover's critique that the ICC may be 'missing

[68] Joseph Hoover, 'Reconstructing Responsibility and Moral Agency in World Politics' (2012) 4 International Theory 233, 234.
[69] Hoover (n 68) 259–60.
[70] Hoover (n 68) 262–63.
[71] Hoover (n 68) 257.
[72] Hoover (n 68) 257.

influential social conditions' in its case selection,[73] perhaps due to problematic understanding of moral agency.[74] This ICC practice is not inevitable, however, since the Rome Statute allows for prosecutions of individuals associated with such social conditions. In fact, by drawing a connection between perceptions about the structural causes of mass violence, and the types of cases that the ICC prosecutes, Hoover ends up suggesting a possible redemptive route towards the Court playing a role in addressing these causes. If ICC judges and lawyers paid closer attention to how their perceptions influence their legal decision-making, they may become more aware of their blind spots over the potential for case selection to address 'the structural causes of mass violence', including the arms trade.

7.4 Conclusion

The empirical research discussed in Chapters 6 and 7 has tracked the interpretative practices through which ICC judges and lawyers apply the Rome Statute doctrines of accomplice liability. A central finding of the research was that most ICC judges and lawyers were reluctant to accept the potential for arms trade cases, but that despite the Court's highly legalistic institutional culture, the practitioners rarely justified this reluctance with reference to the Court's legal framework.

The research suggests that a greater awareness amongst ICC judges and lawyers, about how they frame their aspirations for what the ICC is supposed to do, can inform the ICC's institutional culture and allow it to fulfil its mandate more effectively. At present, when the ICC's actions appear inconsistent with its legal mandate, politicization critiques are common, often reducing case selection to familiar tensions between international law and state sovereignty. However, as the last two chapters have sought to illuminate, the selection of cases also involves perceptions about which types of perpetrator are valuable for the Court to prosecute.

In part, because of the highly legalistic institutional culture of the ICC, the influence of legal culture is easily overlooked. To do so may be perceived as accepting the existence of arbitrariness or irrationality in decision-making, founded on neither law nor political power. While there is perhaps a sense of inevitability in, for example, accepting that political imperatives at the Security Council may influence the ICC's operation, it is less easy for those invested in the Court to accept that their individual ideas, personal views, and prejudices also exert an influential role on legal decision-making. However, as the last two chapters have argued,

[73] Hoover (n 68) 264.
[74] Hoover (n 68) 236.

the interpretive cultural practices of ICC judges and lawyers are not necessarily irrational. The exclusion of arms traders from ICC legal culture can be understood as a logical, albeit unintended, consequence of the culturally constructed aspirations of the Court to end impunity for a particular, familiar type of military or political perpetrator, rather than addressing the full range of structural causes of mass violence.

8
Investigating the Arms Trade in the Second Congo War

8.1 Introduction

The Second Congo War was a multi-actor international armed conflict, fought by nine African countries and at least twenty-five armed groups from August 1998 to May 2003, that resulted in extensive allegations of international crimes centring on the eastern Democratic Republic of the Congo (DRC).[1] The ready availability of weapons was described as an important factor in atrocities and the plunder of Congolese natural resources.[2] As this chapter analyses, UN investigations into the arms trade even identified specific individuals and companies who were responsible for supplying the weapons used in these atrocities. Yet these UN investigations did not result in any criminal accountability, representing a missed opportunity to address the proliferation of small arms in Africa.

As Africa's deadliest conflict, the scale of the Second Congo War still does not seem to register in the public consciousness to the extent it should.[3] According to a much-cited study by the International Rescue Committee, approximately 3.9 million people lost their lives as the direct or indirect victims of armed conflict between August 1998 and April 2004, making it the most lethal period of conflict since World War II.[4] The conflict led to widespread allegations of sexual and gender-based violence and resulted in 3.2 million internally displaced persons and 440,000 refugees.[5]

On 8 September 2003, shortly after the formal cessation of the war, the first ICC Prosecutor, Luis Moreno Ocampo made the announcement to the ASP that '[those

[1] See Philip G Roessler and Harry Verhoeven, *Why Comrades Go to War: Liberation Politics and the Outbreak of Africa's Deadliest Conflict* (Hurst and Co 2017); Gérard Prunier, *Africa's World War: Congo, the Rwandan Genocide, and the Making of a Continental Catastrophe* (OUP 2008).

[2] See Augusta Muchai, 'Arms Proliferation and the Congo War' in John F Clark (ed), *The African Stakes of the Congo War* (Palgrave Macmillan 2002) 185; René Lemarchand, *The Dynamics of Violence in Central Africa* (University of Pennsylvania Press 2012) 5, 244.

[3] See Filip Reyntjens, 'The Congo Wars' (*Oxford Research Encyclopedia of African History*, 1 March 2020) <https://oxfordre.com/africanhistory/> accessed 12 December 2024.

[4] International Rescue Committee, 'Mortality in the Democratic Republic of Congo: Results from a Nationwide Survey' (Burnet Institute 2004). The majority of deaths resulted indirectly from the fighting. See also Benjamin Coghlan and others, 'Mortality in the Democratic Republic of Congo—A Nationwide Survey' (2006) 367 *The Lancet*, 44.

[5] Reyntjens (n 3) 2.

The Arms Trade and International Criminal Law. Tomas Hamilton, Oxford University Press. © Tomas Hamilton 2025.
DOI: 10.1093/oso/9780192868671.003.0008

who] provide weapons' could be 'authors of the crimes', even if they are 'based in other countries'.[6] These words expressed, tentatively, a prosecutorial interest in investigating arms traders in the DRC Situation. In March 2004, the Government of the DRC wrote to the Prosecutor referring the Situation on its territory since 1 July 2002 to the ICC.[7] The Court eventually convicted Mr Lubanga, Mr Katanga, and Mr Ntaganda, and acquitted Mr Ngudjolo Chui. But despite Ocampo's initial interest in investigating arms traders, no public arrest warrant was forthcoming. Thus far, International Criminal Law has provided no accountability for the role of arms brokers in the Second Congo War, with only the mechanisms and instruments of Arms Trade Law playing any role in stemming the flood of weapons into the Great Lakes Region. Chapter 8 analyses the case study before Chapter 9 looks more closely at the ICC Situation.

8.2 A Case Study of the Second Congo War

The central descriptive claim of this chapter is that this transnational assemblage of Arms Trade Law was an ineffective legal response to the Second Congo War. Furthermore, while criminal accountability was absent from this response, it could have strengthened it. Not only did the Security Council embargo system and national export controls fail to prevent the flow of Small Arms and Light Weapons (SALW) to perpetrators of international crimes, but the institutions of international criminal justice also failed to sufficiently recognize that *ex post facto* investigations could have provided a meaningful symbol of accountability.

The Congolese case study is chosen as a poignant historical illustration of the direct links between arms supplies and the perpetration of international crimes. The severity and manner of commission of atrocities in the eastern DRC was only possible with external transfers of SALW and continuous resupplies of ammunition. Specific shipments of weapons were sent by individuals who knew the recipients were carrying out unlawful attacks against civilians and would continue to do so, and in some cases knew that their weapons would assist the carrying out of specific attacks.

The case study is also chosen because it coincides with several watershed moments relevant to the arms trade and International Criminal Law. The establishment of the ICC with temporal jurisdiction over crimes committed from 1 July 2002 was concurrent with the end of the Second Congo War. For the first time, a

[6] Moreno Ocampo, 'Report of the Prosecutor of the ICC Second Assembly of States Parties to the Rome Statute of the International Criminal Court (*ICC Legal Tools Database*, 8 September 2003) 4–5<www.legal-tools.org/doc/8873bd/> accessed 24 June 2020.

[7] Situation in the Democratic Republic of the Congo (Decision) ICC-01/04-1 (5 July 2004), para 4. See Paola Gaeta, 'Is the Practice of 'Self-Referrals' a Sound Start for the ICC?' (2004) 2 Journal of International Criminal Justice 949.

permanent international court existed with the authority to enforce the doctrines of accomplice liability in the Rome Statute. This period was also significant in that the Security Council was defining its relationship with the ICC, while international human rights practice began a shift towards greater criminalization.[8] The focus of UN sanctions bodies and fact-finding mechanisms was shifting towards targeting individuals, groups, or corporate entities, replacing the use of comprehensive sanctions against entire states.[9] And the Second Congo War also coincided with a period of growth in international agreements on the arms trade—at the UN and African regional level—that eventually culminated in the adoption of the Arms Trade Treaty (ATT) in 2013.

Section 8.3 begins by analysing the arms flows while Sections 8.4 looks at the role of the Security Council's powers under Chapter VII to respond to arms trafficking in the Second Congo War, and Section 8.5 examines the role of domestic export controls in regulating the flow of weapons across transnational borders. Sections 8.6 and 8.7 analyse and reflect upon the work of the UN Panel of Experts and its mandate with respect to the arms trade. This leads to a discussion of the findings on the importance of weapons transfers from the neighbouring states of Rwanda and Uganda to non-state armed groups fighting in the eastern DRC, in particular the role of small-scale brokers, transporters, and micro-traders.

8.3 Analysing Arms Flows in the Second Congo War

This section analyses the suppliers and recipients of arms transfers during the Second Congo War. The transfer of weapons is poorly documented, with a lack of on-the-ground reporting about trafficked weapons compounded by limited export data. Within the extensive commentary on the nature and causes of the Second Congo War,[10] including critical scholarship on international aspects of the war,[11] there is limited research specifically on the role of arms transfers.[12] Muchai wrote probably the only in-depth study on the role of weapons.[13] Unconvinced by

[8] See Philip Alston, 'Criminalizing Human Rights' 15(3) Journal of Human Rights Practice (2023) 660–77.

[9] Thomas J Biersteker, Sue E Eckert, and Marcos Tourinho (eds), *Targeted Sanctions* (CUP 2016).

[10] Gérard Prunier, *From Genocide to Continental War: The 'Congolese' Conflict and the Crisis of Contemporary Africa* (Hurst and Co 2009); Filip Reyntjens, *The Great African War: Congo and Regional Geopolitics, 1996–2006* (CUP 2009). See also John F Clark (ed), *The African Stakes of the Congo War* (Palgrave Macmillan 2002); François Ngolet, *Crisis in the Congo: The Rise and Fall of Laurent Kabila* (Springer 2010); Georges Nzongola-Ntalaja, *The Congo: From Leopold to Kabila: A People's History* (Zed Books 2002); Prunier (n 1); Roessler and Verhoeven (n 1); Jason Stearns, *Dancing in the Glory of Monsters: The Collapse of the Congo and the Great War of Africa* (Public Affairs 2012); Thomas Turner, *The Congo Wars: Conflict, Myth and Reality* (Zed Books 2007).

[11] See Séverine Autesserre, *The Trouble with the Congo: Local Violence and the Failure of International Peacebuilding* (CUP 2010). See Thomas Callaghy, Ronald Kassimir, and Robert Latham (eds), *Intervention and Transnationalism in Africa: Global-Local Networks of Power* (CUP 2001).

[12] See Muchai (n 2) 185; Lemarchand (n 2) 244.

[13] Muchai (n 2) 196–97.

the potential of existing arms control laws,[14] Muchai focuses on peacekeeping and disarmament as solutions, rather than strengthening arms control or the potential symbolic role of criminal prosecutions.[15]

Despite the lack of accurate empirical data about the movement of weapons and ammunition, the most important patterns of arms transfers can be discerned. The major flows followed two transnational alliances whose interests were loosely aligned for and against the DRC government in Kinshasa.[16] Before discussing the contemporaneous transfers of arms within these two alliances, it is necessary to consider the longer-term context of arms proliferation in the region.

8.3.1 Background Levels of Arms Proliferation in the Great Lakes Region

The relative importance of new imports weapons and ammunition in the Great Lakes Region for the commission of atrocities during the Second Congo War is dependent, to some extent, on whether the equipment was already available locally. At the start of the Second Congo War in August 1998, vast numbers of SALW were in situ in what is now the eastern DRC.[17] Some weaponry dated back to the Colonial era, and much of it to the Cold War period when the US supported Zaire militarily as a key ally.[18] In the 1980s, the US supplied large quantities of arms to União Nacional para a Independência Total de Angola (UNITA) via Zaire, which accumulated in Angola and the Congo.[19]

The armed conflicts centred on Rwanda and Burundi during the 1990s left the eastern DRC awash with weapons.[20] A significant proportion of the weapons in circulation in the Second Congo War could be traced back to Uganda in the late 1980s, gifted by Ugandan president Yoweri Museveni to the Rwandan Patriotic Front (RPF) who then brought them into Rwanda in 1990.[21] According to Muchai and other sources, another significant influx of arms came from France and Zaire to the Rwandan President Juvénal Habayarimana in 1994, including machetes and SALW that were distributed to Hutu fighters in support of the regime's plan to eliminate Tutsis.[22] Many of these weapons subsequently crossed the Rwandan

[14] Muchai (n 2) 185, 194–95.

[15] Muchai (n 2) 194–95.

[16] Henning Tamm, 'The Origins of Transnational Alliances: Rulers, Rebels, and Political Survival in the Congo Wars' (2016) 41 International Security 147.

[17] Paul Eavis, 'SALW in the Horn of Africa and the Great Lakes Region: Challenges and Ways Forward' (2002) IX Brown Journal of World Affairs 252.

[18] Muchai (n 2) 189.

[19] Muchai (n 2) 189.

[20] Lennart Wholgemuth, 'African Sanctions—The Case of Burundi' in Peter Wallensteen and Carina Staibano (eds), *International Sanctions: Between Words and Wars in the Global System* (Routledge 2005) 126, 130–31.

[21] Prunier (n 1) 93.

[22] Muchai (n 2) 187.

border with Hutu refugees and were eventually used in the Second Congo War. Likewise, the Burundi conflict contributed to the background levels of weaponry in the region, as did Burundi's assistance to Laurent-Désiré Kabila during the First Congo War.[23]

There had been long-standing diversion of arms sold to the DRC military and leakage of existing military and police stockpiles.[24] The DRC exported significant quantities of weapons during this time, including to UNITA in Angola (breaching a Security Council embargo) and the Allied Democratic Forces (ADF) in Uganda (undermining one of Uganda's purposes for intervening in the DRC).[25] In addition to those weapons' use in neighbouring conflicts, notably in the Central African Republic (CAR), a significant proportion were brought back into the DRC during the Second Congo War.[26]

In spite of the existing proliferation of weapons when the Second Congo War began, shipments of new weapons and ammunition, as well as transfers of existing weapons, were pivotal to the scale and nature of the violence. Demand for arms escalated as the conflict became larger, increased demand was self-perpetuating in a localized arms race between non-state armed groups, and ammunition restocks were an essential resource. In other words, although a large quantity of weapons were already available in the eastern DRC, the commission of atrocities was inextricably linked to the availability of fresh supplies, updated weaponry, and the availability of ammunition.

8.3.2 Arms Transfers within the 'Pro-DRC Alliance'

Within the loosely defined 'pro-DRC alliance', the DRC Government was led by President Laurent-Désiré Kabila until his assassination in January 2001, thereafter by his son Joseph Kabila. The DRC was aligned with non-state armed groups fighting in the east of the country.[27]

Weapons intended for use by the Congolese armed forces were funnelled to non-state armed groups in the eastern DRC with the connivance of elites who were well positioned to facilitate the corrupt diversion of weapons.[28] These group can be roughly subdivided into those fighting against Uganda (the LRA, ADF, UNRF

[23] Muchai (n 2) 188.

[24] Muchai (n 2) 186.

[25] Muchai (n 2) 188.

[26] Eric G Berman and Louisa N Lombard, *The Central African Republic and Small Arms: A Regional Tinderbox* (Small Arms Survey 2008) 59–61; Conflict Armament Research, *Non-State Armed Groups in the Central African Republic: Types and Sources of Documented Arms and Ammunition* (Conflict Armament Research 2015) 6.

[27] Prunier (n 1).

[28] *Forces armées congolaises* (FAC).

II, and FNI),[29] those primarily engaged against Rwanda (the ALiR, FDLR, RDR, and RCD-ML),[30] and those fighting Burundi.[31] In addition, 'Mai-Mai' fighters in Eastern Congo became increasingly important to the pro-DRC alliance and in late 2002 were reportedly using heavy weapons provided by the Congolese armed forces.[32]

While these groups were approximately aligned with the interests of the DRC State, a monolithic analysis of the role of flows of weapons from DRC forces to non-state armed groups would ignore the fractures within the state apparatus between Banyamulenge (Congolese Tutsi) and the Katanganese favoured by Laurent-Désiré Kabila.[33] The mode of governance of these factions has been described by Roessler and Verhoeven as reliant on 'co-ethnicity and its norms of reciprocity, social sanctioning mechanisms and dense social networks via overlapping family and kinship ties'.[34] Likewise, frictions between and within the various non-state armed groups, means that arms transfers to and between non-state armed groups were in reality far more diffuse, complex, and decentralized than might first appear.

8.3.3 Arms Transfers from Rwanda and Uganda in the 'Anti-DRC Alliance'

The 'anti-DRC alliance' has been described as Rwanda, Uganda, and Burundi, and various non-state armed groups.[35] Principally, the groups were the RCD, ADFL, RCD-Goma (which received arms from Burundi),[36] and the *Forces du Renouveau* (previously the RCD-K-ML).[37] Additionally, Uganda provided support to

[29] The Lord's Resistance Army (LRA), Allied Democratic Forces (ADF), Uganda National Rescue Front II (UNRF II), and *Front des Nationalistes et Intégrationnistes* (FNI).

[30] The *Armée pour la Libération du Rwanda* (ALiR), *Forces démocratiques de libération du Rwanda* as the main remnant militia of Rwandan *interahamwe* Hutus (FDLR) often referred to as *génocidaires*, the *Rassemblement Républicain pour la Démocratie au Rwanda* (RDR), and the RCD-ML of Mbusa Nyamwisi. See Amnesty International, 'Democratic Republic of Congo: Arming the East' (*Amnesty International*, 4 July 2005) <https://www.amnesty.org/fr/wp-content/uploads/2021/08/afr62006200 5en.pdf> accessed 12 December 2024.

[31] The *Conseil National Pour la Défense de la Démocratie–Forces pour la Défense de la Démocratie* (CNDD-FDD) and the ethnically Hutu *Front de Libération Nationale* (FROLINA).

[32] Human Rights Watch, 'Ituri: 'Covered in Blood', Ethnically Targeted Violence in Northeastern DR Congo' (Human Rights Watch, July 2003) 9 <https://www.hrw.org/report/2003/07/07/covered-blood/ethnically-targeted-violence-northern-drc> accessed 12 December 2024.

[33] Roessler and Verhoeven (n 1) 288–89.

[34] Roessler and Verhoeven (n 1) 289.

[35] See Tamm (n 16).

[36] Amnesty International (n 30) 8, 18; Muchai (n 2), 188.

[37] The core of the *Rassemblement Congolais pour la Démocratie* (RCD) was formed of fighters from the *Alliance of Democratic Forces for the Liberation of Congo* (ADFL) that enabled Laurent-Désiré Kabila to overthrow Mobutu Sese Seko in the First Congo War. The RCD later factionalized into a Goma branch (RCD-Goma). See Gauthier de Villers, 'République démocratique du Congo De la guerre aux élections: L'ascension de Joseph Kabila et la naissance de la Troisième République (janvier 2001–août 2008)' (2009) 75 Cahiers africains 114, 120–31.

Jean-Pierre Bemba's MLC, which came to control a substantial portion of northern DRC, as well as to the RCD-ML and the FIPI.[38]

During 2002, Rwanda is said to have become the main arms supplier to the UPC run by Thomas Lubanga (who was later convicted at the ICC) directly from Rwanda, and indirectly via the RCD-Goma.[39] According to Reyntjens, the alliance between Rwanda and Uganda, initially bound by shared interests and the logic of 'my enemy's enemy is my friend', soured from mid-1998 onwards as the groups that they armed turned against each other, further exacerbating the conflict.[40]

The anti-Angolan UNITA operated in parts of Southern DRC until Jonas Savimbi's death in April 2002.[41] Non-state armed groups of *banyamulenge* and Tutsi-aligned groups also joined the anti-DRC alliance.

8.3.4 Weapons Followed Transnational Alliances

The 'pro-DRC alliance' and 'anti-DRC alliance' supplied weapons to non-state armed groups during the Second Congo War in what are best understood as transnational alliances of mutual dependence.[42] The notion of proxy warfare tends to over-emphasize the interests of states as dominant over pawn-like, non-state armed group proxies. Tamm argues that contrary to conventional political theories of alliance, state-to-non-state armed group support in the Second Congo War was less the product of states' concerns for external threats or opportunities, but rather a means for states to hedge against the internal risk of *coup d'état* or rebellion.[43]

The states in the conflict initially supported non-state armed groups primarily in order to protect their borders and secure influence over their allied non-state armed groups, as in the case of Rwanda and the RCD. Over the course of the war, however, these relationships deepened and became more symbiotic, with states coming to rely on non-state armed groups to maintain a local powerbase and to defend accumulated access to resources in the eastern DRC. As such, as the war progressed, the interdependence of states and non-state armed groups increased. The relationship of mutual dependence meant stronger links between the support provided by the external states and the activities of the armed groups.

[38] *Mouvement de Libération du Congo* (MLC) and *Front pour l'Intégration et la Paix en Ituri* (FIPI). See Amnesty International (n 30) 8.

[39] *Union des Patriotes congolais* (UPC). Human Rights Watch, 'Covered In Blood' (n 32) 10–11; Human Rights Watch, 'Democratic Republic of Congo: The Curse of Gold' (Human Rights Watch, 2 June 2005) 25.

[40] Filip Reyntjens, 'The Privatisation and Criminalisation of Public Space in the Geopolitics of the Great Lakes Region' (2005) 43 The Journal of Modern African Studies 587, 594.

[41] *União Nacional para a Independência Total de Angola* (UNITA).

[42] Tamm (n 16) 152. See Gérard Prunier, 'Rebel Movements and Proxy Warfare: Uganda, Sudan and the Congo (1986–99)' (2004) 103 African Affairs 359, 378–79.

[43] Tamm (n 16).

Following Tamm's analysis, what had previously been a looser affiliation, where Rwanda and Uganda were disinterested in the armed groups' activities as long as their national borders were secured, became over a time an important economic relationship in which the external states had a close knowledge of the resource extraction activities for which they were supporting the armed groups, and an understanding that in order to maintain control of these resources they would need to supply more weapons.[44] This is the context in which the members of the transnational alliances were well aware of the role that arms supplies played in exacerbating and perpetuating the atrocities associated with resource extraction in the eastern DRC.

8.3.5 Arms Transfers from Outside the Great Lakes Region

Additionally, important arms flows came from outside the Great Lakes Region. They involved transfers to Rwanda, Uganda, and Burundi, as well as to the DRC authorities, which eventually found their way to non-state armed groups in the eastern DRC following the alliance patterns described above. But they also involved direct transfers from non-regional states of weapons transported into the hands of the armed groups.

The pro-DRC alliance was supported from outside the Great Lakes Region by the governments of Zimbabwe, Angola, and Namibia.[45] In addition, Chad, the CAR, Libya, and Sudan provided military support to a lesser degree, for instance Sudan reportedly provided weapons to the DRC in 1998 after recently acquiring manufacturing capabilities.[46] France was broadly in support of the pro-DRC alliance at this time, and had encouraged Chad to support the DRC as a means of regaining influence in territory lost by the French after the Rwandan genocide.[47]

The anti-DRC alliance was supported by a number of non-regional states. At the start of the war, the US was described as broadly in support of Rwanda and Uganda achieving regime change in the DRC.[48] Supply states from beyond Europe also included North Korea, Iran, and Brazil.[49] Belgium had reportedly provided large quantities of weapons into the region since the early 1990s.[50] Transit states outside of Africa included Albania and Israel.[51] Elements of both the pro-DRC and

[44] Muchai (n 2) 190–91.
[45] Prunier, 'Rebel Movements' (n 42) 378.
[46] Prunier, 'Rebel Movements' (n 42) 378.
[47] International Crisis Group, 'Congo at War: A Briefing of the Internal and External Players in the Central African Conflict' (International Crisis Group, 17 November 1998) <https://www.crisisgroup.org/africa/central-africa/democratic-republic-congo/congo-war> accessed 12 December 2024.
[48] International Crisis Group (n 101).
[49] Muchai (n 2) 189–90.
[50] Muchai (n 2) 189.
[51] Muchai (n 2) 189–90.

anti-DRC alliances were supported at various times by Russia, Belarus, Romania, and Slovakia and other Warsaw Pact states including Bulgaria, supplying arms from Cold War stockpiles as well as from more recent manufacture.[52]

There were other African transit states in which arms supplies were transshipped for onward movement into the conflict zone.[53] Transshipments via Eritrea, Mozambique, Guinea, Tanzania, Djibouti, Somalia, Kenya, Liberia, and Burkina Faso have also been reported.[54] Another source of weapons came from within African states with significant domestic manufacture capacity, principally the domestic arms manufacturing industries in Egypt and South Africa, with South African companies reportedly selling weapons to both the pro-DRC and anti-DRC alliances.[55]

In terms of the connection of arms transfers from outside the Great Lakes Region to the atrocities in the eastern DRC, there are important differences between, on the one hand, the arms transfers to belligerent states, and on the other hand, arms shipments that non-regional actors supplied directly to the armed groups. In the former case, non-regional states may have indirectly supported the commission of atrocities by sending weapons to the DRC, Rwanda, Uganda or other countries knowing that they would be onward shipped to the rebel groups.[56] However, the recipient states had lawful military and security needs and in most cases the onward shipment of weapons for unlawful purposes may not have been clear to external states. Moreover, while there are active questions about the role of non-regional states in the Second Congo War, from the perspective of criminal law, indirect and fungible arms supplies via another state are unlikely to show that the state assisted the eventual perpetrators of the crimes. As Muchai recognizes: 'The worlds of the manufacturers and the end users in Congo are far apart. The many parties involved in a single weapons purchase bridge the distance.'[57]

In the latter case, however, where an external actor sold weapons directly to an armed groups in the eastern DRC, the direct nature of the contribution to the commission of atrocity may be more apparent. This is where international arms brokers played a particularly important role. These brokers were lynchpins for

[52] Stockholm Institute for Peace Research, 'SIPRI Yearbook 1999: Armaments, Disarmament, and International Security' (July 1999); Wairagala Wakabi and Ogoso Opolot, 'Museveni Shopped for Guns in Belarus' *The East African* (24 April 2000) 1.

[53] Muchai (n 2) 190.

[54] Muchai (n 2) 190.

[55] Muchai (n 2) 186. South African and Zambia also acted as mediators during the conflict, first with the SADC then OAU.

[56] Similarly, international aid money to Uganda, Rwanda, and the DRC enabled the purchase of weapons which, in turn, assisted the commission of atrocities. Human Rights Watch, 'Covered in Blood' (n 32) 53 points out that donors who provided this financial assistance may not have been in a position to know that aid money was to be used in this way, and by its fungible nature, often it would not be possible to identify that financing was in fact bound to be used in this way. See Zoë Marriage, 'Ambiguous Agreements: Aid in Negotiating Processes' (2008) 8 Conflict, Security and Development 1; Zoë Marriage, *Formal Peace and Informal War. Security and Development in Congo* (Routledge 2013).

[57] Muchai (n 2) 190.

the shipment of weapons and ammunition from Rwanda and Uganda, as well as sources outside the Great Lakes Region, directly to the perpetrators of atrocities in the conflict zone.

8.3.6 The Pivotal Role of Arms Brokers

To sum up the preceding analysis, insofar as it is possible to identify the key flows of weapons and ammunition during the Second Congo War, they appear to have been: (i) from the DRC authorities to an agglomeration of *ex-FAR* or *Interahamwe* or *génocidaire* non-state armed groups in the eastern DRC,[58] (ii) from Rwanda to its own armed forces (at the start of the war) and to various non-state armed groups (at a significantly increased level from 2001 onwards),[59] and (iii) from Uganda to non-state armed groups in Ugandan-controlled DRC.[60] The central importance of the Rwandan and Ugandan arms flows is consistent with the findings of the UN Panel in the October 2003 Confidential Supplement discussed below in relation to the maintenance of patterns of resource extraction.

Alongside these three main flows of weapons and ammunition, large quantities were left over from previous conflicts. Additionally, from outside the Great Lakes Region, other African states fed weapons into the conflict, notably Angolan and Namibian military aid on which the DRC was dependent, as well as numerous actors from non-regional states involved in different stages of the supply chain.

Most of these arms flows depended on the small-scale arms brokers, transporters, and micro-traders identified in Chapter 1 to ensure weapons arrived at the local level where the fighting occurred. Shipments from Rwanda, Uganda, Burundi, and Angola and non-regional states often depended on 'middlemen' operations at a local level in the DRC. The reason these actors are so interesting from a criminal law perspective is that they would usually be the closest actors in the supply chain to the perpetrators, rendering them causally, geographically, and temporally most proximate to the commission of crimes. This would also mean they often had close knowledge of what their buyers were planning to do imminently with the weapons they supplied. Furthermore, they would often be individual people with personal responsibility for coordinating the operations and logistics of the arms supplies, as opposed to officials in state structures or large corporations where an individual's personal contribution is more defuse.

The importance of arms brokers in the Second Congo War can be understood through scholarship on the informalization of conflict economies, which

[58] Roessler and Verhoeven (n 1) 330–33, 340.

[59] Prunier (n 1) 102.

[60] Human Rights Watch, 'Uganda in Eastern DRC Fueling Political and Ethnic Strife' (Human Rights Watch, March 2001) 6.

according to Mkandawire, has played a growing role in African wars by providing 'perfect cover' for the movement of resources to finance arms purchases.[61] Elite actors involved in micro-trades of weapons are often well positioned to take advantage of these informal economies since they are local to the conflict zone and have access to significant material and political resources, even where these elites have no connection to larger transnational organized crime groups.[62]

Data from the Small Arms Survey suggest the importance of informalized 'micro-transfers' is widely underestimated: 'the multi-ton, inter-continental shipments organized by the "merchants of death" account for only a small fraction of illicit transfers'.[63] The popular image of brokers, such as Victor Bout (who was described as 'the merchant of death')[64] single-handedly equipping conflicts and terrorist groups across the world, is not necessarily inaccurate. But this account must be nuanced by acknowledging the cumulative effects of the so-called 'ant trade' of elite actors involved in lawful or grey-area activities involving lawfully registered companies and corrupt state officials.

The role of private brokers in the DRC is also better understood by reflecting on the historical dependence of Congolese military and security forces on private sources of military support, to an extent that differs from other African states.[65] The dominance of private interests in the DRC and the role of external weapons suppliers can be traced back to King Leopold II's private ownership of the Congo Free State from 1885. Unusually in the history of African colonialism, the Free State was at this time 'neither a colony, nor a protectorate, nor a Belgian province but the personal estate of an individual'.[66]

Lacking the public funds, military organization ,and infrastructure of a colonial State, King Leopold II was dependent on privately financed resource exploitation of the Congo, privately acquired mercenaries, and arms purchased in Europe.[67] This 'extreme paternalism' of the Free State and its military dependency continued after it was bequeathed to Belgium as a colony. Privately sourced weapons supplies continued to be important and contributed to massive weapons proliferation.[68] The resource-rich eastern DRC thus has long-standing patterns of weapons and

[61] Thandika Mkandawire, 'The Terrible Toll of Post-Colonial Rebel Movements' (2002) 40 The Journal of Modern African Studies 181, fn 19.

[62] Mkandawire (n 61) 181, fn 19.

[63] Small Arms Survey, 'Illicit Trafficking' (*Small Arms Survey website*, 2020) <www.smallarmssurvey.org/de/weapons-and-markets/transfers/illicit-trafficking.html> accessed 4 August 2024.

[64] Douglas Farah and Stephen Braun, *Merchant of Death: Money, Guns, Planes, and the Man Who Makes War Possible* (John Wiley and Sons 2007).

[65] See Michael Wallace Nest, Francois Grignon, and Emizet F Kisangani, *The Democratic Republic of Congo: Economic Dimensions of War and Peace* (Lynne Rienner 2006).

[66] Roessler and Verhoeven (n 1) 88.

[67] Roessler and Verhoeven (n 1) 88–89. As Roessler and Verhoeven write, this 'privatised colonialism' exacerbated the cruelty and terror of resource extraction in the Free State since its people lacked *even* the legal status of citizens or colonial subjects.

[68] Roessler and Verhoeven (n 1) 88–89.

ammunition transfers reliant on private small-scale brokers, transporters, and micro-traders, compared to other armed conflicts around the globe where exports from major arms manufacturing corporations are more significant.

8.3.7 Linking Arms Transfers to Atrocity

There is little disagreement that human rights violations amounting to international crimes occurred on a large scale during the Second Congo War, primarily in the eastern DRC. In 2010, the Office of the United Nations High Commissioner for Human Rights (OHCHR) published a mapping exercise of 'the most serious violations of human rights and international humanitarian law committed within the territory of the DRC between March 1993 and June 2003', finding 617 separate incidents involving the possible commission of gross violations of human rights or international humanitarian law.[69] The OHCHR data was based on corroborated witness accounts and supplemented by documentary evidence.[70] Individuals in both the pro-DRC and anti-DRC alliances are alleged to have committed international crimes.[71]

Assault rifles such as the AK-47 and other SALW were the main weapons used in killings in the Second Congo War.[72] Despite the scale of the war, Major Conventional Weapons (MCW) were used to a relatively limited extent compared to other international armed conflicts of the same era,[73] although in some incidents the availability of MCW amplified the severity of the fighting in the eastern DRC.[74] Inevitably, the usage of SALW and MCW over a four-year period also required large quantities of ammunition.

A lack of accurate publicly available information about specific arms transfers in the Second Congo War, as well as high background levels of proliferation, makes it challenging to identify publicly available evidence of specific guns or ammunition that were used in specific incidents of violence. However, as discussed in this chapter, the UN Panel of Experts was able to identify and name key individual and companies. In cases where it is possible to prove that a shipment of weapons

69 OHCHR, 'Report of the Mapping Exercise documenting the most serious violations of human rights and international humanitarian law committed within the territory of the Democratic Republic of the Congo between March 1993 and June 2003' (No UN Doc number August 2010) <www.ohchr.org/EN/Countries/AfricaRegion/Pages/RDCProjetMapping.aspx> accessed 4 August 2024

70 OHCHR (n 69).

71 Benjamin Coghlan and others (n 4) 44–51; Prunier (n 1) 103.

72 Muchai (n 2) 186.

73 Muchai (n 2) 187; Mike Bourne, 'Militarization and Conflict in the Great Lakes' in Owen Green and others, *Light Weapons and Peacebuilding in Central and East Africa* (International Alert 1998) 5; Human Rights Watch, 'Covered In Blood' (n 32) 9.

74 Roessler and Verhoeven (n 1) 203–06, 233. This stands in contrast to the First Congo War in 1996 and 1997 that was fought with 'no tanks or air support used by the RPA/AFDL' who 'had to make do with basic automatic rifles' until the arrival in April 1997 of an Angolan force with heavy artillery.

or ammunition was supplied to an armed group that soon afterwards perpetrated atrocities, an important question for the legal analysis will be whether the supplied weapons were a sufficiently significant form of assistance. At least three features of the Second Congo War are salient in this analysis.

First, there was a sharp upswing in demand for weapons in the eastern DRC as the Second Congo War unfolded. On the one hand, this makes it harder to identify the impact of a specific arms transfer due to the large and complex web of transfers taking place. On the other hand, in a context where supply of weapons was unable to keep up with demand, a single shipment of weapons could play a pivotal role. It is certain that from August 1998, the severity of violence in the eastern DRC increased exponentially, and this corresponded to an increase in reports of atrocities and ramped up demand for external supplies of weapons.

As the Second Congo War continued, a localized arms race developed in the eastern DRC between competing non-state armed groups who needed to 'arm-up' to maintain control of natural resources over their adversaries, requesting their allied states to provide more and more weapons as part of the key transnational alliances discussed above. The knock-on effect on human security across the DRC was an 'increase in violent crime and domestic assaults, creating a culture of violence where disputes are settled with deadly force'.[75] This escalating gun violence inevitably meant further demand for weapons. In this scenario, where heightened demand outstripped supply (even accounting for background levels of arms proliferation), a single shipment from an arms broker could play a more pivotal role in an attack, more easily constituting a significant factor in determining whether or not an attack would go ahead, in the same manner, and with the same degree of ferocity.

Second, there was 'arming-up' of new fighters who did not previously have weapons, which again meant that a single arms shipment could be responsible for enabling these new fighters to carry out an attack. In the course of the Second Congo War, large numbers of the unarmed rural agricultural population were drawn into the conflict and became armed for the first time. Mkandawire argues that, in common with the growth of other rebel movements in African conflicts, the ability to purchase arms in the Second Congo War was what enabled formerly small-scale guerrilla groups to undergo a 'hasty transformation to conventional warfare'.[76] In eastern DRC in late 1996, the availability of weapons was said to be the primary limiting factor on the number of new *kadogo* youth fighters recruited by Kabila to join the conflict.[77] At this time, according to Prunier, 'the only limit to enrolment was the available number of AK-47s'.[78]

[75] Eavis (n 17) 253.
[76] Thandika Mkandawire (n 61) 206.
[77] Prunier (n 1) 164.
[78] Prunier (n 1) 164.

Third, ammunition is an exhaustible commodity that required replenishment throughout the conflict. Old AK-47s also have to be replaced eventually, but the depletion of ammunition has a more immediate effect on reducing the severity of a conflict. With limited domestic industrial or artisanal production in the DRC, resupplies of ammunition had to be imported across borders. A singular shipment of ammunition could thus play a decisive role in the commission, including the manner of commission, of an attack.

As such, the availability of fresh arms and ammunition was an important factor for the continuation and exacerbation of the conflict, yet obtaining evidence of sufficient links between the supply of weapons and the commission of crimes remains a challenge for criminal liability. In these circumstances, the strongest allegations would be against those individuals who were closest to the perpetrators of international crimes, notably the brokers that facilitated shipments from Rwanda and Uganda to the militia groups in the eastern DRC who were increasingly dependent on transnational shipments of weapons to maintain control of sites of natural resource extraction as the conflict wore on.

8.4 Arms Export Regulation During the Second Congo War

Having analysed the key arms flows in the Second Congo War, this chapter now turns to consider how the existing transnational assemblage of Arms Trade Law failed to prevent weapons flowing into the eastern DRC on a massive scale from Rwanda and Uganda and further afield. It examines arms export regulations, arms embargoes, and the UN fact-finding on the DRC in relation to arms flows.

Some Global North manufacturing states took steps during the Second Congo War to change their export policies to some belligerent states. The US Senate sought to prevent weapons flows to Laurent-Désiré Kabila on 16 July 1997, shortly after he took power. The Foreign Assistance Appropriation Act prohibited direct assistance to Kinshasa 'until the DRC government is cooperating fully with UN investigators' or 'any other international relief organizations in accounting for human rights violations or atrocities committed in Congo or adjacent countries'.[79] In September 1999, the US announced it would not sell arms 'to regions of conflict not already covered by arms embargoes [and] encourage[d] other nations to establish and observe such moratoria'.[80] At this time prior to the ATT of 2013, however,

[79] US State Department, Bureau of Intelligence, 'Arms Flows to Central Africa/Great Lakes Fact Sheet' (November 1999) <https://1997-2001.state.gov/global/arms/bureau_pm/fs_9911_armsflows.html> accessed 26 June 2020.

[80] Madeleine Albright, 'Statement by Secretary of State Madeleine Albright to the UN Security Council Ministerial on Small Arms' (New York, 24 September 1999). See also US State Department, 'Section 655 Annual Report for Fiscal Year 1998' (30 June 1999); Arms Export Control Act: Restraint in arms sales to Sub-Saharan Africa 22 USC §2773.

there was no multilateral treaty binding the manufacturing states to arms export standards that would have required them to assess the risk of use in atrocities in the eastern DRC.

Interestingly, several of the belligerent states to the Second Congo War sought to mutually regulate the influx of weapons into the Great Lakes Region during this period. On 15 March 2000, in the midst of the war, the DRC, Rwanda, Uganda, Burundi, and Sudan met with five other African states to conclude the Nairobi Declaration.[81] The signatories made non-binding commitments to reduce illicit arms flows and urged 'source countries to ensure that all manufacturers, traders, brokers, financiers and transporters of small arms and light weapons are regulated through licensing'.[82]

The subsequent Nairobi Protocol adopted in August 2001 required signatory states to legislate criminal sanctions for illicit trafficking in SALW, emphasized the need for 'effective controls of arms transfers by suppliers and brokers outside the region (including measures against transfer of surplus arms)', and recognized the inadequate capacity of regional states to control the proliferation of SALW.[83] Likewise, in the Bamako Declaration adopted on 1 December 2000,[84] the OAU appealed to the 'wider international community and, particularly, to arms supplier countries' to take action to regulate the arms trade.[85]

The UN Conference on SALW was also developing at this time and led to the adoption of the UN PoA. This process failed to address arms transfers to non-state armed groups, mainly because the US insisted at the outset of the Conference that it would not consider any restrictions on sales of arms to non-state armed groups.[86]

[81] The Nairobi Declaration on the Problem of the Proliferation of Illicit Small Arms and Light Weapons in the Great Lakes Region and the Horn of Africa (signed 15 March 2000) (Nairobi Declaration). The declaration was agreed at a sub-regional conference that preceded the UN Conference on SALW.

[82] Nairobi Declaration (n 81) 3. The broad language of the Nairobi Declaration was subsequently developed, also on the basis of SADC initiatives on regional arms regulation that had begun in August 1999, into the legally binding requirements of the Nairobi Protocol. SADC, The Protocol on the Control of Firearms, Ammunition and Other Related Material in the Southern African Development Community Region (adopted 14 August 2001, entered into force 8 November 2004); UNGA 'SADC Council Decisions, 13–14 August 1999: Prevention and Combating of Illicit Trafficking in Small Arms and Related Crimes' (21 October 1999) UN Doc A/54/488, S/1999/1082. Nairobi Protocol for the Prevention, Control and Reduction of Small Arms and Light Weapons in the Great Lakes Region and the Horn of Africa (adopted 21 April 2004, entered into force 5 May 2005) (Nairobi Protocol). The Nairobi Protocol led to the establishment of the RECSA regional monitoring mechanism. See Regional Centre on Small Arms in the Great Lakes Region, the Horn of Africa and Bordering states, website <https://recsasec.org> accessed on 24 June 2020.

[83] Nairobi Protocol (n 82) 2.

[84] OAU, Bamako Declaration on an African Common Position on the Illicit Proliferation, Circulation and Trafficking of Small Arms and Light Weapons (adopted 1 December 2000) (Bamako Declaration).

[85] Bamako Declaration, para V(4). The Bamako Declaration led the AU to adopt the 'Windhoek Common Position' on 16 December 2005. AU, African Common Position to the Review Conference on Progress Made in the Implementation of the UN Programme of Action to Prevent, Combat and Eradicate the Illicit Trade in Small Arms and Light Weapons in All Its Aspects (adopted 16 December 2005).

[86] UN Conference on Illicit Trade in Small Arms (2001) 95 AJIL 901, 901. This US position was contrary to its representations in the Preparatory Committees.

African states initially voiced strong disagreement, but eventually backed down to allow the agreement of the United Nations Programme of Action on Small Arms and Light Weapons (UN PoA). The UN PoA document focused on state-to-state transfers.[87]

As such, the Second Congo War was a period of significant development for African regional arms agreements.[88] The DRC, Rwanda, and Uganda were publicly acknowledging the transnational and supraregional dimensions of arms proliferation at this time in agreements that were in some respects more progressive than the later ATT. Ultimately, however, there is little evidence that these efforts had any impact on the arms flows from those states to the armed groups in the eastern DRC along the transnational alliances that were of central importance to the atrocities of the Second Congo War.[89]

8.5 Arms Embargoes During the Second Congo War

It was only on 28 July 2003, after years of inaction in the face of massive flows of weapons into the conflict zone,[90] that the Security Council eventually embargoed the DRC in Resolution 1493.[91] This came on the heels of the peace accords of May 2003 in the Global and All-inclusive Agreement that ended the Second Congo War.

The arms embargo was drafted to permit weapons to flow to the newly installed DRC government while restricting weapons to the armed groups in the eastern DRC. The operative part of Resolution 1493 required UN Member States to take the 'necessary measures to prevent the direct or indirect supply, sale or transfer of arms and any related material, and the provision of any assistance, advice or training related to military activities, to all foreign and Congolese armed groups and militias operating in the territory of North and South Kivu and of Ituri, and to groups not party to the Global and All-inclusive agreement'.[92] The EU acted in tandem. While an EU arms embargo had been in place since as long ago as 7 April 1993 with the aim of preventing weapons reaching Congolese State authorities,[93] in mid-2003 the EU modified the embargo to cover non-state armed groups only.

[87] The Conference relied extensively on a report prepared by a Group of Governmental Experts. UNGA, Report of the Group of Governmental Experts established pursuant to General Assembly resolution 54/54 V (15 December 1999).

[88] See Gani Yoroms, 'Approaches and Challenges in ECOWAS Security Sector Reform and Governance in West Africa' (2014) 1 Journal of African Foreign Affairs 30.

[89] Edward J Laurance, 'The Small Arms Problem as Arms Control: A Policy Driven Research Agenda' in Peter Batchelor and Kai Michael Kenkel (eds), *Controlling Small Arms: Consolidation, Innovation and Relevance in Research and Policy* (Routledge 2013) 13.

[90] OHCHR, Mapping Report (n 69).

[91] UNSC Res 1493 (2003) UN Doc S/RES/1493.

[92] UNSC Res 1493 (n 91).

[93] Declaration (EC) 33/93 on Zaire (entered into force 7 April 1993) [1993]. See also Council Common Position of 21 October 2002 on the supply of certain equipment into the Democratic Republic of Congo (2002/829/CFSP) [2002] OJ L285/1.

In effect, the terms of the UN embargo, and the revised EU embargo, supported the new Transitional Government in consolidating power in the eastern DRC and in its disarmament efforts.[94] They were unlike the earlier Somalia and Eritrea/Ethiopia embargoes, or the 'general and complete' embargo on Yugoslavia applicable to arms trades across the entirety of a state's territory. Instead, the DRC embargo was akin to the UNITA, Rwanda, Sierra Leone, and Iraq embargoes that served to strengthen the hand of a government against a rebel movement.[95]

That the embargo came after the conclusion of the Global and All-inclusive Agreement that officially ended the Second Congo War in May 2003 meant the Security Council was too late to prevent the war's atrocities. Even then, the Security Council decided not to establish a sanctions committee to monitor embargo breaches and not to impose travel bans and asset freezing measures that could have gone some way to sanctioning and deterring arms traffickers. A year later, Resolution 1533 established a Sanctions Committee and THE United Nations Organization Mission in the Democratic Republic of the Congo (MONUC) was authorized to monitor, collect, and dispose of arms that violated the embargo.[96] In 2005, Resolution 1596 imposed travel bans for all persons acting in violation of the embargo,[97] but retained an exemption for Congolese government forces.[98] In essence, the international arms embargo system failed to prevent weapons from fuelling atrocity during the Second Congo War, even though there had been a strong case for embargoing the whole country since at least 1998.

8.6 Politicization Critiques of Arms Embargoes

The dynamics of Security Council inaction during the Second Congo War reveal certain limitations of the international embargo system. In doing so, they also reveal possible routes for International Criminal Law to impact arms trafficking in scenarios where embargoes cannot.

The strategic use of embargoes in armed conflict is by no means unusual as a tool of state 'coercive diplomacy'.[99] It has been convincingly argued that since the 1990s sanctions have been increasingly 'aimed at affecting the internal balance of

[94] Council Regulation (EC) No 1727/2003 of 29 September 2003 concerning certain restrictive measures in respect of the Democratic Republic of Congo [2003] OJ L249/5. See also Council Common Position 2003/680/CFSP of 29 September 2003 [2003] OJ L249/64.

[95] Carina Staibano, 'Trends in UN Sanctions' in Peter Wallensteen and Carina Staibano (eds), *International Sanctions: Between Words and Wars in the Global System* (Routledge 2005) 36.

[96] UNSC Res 1533 (2004) UN Doc S/RES/1533.

[97] UNSC Res 1596 (2005) UN Doc S/RES/1596.

[98] UNSC Res 1533 (2004) UN Doc S/RES/1533.

[99] Natalino Ronzitti, 'Sanctions as Instruments of Coercive Diplomacy: An International Law Perspective' in Natalino Ronzitti (ed), *Coercive Diplomacy, Sanctions and International Law* (Martinus Nijhoff 2016) 1.

power in conflict situations'.[100] The Security Council's inaction during the Second Congo War should be seen in light of France's generally supportive attitude towards the pro-DRC alliance,[101] and the US being broadly in support of Rwanda and Uganda achieving regime change in the DRC.[102]

At the time of the war, the need for a Security Council embargo or a comprehensive EU embargo appears to have received surprisingly little attention from states or civil society. Human Rights Watch reported EU discussions in 1997 about extending the EU embargo on the DRC across the entire Great Lakes region, which would have aimed to reduce supplies of new weapons and ammunition to non-state armed groups in the eastern DRC.[103] In general, however, the Global North states appeared to remain passive, or deadlocked, pending an outcome of the war in which they could consolidate support for a winning side.[104]

This was not a new approach to embargoes in the Great Lakes Region. The UN embargo of UNITA in Angola from 1998 to 2002 was criticized as serving US foreign policy interests, no embargo being imposed for many years prior, despite extensive allegations of human rights abuses.[105] Following peace accords, a mutually shared interest emerged between former adversaries in avoiding arming-up.[106] Similarly, US efforts at the Security Council in July 1995 to lift the Rwandan arms embargo were criticized as taking sides with the Rwandan government.[107] The multilateral embargo imposed by Great Lakes Region states on Burundi on 6 August 1996 was widely seen as ineffective[108] and breaches of the sanctions by air transport increasingly diluted their impact.[109] Indeed, the Burundi and Rwanda embargoes were not only criticized as 'never serv[ing] any useful purpose' but also that the potential negative effects of such embargoes included shifting the trade 'into the hands of criminal networks'.[110]

In the Second Congo War, consistent with Burundi, Rwanda, and Angola, the Security Council's non-embargo of the DRC appears to have been shaped by a

[100] Staibano (n 95) 35.

[101] International Crisis Group, 'Congo at War: A Briefing of the Internal and External Players in the Central African Conflict' (International Crisis Group 17 November 1998).

[102] International Crisis Group (n 101).

[103] Human Rights Watch, 'Human Rights Watch World Report 1998—Rwanda' (Human Rights Watch, 1 January 1998).

[104] A passive attitude towards arms embargo unless it is in the manufacturing states' interest is consistent with Grillo's description of a 'great-power consensus' against stronger arms control Grillot (n 52) 542.

[105] UNSC Res 1173 (1998) UN Doc S/RES/1173. This led to the UN-commissioned Fowler Report and the Kimberley Process Certification Scheme for 'blood diamonds'.

[106] Roessler and Verhoeven (n 1) 376.

[107] See UNSC Res 997 (1995) UN Doc S/RES/997; Wholgemuth (n 20) 130; Muchai (n 12) 195.

[108] See Eric Hoskins, Samantha Nutt, and TJ Watson Jr, *The Humanitarian Impacts of Economic Sanctions on Burundi* (Institute for International Studies 1997). See also Gerald Prunier, 'Burundi: A Manageable Crisis?' (1994) Writenet 52.

[109] Wholgemuth (n 20) 130–31.

[110] Muchai (n 2) 195.

lack of any clear self-interest amongst the Permanent Members.[111] According to Roessler and Verhoeven, fading Cold War concerns meant that states had less interest in intervening in regional conflicts for the purposes of alliance building.[112] The US had little interest in preventing weapons flows to non-state armed groups in the eastern DRC as this would have hampered the possibility of removing Laurent-Désiré Kabila who had proved less cooperative with the US than anticipated.[113]

After the Second Congo War, with the installation of Joseph Kabila and the DRC's increasing economic cooperation, there was greater interest in reducing violence and stabilizing the eastern DRC. As Roessler and Verhoeven argue, US foreign policy towards the DRC from the end of the Cold War was largely one of indifference, as the Great Lakes region fell down the list of US strategic priorities.[114] After the war, both the Security Council and EU embargoes can be interpreted as Western states moving to 'take sides' and bolster the peace agreement.[115]

The politicization critiques of arms embargoes are a powerful reminder of the fundamental limitations of the Security Council's collective security apparatus in preventing arms from contributing to atrocity. These critiques both support and undermine the potential role of International Criminal Law. On the one hand, where the Security Council is hamstrung or disinterested, the ICC or another international(ized) or domestic jurisdictions could take action to prosecute arms traffickers who take advantage of the absence of an embargo to sell weapons that contribute to atrocity. International criminal law could play an *ex post facto* role where the preventative *ex ante* embargo system has failed. On the other hand, the political pressures on the institutions of International Criminal Law are similar to those exerted on UN bodies; they too must negotiate geopolitical demands and enforcement asymmetries.[116] Although as a judicial institution the ICC would be bound to investigate arms traffickers without fear or favour, as a political institution dependent on state cooperation, the ICC may end up just as hamstrung or disinterested at the Security Council.

Politicization critiques, however pervasive, are not the only explanation for the ineffectiveness of the UN embargo system during the Second Congo War. The familiar portrayal of the Security Council—from statist and realist perspectives—posits the self-interested use of the P5 veto as axiomatic. But this perspective must guard against what Niezen calls 'knee-jerk reactions to the most visible powers and

[111] Roessler and Verhoeven (n 1) ch 6. Furthermore, Roessler and Verhoeven argue that in the First Congo War from 1996 to 1997, an embargo would have undermined US strategic interests in seeing Mobutu Sese Seko overthrown.

[112] Roessler and Verhoeven (n 1) ch 6.

[113] Roessler and Verhoeven (n 1) ch 6.

[114] Roessler and Verhoeven (n 1) 106–07.

[115] Staibano (n 95) 35.

[116] Sergey Vasiliev, 'Watershed Moment or Same Old? Ukraine and the Future of International Criminal Justice' (2022) 20 Journal of International Criminal Justice.

incapacities' of international institutions.[117] Excessive attention to the power dynamics of the Security Council may obscure its actual decision-making processes, including on how it should respond to arms trafficking.[118] The Security Council's failure to take opportunities to act on weapon transfers during the Second Congo War may have been influenced not only by the real politics of the P5, but by perceptions, notions, and assumptions about the arms trade.

In a similar way to the institutional culture of the ICC examined in Chapter 7 and this chapter, which appeared to reject out-of-hand the idea of the Court tackling the arms trade, the Security Council status quo on embargoes may have overlooked alternative ways of responding to the arms trade. These included the potential for *ex post facto* criminal investigations, as well as closer integration with the institutions of International Criminal Law, including by ensuring the mandates granted to UN fact-finding bodies took into account the arms trade.

8.7 The Panel of Experts: Resource Extraction and Arms Trafficking

On 2 June 2000, in the midst of the Second Congo War, the Security Council requested the Secretary-General to establish an expert panel on the illegal exploitation of natural resources and other forms of wealth of the DRC (Panel of Experts).[119] The following section looks at the panel's work and how its mandate from the Security Council shaped the international response to arms trafficking in the Second Congo War.

8.7.1 The Resource Extraction Mandate

The initial mandate of the Panel of Experts was centred on the links between the exploitation of natural resources and the continuation of the conflict.[120] This reflected that the violence of the Second Congo War became inextricably linked to the control of resources in the areas of Ituri and the Kivus in the eastern DRC.[121]

[117] Ronald Niezen and Maria Sapignoli (eds), *Palaces of Hope: The Anthropology of Global Organizations* (CUP 2017); Richard Wilson (ed), *Human Rights, Culture and Context* (Pluto 1997).

[118] Niels Nagelhus Schia, 'Horseshoe and Catwalk: Power, Complexity, and Consensus-Making in the United Nations Security Council' in Niezen and Sapignoli (n 117) 55.

[119] UNSC, 'Statement by the President of the Security Council' (2 June 2000) UN Doc S/PRST/2000/20; UNSC, 'Letter from the Secretary-General' (14 August 2000) UN Doc S/2000/796.

[120] UNSC, 'Statement by the President of the Security Council' (2 June 2000) UN Doc S/PRST/2000/20, para 4.

[121] See UNSC, 'Interim report of the United Nations Expert Panel on the Illegal Exploitation of Natural Resources and Other Forms of Wealth of the Democratic Republic of the Congo' (16 January 2001) UN Doc S/2001/49; UNSC, 'Interim report of the United Nations Expert Panel on the Illegal Exploitation of Natural Resources and Other Forms of Wealth of the Democratic Republic of the Congo' (22 May 2002) UN Doc S/2002/565.

Prunier charts how resources drove the origins of war, arguing that in September 1997, allegations of refugee massacres were '[only of concern] to *some members* of the international community [...] for many others the main worry seemed to be about how business as usual could be reinstated'.[122] Despite Laurent-Désiré Kabila's stated intention to establish new relationships with US mining companies, as Prunier puts it, Kabila ended up renewing deals with 'the traditional South African and Belgian predators'.[123] This view underscores that geopolitical contestation of natural resources in the eastern DRC was central to how the Second Congo War unfolded.

Civil society organizations recognized the need to restrict the extraction of conflict minerals, gold, coltan, and other natural resources that was contributing to atrocity, by regulating 'the transport of [coltan] ore to European destinations [and] mechanisms to monitor the minerals trade from the Great Lakes and other conflict regions'.[124] Like the initial mandate of the Panel of Experts, international responses to the Second Congo War centred on resource extraction and on improving ethical standards in supply chains that would allow extraction to continue. As Roessler and Verhoeven point out, characterizations of the Second Congo War as a 'resource war' were overly dominant in literature and policy.[125]

The initial mandate granted by the Security Council on 2 June 2000 limited the analysis of the Panel of Experts to resource extraction as a relatively isolated phenomenon. The experts' interpretation of their mandate would frame the range of conclusions they could reach.[126] While drawn from global civil society and nominally independent, such experts are ultimately appointed by the UN and restricted by the terms of the Resolutions that renew their tenure.[127] The problem with the approach taken in the Security Council's initial mandate was that it overlooked the reality of arms trafficking on the ground: fresh supplies of weaponry were necessary for armed groups obtaining control over the mines in the eastern DRC, and the sale of extracted resources funded the purchase of further weaponry.

8.7.2 Initial Findings on Arms Supplies

The Panel of Experts nonetheless documented the role of the arms trade in the DRC. Its report of 12 April 2001 referred to the role of arms brokers including

122 Prunier (n 1) 159 (emphasis original).
123 Prunier (n 1) 167.
124 Jeroen Cuvelier and Tim Raeymaekers, 'European Companies and The Coltan Trade: An Update Part 2' (International Peace Information Service, September 2002) 3.
125 Roessler and Verhoeven (n 1).
126 Turner (n 10) 163.
127 John Keane, *Global Civil Society?* (CUP 2003); Mary Kaldor, 'The Idea of Global Civil Society' (2003) 79 International Affairs 583.

Viktor Bout.[128] The report found 'a number of companies have been involved and have fuelled the war directly, trading arms for natural resources. Others have facilitated access to financial resources, which are used to purchase weapons.'[129] It recommended an immediate arms embargo on the supply of weapons to 'the rebel groups operating in the DRC' and 'to consider extending this embargo to the States that support or assist those groups'.[130] This report was made confidential and was not released until December 2009.

An addendum dated 13 November 2001 discussed the supply of arms from the DRC authorities,[131] while referring to the security concerns of Rwanda and Uganda in invading the DRC.[132] A subsequent report issued on 22 May 2002 indicated, without making specific findings, that '[t]he relationship between the exploitation activities and arms trafficking and other organized criminal activities is also a part of the Panel's investigations'.[133]

By the time of its report on 16 October 2002, the Panel of Experts was identifying specific individuals involved in arms trafficking. As well as the mining companies, financiers, and resource transporters, the Panel now emphasized the nexus between arms transfer conduct and resource exploitation and its links to conflict and insecurity.[134] It listed in its Annexes a number of Belgian and French companies involved in supplying weapons and ammunition to the DRC government, and the brokers Viktor Bout and Leonard Minin, Belgian ammunition manufacturer George Forrest, businessman John Bredenkamp, and other individuals and companies.[135] Its conclusions mentioned that 'Restrictive measures nevertheless need to be taken vis-à-vis the role of companies and individuals involved in arms supply and resource plundering', but at this time the Panel did not draw explicit conclusions about the role of Uganda or Rwanda in supplying weapons.[136]

[128] UNSC, 'Report of the Panel of Experts on the Illegal Exploitation of Natural Resources and Other Forms of Wealth of the Democratic Republic of the Congo' (12 April 2001) UN Doc S/2001/357, paras 73, 74, 91.

[129] UNSC (n 128) para 215.

[130] UNSC (n 128).

[131] UNSC, 'Addendum to the report of the Panel of Experts on the Illegal Exploitation of Natural Resources and Other Forms of Wealth of the Democratic Republic of the Congo' (13 November 2001) UN Doc S/2001/1072, paras 67, 136.

[132] UNSC (n 131) paras 91, 95.

[133] UNSC, 'Interim report of the United Nations Expert Panel on the Illegal Exploitation of Natural Resources and Other Forms of Wealth of the Democratic Republic of the Congo' (22 May 2002) UN Doc S/2002/565.

[134] UNSC, 'Final Report of the Panel of Experts on the Illegal Exploitation of Natural Resources and Other Forms of Wealth of the Democratic Republic of the Congo' (16 October 2002) UN Doc S/2002/1146.

[135] UNSC (n 134) paras 29–31.

[136] UNSC (n 134).

8.7.3 Revising the Annexes

On 20 June 2003, an Addendum to the previous report was issued setting out the responses from the named individual and companies.[137] The Panel's report clearly had some impact. A Belgian diamond company submitted that: 'The result [of the Panel report] for people and companies mentioned was devastating.'[138] The 20 June 2003 Addendum removed from the Annexed individuals and companies that had change their practices, without considering the need for *ex post facto* accountability. The Panel nonetheless recognized the negotiated compromise it had entered into: 'It should be stressed that resolution should not be seen as invalidating the Panel's earlier findings with regard to the activities of those actors.'[139]

The Panel stated it 'was able to show the companies concerned that their behaviour was widely perceived to be suspect'.[140] It was unclear whether the Panel's exoneration of the individuals and companies removed from the revised version of the Report was contingent on the entities making long-term changes to their operations. In some cases, the Panel accepted the response of a company, thereby engaging in a sort of quasi restorative justice: 'it became apparent that their business practices could be viewed as acceptable in that they make positive contributions to their communities in providing goods and services, as well as jobs for local people'.[141] The potential for accountability was not at the forefront of the Panel's findings.

8.7.4 A New Mandate on Arms Trafficking

By revising the mandate of the Panel of Experts on 13 August 2003,[142] the Security Council included the role of arms trafficking in the eastern DRC. But it did this only after the war finished, following the Global and All-inclusive Agreement in May 2003 and the Security Council embargo on 28 July 2003 on non-state armed groups in the eastern DRC.[143] The new mandate added additional areas, explicitly requesting the experts to consider the connection between resource exploitation and 'the illicit trade of small arms and light weapons'.[144] It was not until 23 October

[137] UNSC, 'Addendum to the Final Report of the Panel of Experts on the Illegal Exploitation of Natural Resources and Other Forms of Wealth of the Democratic Republic of the Congo' (20 June 2003) UN Doc S/2002/1146/Add.1.

[138] UNSC (n 137) 358.

[139] UNSC, 'Final Report of the Panel of Experts on the Illegal Exploitation of Natural Resources and Other Forms of Wealth of the Democratic Republic of the Congo' (23 October 2003) UN Doc S/2003/1027 9 (emphasis added).

[140] UNSC Revised Final Report of the Panel of Experts (n 139) 10.

[141] UNSC Revised Final Report of the Panel of Experts (n 139) 11.

[142] Resolution 1499 (2003) UN Doc S/RES/1499.

[143] UNSC Res 1493 (2003) UN Doc S/RES/1493.

[144] UNSC Res 1499 (2003) UN Doc S/RES/1499, para 6.

2003 that the Panel of Experts issued its report that reflected the revised mandate and was very much focused on the role of the arms trade. Now the Panel concluded 'it is very difficult to stem or halt illegal exploitation [of resources] without also tackling the issue of arms trafficking'.[145] In sum, after the war was over, the Security Council's revisions to the mandate, in effect, bolstered the one-sided embargo on weapons to armed groups by drawing attention to the Panel's work on arms trafficking in the eastern DRC.

8.7.5 Implicating Rwanda and Uganda

In November 2003, the Panel of Experts sent a Confidential Supplement to the Security Council in which it detailed the transfer of arms from Rwanda and Uganda to eastern DRC (the 'anti-DRC alliance').[146] It was not until Human Rights Watch and Amnesty International republished findings from the leaked Confidential Supplement in mid-2005 that it was widely known that the Panel had made extensive findings of Rwandan and Ugandan weapons transfers to the eastern DRC.

The Panel made extensive allegations that mortars, machine guns, and ammunition were sent from Rwanda to the UPC in Ituri between November 2002 and January 2003.[147] Rwanda rented arms to the RCD-Goma,[148] and trained UPC combatants.[149] Rwandan airline companies flew weapons to Goma.[150] The UPC had received arms from the Balkans and South Africa.[151] Key UPC commanders reported directly to the Rwandan army high command,[152] and funds were transferred directly from the Ugandan Office of the Presidency to support armed groups in Ituri, with arms and military supplies provided to these groups on a coordinated, institutional basis.[153] Meanwhile, the DRC government received SALW shipments from Jordan,[154] and arms from the DRC government were provided to ex-FAR/Interahamwe and a Mai Mai commander in South Kivu.[155]

Moreover, Human Rights Watch, in publicizing the November 2003 Supplement deliberately recognized the potential of International Criminal Law accountability for individuals involved in arms transfers from Rwanda and Uganda to allied non-state armed groups in the eastern DRC.[156] In the final recommendations of its

145 UNSC Revised Final Report of the Panel of Experts (n 139) para. 47.
146 Human Rights Watch, Curse of Gold (n 39) 25. Amnesty International, 'Democratic Republic of Congo: Arming the East' (Amnesty International, 4 July 2005).
147 Human Rights Watch, Curse of Gold (n 39) 25, 35, 124. See also 39.
148 Amnesty International (n 146) 34.
149 Human Rights Watch, Curse of Gold (n 39) 24.
150 Amnesty International (n 146) 36.
151 Amnesty International (n 146) 24.
152 Human Rights Watch, Curse of Gold (n 39) 27.
153 Human Rights Watch, Curse of Gold (n 39) 123.
154 Amnesty International (n 146) 38.
155 Amnesty International (n 146) 5960.
156 See Human Rights Watch, Curse of Gold (n 39) 63, 127.

report 'Curse of Gold', Human Rights Watch called upon the ICC to 'investigate the links between individuals and armed groups involved in natural resources extraction who may have contributed to war crimes and crimes against humanity in Ituri'.[157] Later, in 2006, the NGO commented that in the DRC Situation, '[w]e believe that the prosecutor's investigation should include those who armed and supported militia groups operating in Ituri, which may extend to senior officials in Kinshasa, Kampala and Kigali'.[158] And soon after, it noted with concern that the ICC had still not issued arrest warrants against senior political figures, not only in the DRC, but also in Uganda or Rwanda who 'backed [...] armed groups' in the DRC.[159]

The inner machinations of the Panel of Experts and its relationship to the Security Council are beyond the scope of this book,[160] but even from this analysis it is clear that there was a tension between the Security Council's restrictive initial mandate granted to the experts, and the shift at the end of the Second Congo War to a mandate looking at the 'insecurity problem' in the eastern DRC, and the increasing attempts of the Panel of Experts to make detailed allegations against arms traders, specifically involving brokers involved in shipping weapons from Rwanda and Uganda to allied non-state armed groups in the eastern DRC.

8.8 Conclusion

Arms transfers came to play an increasingly important role in atrocities committed in the Second Congo War—even with existing levels of arms proliferation, the scale and manner of commission of atrocities would not have been the same without renewed in-flows of weapons. During the war, the existing mechanisms of Arms Trade Law—export regulation, international agreements, and UN and EU arms embargoes—were largely ineffective at preventing these weapons from reaching atrocities. Analysing the Security Council's embargo practice and its mandate to the Panel of Experts reveals that Arms Trade Law was deployed strategically at the end of the conflict rather than in response to the threat of international crimes during the conflict, for example through the imposition of a much

157 See Human Rights Watch, Curse of Gold (n 39) 8.

158 Human Rights Watch, 'The Selection of Situations and Cases for Trial before the International Criminal Court: A Human Rights Watch Policy Paper' (Human Rights Watch, October 2006) citing Human Rights Watch, 'D.R. Congo: ICC Arrest First Step to Justice' (*Human Rights Watch news release*, 17 March 2006) <www.hrw.org/news/2006/03/17/dr-congo-icc-arrest-first-step-justice> accessed 25 June 2020.

159 Human Rights Watch, 'Democratic Republic of Congo and the International Criminal Court, Report on the Hearing to Confirm the Charges against Thomas Lubanga Dyilo' (Human Rights Watch, November 2006) 7.

160 Catherine Harwood, 'Contributions of International Commissions of Inquiry to Transitional Justice' in Cheryl Lawther, Luke Moffett, and Dov Jacobs, *Research Handbook on Transitional Justice* (Edward Elgar Publishing 2017) 401–23.

called-for embargo. For the victims of atrocity in the eastern DRC, this was too little, too late.

International arms brokers were able to play an indispensable role in funnelling weapons to the perpetrators of atrocity with virtually no *ex ante* preventative legal regulation, and experiencing *ex post facto* impunity. While the role of major arms manufacturing corporations and transnational organized crime groups in the arms trade is often emphasized in commentary on the arms trade, the Second Congo War shows the essentiality of elite actors at the local level and brokers who were geographically and causally proximate to the atrocities. These individuals, rather than major arms manufacturing corporations or complex transnational organized crime groups, were at the forefront of enabling the DRC, Rwanda, and Uganda to supply weapons to their allied non-state armed groups in the eastern DRC.

The rules on complicity in International Criminal Law were applicable to, but were not enforced against, international arms brokers in the conflict. Their individual conduct in transferring weapons and ammunition may have in some cases contributed to the commission of specific international crimes. Insofar as the Security Council and Panel of Expert were concerned with the arms trade, the only legal responses under consideration appeared to be embargoes and the strengthening of domestic export regulations. This perspective viewed regulation through the preventative lens of Arms Trade Law, paying insufficient attention to the lens of international criminal accountability. As Autesserre has articulated, the Security Council's focus on resource extraction in the eastern DRC restricted its ability to see other potential responses to the conflict.[161] Those responses could have included shutting down key international arms brokers, including by recognizing the potential involvement of the newly operational ICC, as reflected in Ocampo's announcement from September 2003, and reiterated by Human Rights Watch in its call in 2005, for the Court to investigate arms traders. With this in mind, Chapter 9 returns to consider the potential role of the ICC and the relevance of legal culture in shaping how the Situation in the DRC unfolded.

[161] Séverine Autesserre, 'Dangerous Tales: Dominant Narratives on the Congo and their Unintended Consequences' (2012) 111 African Affairs 202.

9
Overlooking Arms Brokers in the ICC's Situation in the DRC

9.1 Introduction

In its formative years after the commencement of the ICC's temporal jurisdiction on 1 July 2002, the atrocities of the Second Congo War presented an early opportunity to enforce International Criminal Law. The expressed intention of Prosecutor Ocampo to examine international arms suppliers and the exploitation of resources[1] could have led to an arrest warrant based on charges for arms transfer conduct under Article 25(3)(d)(ii) liability.[2] This would have offered a powerful symbol that the Court's fight against impunity was directed not only at military and political figures but also at commercial actors such as the small-scale arms brokers, transporters, and micro-traders whose activities are poorly regulated by Arms Trade Law.[3] Chapter 8 provided a fine-grained analysis of those activities and their poor regulation.

This chapter now examines the ICC's DRC Situation and the unfulfilled potential to prosecute arms traders, in light of the earlier chapters about the Court's institutional culture, in which arms transfers were viewed through the lens of Arms Trade Law rather than international criminal accountability.[4] Going beyond the familiar dialectic between law and politics reveals as to how the assumptions, beliefs, and commitments of ICC judges and lawyers play a role in shaping case selection. The DRC Situation illustrates how the scope of application of the Rome Statute's modes of liability can become narrowed when case selection focuses on certain priorities and justifications. This narrowing is characterized in this chapter in terms of four 'blind spots', which contributed to obscuring the arms trade in the DRC Situation. These are blind spots over: (i) politically viable arms trade cases;

[1] Luis Moreno Ocampo, 'Report of the Prosecutor of the ICC Second Assembly of States Parties to the Rome Statute of the International Criminal Court' (*ICC Legal Tools Database*, 8 September 2003) <www.legal-tools.org/doc/8873bd/> accessed 24 June 2020: 'those who direct mining operations, sell diamonds or gold extracted in these conditions, launder the dirty money or provide weapons could also be authors of the crimes, even if they are based in other countries'. See Human Rights Watch, 'Democratic Republic of Congo: The Curse of Gold' (Human Rights Watch, 2 June 2005) 8, 63, 127.

[2] See Chapters 4 and 5.

[3] See Chapters 1 to 3.

[4] See Chapter 6.

The Arms Trade and International Criminal Law. Tomas Hamilton, Oxford University Press. © Tomas Hamilton 2025.
DOI: 10.1093/oso/9780192868671.003.0009

(ii) 'pragmatic' arms trade prosecutions; (iii) the interests of victims in arms trade cases; and (iv) horizontal selectivity.

In describing the focus of the ICC's attention in the DRC Situation in terms of 'blind spots', this chapter seeks a thicker understanding of case selection based on Garland's observation that the institutional frameworks of criminal law tend to 'narrow our perceptions of punishment'.[5] Lodge describes blind spots as a feature not only of how 'organizations and policies are designed and operated', but also how 'these operations are studied and evaluated'.[6] In other words, blind spots are not concerned simply with *not seeing*, they are concerned with *not seeing the not seeing*.

Blind spots are associated with unintended consequences, and rather than depending on irrationality or bias, they involve organizations not even realizing what is being excluded from view.[7] The ICC's blind spots therefore highlight, firstly, the ways in which the Prosecutor's initial view of a broad range of actors in the DRC Situation came to be narrowed to exclude the arms trade, but secondly, how this narrowing may not have been recognized in the awareness of ICC practitioners (nor in commentary literature on the ICC). The chapter draws on scholarship referred to earlier in the book, whose critiques of the ICC recognize similar blind spot processes. Section 9.2 discusses the potential arms trade cases in the DRC Situation that could have been selected for investigation and prosecution. Sections 9.3 to 9.6 address each of the four blind spots.

9.2 Recognizing Potential Arms Trade Cases in the DRC Situation

The announcement of the ICC Prosecutor on 8 September 2003 showed that Ocampo was already considering arms traders as potential suspects for the DRC Situation.[8] The Prosecutor's approach to case selection is reflected in the draft Policy Paper publicly disseminated as early as June 2003,[9] which was the precursor to the OTP Regulations, in interim form, an aim of which was to legitimate the Prosecutor's case selection decisions.[10] As such, even though they were formalized

[5] David Garland, *Punishment and Modern Society: A Study in Social Theory* (Clarendon Press 1991) 1.

[6] Martin Lodge, 'Accounting for Blind Spots' in Tobias Bach and Kai Wegrich (eds), *The Blind Spots of Public Bureaucracy and the Politics of Non-Coordination* (Palgrave Macmillan 2019) 29, 32.

[7] Lodge (n 6) 32.

[8] Moreno Ocampo (n 1).

[9] OTP, 'Draft paper on some policy issues before the Office of the Prosecutor for discussion at the public hearing in The Hague on 17 and 18 June 2003' (18 June 2003) <www.legal-tools.org/doc/abb9f7/> accessed 10 May 2020.

[10] OTP, 'Paper on some policy issues before the Office of the Prosecutor' (5 September 2003) <www.legal-tools.org/doc/f53870/> accessed 10 May 2020.

subsequently, the OTP Regulations provide insight into the Prosecutor's case selection policy in the DRC Situation.[11]

At some point in negotiating with the DRC government, the Prosecutor narrowed his initially broad scope of potentially liable individuals for investigation: the arms trade cases were excluded from consideration. This is clear from the Prosecutor's diplomatic briefing on 12 February 2004, at which point the Prosecutor had already developed 'a division of labour' with the Congolese government, whereby the OTP would 'prosecute the leaders who bear the greatest responsibility', and the DRC 'with the assistance of the international community, could implement appropriate mechanisms to address other responsible individuals'.[12] The DRC then referred the Situation in its territory to the ICC on 3 March 2004, some six months after the Prosecutor's announcement about arms traders.[13]

The Prosecutor's announcement of 8 September 2003 came while the Panel of Experts was preparing its final report (dated 15 October 2003). The Panel was now working in accordance with its revised mandate from the Security Council on arms trafficking, which had followed from the recent imposition of the Security Council arms embargo on 28 July 2003.[14] The Prosecutor indicated he was awaiting the publication of the Panel's report in the context of investigations into those implicated in resource extraction.[15] Later, the Lubanga trial proceedings decided not to admit into evidence the findings of the Panel of Experts, including on the role of Rwanda and Uganda in the eastern DRC.[16] The mid-2003 shift of stance of the Security Council on weapons supplies to the eastern DRC may help explain why the Prosecutor had arms trade suspects in mind.

When the Security Council and the Panel of Experts made reference to the potential response to the individuals and companies implicated in the supply of arms linked to resource extraction during the Second Congo War,[17] they did not refer to international criminal accountability, instead focusing on the potential of embargoes and export regulations. In particular, when the Panel of Experts recommended on 23 October 2003 that 'information and documentation could be useful for an arms monitoring mechanism', the Panel could have also recognized the potential role for international crimes prosecutions of arms trades.[18]

11 OTP, Policy Paper (n 10) preamble.

12 Luis Moreno Ocampo, 'Statement of the Prosecutor Luis Moreno Ocampo to Diplomatic Corps, The Hague, Netherlands' (*ICC Legal Tools Database*, 12 February 2004) 4<www.legal-tools.org/doc/6dvm3d/>.

13 The DRC had ratified the Rome Statute in April 2002. This was the second State Party referral to the ICC of a situation on its territory following Uganda's referral of the situation on its territory on 29 January 2004.

14 Chapter 7.

15 Moreno Ocampo (n 1).

16 ICC-01/04-01/06-2135, 22 September 2009, paras 26–34.

17 Chapter 7.

18 UNSC, 'Final Report of the Panel of Experts on the Illegal Exploitation of Natural Resources and Other Forms of Wealth of the Democratic Republic of the Congo' (23 October 2003) UN Doc S/2003/1027, para 47.

Members of civil society did recognize this potential. Soon after the publication of the Panel of Expert's final report on 23 October 2003, the NGO Transparency International explicitly identified that the findings of the Panel of Experts could be part of the ICC's nascent investigation in the DRC Situation, calling for the Security Council to support the ICC's investigations into arms traders.[19] The OTP would certainly have been aware of the potential support from civil society for these arms trade cases at this time.

The UN Panel of Experts identified individuals who would be within the jurisdiction of the ICC, including international arms broker Victor Bout.[20] His alleged notoriety and wide ranging brokering activities across several jurisdictions, to feed numerous conflicts including the DRC, and his alleged record of violating export regulations, made him a candidate for investigations.[21] Bout had been named in UN reports since at least 1998, had Interpol Red Notices issued against him, and was later arrested in 2008 and convicted in New York in 2011.[22] If the ICC Prosecutor had wanted a high-profile suspect at the start of the ICC's work to send a symbolic message that the Court took the structural causes of violence seriously, international brokers such as Bout could have proved suitable targets.

In assessing the Prosecutor's decision not to prosecute the arms trade cases, it is important to recall the legal framework for ICC case selection analysed in Chapter 7 and its deficiencies in providing determinate legal rules, which mean that case selection relies on a broad prosecutorial and judicial discretion.[23] In this legal context, blind spots over the potential to select certain types of case can come to play a more significant role in case selection than they would otherwise in a system of more structured discretion.

9.3 Blind Spot 1: Politically Viable Arms Trade Cases

Critiques of the ICC's intervention in the DRC have often focused on political compromises made by the Court in securing suspects for its earliest trials.[24] While political constraint may explain why certain cases were chosen in the DRC Situation and not others, it is insufficient to fully explain the non-selection of arms trade cases. ICC judges and lawyers may not have imagined arms trade cases as 'appropriate' for the DRC Situation, for reasons that have less to do with the Rome

[19] Transparency International, 'UN Should Support ICC Investigations into Links Between Corrupt Business and War Crimes in DRC (Transparency International, 4 November 2003).

[20] Chapter 7.

[21] UNSC, Revised Final Report of the Panel of Experts (n 18).

[22] Chapter 8.

[23] See Chapter 7.

[24] Phil Clark, *Distant Justice: The Impact of the International Criminal Court on African Politics* (CUP 2018).

Statute and more to do with the ICC's legal culture, as seen in the two 'frames' in Chapter 6.

The first four suspects in the DRC Situation were all leaders of non-state armed groups in Ituri province—Thomas Lubanga, Bosco Ntaganda, Germain Katanga, and Mathieu Ngudjolo. According to Clark's analysis, the charges against these individuals, came about as a result of a negotiated compromise between the Prosecutor and senior members of the Congolese executive in Kinshasa, a compromise that was not shared by senior judicial officials in Ituri, some of whom considered that 'the ICC should [have been] handling bigger cases than [it was prosecuting]'.[25] The Prosecutor was eager for the DRC to make a self-referral to the ICC to avoid using his *proprio motu* power to initiate proceedings.[26] Furthermore, the Prosecutor had been 'actively on the lookout for the Ituri situation in north-eastern DRC' since he was sworn in.[27] In Clark's account, the ICC was so concerned with the threat of non-cooperation from states that it overlooked the extent to which states were interested in manipulating case selection for their own political gain.[28]

Similarly, Schiff argues that Joseph Kabila instrumentalized the ICC as a tool for post-conflict consolidation of power, while the Prosecutor saw potential in Kabila's cooperativeness.[29] In Burke-White's view, Kabila's calculated self-interest in consolidating power against opponents for the Presidency and disassociating himself from the violence of the past,[30] led him to make the ICC referral and subsequently to support the ICC's investigations.[31] This would, accordingly, reduce domestic political threats to Kabila while allowing an externalization of the political costs involved.[32] The ICC thus offered a means to neutralize domestic opponents who had been involved in the conflict.

The narrowing of DRC Situation case selection to exclude arms traders is consistent with Cryer's claim that early ICC practice contributed to a narrowing of the scope of application of International Criminal Law.[33] State Parties regarded the ICC as an 'unsafe' tribunal posing unpredictable threats to their interests (due its broad jurisdictional range over many states and individuals and the case selection powers

[25] Clark, *Distant Justice* (n 24) 179.

[26] Clark, *Distant Justice* (n 24) 105.

[27] Clark, *Distant Justice* (n 24) 105.

[28] Clark, *Distant Justice* (n 24) 182.

[29] Benjamin N Schiff, *Building the International Criminal Court* (CUP 2008) 213.

[30] His four Vice-Presidents, including Jon-Pierre Bemba, were considered potential threats to his Presidency.

[31] William W Burke-White, 'Complementarity in Practice: The International Criminal Court as Part of a System of Multi-level Global Governance in the Democratic Republic of Congo' (2005) 18 Leiden Journal of International Law 557, 564.

[32] Burke-White (n 31) 567: 'Kabila [could] let the international community do his bidding, without bearing the domestic political costs of prosecution'.

[33] Robert Cryer, 'Prosecuting the Leaders: Promises, Politics and Pragmatics' (2009) 1 Göttingen Journal of International Law 45.

of the Prosecutor).[34] The ICC was thus distinguished from 'safe' tribunals' like the ICTR with their more limited and prescribed mandates.[35] Cryer's account would suggest a significant political pressure on the first Prosecutor to be seen as non-threatening to States Parties in his early work. And in this context, the Prosecutor may have reached for the more predictable types of cases against militia leaders, considering that these would satisfy political constraints. In so doing, he may have overlooked that international arms brokers could also have been politically feasible cases.

In focusing on political constraint, the law-versus-politics critiques inadequately represents the breadth of cases that could have been acceptable to Kabila. Politicization may explain why cases against Ituri rebel leaders were selected, while DRC government officials avoided prosecution. But a politicization critique does not adequately explain why arms traders were not selected. Certain arms suppliers may have been in Kabila's interest to prosecute; he already stood to benefit from the Security Council's post-war embargo that was aimed at preventing transfers to non-state armed groups in the eastern DRC to consolidate Kabila's new government. And he must have been aware that the Security Council Panel of Experts had investigated individuals including Victor Bout whose cases could have been part of a negotiated compromise with the ICC.

At the same time, according to these critiques, the Prosecutor may have been wary of implicating the involvement of actors, particularly Rwanda and Uganda, in the provision of weapons used in the eastern DRC. In Danner's critical scholarship on the ICC, the Prosecutor's autonomy is restricted by the fact that it is pragmatically accountable to states, even including non-party states.[36] Adopting Danner's perspective, the Prosecutor's selection of cases in the DRC would have needed to take into account the potential threat of a Security Council deferral of the DRC investigation; the risk of losing funding from donations, whether from individual State's withdrawal of voluntary contributions, or collectively through the UNGA's non-support for funding; and the constant danger of reduced international co-operation and judicial assistance of states.[37]

Danner describes how the EU and France took an active role in influencing the DRC to make a self-referral to the ICC—pressuring Kabila to improve his international standing.[38] Woudenberg notes the international pressure to prosecute charges against Lubanga concerning the killing of Bangladeshi MONUC peacekeepers.[39] In addition, states in the Great Lakes Region had an interest in

[34] Robert Cryer, 'The Boundaries of Liability in International Criminal Law, or Selectivity by Stealth' (2001) 3 Journal of Conflict and Security Law 6.

[35] Cryer (n 34) 100, 315.

[36] Allison Marston Danner, 'Enhancing the Legitimacy and Accountability of Prosecutorial Discretion at the International Criminal Court' (2003) 97 AJIL 525 ff.

[37] Danner (n 36) 527.

[38] Schiff (n 29) 212–13.

[39] Anneke van Woudenberg, 'Arrest All Ituri Warlords' (11 March 2005) *Le Potentiel*.

the outcome of the ICC's involvement in the DRC Situation, such as the Rwandan and Ugandan interest in avoiding prosecutions that would emphasize their role in the conflict. Nonetheless, the Prosecutor may not have been aware that he was overlooking opportunities and possibilities of arms trade cases that would have been attractive to external political actors.

In sum, critiques of the ICC have emphasized the overriding impact of political viability in DRC case selection. Yet the 'law versus politics' dialectic can be reductive, overemphasizing the intentionality and foresight of the actors involved while under-acknowledging the role of cultural assumptions, beliefs, and commitments. It may not have been a deliberate intention of Kabila and the Prosecutor to rule out arms traders from consideration. Both may have wanted cases that were politically feasible, and the rebel militia leaders were prima facie the most obvious targets. But they were not necessarily the only feasible cases, and the Prosecutor might well have found unexpected support for arms traders prosecutions at the UN, EU, or amongst regional states. Moving against international arms brokers could also have been consistent with mutually beneficial compromise, had this avenue been more prominent in the minds of ICC and DRC decision-makers.

It is more likely that, after the Prosecutor's initial enthusiasm for arms trader cases in the 8 September 2003 announcement, the DRC referral began to materialize, and the focus of the discussions turned to what were understood to be the most politically acceptable cases—the Ituri warlords—the unintended consequence of which was to overlook whole categories of actors. This would be consistent with the findings of Chapter 6, that arms traders tended to be overlooked or dismissed as potential cases for the ICC; they were not a type of perpetrator readily envisaged in the Court's institutional culture.

9.4 Blind Spot 2: Pragmatic Arms Trade Prosecutions

Consistent with Clark's analysis of the ICC's negotiations with Kabila in the DRC Situation, the Ituri warlord suspects were perceived to be not only politically viable targets for prosecution; they were also viewed as 'pragmatic' in the sense of being relatively 'convenient', 'easy', and 'safe' to prosecute. In focusing on these cases, the OTP may have overlooked the potential for arms trade prosecutions that could also have been pragmatic choices.

In terms of 'convenience, Lubanga, for instance, was viewed as a convenient choice since he was already available to the Prosecutor under house arrest in the Grand Hotel in Kinshasa. Obtaining other potential suspects may have involved putting more ICC investigators into the field in eastern DRC. Other cases may have been relatively difficult to investigate or prosecute due to the DRC government's lack of ability to apprehend them or carry out investigations in the eastern DRC.[40]

The Ituri warlord cases were seen as relatively 'easy' cases because the investigation would be facilitated by the progress of in-country evidence collection and the development of the DRC judiciary in Ituri province (notwithstanding that the DRC self-referral implied that the ICC would itself be investigating and prosecuting these cases).[41] The Prosecutor recognized that Article 17 of the Rome Statute in effect meant that he should focus his energies on cases that DRC authorities were unwilling or unable to investigate and prosecute,[42] and it was true that the central DRC authorities had taken minimal steps to investigate Lubanga.[43] However, it has been argued that the Prosecutor chose cases where the local (eastern DRC) authorities' ability and willingness to prosecute was in fact relatively enhanced.[44] Ituri had recently received external assistance improving the capacity of the local judicial system and these cases might have been pursued in the DRC.[45]

There was pressure on the Prosecutor to select cases that were seen as 'safe' in light of legal ambiguities in the Rome Statute that would make cases less likely to succeed at trial.[46] As the DRC Situation progressed, internal tensions between the Office of the Prosecutor of the International Criminal Court (OTP) and the Pre-Trial Chamber (PTC) grew over procedural issues and the issuance of arrest warrants, as both organs asserted greater control over the investigations.[47] In this regard, arms trade cases could have been viewed as less certain to fall within the ambit of the Article 25 modes of liability. Yet the legal basis analysed in Chapters 4 and 5 could have reassured these doubts had arms traders been given careful consideration as potential suspects.

Thus the Ituri warlords seemed like the most 'convenient', 'easy', and 'safe' prosecutions to aim for, while decision-makers at the Court may have overlooked whether investigations into arms brokers could also satisfy these criteria. This recalls Chapter 6's discussion of the assumptions, beliefs, and commitments of ICC

[40] Burke-White (n 31) 586.

[41] Phil Clark, 'Grappling in the Great Lakes: The Challenges of International Justice in Rwanda, the Democratic Republic of Congo and Uganda' in Brett Bowden, Hilary Charlesworth, and Jeremy Farrall (eds), *Great Expectations: The Role of International Law in Restructuring Societies after Conflict* (CUP 2009).

[42] Ocampo stated that 'As a general rule, the policy of the Office of the Prosecutor will be to undertake investigations only where there is a clear case of failure to act by the State or states concern(ed).' See OTP, Draft Policy Paper (n 9) 5.

[43] Human Rights Watch, 'Democratic Republic of Congo and the International Criminal Court, Report on the Hearing to Confirm the Charges against Thomas Lubanga Dyilo' (Human Rights Watch, November 2006) 7.

[44] Phil Clark, 'Law, Politics and Pragmatism: The ICC and Case Selection in the Democratic Republic of Congo and Uganda' in Nicholas Waddell and Phil Clark (ed), *Courting Conflict: Justice, Peace and the ICC in Africa* (Royal African Society 2008).

[45] Clark, 'Law, Politics and Pragmatism' (n 44).

[46] Schiff (n 29) 215–19.

[47] Schiff (n 29) 215–19.

judges and lawyers about the pragmatic constraints on prosecuting arms trader cases, which were perceived as too 'difficult', 'dangerous', or 'technically complex'. The notion that Ocampo's decision not to press ahead with arms trader cases was shaped by a presumption that the Ituri warlord cases would be more pragmatic is supported by a comment made by the ICC head of investigations at the time:

> [w]hen the idea [of investigating the link between finance and conflict] was initially presented, we encountered resistance to it, externally but even internally because it was not in line with more traditional ways of approaching crimes committed in conflict zones.[48]

This comment was made in the context of a briefing about the Court's work in which De Smedt discussed the damaging effects of the arms trade, ICC investigations into finance and resource extraction, and the problem that small arms 'continue[d] to fuel the conflict in the DRC'.[49] His insight supports the notion that ICC investigations into resource extraction in the DRC lost traction in part because they were not consistent with the status quo on 'traditional ways' of approaching case selection.

9.5 Blind Spot 3: Imagined Victims, Imagined Perpetrators

The non-prosecution of arms trade cases in the DRC Situation can be understood in terms of how victim interests are imagined within the ICC's legal culture, as well as how the perpetrators are imagined. Whether ICC decision-makers were blinded from seeing the potential for arms trader prosecutions depends not only on whether they imagined that victims' interests would be served by such prosecution, but also whether arm trade perpetrators were imagined to be appropriate targets for prosecution. It appears that Ocampo viewed arms traders as prima facie possible 'authors of the crimes'. But as Chapter 6 explored, certain perpetrator archetypes were predominant in the imaginary of ICC judges and lawyers, tending to exclude arms traders from view.

There is limited empirical research into how the interests of victims at the ICC influences the selection of specific cases.[50] This is surprising for at least three reasons. First, Article 53(1)(c) of the Rome Statute imposes a specific obligation

[48] Michael de Smedt, 'Speech on The Role of Companies in Conflicts within the Court's Jurisdiction' (*ICC website*, 29 October 2010) <https://www.icc-cpi.int/news/speech-head-investigation-michel-de-smedt-role-companies-conficts-within-courts-jurisdiction> accessed 4 August 2024.

[49] De Smedt (n 48) 1, 5, 6.

[50] Studies of victimhood in international criminal justice have focused on the legal status of victims before the ICC, the role of victims in the courtroom process, procedural rights at the preliminary examination, investigation, pre-trial, trial, and reparation stages, and the broader modalities of engaging victims in the justice process.

on the Prosecutor to consider the interests of victims in deciding whether or not to initiate an investigation. Second, the Court's legal framework does not elaborate criteria by which the Prosecutor should take into account victims' interests under Article 53.[51] Third, it had often been said that the effectiveness of the ICC's case selection strategy is highly dependent on ensuring that dialogue with victims is at the heart of the Court's work.[52]

The requirement under Article 53(1)(c) for the Prosecutor to consider 'victims' interests' does not state whether this means prosecuting the most notorious perpetrators, towards whom, perhaps, the most widely felt grievances are directed. Alternatively, Article 53(1)(c) could be interpreted as meaning that the Court's role extends to bringing to light the less visible structural causes of collective violence by prosecuting a range of individual perpetrators from across the spectrum of those who are criminally responsible. In a context of legal indeterminacy, as discussed in Chapter 7, the forms of victimhood that are imagined in the DRC Situation, and the corresponding imagined perpetrators, can come to play a significant role in case selection.

The centrality of victim interests for case selection in the DRC Situation was highlighted by the Prosecutor.[53] In the first years of investigation, multiple missions to Kinshasa and Ituri were conducted for the purpose of 'consulting with civil society groups and victim representatives with a view to understanding the concerns of local populations' and three missions were sent to Kinshasa, Bunia, and Ituri by multidisciplinary teams 'to analyse the probable consequences of OTP action for local populations, including victims and witnesses'.[54] On the other hand, in Clark's account of the DRC investigations, the Court overlooked victims' interests while taking advantage of the opportunities offered by the Congolese government, MONUC, and the existing EU-bolstered investigations in Ituri: 'self-serving pragmatism, rather than pragmatism geared to the needs of the Congolese population [was] the primary consideration in the ICC's case selection'.[55]

Ultimately, among the diverse range of perpetrators who could have met victims' interests, only a narrow category of perpetrator types was covered (ie the Ituri warlords) and the resource extraction nexus to the violence did not result in arrest warrants for arms traders.[56] This narrow range of actors prosecuted in the DRC Situation is consistent with a more restricted view of the types of cases that serve

[51] Rome Statute, art 53. See *Situation in the Democratic Republic of Congo* (Judgment) ICC-01/04-556 (19 December 2008).

[52] Ambos and Stegmiller (n 42) 431–32. Ambos and Stegmiller discuss the procedural participatory rights of victims and comment that 'efforts to address victims and to include them in dialogue would be entirely undermined by a selection strategy which is felt to ignore them'.

[53] OTP, 'Policy Paper on the Interests of Justice' (*ICC Legal Tools Database*, 1 September 2007) <www.legal-tools.org/doc/bb02e5/a6> accessed 4 August 2024.

[54] OTP, 'Policy Paper on the Interests of Justice' (*ICC Legal Tools Database*, 1 September 2007) <www.legal-tools.org/doc/bb02e5/a6> accessed 4 August 2024.

[55] Clark, 'Law, Politics and Pragmatism' (n 44) 41.

[56] Katanga's conduct included distributing weapons. *Katanga* (Trial Judgment) (n 19) paras 642–51.

the interests of victims. To understand more about how the DRC case selection was narrowed, we can look to concepts of 'victimhood' in the critical legal scholarship on the ICC that is concerned with identification of victims and the nature of their interests.[57] The social construction of the 'ideal victim' in the ICC's legal culture is described as a context-dependent, dynamic process that differs from situation to situation and can evolve over time.[58]

Our understanding of how the Ituri warlords may have been imagined in ICC legal culture as idealized perpetrators, whose prosecution would serve the interests of idealized victims, is illuminated by several studies that build-on the recognition that 'there is a gap between imagined and real victims'.[59] In domestic criminology, conceptual underpinnings are found in research on 'ideal victims' who, according to Christie, correspond to and necessitate 'ideal perpetrators'.[60] In this vein, McEvoy and McConnachie argue that '[t]he "innocent" victim should be the binary opposite of what [has been] termed the guilty "Bogeyman" who perpetrates wickedness'.[61] As Stahn notes, 'idealized perpetrators' are preferred by prosecutors because they reinforce assumed didactic functions of trials,[62] while Niezen likens the unreality of these idealizations to the 'piecemeal utopias' of consumer society.[63]

What these studies have in common is their recognition that when we narrow our view of criminality to an essentialized 'ideal', our view of who should be held responsible tends to become restricted too. In Federman's work, the French train company SNCF was identified as an 'ideal perpetrator' against which to construct accountability for Holocaust deportations.[64] Importantly, SNCF was ideal not due to its level of culpability, but because it provided a strong, abstractable, representation of the criminality involved, and had a champion-opponent to focus attention on it.[65] Bringing this perspective to the DRC Situation, the focus of OTP

[57] Luke Moffett, *Justice for Victims before the International Criminal Court* (Routledge 2014) Luke Moffett, 'Elaborating Justice for Victims at the International Criminal Court: Beyond Rhetoric and The Hague' (2015) 13.2 Journal of International Criminal Justice 281–311.

[58] Christine Schwöbel-Patel, 'The "Ideal" Victim of International Criminal Law' (2018) 29 European Journal of International Law 703; Carolyn Hoyle and Leila Ullrich, 'New Court, New Justice? The Evolution of "Justice for Victims" at Domestic Courts and at the International Criminal Court' (1 September 2014) 12.4 Journal of International Criminal Justice 681–703.

[59] Laurel E Fletcher, 'Refracted Justice: The Imagined Victim and the International Criminal Court' in Christian De Vos, Sara Kendall, and Carsten Stahn (eds), *Contested Justice: The Politics and Practice of International Criminal Court Interventions.* (CUP 2015) 324–25.

[60] Nils Christie, 'The Ideal Victim' in Ezzat Fattah (ed), *From Crime Policy to Victim Policy* (Palgrave 1986) 17.

[61] Kieran McEvoy and Kirsten McConnachie, 'Victimology in Transitional Justice: Victimhood, Innocence and Hierarchy' (2012) 9 European Journal of Criminology 527, 531.

[62] Carsten Stahn, *Justice as Message: Expressivist Foundations of International Criminal Justice* (OUP 2020) 276–77. See Sofia Stolk, 'A Sophisticated Beast? On the Construction of an 'Ideal' Perpetrator in the Opening Statements of International Criminal Trials' (2018) 29 European Journal of International Law 677.

[63] Ronald Niezen, *#HumanRights: The Technologies and Politics of Justice Claims in Practice* (Stanford University Press 2020).

[64] Sarah Federman, 'The "Ideal Perpetrator": The French National Railways and the Social Construction of Accountability' (2018) 49 Security Dialogue 327.

[65] Federman (n 64).

investigations came to centre on the Ituri warlords not because they were necessarily the only culpable perpetrators under the Rome Statute modes of liability, but because they offered a strong emblem of the immediate causes of violence in Ituri. The less visible, more structural causes—ie the nexus between resource extraction and arms trafficking—fell into the background.

In constructing these perceptions as to which prosecutions in the DRC Situation would best serve victims' interests, NGOs played a significant mediating role.[66] NGO advocacy focused on the scope of victim interests, their legal representation and its financing, and the structure of the ICC's office for victim representation.[67] NGOs projected their own understandings of victim interests when formulating proposals for ICC case selection, specifically on the links between victim interests and the role of arms transfers to non-state armed groups in the eastern DRC.[68] This NGO influence may have been more significant than is often acknowledged. As Krause puts it, 'a focus on states as the main actor in world politics is not helpful in understanding domains in which effective forms of influence (especially of individuals, grassroots organizations, transnational NGOs and "political or moral entrepreneurs") are wielded within or parallel to state-centred pathways of power'.[69]

The very practice of representing victimhood can have tangible effects on ICC decision-making including which perpetrators were considered viable for prosecution.[70] In the DRC Situation, a 'richer narrative' of victimhood[71] could have gone beyond more familiar accounts of retribution against direct perpetrators (eg killers of a victim's family members), or local militia leaders, to a more systemic representation of responsibility based on the full spectrum of liable actors. Interpreting the requirement under Article 53(1)(c) for the Prosecutor to consider 'victims' interests' via a richer narrative of victimhood could have led to a more diverse range of prosecutions, which in turn could have better represented the nuanced multiple causes of violence in the DRC Situation.

Arms transfer regulation was emerging as a key 'problematic' at the time of the Second Congo War, yet international criminal accountability was not generally

[66] See Danner (n 36) 533–34.

[67] See REDRESS, May 2005, *Ensuring the Effective Participation of Victims before the International Criminal Court: Comments and Recommendations Regarding Legal Representation for Victims (DRC Report)*. REDRESS, *Making the ICC relevant to affected communities*, 3 December 2007, 10.

[68] Human Rights Watch, 'Covered In Blood' (n 32); Human Rights Watch, Curse of Gold (n 39); Human Rights Watch, 'State Responsibility in the Arms Trade and the Protection of Human Rights' (Human Rights Watch, 17 February 1999) 3, 5. See also Section 8.7.5.

[69] Keith Krause, 'Facing the Challenge of Small Arms: The UN and Global Security Governance' in Richard M Price and Mark W Zacher (eds), *The United Nations and Global Security* (Palgrave Macmillan 2004) 21–38.

[70] See Sara Kendall and Sarah Nouwen, 'Representational Practices at the International Criminal Court: The Gap between Juridified and Abstract Victimhood' (2013) 76 Law and Contemporary Problems 236.

[71] Mark A Drumbl, 'Victims Who Victimize: Transcending International Criminal Law's Binaries' (2016) 4(2) London Review of International Law 27.

seen as part of the range of potential solutions.[72] The establishment of the ICC occurred during a decade of significant development of Arms Trade Law, particularly the UN Firearms Protocol, the United Nations Programme of Action on Small Arms and Light Weapons (UN PoA), and the United Nations International Tracing Instrument (UN ITI), and the eventual development of the ATT in 2013. Rather than the ICC being seen as providing a potential form of *ex post facto* accountability for arms transfer complicity, the potential of International Criminal Law was largely ignored, reinforcing the perception that the arms trade was uniquely regulated under Arms Trade Law. Wood and Peleman's important report on arms brokers in 2000 commented extensively on the role of arms transfer conduct in enabling genocide and crimes against humanity.[73] Their analysis refers briefly to the establishment of the ICC,[74] and was oriented towards the development of international agreements presaging the ATT.[75] Likewise, Mack and Wood's analysis in 2009 focused on the ATT and did not mention the ICC as a potentially relevant actor.[76] A UN publication from 2006 considered novel legal approaches to arms regulation but did not mention International Criminal Law.[77]

Ultimately, it was the Ituri warlords—relatively proximate to the crimes—who were indicted in the DRC Situation while structurally and geographically remote perpetrators were not. In this regard, the narrowing of liability in the DRC Situation to certain types of (military and political) perpetrators also involves a narrower causal and geographical perspective. The lack of attention to remote perpetrators should cause us to reflect on the uninterrogated assumptions and deeply rooted notions as to the causes of social upheaval and violence in Africa. Schwöbel-Patel has spoken of the 'spectacularised construction of the victim of international crime as a replica of the familiar fundraising image of victimhood'[78] through which International Criminal Law tends to focus on an 'ideal' victim accompanied by certain aesthetic qualities.[79] The construction of victimhood by the 'institutions of International Criminal Law, NGOs, governments and others acting in the name of humanity' is linked to certain images of perpetrators.[80]

72 Keith Krause, *Norm-building in Security Spaces: The Emergence of The Light Weapons Problematic* (Research Group in International Security Occasional Paper 2001).

73 Brian Wood and Johan Peleman, 'The Arms Fixers. Controlling the Brokers and Shipping Agents' (Peace Research Institute Oslo, 2000) ch 3.

74 Wood and Peleman (n 73) ch 10, 8.

75 Wood and Peleman (n 73) ch 11, 1.

76 Daniel Mack and Brian Wood 'Civil Society and the Drive Towards an Arms Trade Treaty' (United Nations Institute for Disarmament Research February 2009).

77 John Borrie and Vanessa Martin Randin, 'Thinking Outside the Box in Multilateral Disarmament and Arms Control Negotiations' (United Nations Institute for Disarmament Research 2006) 3.

78 Christine Schwöbel-Patel, 'Spectacle in International Criminal Law: The Fundraising Image of Victimhood' (2016) 4 London Review of International Law 247.

79 Schwöbel-Patel (n 58).

80 Schwöbel-Patel (n 78) 257.

According to Schwöbel-Patel, the image of the victim of international crime and that of the perpetrator are interdependent—a portrayal of perpetrators as 'strong and warlord-like' provides a 'spectacular' contrast to the victim whose vulnerable and helpless status is thereby emphasized.[81] Such a focus on 'strong and warlord-like' perpetrators would tend to obscure economic actors from view and a reluctance to contemplate prosecution of economic actors from outside the eastern DRC, such as international arms brokers, may also carry dimensions of racial, ethnic, or national discrimination.[82] By focusing the narrative on the Ituri warlords, responsibility for atrocities is thus decoupled from the external role played by business actors who were racially, ethnically, or nationally distinct from the imagined perpetrators.

The empirical work of Chapter 6 adds to the understanding and explanation of how this spectacular victimhood and archetypal perpetratorship were simultaneously constructed in the DRC Situation. That arms traders were not amongst these perpetrators imagined in ICC legal culture as responsible for international crimes suggests a cultural commitment to certain portrayals of victims in the Second Congo War that focused on more proximate perpetrators, tending to exclude more structurally and geographically distant arms traders.

9.6 Blind Spot 4: Horizontal Selectivity

The prioritization of suspects in the DRC Situation appears to have centred on their hierarchical importance and seniority, leaving an unseen blind spot over the range of different actors who could have been considered. The Prosecutor's attention to 'vertical' selectivity (ie choosing individuals who were considered to be at an appropriate hierarchical level to prosecute, not 'too high' or 'too low') left a blind spot over 'horizontal' selectivity (ie whether there were other types of perpetrators outside those hierarchies who could have been important).

As early as September 2003, the Prosecutor developed a general policy of selecting the 'most responsible' individuals in a conflict.[83] The policy was described by a senior member of the OTP as prioritizing 'first and foremost those situated at the highest echelons of responsibility [...] such as those persons holding leadership positions' after which the Prosecutor would 'consider *moving down the chain*'.[84] The policy thus emphasized vertical positioning within structured hierarchies.

[81] Schwöbel-Patel (n 78) 256.

[82] See Randle C DeFalco and Frédéric Mégret, 'The Invisibility of Race at the ICC: Lessons from the US Criminal Justice System' (2019) 7 London Review of International Law 55.

[83] OTP, Policy Paper (n 10) 7.

[84] Fabricio Guariglia, 'The Selection of Cases by the Office of the Prosecutor of the International Criminal Court' in Carsten Stahn and Göran Sluiter (eds), *The Emerging Practice of the International Criminal Court* (Brill 2009) 209, 214–15 (emphasis added).

It paid less attention to actors who were horizontally displaced outside those hierarchies, such as economic actors.

As noted already in this book, it is worth emphasizing that the vertical approach to ICC case selection is prosecutorial policy rather than law. The Rome Statute does not stipulate a personal jurisdiction threshold of 'those most responsible' (unlike some international criminal tribunals).[85] The preamble to the Rome Statute affirms '*the most serious crimes* of concern to the international community as a whole must not go unpunished', but the Statute does not restrict cases to the 'upper echelons'. Cryer emphasized that the potential breadth of liability in the Statute is juxtaposed with the extent to which the practice of ICC case selection has been narrowly construed.[86]

In the early ICC jurisprudence on requests for arrest warrants in the DRC Situation, the refusal decision from PTC1 was on the grounds that the alleged perpetrator was not a 'senior leader' and the case was inadmissible due to a lack of 'sufficient gravity'.[87] The Appeals Chamber considered PTC1's view wrong in law, such that 'automatically exclud[ing] [...] any perpetrators other than those at the very top [...] from the exercise of the jurisdiction of the Court' would be contrary to the Court's deterrence role.[88] The Appeals Chamber confirmed the absence of a 'senior leader' provision in the Rome Statute and rejected PTC1's erroneous interpretation of 'gravity'. It is important to recognize that while the Appeals Chamber construed the issue in terms of whether the suspects were 'at the very top' of a military or political hierarchy, the decision has implications for both vertical and horizontal selectivity. PTC1's restrictive focus on 'senior leaders' would exclude from case selection not only the individuals who are lower down in military and political hierarchies, but also those who are outside of these hierarchies. In other words, the Appeals Chamber jurisprudence implicitly acknowledges that the exclusion of economic actors from case selection would be wrong in law and contrary to the Court's deterrence role.

Several other aspects of the DRC Situation contributed to obscuring the question of horizontal selectivity. In Clark's analysis, the Prosecutor entered into a 'negotiated compromise' with Kabila that focused the investigations on the Ituri warlords. Accordingly, the Prosecutor's initial attention to arms traders was overshadowed by concerns for rebutting criticisms of political bias, allegations that he was investigating only certain non-state armed groups to the exclusion of others, critiques based on 'victor's justice', and the need to justify the tacet agreement with

[85] Ward Ferdinandusse and Alex Whiting, 'Prosecute Little Fish at the ICC' (2021) 19 Journal of International Criminal Justice.

[86] Cryer and others (n 34); Cryer (n 33).

[87] See *Situation in the Democratic Republic of the Congo* (Decision) ICC-01/04-02/06-20-Anx2 (10 February 2006).

[88] *Situation in the Democratic Republic of the Congo* (Judgment) ICC-01/04-169 (13 July 2006) para 74.

the DRC authorities not to investigate governmental actors. A focus on these concerns drew attention away from considering other perpetrator types.

In defending the impartiality of the Prosecutor's actions in the DRC Situation, a Policy Paper commented on which '*groups* must be prosecuted'.[89] The Prosecutor had also depicted himself as a welcome arbiter of conflict by stating: '[g]roups bitterly divided by conflict may oppose prosecutions at each others' hands and yet agree to a prosecution by a Court perceived as neutral and impartial'.[90] This focus on non-state armed groups framed the debate over case selection narrowly, portraying it as a choice between which of these groups would be prosecuted in the DRC Situation, rather than considering the full range of actors who had played diverse roles in the Congolese conflict.[91] In this way, the Prosecutor became focused on justifying the selection of the Ituri warlord cases as sufficiently senior (within the hierarchies of the militia groups), and sufficiently impartial (in targeting exclusively these militia groups). This contributed to a blind spot over the full extent of potential suspects in the DRC Situation.

The blind spot over horizontal selectivity is mirrored in commentary literature on the ICC, which has tended to critique case selection in terms of vertical selectivity. In Robinson's careful extrapolation of critiques of the ICC, he describes an oscillation between 'too high' critiques of the Prosecutor's case selection and 'too low' critiques.[92] The oscillation posited by Robinson can be seen in the DRC Situation, wherein Clark criticized the Prosecutor for taking the 'easy option' in Ituri of accessible, relatively low-level militia leaders, in the negotiated compromise that effectively shielded members of the DRC executive from prosecution.[93]

Robinson views this inescapable dyad as a 'no-win' predicament for the Court. Yet the analysis of this dyad is itself framed within a concern for vertical selectivity (too-high versus too-low), sidelining the question of horizontal selectivity (is the selection of cases 'too broad' or 'too narrow'?). An escape from this up-down dyad may be to prosecute cases outside of the conventional military and political hierarchies. In this sense, commentary on ICC case selection has often centred on whether there is sufficient attention to lower level perpetrators, leaving aside the issue of whether individuals from outside military and political hierarchies could also be prosecuted.[94] Building on Robinson's dyads critique, one way for the ICC to 'escape' the vertical selection dyad could be to attend to the full horizontal range of cases within the Court's jurisdiction.

89 Guariglia (n 84) 212 (emphasis added).
90 Moreno Ocampo (n 1) 4.
91 See Human Rights Watch (n 68) 5.
92 Darryl Robinson, 'Inescapable Dyads: Why the International Criminal Court Cannot Win' (2015) 28 Leiden Journal of International Law 323.
93 See Clark, 'Law, Politics and Pragmatism' (n 44).
94 Ferdinandusse and Whiting (n 85).

In sum, the Prosecutor's justifications for case selection in the DRC Situation came to focus on whether the indicted suspects were 'too high' or 'too low', moving away from the Prosecutor's initial attention to economic actors. Consistent with the framing of arms traders in ICC legal culture in Chapter 6, there may have been a lack of awareness within the Court about the real potential for arms broker cases. If it had been better understood that the Prosecutor's policy of aiming for 'high level' cases against militia leaders was not inevitable, this may have brought to the foreground other perpetrators, not only those at the lower end of the vertical spectrum, but also arms traders at the outer edges of the horizontal spectrum.

'Seeing what the Prosecutor was not seeing' in this blind spot could have brought attention to the remotely contributing individuals from outside the DRC, specifically, the suppliers of weapons along the transnational alliances between the non-state armed groups in the eastern DRC and Rwanda and Uganda, and even further afield to non-regional states involved in the arms trade. Ultimately, these shifts of focus could have engaged the ICC in a more nuanced, representative, and authentic post-conflict response in the DRC Situation than simply 'aiming high' within certain militia groups, bringing attention to the regional and international dimensions of the Congolese violence.

9.7 Conclusion

In the DRC Situation, the Prosecutor's initially broad perspective of case selection was soon narrowed. The announcement of 8 September 2003 became emblematic of the Court's latent potential to make use of UN Security Council-mandated fact-finding on the eastern DRC to provide some accountability for illicit arms trafficking. Ultimately, the international response to arms transfers was left to the strikingly ineffective system of export regulations and embargoes.

A broad range of factors influenced the Prosecutor's non-selection of arms trade cases in the DRC Situation. Four blind spots have been described here as obscuring cases that could have been feasible, such as the prosecution of regionally active international brokers like Victor Bout (who had been named by the UN Panel of Experts). These blind spots were not intrinsically benign. Indeed, Lodge describes blind spots as both problematic and essential if organizations are to have any meaningful goals.[95] And some degree of 'tunnel vision' may have been important for the Prosecutor's early work in the DRC Situation.

The Second Congo War, which was being fought when the Rome Statute entered into force on 1 July 2002, was the first armed conflict to be subject to both the

[95] Lodge (n 6) 39.

existing Arms Trade Law described in Chapters 2 and 3, and the jurisdiction of the nascent ICC as per Chapters 4 to 5. It became the staging post for the first, formative, interaction between two legal orders for regulating the arms trade—the existing system of global Arms Trade Law and the nascent possibility of International Criminal Law. The DRC Situation came to represent a missed opportunity to exercise jurisdiction over a vertically and horizontally diverse range of perpetrators and to represent the full scope of international criminal liability, as the Nuremburg trials did, rather than the restricted small number of cases focused on senior militia leaders.

Chapters 8 and 9 have explored how the case study of the Second Congo War and the DRC Situation at the ICC illustrate the under-recognized potential of International Criminal Law in relation to the arms trade. Subsequently, the potential for syncretism has remained. The Security Council's Group of Experts on the DRC and the DRC Sanctions Committee have increasingly identified specific individuals involved in arms trafficking, rather than whole groups.[96] The Group of Experts has increasingly recommended individual asset freezing orders and travel bans, and has increasingly used the language of individual criminal responsibility to recommend penal sanctions.[97]

Meanwhile at the ICC, despite these increased opportunities for syncretism, there has not been further action on economic actors in the DRC Situation. Could this still happen? There would be no statute of limitations for the alleged crimes in the DRC Situation, pursuant to Article 29 of the Rome Statute. Furthermore, the temporal period during which the Prosecutor may issue an arrest warrant in the DRC Situation appears extensive.[98] The PTC held in the DRC Situation that crimes committed subsequent to the referral date could fall within the jurisdiction of the Court 'when sufficiently linked to that particular situation of crisis'.[99] In doing so, the PTC appeared to set no fixed temporal bounds to the crimes that could be sufficiently linked to the facts of that crisis, even many years after March 2004.[100]

Because of how the DRC Situation unfolded, the specificities of the initial Ituri warlord cases came to contribute to the OTP's policies on case selection. The experience of the OTP in the DRC Situation must also have shaped the perceptions of ICC judges and lawyers as to which types of perpetrators are appropriate

[96] UNSC, 'Final report of the Group of Experts on the DRC submitted in accordance with paragraph 8 of Security Council resolution 1857 (2008)' (23 November 2009) UN Doc S/2009/603, para 344.

[97] UNSC, 'Interim report of the Group of Experts on the DRC submitted in accordance with paragraph 8 of Security Council resolution 1857 (2008)' (18 May 2009) UN Doc S/2009/253, paras 89–90.

[98] See Rebecca Hamilton, 'The ICC's Exit Problem' (2014) 47 New York University Journal of International Law and Policy 1.

[99] *Prosecutor v Callixte Mbarushimana* (Defence Filing) ICC-01/04-01/10-451 (26 October 2011).

[100] *Prosecutor v Callixte Mbarushimana* (Defence Filing) ICC-01/04-01/10-451 (26 October 2011) 37.

targets for ICC investigation. The continued exclusion of these cases (while the resource extraction dimensions of ongoing Congolese violence are widely known) echoes Cryer's contention; that the narrowing of the modes of liability in the practice of International Criminal Law poses a significant challenge to its legitimacy.[101]

[101] See Cryer and others (n 34); Cryer (n 33).

10
Conclusion

This book has examined the challenging and relatively uncharted topic of criminal complicity in the arms trade from a variety of legal and practical angles. It has explored International Criminal Law's relationship with a leading systemic cause of mass violence in society. From a doctrinal standpoint, there is little doubt that the modes of liability in the Rome Statute can criminalize certain actions of individual in the arms trade, from the executives of major manufacturing corporations to heads of transnational organized crime groups, as well as smaller-scale brokers. The breadth of International Criminal Law demonstrates its potential to complement existing regulation due to features of its liability, its jurisdiction, and the values and interests it seeks to protect.

The global trade is made up of a diversity of different actors and conduct in the 'lawful' and 'illicit' trades at international, national, and local levels, mirrored in the plurality of legal regimes that impact arms transfers. After mapping the contours of national export regulation, international agreements, and arms embargoes, a range of sources of a putative field of Arms Trade Law were identified, including human rights law, international humanitarian law, the law of state responsibility, the *jus ad bellum*, the law of neutrality, counterterrorism law, international economic law, and related areas of Transnational Criminal Law, cyber law, and anti-corruption law. This Arms Trade Law assemblage imposes standards for the pre-emptive prevention of transfers that may be used in international crimes, but does not provide criminal accountability.

The book makes several contributions to existing scholarship. Chapters 2 and 3 shed light on how criminal complicity differs fundamentally from existing Arms Trade Law: International Criminal Law punishes individuals for their complicity in international crimes, rather than a breach of export regulations or embargoes, or other infraction; it has a potential jurisdiction over all individuals in contrast to the unevenly differentiated patchwork of regulatory fields of export authorities; it applies to all types of objects since it is based on criminal *actus reus* and *mens rea* rather than the regulation of certain items; it does not require a cross-border element; and it assesses the actual contribution of arms transfer conduct to the commission of a crime. Most distinctively, however, a symbolic international criminal prosecution of an arms trader would express societal condemnation of the heinousness of profiting from atrocity.

A detailed interpretation of Rome Statute complicity was developed in Chapters 4 and 5 which contributes to the extensive scholarship on modes of

The Arms Trade and International Criminal Law. Tomas Hamilton, Oxford University Press. © Tomas Hamilton 2025.
DOI: 10.1093/oso/9780192868671.003.0010

liability by showing the significance of 'contributing to a group crime' under Article 25(3)(d)(ii). This provision criminalizes the arms transfer conduct of disinterested individuals involved in the sale of weapons to a group that they know intends to commit an international crime. Chapter 5 argued that the application of Article 25(3)(d)(ii) is highly dependent on the interpretation of the *mens rea* requirement of 'knowledge of the group's intention'. It is never possible for an accomplice to know a principal's intentions with the same certainty as their own, and, in practice, factual assessments would centre on the supplier's assumption of unacceptable risks that specific crimes will be committed with their weapons.

The existing system of Arms Trade Law provides a source of standards of what constitutes an 'unacceptable risk' in different legal regimes, and a factual source of evidence that can be used to assess an accomplice's guilty knowledge to prove *mens rea* (eg Security Council arms embargoes, UN fact-finding reports, expert evidence on the arms trade, and journalism, and NGO reports). Assessments made by a state's licensing body in authorizing an export may be the basis on which a state meets its obligations in accordance with Arms Trade Law, but the permission granted by such an authorization does not necessarily remove the possibility of an individual knowing that the weapons they sell will contribute to international crimes.

Chapter 6 carried out an open-ended empirical inquiry into the assumptions, beliefs, and commitments of International Criminal Court (ICC) judges and lawyers, to understand and explain how the Court's institutional culture is constitutive of decisions on case selection. The chapter found the idea of prosecuting arms traders was usually viewed through the lens of existing Arms Trade Law, rather than from a perspective of individual criminal responsibility. The professional intuitions of ICC judges and lawyers viewed other forms of arms regulation as predominant, while perceiving insurmountable pragmatic constraints to the ICC ever taking on this type of defendant.

Importantly, Chapter 7 helped to explain how the aspirations of International Criminal Law are culturally contingent, focusing attention on a narrow category of 'ideal perpetrators' of international crimes. The typical defendant—a military or political leader—is unrepresentative of the range of conduct that is criminalized by Rome Statute doctrines. The exclusion of arms traders from International Criminal Law's aspirations is not inevitable, nor even grounded in the legal doctrines of complicity. Studying the arms trade therefore tells us that the development of International Criminal Law is mediated by the content of its practitioners' aspirations in ways that narrow the scope of its application.

The case study of the Second Congo War in Chapter 8 showed the limitations of domestic export regulation and the Security Council arms embargo system. Only after the formal cessation of the armed conflict did the Security Council impose an embargo and revise the selective mandate of the UN Panel of Experts to include the arms trade. The Panel made confidential findings on arms transfers from Rwanda and Uganda to non-state armed groups in the eastern Democratic Republic of the Congo (DRC) but these were not made public. The Panel identified specific arms brokers who could have been eminently suitable for the Court's investigation and prosecutions, and perhaps suited the first Prosecutor's apparent wish to prosecute high profile cases to garner attention and legitimacy in the early days of the Court.

Chapter 9 found that those same individuals were obscured from the Prosecutor's view in the DRC Situation and did not lead to cases, while the apparent negotiated compromise with the new DRC Government focused narrowly on the 'warlord' suspects. Familiar critiques based on 'law versus politics' are insufficient to explain this non-selection. A greater awareness of the assumptions, beliefs, and commitments in the Court's institutional culture could illuminate the factors that influence case selection. In the DRC Situation, blind spots may have obscured arms trade cases that were politically viable, 'pragmatic', served the interests of victims, would have ameliorated horizontal selectivity, and could have achieved modes goals in line with the ICC's broader goals of ending impunity. In this way, reflecting on the non-selection of arms trade cases can contribute to a better understanding of how the Court lost an opportunity in the DRC Situation to prosecute a more comprehensive selection of the range of actors responsible for international crimes.

Returning to 8 September 2003 in the DRC Situation, the ICC Prosecutor's announcement about prosecuting 'those who provide weapons' reminds us that international criminal justice, with its normatively infused character, could still move in unexpected directions. At the time of writing, Prosecutor Khan's actions in the Situations in Ukraine, Palestine, and Sudan could not have been easily predicted. Perhaps in future, the Office of the Prosecutor of the International Criminal Court (OTP) will be part of a growing movement towards greater corporate accountability and the Prosecutor will once again consider 'those who provide weapons' in their policies. While this book did not set out to call for the investigation and prosecution of an arms broker at the ICC, it became a call for practitioners and commentators to engage with understanding why the Court has not yet addressed the full range of actors who are complicit under the Rome Statute. Reflecting on the unfulfilled legal basis of accomplice liability might help to appreciate the ICC's *aspirational* nature. As Pirie puts it, international criminal justice remains particularly prone to claiming legitimacy when in fact it has thus far attained only aspiration.[1] What this book adds to Pirie's observation is that the development of International Criminal Law is not defined by a single aspiration to 'fight impunity': it is also a struggle to define the content of its aspirations and to attend to their consonance with the doctrine of individual criminal responsibility.

[1] Fernanda Pirie, 'Law Before Government: Ideology and Aspiration' (2010) 30 OJLS 207.

Bibliography

Books

Aksenova M, *Complicity in International Criminal Law* (Bloomsbury 2016)
Anthony I (ed), *Arms Export Regulations* (OUP 1991)
Ashworth A and Horder J, *Principles of Criminal Law* (7th edn, OUP 2013)
Aust HP, *Complicity and the Law of State Responsibility* (CUP 2011)
Autesserre S, *The Trouble with the Congo: Local Violence and the Failure of International Peacebuilding* (CUP 2010)
Berman PS, *Global Legal Pluralism: A Jurisprudence of Law beyond Borders* (CUP 2012)
Biersteker TJ, Eckert SE, and Tourinho M (eds), *Targeted Sanctions* (CUP 2016)
Block J, *Reconciling Responsibility with Reality: A Comparative Analysis of Modes of Active Leadership Liability in International Criminal Law* (Springer 2023)
Boister N, *An Introduction to Transnational Criminal Law* (1st edn, OUP 2012)
—— *An Introduction to Transnational Criminal Law* (2nd edn, OUP 2018)
Boister N and Currie RJ, *Routledge Handbook of Transnational Criminal Law* (Routledge 2014)
Bosco D, *Rough Justice: The International Criminal Court in a World of Power Politics* (OUP 2013)
Bourdieu and others, *The Weight of the World: Social Suffering in Contemporary Society* (Polity 1999)
Brinkmann S and Kvale S, *InterViews: Learning the Craft of Qualitative Research Interviewing* (3rd edn, Sage 2014)
Brzoska M and Pearson FS, *Arms and Warfare: Escalation, De-escalation, and Negotiation* (University of South Carolina Press 1998)
Buzan B and Herring E, *The Arms Dynamic in World Politics* (Lynne Rienner 1998)
Callaghy T, Kassimir R, and Latham R (eds), *Intervention and Transnationalism in Africa: Global-Local Networks of Power* (CUP 2001)
Carisch E, Rickard-Martin L, and Meister SR, *The Evolution of UN Sanctions: From a Tool of Warfare to a Tool of Peace, Security and Human Rights* (Springer 2017)
Cartner J and others, *The International Law of the Shipmaster* (Routledge 2013)
Casey-Maslen S (ed), *Weapons Under International Human Rights Law* (CUP 2014)
Cassese A, *International Criminal Law* (2nd edn, OUP 2008)
Clapham A, *Human Rights Obligations of Non-State Actors* (OUP 2006)
—— Human Rights and Non-State Actors (ed) (Elgar 2013)
Clapham A and Paolo Gaeta (eds), *The Oxford Handbook of International Law in Armed Conflict* (OUP 2014)
Clapham A and others, *The Arms Trade Treaty: A Commentary* (OUP 2016)
Clark JF (ed), *The African Stakes of the Congo War* (Palgrave Macmillan 2002)
Clark P, *The Gacaca Courts, Post-Genocide Justice and Reconciliation in Rwanda: Justice Without Lawyers* (CUP 2010)
—— *Distant Justice: The Impact of the International Criminal Court on African Politics* (CUP 2018)
Coleman K, *A History of Chemical Warfare* (Palgrave Macmillan 2005)
Combs NA, *Fact-Finding without Facts: The Uncertain Evidentiary Foundations of International Criminal Convictions* (CUP 2010)
Cownie F, *Legal Academics: Culture and Identities* (Hart 2004)
Crawford J, *The International Law Commission's Arts on State Responsibility: Introduction, Text and Commentaries* (CUP 2002)
—— *Brownlie's Principles of Public International Law* (OUP 2019)

Cronin A, *Corporate Criminality and Liability for Fraud* (Routledge 2018)
Cryer R, *Prosecuting International Crimes: Selectivity and The International Criminal Law Regime* (CUP 2005)
Cryer R and others, *An Introduction to International Criminal Law and Procedure* (2nd edn, CUP 2010)
—— *Research Methodologies in International and EU Law* (Hart 2011)
—— *An Introduction to International Criminal Law and Procedure* (3rd edn, CUP 2014)
D'Aspremont J, *Formalism and The Sources of International Law: A Theory of the Ascertainment of Legal Rules* (OUP 2011)
da Silva C and Wood B (eds), *The Arms Trade Treaty: Weapons and International Law* (Intersentia 2021)
Denscombe M, *The Good Research Guide: For Small-Scale Social Research Projects* (McGraw-Hill 2014)
De Vos C, Kendall S, and Stahn C (eds), *Contested Justice: The Politics and Practice of International Criminal Court Interventions* (CUP 2015)
Erickson JL, *Dangerous Trade: Conventional Arms Exports, Human Rights, and International Relations* (Columbia University Press 2015)
Farah D and Braun S, *Merchant of Death: Money, Guns, Planes, and the Man Who Makes War Possible* (John Wiley and Sons 2007)
Festinger L, *A Theory of Cognitive Dissonance* (Stanford University Press 1957)
—— (ed), *Conflict, Decision, and Dissonance* (Stanford University Press 1964)
Festinger L, Riecken H, and Schachter S, *When Prophecy Fails: A Social and Psychological Study of a Modern Group that Predicted the Destination of the World* (Harper 1956)
Fish S, *Is There a Text in This Class?: The Authority of Interpretive Communities* (Harvard University Press 1982)
Fraser J and McGonigle Leyh B (eds), *Intersections of Law and Culture at the International Criminal Court* (Edward Elgar Publishing 2020)
Garland D, *Punishment and Modern Society: A Study in Social Theory* (Clarendon Press 1991)
Geertz C, *The Interpretation of Cultures* (Basic Books 1973)
Geldenhuys G, *Isolated States: A Comparative Analysis* (CUP 1990)
Gelsthorpe L and Padfield N, *Exercising Discretion: Decision-Making in the Criminal Justice System and Beyond* (Willan 2003)
Giumelli F, *The Success of Sanctions* (Routledge 2019)
Glaser B and Strauss A, *The Discovery of Grounded Theory: Strategies for Qualitative Research* (Aldine 1967)
Harkavy RE, *The Arms Trade and International Systems* (Ballinger 1975)
Harwood C, *The Roles and Functions of Atrocity-related United Nations Commissions of Inquiry in the International Legal Order: Navigating Between Principle and Pragmatism* (Brill Nijhoff 2020)
Heller K, *The Nuremberg Military Tribunals and the Origins of International Criminal Law* (OUP 2011)
Heller K and others (eds), *The Oxford Handbook of International Criminal Law* (OUP 2020)
Higgins R and others, *Oppenheim's International Law: United Nations* (OUP 2018)
Holsti KJ, *International Politics: A Framework for Analysis* (Prentice-Hall Englewood Cliffs 1995)
Hoskins E, Nutt S, and Watson TJ, *The Humanitarian Impacts of Economic Sanctions on Burundi* (Institute for International Studies 1997)
Husabø E and Bruce I, *Fighting Terrorism Through Multilevel Criminal Legislation* (Brill Nijhoff 2009)
Ingold T, *Companion Encyclopedia of Anthropology: Humanity, Culture, and Social Life* (Routledge 1994)
Jackson M, *Complicity in International Law* (OUP 2015)
Jain N, *Perpetrators and Accessories in International Criminal Law: Individual Modes of Responsibility for Collective Crimes* (Bloomsbury 2014)
James W, *The Ceremonial Animal: A New Portrait of Anthropology* (OUP 2005)

Jessup PC, *Transnational Law* (Yale University Press 1956)
Kahn PW, *The Cultural Study of Law: Reconstructing Legal Scholarship* (2nd edn, University of Chicago Press 1999)
Kamminga, MT and Zia-Zarifi S (eds), *Liability of Multinational Corporations under International Law* (Springer 2000)
Kassin S, Fein S, and Markus HR (eds), *Social Psychology* (9th edn, Cengage 2014)
Keane J, *Global Civil Society?* (CUP 2003)
Kelsall T, *Culture under Cross-Examination: International Justice and the Special Court for Sierra Leone* (CUP 2009)
Kennedy D, *A World of Struggle: How Power, Law, and Expertise Shape Global Political Economy* (Princeton University Press 2018)
Kersten M, *Justice in Conflict: The Effects of the International Criminal Court's Interventions on Ending Wars and Building Peace* (OUP 2016)
Krause K, *Arms and The State: Patterns of Military Production and Trade* (CUP 1995)
Kutz C, *Complicity: Ethics and Law for a Collective Age* (CUP 2007)
Laurance EJ, *The International Arms Trade* (Lexington 1992)
Lemarchand R, *The Dynamics of Violence in Central Africa* (University of Pennsylvania Press 2012)
Lohne K, *Advocates of Humanity: Human Rights NGOs in International Criminal Justice* (OUP 2019)
Louscher DJ, *Marketing Security Assistance: New Perspectives on Arms Sales* (Free Press 1987)
Lowe V, *International Law* (OUP 2007)
Luban D, O'Sullivan JR, and Stewart DP, *International and Transnational Criminal Law* (Aspen 2010)
Lustgarten L, *Law and the Arms Trade: Weapons, Blood and Rules* (Bloomsbury 2020)
Marriage Z, *Formal Peace and Informal War. Security and Development in Congo* (Routledge 2013)
McEvoy K and McGregor L (eds), *Transitional Justice from Below: Grassroots Activism and the Struggle for Change* (Bloomsbury 2008)
Moore MS, *Causation and Responsibility: An Essay in Law, Morals, and Metaphysics* (OUP 2009)
Mosse D, 'Cultivating Development: An Ethnography of Aid Policy and Practice (Pluto Press 2004)
Neuman SG, *Military Assistance in Recent Wars: The Dominance of The Superpowers* (Praeger 1986)
Ngolet F, *Crisis in the Congo: The Rise and Fall of Laurent Kabila* (Springer 2010)
Niezen R, *#HumanRights: The Technologies and Politics of Justice Claims in Practice* (Stanford University Press 2020)
Niezen R and Sapignoli M (eds), *Palaces of Hope: The Anthropology of Global Organizations* (CUP 2017)
Nouwen S, *Complementarity in the Line of Fire: The Catalysing Effect of the International Criminal Court in Uganda and Sudan* (CUP 2013)
Novak A, *The International Criminal Court: An Introduction* (Springer 2015)
Nzongola-Ntalaja G, *The Congo: From Leopold to Kabila: A People's History* (Zed Books 2002)
O'Keefe R, *International Criminal Law* (OUP 2015)
Padfield N, *Criminal Law* (8th edn, OUP 2012)
Palmer N, *Courts in Conflict: Interpreting the Layers of Justice in Post-Genocide Rwanda* (OUP 2015)
Pirie F, *The Anthropology of Law* (OUP 2013)
Posner E, *The Perils of Global Legalism* (University of Chicago Press 2009)
Posner RA, *How Judges Think* (Harvard University Press 2010)
Prunier G, *From Genocide to Continental War: The 'Congolese' Conflict and the Crisis of Contemporary Africa* (Hurst and Co 2009)
—— *Africa's World War: Congo, the Rwandan Genocide, and the Making of a Continental Catastrophe* (OUP 2008)

Rastell J and Rastell W, *Les Termes de la Ley: or, Certaine Difficult and Obscure Words and Termes of the Common Lawes and Statutes of this Realme* (1st edn, Beale and Hearne 1523)
Reyntjens F, *The Great African War: Congo and Regional Geopolitics, 1996–2006* (CUP 2009)
Roessler PG and Verhoeven H, *Why Comrades Go to War: Liberation Politics and the Outbreak of Africa's Deadliest Conflict* (Hurst and Co 2017)
Rosen L, *The Anthropology of Justice: Law as culture in Islamic Society* (CUP 1989)
Saul B, *Defining Terrorism in International Law* (OUP 2010)
Schiff BN, *Building the International Criminal Court* (CUP 2008)
Schroeder M, Smith D, and Stohl R, *The Small Arms Trade: A Beginner's Guide* (Oneworld Publications 2012)
Shklar JN, *Legalism: Law, Morals, and Political Trials* (Harvard University Press 1964)
Simester A and others, *Criminal Law: Theory and Doctrine* (6th edn, Hart 2016)
Smeulers A and Haveman R (eds), *Supranational Criminology: Towards a Criminology of International Crimes* (Intersentia 2008)
Smith KJM, *A Modern Treatise on the Law of Criminal Complicity* (Clarendon Press 1991)
Stahn C, *A Critical Introduction to International Criminal Law* (CUP 2019)
Staibano C and Wallensteen P (eds), *International Sanctions: Between Wars and Words* (Routledge 2005)
Stearns J, *Dancing in the Glory of Monsters: The Collapse of the Congo and the Great War of Africa* (Public Affairs 2012)
Steger M, *The Rise of the Global Imaginary: Political Ideologies from the French Revolution to the Global War on Terror* (OUP 2008)
Stockholm Institute for Peace Research, *The Arms Trade with the Third World* (Pelican 1971)
Stohl R and Grillot S, *The International Arms Trade* (Polity 2009)
Stroud's Judicial Dictionary (9th edn, Sweet and Maxwell 2018)
Tan A (ed), *The Global Arms Trade: A Handbook* (Routledge 2014)
Taylor C, *Modern Social Imaginaries* (Duke University Press 2004)
Thayer G, *The War Business: The International Trade in Armaments* (Weidenfield and Nicolson 1969)
Turner T, *The Congo Wars: Conflict, Myth and Reality* (Zed Books 2007)
Van Hoecke M (ed), *Methodologies of Legal Research: Which Kind of Method for What Kind of Discipline?* (Bloomsbury 2011)
Van Sliedregt E, *Individual Criminal Responsibility in International Law* (OUP 2012)
Van Sliedregt E and Vasiliev S (eds), *Pluralism in International Criminal Law* (OUP 2014)
Webb P, *International Judicial Integration and Fragmentation* (OUP 2013)
Werle G and Jessberger F, *Principles of International Criminal Law* (OUP 2014)
Whitehead N and Finnström S (eds), *Virtual War and Magical Death: Technologies and Imaginaries for Terror and Killing* (Duke University Press 2013)
Wilson RA (ed) *Human Rights, Culture and Context* (Pluto 1997)
—— *Writing History in International Criminal Trials* (CUP 2011)
—— *Incitement on Trial: Prosecuting International Speech Crimes* (CUP 2017)
Yihdego Z, *The Arms Trade and International Law* (Bloomsbury 2007)
Zierler D, *The Invention of Ecocide: Agent Orange, Vietnam, and the Scientists who Changed the Way We Think about the Environment* (University of Georgia Press 2011)

Book Chapters and Sections

Ambos K, 'The ICC and Common Purpose: What Contribution Is Required Under Article 25(3)(d)?' in Carsten Stahn (ed), *The Law and Practice of the International Criminal Court* (OUP 2015) 595
—— 'Comments on Article 25' in Kai Ambos and Otto Triffterer (eds), *Commentary on the Rome Statute of the International Criminal Court* (Hart 2016)
Bellal A, 'Arms Transfers and International Human Rights Law' in Stuart Casey-Maslen (ed), *Weapons Under International Human Rights Law* (CUP 2014) 448
Bitti G, 'Article 21 and the Hierarchy of Sources of Law before the ICC' in Carsten Stahn (ed), *The Law and Practice of the International Criminal Court* (OUP 2015) 427

Bitzinger RA, 'Globalization Revisit(ed)' in Andrew Tan (ed), *The Global Arms Trade: A Handbook* (Routledge 2014) 208

Bourne M, 'Militarization and Conflict in the Great Lakes' in Owen Green and others, *Light Weapons and Peacebuilding in Central and East Africa* (International Alert 1998) 5

Chehtman A, 'Terrorism and the Conceptual Divide Between International and Transnational Criminal Law' in Harmen Van Der Wilt and Christophe Paulussen (eds), *Legal Responses to Transnational and International Crimes: Towards an Integrative Approach?* (Edward Elgar 2017) 15

Christensen MJ, 'The Symbolic Economy of International Criminal Justice: Shaping the Discourse of a New Field of Law' in Joanna Nicholson (ed), *Strengthening the Validity of International Criminal Tribunals* (Brill 2018)

—— 'The Creation of an Ad Hoc Elite and the Value of International Criminal Law Expertise on a Global Market' in Kevin Heller and others (eds), *The Oxford Handbook of International Criminal Law* (OUP 2020) 89

Christie N, 'The Ideal Victim' in Ezzat Fattah (ed), *From Crime Policy to Victim Policy* (Palgrave 1986) 17

Clapham A, 'Sanctions and Economic, Social and Cultural Rights' in Vera Gowlland-Debbas (ed), *United Nations Sanctions and International Law* (Kluwer 2001) 131

—— 'Corporations and Criminal Complicity' in Gro Nystuen, Andreas Follesdal, and Ola Mestad (eds), *Human Rights, Corporate Complicity and Disinvestment* (CUP 2011) 222

—— 'Weapons and Armed non-state actors' in Stuart Casey-Maslen (ed), *Weapons Under International Human Rights Law* (CUP 2014)

—— 'Focusing on armed Non-state Actors' in Andrew Clapham and Paola Gaeta (eds), *The Oxford Handbook of International Law in Armed Conflict* (OUP 2014)

—— 'Article 6' in Andrew Clapham and others, *The Arms Trade Treaty: A Commentary* (OUP 2016) 204

—— 'Article 7' in Andrew Clapham and others, *The Arms Trade Treaty: A Commentary* (OUP 2016) 255

—— 'Human Rights and International Criminal Law' in William A Schabas (ed), *The Cambridge Companion to International Criminal Law* (CUP 2016) 11

Clark P, 'Law, Politics and Pragmatism: The ICC and Case Selection in the Democratic Republic of Congo and Uganda' in Nicholas Waddell and Phil Clark (eds), *Courting Conflict: Justice, Peace and the ICC in Africa* (Royal African Society 2008) 37

—— 'Grappling in the Great Lakes: The Challenges of International Justice in Rwanda, the Democratic Republic of Congo and Uganda' in Brett Bowden, Hilary Charlesworth, and Jeremy Farrall (eds), *Great Expectations: The Role of International Law in Restructuring Societies after Conflict* (CUP 2009)

Crowley M, 'International Legal Constraints upon the Weaponization of Toxic Chemicals' in Michael Crowley, Malcolm Dando, and Lihao Shang (eds), *Preventing Chemical Weapons: Arms Control and Disarmament as the Sciences Converge* (Royal Society of Chemistry 2018) 146

D'Aspremont J, 'The Two Cultures of International Criminal Law' in Kevin Heller and others (eds), *The Oxford Handbook of International Criminal Law* (OUP 2020) 400

Feinstein A and Holden P, 'Arms Trafficking', *The Oxford Handbook of Organized Crime* (OUP 2014) 444

Finnström S, 'Today He Is No More: Magic, Intervention, and Global War in Uganda' in Neil Whitehead and Sverker Finnström (eds), *Virtual War and Magical Death: Technologies and Imaginaries for Terror and Killing* (Duke University Press 2013)

Geertz C, 'Local Knowledge: Fact and Law in Comparative Perspective' in Clifford Geertz, *Local Knowledge: Further Essays in Interpretive Anthropology* (Basic Books 1983) 184

Gillet P and Salaber-Ayton J, 'The Recent Development and Performance of Ethical Investments' in Othmar M Lehner (ed), *Routledge Handbook of Social and Sustainable Finance* (Routledge 2017) 2

Guariglia F, 'The Selection of Cases by the Office of the Prosecutor of the International Criminal Court' in Carsten Stahn and Göran Sluiter (eds), *The Emerging Practice of the International Criminal Court* (Brill Nijhoff 2009) 209

Guilfoyle D, 'Transnational Crimes' in Kevin Heller and others (eds), *The Oxford Handbook of International Criminal Law* (OUP 2020) 791

Hagelin B, 'International Armament Embargoes and the Need for End-Use Documents' in Carina Staibano and Peter Wallensteen (eds), *International Sanctions: Between Wars and Words* (Routledge 2005)

Halliday S, 'The Role of Empirical Legal Research in the Study of UK Public Law' in Caroline Hunter (ed), *Integrating Socio-Legal Studies Into The Law Curriculum* (Palgrave MacMillan 2012) 14

Hamilton T, 'Arms Transfer Complicity under Article 25(3)(d)(ii) of the Rome Statute' in Nina HB Jørgensen (ed), *International Criminal Responsibility of War's Funders and Profiteers* (CUP 2020)

Harwood C, 'Contributions of International Commissions of Inquiry to Transitional Justice' in Cheryl Lawther, Luke Moffett, and Dov Jacobs (eds), *Research Handbook on Transitional Justice* (Edward Elgar Publishing 2017) 401–23

Heller KJ, 'The Rome Statute in Comparative Perspective' in Kevin Heller and Markus Dubber (eds), *The Handbook of Comparative Criminal Law* (Stanford Law Books 2010)

Hopkins R, 'Catching Wars' Funders and Profiteers: The Disjointed Web of Corporate Criminal Liability in England and Wales' in Nina HB Jørgensen (ed), *International Criminal Responsibility of War's Funders and Profiteers* (CUP 2020)

Jørgensen N, 'Charles Taylor Inc: Lessons from the Trial of a President, Businessman and Warlord' in Nina HB Jørgensen (ed), *International Criminal Responsibility of War's Funders and Profiteers* (CUP 2020)

Kaufmann C, 'World Customs Organization' in Frauke Lachenmann and Rüdiger Wolfrum (eds), *International Economic Law: The Max Planck Encyclopedia of Public International Law* (OUP 2015) 904

Kersten M, 'A Fatal Attraction? The UN Security Council and the Relationship between R2P and the International Criminal Court' in Jeff Handmaker and Karin Arts (eds), *Mobilising International Law for 'Global Justice'* (CUP 2018) 142

Krever T, 'Unveiling (and Veiling) Politics in International Criminal Trials' in Christine Schwöbel-Patel (ed), *Critical Approaches to International Criminal Law: An Introduction* (Routledge 2014) 117

Laurance EJ, 'The Small Arms Problem as Arms Control: A Policy Driven Research Agenda' in Peter Batchelor and Kai Michael Kenkel (eds), *Controlling Small Arms: Consolidation, Innovation and Relevance in Research and Policy* (Routledge 2013) 13

Lodge M, 'Accounting for Blind Spots' in Tobias Bach and Kai Wegrich (eds), *The Blind Spots of Public Bureaucracy and the Politics of Non-Coordination* (Palgrave Macmillan 2019) 29

May C, 'The Rule of Law as a Social Imaginary' in Christopher May (ed), *The Rule of Law: The Common Sense of Global Politics* (Elgar 2014)

Meierhenrich J, 'The Evolution of the Office of the Prosecutor at the International Criminal Court: Insights from Institutional Theory' in Martha Minow, Cora C True-Frost, and Alex Whiting (eds), *The First Global Prosecutor: Promise and Constraints. Law, Meaning, and Violence* (University of Michigan Press 2015) 97

Messner C, 'Observing Victims: Global Insecurities and the Systemic Imagination of Justice in World Society' in Ronnie Lippens (ed), *Imaginary Boundaries of Justice Social and Legal Justice across Disciplines* (Hart 2004)

Michel N, 'The Creation of the Tribunal in its Context' in Amal Alamuddin, Nidal Nabil Jurdi, and David Tolbert (eds), *The Special Tribunal for Lebanon: Law and Practice* (OUP 2014)

Muchai A, 'Arms Proliferation and the Congo War' in John F. Clark (ed), *The African Stakes of the Congo War* (Palgrave Macmillan 2002) 185

Nerlich V, 'The Status of ICTY and ICTR Precedent in Proceedings before the ICC' in Carsten Stahn and Göran Sluiter (eds), *The Emerging Practice of the International Criminal Court* (Brill Nijhoff 2009) 314

Nouwen S, 'Justifying Justice' in James Crawford and Martti Koskenniemi (eds), *The Cambridge Companion to International Law* (CUP 2012) 337

Ohlin J, 'Peace, Security, and Prosecutorial Discretion.' in Carsten Stahn and Göran Sluiter (eds), *The Emerging Practice of the International Criminal Court* (Brill Nijhoff 2009) 183

Palmer N, 'The Place of Consultation in the International Criminal Court's Approach to Complementarity and Cooperation' in Olympia Bekou and Daley Birkett (eds), *Cooperation and the International Criminal Court: Perspectives from Theory and Practice* (Brill Nijhoff 2016) 210

Pellet A and Miron A, 'Sanctions' in *Max Planck Encyclopedia of Public International Law* (OUP 2013)

Perlo-Freeman S, 'The United Kingdom Arms Industry in a Globalized World' in Andrew Tan (ed), *The Global Arms Trade: A Handbook* (Routledge 2014)

Polner M and Moell D, 'Interagency Collaboration and Combating Wildlife Crime' in Grant Pink and Rob White (eds), *Environmental Crime and Collaborative State Intervention* (Palgrave Studies in Green Criminology 2016) 59

Prunckun H, 'The Rule of Law: Controlling Cyber Weapons' in Henry Prunckun (ed), *Cyber Weaponry: Issues and Implications of Digital Arms* (Springer 2018) 87

Rastan R, 'Can the ICC Function Without State Compliance?' in Margaret M deGuzman and Valerie Oosterveld (eds), *The Elgar Companion to the International Criminal Court* (Edward Elgar 2020)

Saland P, 'International Criminal Law Principles' in Roy Lee (ed), *The International Criminal Court: The Making of the Rome Statute* (Martinus Nijhoff 1999) 189

Schabas W, 'Selecting Situations and Cases' in Carsten Stahn (ed), *The Law and Practice of the International Criminal Court* (OUP 2014) 368

Scheele J, 'In Praise of Disorder: Breaking the Rules in Northern Chad' in Paul Dresch and Judith Scheele (eds), *Legalism: Rules and Categories* (OUP 2015) 153

Schia NN, 'Horseshoe and Catwalk: Power, Complexity, and Consensus-Making in the United Nations Security Council' in Ronald Niezen and Maria Sapignoli (eds), *Palaces of Hope: The Anthropology of Global Organizations* (CUP 2017) 55

Schwöbel-Patel C, 'The Core Crimes of International Criminal Law' in Kevin Heller and others (eds), *The Oxford Handbook of International Criminal Law* (OUP 2020) 768

Seger P, 'The Law of Neutrality', in Andrew Clapham, and Paola Gaeta (eds), *The Oxford Handbook of International Law in Armed Conflict* (OUP 2014) 248

Signori S, 'Socially Responsible Investors: Exploring Motivations and Ethical Intensity' in Leire San-Jose, José Luis Retolaza, and Luc van Liedekerke (eds), *Handbook on Ethics in Finance* (Springer 2020) 1

Sluiter G and Yau S, 'Aiding and Abetting and Causation in the Commission of International Crimes —The Cases of Dutch Businessmen van Anraat and Kouwenhoven' in Nina HB Jørgensen (ed), *The International Criminal Responsibility of War's Funders and Profiteers* (CUP 2020) 304

Stahn C, 'Justice Civilisatrice? The ICC, Post-colonial Theory, and Faces of "the Local"' in Christian De Vos, Sara Kendall, and Carsten Stahn (eds), *Contested Justice: The Politics and Practice of International Criminal Court Interventions* (CUP 2015) 46

Staibano C, 'Trends in UN Sanctions' in Peter Wallensteen and Carina Staibano (eds), *International Sanctions: Between Words and Wars in the Global System* (Routledge 2005) 35

Stewart JG, 'The Strangely Familiar History of the Unitary Theory of Perpetration' in Bruce Ackerman and others (eds), *Visions of Justice, Essays in Honor of Professor Mirjan Damaška* (Duncker and Humblot 2016)

Sugarman D and Warrington R, 'Land Law, Citizenship, and the Invention of "Englishness"' in John Brewer and Susan Staves (ed), *Early Modern Conceptions of Property* (Routledge 1996) 111

Sullivan B, 'Reformulating Bribery: A Legal Critique of the Bribery Act 2010' in Jeremy Horder and Peter Alldridge (eds), *Modern Bribery Law: Comparative Perspectives* (CUP 2013) 13

Van Hoecke M, 'Legal Doctrine: Which Methods for What Kind of Discipline' in Mark Van Hoecke, *Methodologies of Legal Research: Which Kind of Method for What Kind of Discipline?* (Bloomsbury 2011)

Webb P, 'Individual Criminal Responsibility' in Amal Alamuddin, Nidal Nabil Jurdi, and David Tolbert (eds), *The Special Tribunal for Lebanon: Law and Practice* (OUP 2014) 88

—— 'The Participation of Non-State Actors in the Multilateral Treaty Process' in Simon Chesterman, David M Malone, and Santiago Villalpando (eds), *The Oxford Handbook of UN Treaties* (OUP 2019)

Wezeman ST, 'The Global Arms Trade After the Cold War' in Andrew Tan (ed), *The Global Arms Trade: A Handbook* (Routledge 2014) 193

Wholgemuth L, 'African Sanctions—The Case of Burundi' in Peter Wallensteen and Carina Staibano (eds), *International Sanctions: Between Words and Wars in the Global System* (Routledge 2005) 126

Wiley B and Jørgensen NHB, 'Linking Economic Actors to the Core International Crimes of the Syrian Regime' in Nina HB Jørgensen (ed), *International Criminal Responsibility of War's Funders and Profiteers* (CUP 2020) 93

Journal Articles

Akerman A and Seim AL, 'The Global Arms Trade Network 1950–2007' (2014) 42 Journal of Comparative Economics 535

Aksenova M, 'The Modes of Liability at the ICC: The Labels that Don't Always Stick' (2015) 15 International Criminal Law Review 629

Alston P, 'Criminalizing Human Rights' (2023) 15(3) Journal of Human Rights Practice 660–77

Ambos K and Stegmiller I, 'Prosecuting International Crimes at the International Criminal Court: Is There a Coherent and Comprehensive Prosecution Strategy?' (2013) 59 Crime, Law and Social Change 415

Anders G, 'Testifying about "Uncivilized Events": Problematic Representations of Africa in the Trial Against Charles Taylor' (2011) 24 Leiden Journal of International Law 937

Anderson ES and Pildes RH, 'Expressive Theories of Law: A General Restatement' (2000) 148 University of Pennsylvania Law Review 1503

Autesserre S, 'Dangerous Tales: Dominant Narratives on the Congo and their Unintended Consequences' (2012) 111 African Affairs 202

Bernaz, N, 'Conceptualizing Corporate Accountability in International Law: Models for a Business and Human Rights Treaty' (2021) 22 Human Rights Review 45

Boister N, 'Transnational Criminal Law?' (2003) 14 European Journal of International Law 953

—— 'Further reflections on the concept of transnational criminal law' (2015) 6 Transnational Legal Theory 9

Boivin A, 'Complicity and Beyond: International Law and the Transfer of Small Arms and Light Weapons' (2005) 87 International Review of the Red Cross 467

Boon A, Flood J, and Webb J, 'Postmodern Professions? The Fragmentation of Legal Education and the Legal Profession' (2005) 32 Journal of Law and Society 473

Bothe M and Marauhn T, 'The Arms Trade: Comparative Aspects of Law' (1993) 26 Revue Belge de Droit International 20

Bove V and Böhmelt T, 'Arms Imports in the Wake of Embargoes' (2021) 27(4) European Journal of International Relations 1114–35

Brandes M, 'All's Well That Ends Well, or Much Ado about Nothing: A Commentary on the Arms Trade Treaty' (2013) 5 Goettingen Journal of International Law 399

Bryk L and Saage-Maaß M, 'Individual Criminal Liability for Arms Exports under the ICC Statute: A Case Study of Arms Exports from Europe to Saudi-led Coalition Members Used in the War in Yemen' (2019) 17 Journal of International Criminal Justice 1117

Burchard C, 'Ancillary and Neutral Business Contributions to "Corporate–Political Core Crime": Initial Enquiries Concerning the Rome Statute' (2010) 8 Journal of International Criminal Justice 919

Burke-White WW, 'International Legal Pluralism' (2003) 25 Michigan Journal of International Law 963

—— 'Complementarity in Practice: The International Criminal Court as Part of a System of Multi-level Global Governance in the Democratic Republic of Congo' (2005) 18 Leiden Journal of International Law 557

Caron D, 'The ILC Arts on State Responsibility: The Paradoxical Relationship between Form and Authority' (2002) 96 AJIL 857dd

Christensen MJ, 'Preaching, Practicing and Publishing International Criminal Justice: Academic Expertise and the Development of an International Field of Law' (2017) 17 International Criminal Law Review 239

Christensen MJ and Kjeldgaard-Pedersen A, 'Competing Perceptions of Hybrid Justice: International v. National in the Extraordinary Chambers of the Courts of Cambodia' (2018) 18 International Criminal Law Review 127

Ciorciari J, 'China and the Pol Pot Regime' (2014) 14 Cold War History 215

Clancy P, 'Neutral Arms Transfers and the Russian Invasion of Ukraine' (2023) ICLQ 72(2) 527–43

Clapham A, 'Extending International Criminal Law Beyond the Individual to Corporations and Armed Opposition Groups' (2008) 6 Journal of International Criminal Justice 899

—— 'Three Tribes Engage on the Future of International Criminal Law' (2011) 9 Journal of International Criminal Justice 689

Coghlan B and others, 'Mortality in the Democratic Republic of Congo—A Nationwide Survey' (2006) 367 The Lancet 44

Cooper N, 'What's the Point of Arms Transfer Controls?' (2006) 118 Contemporary Security Policy 27, 119–20

—— 'Race, Sovereignty, and Free Trade: Arms Trade Regulation and Humanitarian Arms Control in the Age of Empire' (2018) 3 Journal of Global Security Studies 444

Cryer R, 'The Boundaries of Liability in International Criminal Law, or Selectivity by Stealth' (2001) 3 Journal of Conflict and Security Law

—— 'Prosecuting the Leaders: Promises, Politics and Pragmatics' (2009) 1 Göttingen Journal of International Law 45

Dan-Cohen M, 'Listeners and Eavesdroppers: Substantive Legal Theory and its Audience' (1992) 63 University of Colorado Law Review 569

Danner AM, 'Enhancing the Legitimacy and Accountability of Prosecutorial Discretion at the International Criminal Court' (2003) 97 AJIL 510

DeFalco RC and Mégret F, 'The Invisibility of Race at the ICC: Lessons from the US Criminal Justice System' (2019) 7 London Review of International Law 55

deGuzman M, 'Giving Priority to Sex Crime Prosecutions: The Philosophical Foundations of a Feminist Agenda' (2011) 11 International Criminal Law Review 515

—— 'Choosing to Prosecute: Expressive Selection at the International Criminal Court' (2012) 33 Michigan Journal of International Law 265

Del Carmen García-Alonso and Paul Levine, 'Arms Export Controls, Subsidies and the WTO Exemption' (2005) 52 Scottish Journal of Political Economy 305

De Waal A, 'The Humanitarians' Tragedy: Escapable and Inescapable Cruelties' (2010) 34 Disasters s130

Dhooge LJ, 'We Arm The World: The Implications of American Participation in the Global Armaments Trade' (1999) 16 Arizona Journal of International and Comparative Law 577

Dixon P and Tenove C, 'International Criminal Justice as a Transnational Field: Rules, Authority and Victims' (2013) 7 International Journal of Transitional Justice 393

Drumbl M, 'Victimhood in Our Neighborhood: Terrorist Crime, Taliban Guilt, and the Asymmetries of the International Legal Order' (2002) North Carolina Law Review 81

Eavis P, 'SALW in the Horn of Africa and the Great Lakes Region: Challenges and Ways Forward' (2002) IX Brown Journal of World Affairs 252

Efrat A, 'Toward Internationally Regulated Goods: Controlling the Trade in Small Arms and Light Weapons' (2010) 64 International Organization 97

El Zeidy MM, 'The Principle of Complementarity: A New Machinery to Implement International Criminal Law' (2001) 23 Michigan Journal of International Law 869

Erickson JL, 'Punishing the Violators? Arms Embargoes and Economic Sanctions as Tools of Norm Enforcement' (2020) 46 Review of International Studies 96

Falk RA, 'The Shimoda Case: A Legal Appraisal of the Atomic Attacks upon Hiroshima and Nagasaki' (1965) AJIL 759

Farrell N, 'Attributing Criminal Liability to Corporate Actors: Some Lessons from the International Tribunals' (2010) 8 Journal of International Criminal Justice 873

Federman S, 'The "Ideal Perpetrator": The French National Railways and the Social Construction of Accountability' (2018) 49 Security Dialogue 327

Feinstein A and Holden P, 'The Failure of Regulation of the Global Arms Trade as a Consequence of High-Level Conflicts in Interest' (2020) 27 Brown Journal of World Affairs 23

Ferdinandusse W and Whiting A, 'Prosecute Little Fish at the ICC' (2021) 19 Journal of International Criminal Justice 759

Finnin S, 'Elements of Accessorial Modes of Liability: Article 25(3)(b) and (c) of The Rome Statute of The International Criminal Court' (2012) 61 ICLQ 325

Fuller C, 'Legal Anthropology: Legal Pluralism and Legal Thought' (1994) 10 Anthropology Today 9

Gaeta P, 'Is the Practice of 'Self-Referrals' a Sound Start for the ICC?' (2004) 2 Journal of International Criminal Justice 949

Gallmetzer R, 'Prosecuting Persons Doing Business with Armed Groups in Conflict Areas: The Strategy of the Office of the Prosecutor of the International Criminal Court' (2010) 8 Journal of International Criminal Justice 947

Gardner J, 'Complicity and Causality' (2007) 1 Criminal Law and Philosophy 127

—— 'Moore on Complicity and Causality' (2008) 156 University of Pennsylvania Law Review 432

Garland D, 'Concepts of Culture in the Sociology of Punishment' (2006) 10 Theoretical Criminology 419

Gaskarth J, 'The Virtues in International Society' (2012) 18 European Journal of International Relations 431

Ghafur S and others, 'A Retrospective Impact Analysis of the WannaCry Cyberattack on the NHS' (2019) 2 Nature Partner Journals: Digital Medicine 98

Gillett M, 'Testing the Limits of the Law against Those Who Test the Tribunal's Limits: Contempt Proceedings at the Special Tribunal for Lebanon' (2017) 15 Journal of International Criminal Justice 775

Goose S and Smyth F, 'Arming Genocide in Rwanda' (1994) 73 Foreign Affairs 86

Greene O, 'Examining International Responses to Illicit Arms Trafficking' (2000) 33 Crime, Law and Social Change 151

Grillot SR, 'Global Gun Control: Examining the Consequences of Competing International Norms' (2011) 17 Global Governance 529

Guilfoyle D, 'Responsibility for Collective Atrocities: Fair Labelling and Approaches to Commission in International Criminal Law' (2011) 64 Current Legal Problems 255

Habteslasie A, 'A Humanitarian Intervention? The Court of Appeal Decision in *CAAT v Secretary of State for Trade*' (2019) Judicial Review 169

Hamilton R, 'The ICC's Exit Problem' (2014) 47 New York University Journal of International Law and Policy 1

Hamilton T, 'Outside, Inside, and Courtside: Taking Stock of the ICC' (2016) 27 Criminal Law Forum 99

—— 'Situating 'Law' as 'Culture' in Scholarly Discourse on the International Criminal Court' (2022) 18 International Journal of Law in Context 517

Hamilton T and Sluiter S, 'Principles of Reparations at the International Criminal Court: Assessing Alternative Approaches' (2022) 25 Max Planck Yearbook of United Nations Law 272

Hamilton T, Lucas N, Prezanti A, Smith M, and Strayer A, 'Targeted Sanctions as a Pathway to Accountability: An Active Role for Civil Society?' (2024) Journal of International Criminal Justice

Hansel M, Mutschler M, and Dickow M, 'Taming Cyber Warfare: Lessons from Preventive Arms Control' (2018) 3 Journal of Cyber Policy 44

Hansen S, 'Exploiting and Constructing Legal Ambiguity. UK Arms Exports to Saudi Arabia during the War in Yemen' (2023) European Security 32(4) 607

Hathaway JC, 'The Human Rights Quagmire of "Human Trafficking"' (2008) 49 Virginia Journal of International Law 1

Heise M, 'Past, Present, and Future of Empirical Legal Scholarship: Judicial Decision Making and the New Empiricism' (2002) The University of Illinois Law Review 819

Heller K, 'Who Is Afraid of the Crime of Aggression?' (2021) Journal of International Criminal Justice 19(4) 999

Heller KJ and Trabucco L, 'The Legality of Weapons Transfers to Ukraine Under International Law' (2022) Journal of International Humanitarian Legal Studies 13(2) 251–74

Henry R, *Jurisprudence Constante* and *Stare Decisis* Contrasted' (1929) 15 American Bar Association Journal 11

Holtom P and Bromley M, 'The International Arms Trade' (2010) 40 Arms Control 8

Hoover J, 'Reconstructing Responsibility and Moral Agency in World Politics' (2012) 4 International Theory 233

Jackson M, 'The Attribution of Responsibility and Modes of Liability in International Criminal Law' (2016) 29 Leiden Journal of International Law 879

—— 'Virtuous Accomplices in International Criminal Law' (2019) 68 International and Comparative Law Quarterly 817

Jackson RH, 'Justice Jackson's Report to President Truman on the Legal Basis for Trial of War Criminals' (1946) 19 Temple Law Quarterly 144

Jalloh CC, 'Special Court for Sierra Leone: Achieving Justice' (2011) 32 Michigan Journal of International Law 395

Jeßberger F, 'On the Origins of Individual Criminal Responsibility under International Law for Business Activity: IG Farben on Trial' (2010) 8 Journal of International Criminal Justice 783

Jo H and Simmons B, 'Can the International Criminal Court Deter Atrocity?' (2017) 71 International Organization 419

Jodoin S, 'Understanding the Behavior of International Courts: An Examination of Decision-Making at the Ad Hoc International Criminal Tribunals' (2010) 6 Journal of International Law and International Relations 1

Johnson RAI and Willardson SL, 'Human Rights and Democratic Arms Transfers: Rhetoric versus Reality with Different Types of Major Weapon Systems' (2018) 62 International Studies Quarterly 453

Jørgensen NHB, 'State Responsibility for Aiding or Assisting International Crimes in the Context of the Arms Trade Treaty' (2014) 108 AJIL 722

Kaldor K, 'The Idea of Global Civil Society' (2003) 79 International Affairs 583

Kelly MJ, '"Never Again"? German Chemical Corporation Complicity in the Kurdish Genocide' (2013) 31 Berkeley Journal of International Law 348

Kendall S and Nouwen S, 'Speaking of Legacy: Toward an Ethos of Modesty at the International Criminal Tribunal for Rwanda' (2016) 110 AJIL 212

Keppler E, 'Comment, Preventing Human Rights Abuses by Regulating Arms Brokering: The U.S. Brokering Amendment to the Arms Export Control Act' (2001) 19 Berkeley Journal of International Law 381

Kessler G, 'Judges' Awareness, Understanding, and Application of Digital Evidence' (2011) 6 Journal of Digital Forensics, Security and Law 55

Khoury S and Whyte D, 'Sidelining Corporate Human Rights Violations: The Failure of the OECD's Regulatory Consensus' (2019) 18 Journal of Human Rights 363

Kiss A, 'La contribución en la comisión de un crimen por un grupo de personas en la jurisprudencia de la Corte Penal Internacional' (2013) 2 InDret 1

Klare M, 'The Kalashnikov Age' (1999) 55 Bulletin of the Atomic Scientists 18

Koh HH, 'A World Drowning in Guns' (2002) 71 Fordham Law Review 2333

—— 'Why Transnational Law Matters' (2005) 24 Penn State International Law Review 745

—— 'International Criminal Justice 5.0' (2013) 38 Yale Journal of International Law 525

Koller DS, 'The Faith of the International Criminal Lawyer' (2007) 40 New York University Journal of International Law and Politics 1019

Kopel DB, Gallant P, and Eisen JD, 'The Arms Trade Treaty: Zimbabwe, the Democratic Republic of the Congo, and the Prospects for Arms Embargoes on Human Rights Violators' (2010) 114 Penn State Law Review 101

Koskenniemi M and Leino P, 'Fragmentation of International Law? Postmodern Anxieties' (2002) 15 Leiden Journal of International Law 553
Kotiswaran P and Palmer N, 'Rethinking the 'International Law of Crime': Provocations From Transnational Legal Studies' (2015) 6 Transnational Legal Theory 55
Kranz K, 'European Union Arms Embargoes: The Relationship between Institutional Design and Norms' (2016) 29 Cambridge Review of International Affairs 970
Krause K, 'The Political Economy of the International Arms Transfer System: The Diffusion of Military Technique via Arms Transfers' (1990) 45 International Journal 687
Kuo R and Spindel J, 'The Unintended Consequences of Arms Embargoes' (2023) 19(1) Foreign Policy Analysis
Kutz C, 'Causeless Complicity' (2007) 1 Criminal Law and Philosophy 289
Lester M and Kennelly B, 'Judicial Review of Sanctions Decisions: "The Wrong Point in the Wrong Court with the Wrong Defendant"?' (2013) 18 Judicial Review 206
Levy PI, 'Sanctions on South Africa: What Did They Do?' (1990) 89 The American Economic Review 415
Lowe V, 'Responsibility for the Conduct of Other States' (2011) 4 Japanese Journal of International Law 12
Lustgarten L, 'The Arms Trade Treaty: Achievements, Failings, Future' (2015) 64 ICLQ 569
Macintyre D and others, 'Letter: Divestment for Health: Consider the Arms Industry' (28 February 2020) 368 BMJ 765
Mack K and Anleu SR, 'The National Survey of Australian Judges: An Overview of Findings (2008) 18 Journal of Judicial Administration 5
Marriage Z, 'Ambiguous Agreements: Aid in Negotiating Processes' (2008) 8 Conflict, Security and Development 1
McCrudden, 'Legal Research and the Social Sciences' (2006) 122 LQR 632
McEvoy K, 'Beyond Legalism: Towards a Thicker Understanding of Transitional Justice' (2007) 34 Journal of Law and Society 411
McEvoy K and McConnachie K, 'Victimology in Transitional Justice: Victimhood, Innocence and Hierarchy' (2012) 9 European Journal of Criminology 527
Mégret F, 'International Criminal Justice as a Juridical Field' (2016) 13 Champ Pénal 1
Meierhenrich J, 'The Practice of International Law: A Theoretical Analysis' (2014) 76 Law and Contemporary Problems 1
—— 'The Practices of the International Criminal Court' (2013) Law and Contemporary Problems i–x
Merry SE, 'Legal Pluralism' (1988) 22 Law and Society Review 869
Meyer DS, 'Framing National Security: Elite Public Discourse on Nuclear Weapons during the Cold War.' (1995) 12 Political Communication 173
Milanovic M, 'Intelligence Sharing in Multinational Military Operations and Complicity under International Law' (2021) 97 International Law Studies 1269
Mkandawire T, 'The Terrible Toll of Post-Colonial Rebel Movements' (2002) 40 The Journal of Modern African Studies 181
Moore M, 'Arming the Embargoed: A Supply-Side Understanding of Arms Embargo Violations' (2010) 54 Journal of Conflict Resolution 593
Mosse D, 'Anti-social Anthropology? Objectivity, Objection, and the Ethnography of Public Policy and Professional Communities' (2006) 12 Journal of the Royal Anthropological Institute 935
Murray DR, 'Handguns, Gun Control Laws and Firearm Violence' (1975) 23 Social Problems 81
Musa S, 'The Saudi-Led Coalition in Yemen, Arms Exports and Human Rights: Prevention Is Better Than Cure' (2017) 22(3) Journal of Conflict and Security Law 433
Nelken D, 'Using The Concept of Legal Culture' (2004) 29 Australian Journal of Legal Philosophy 1
—— 'Thinking About Legal Culture' (2014) 1 Asian Journal of Law and Society 255
—— 'Comparative Legal Research and Legal Culture: Facts, Approaches, and Values' (2016) 12 Annual Review of Law and Social Science 45

Nerlich V, 'Core Crimes and Transnational Business Corporations' (2010) 8 Journal of International Criminal Justice 895

Nouwen S, 'The Importance of Frames: The Diverging Conflict Analyses of the United Nations and the African Union' (2013) 107 Proceedings of the American Society of International Law 330

Nouwen S and Werner W, 'Monopolizing Global Justice: International Criminal Law as Challenge to Human Diversity' (2015) 13 Journal of International Criminal Justice 157

Ohlin J, 'Joint Criminal Confusion' (2009) 12 New Criminal Law Review 408

Olson KB, 'Aum Shinrikyo: Once and Future threat?' (1999) 5 Emerging Infectious Diseases 513

Orlovsky K, 'International Criminal Law: Towards New Solutions in the Fight Against Illegal Arms Brokers' (2006) 29 Hasting International and Comparative Law Review 343

Palmer MG, 'The Case of Agent Orange: International Perspectives and an Homage to Victims' (2007) 29 Contemporary Southeast Asia: A Journal of International and Strategic Affairs 172

Palmer N, 'International Criminal Law and Border Control: The Expressive Role of the Deportation and Extradition of Genocide Suspects to Rwanda' (2020) Leiden Journal of International Law 1

Palmer N and Hamilton T, 'Legal Humility and Perceptions of Power in International Criminal Justice' (2022) International Criminal Law Review 1

Palmer N, Jones B, and Viebach J, 'Ways of Knowing Atrocity: A Methodological Enquiry into the Formulation, Implementation, and Assessment of Transitional Justice' (2015) 30 Canadian Journal of Law and Society 173

Palmer N and Kroner F, 'Anthropology, Transitional Justice and Criminal Law' (2019) 13 International Journal of Transitional Justice 398

Paretzky R, 'The United States Arms Embargo Against South Africa: An Analysis of the Laws, Regulations, and Loopholes' (1987) 12 Yale Journal of International Law 133

Paternoster R and Simpson S, 'Sanction Threats and Appeals to Morality: Testing a Rational Choice Model of Corporate Crime' (1996) 30 Law and Society Review 549

Perkins R and Neumayer E, 'The Organized Hypocrisy of Ethical Foreign Policy: Human Rights, Democracy and Western Arms Sales' (2010) 41 Geoforum 247

Petrochilos G, 'The Relevance of the Concepts of War and Armed Conflict to the Law of Neutrality' (1998) 31 Vanderbilt Transnational Law Journal 575, 605

Picinali F, 'The Denial of Procedural Safeguards in Trials for Regulatory Offences: A Justification' (2017) 11 Criminal Law and Philosophy 681

Pirie F, 'Law Before Government: Ideology and Aspiration' (2010) 30 OJLS 207

Platte H and Leuffen D, 'German Arms Exports: Between Normative Aspirations and Political Reality' (2016) 25 German Politics 561

Prunier G, 'Rebel Movements and Proxy Warfare: Uganda, Sudan and the Congo (1986–99)' (2004) 103 African Affairs 359

—— 'Burundi: A Manageable Crisis?' (1994) Writenet 252

Ramsden M and Hamilton T, 'Uniting Against Impunity: the UN General Assembly as a Catalyst for Action at the ICC' (2017) 66 ICLQ 893

Rastan R, 'What Is a 'Case' for the Purpose of the Rome Statute?' (2008) 19 Criminal Law Forum 435

—— 'What is "Substantially the Same Conduct"? Unpacking the ICC's "First Limb" Complementarity Jurisprudence' (2017) 15 Journal of International Criminal Justice 1

Raustiala K, 'Law, Liberalization and International Narcotics Trafficking' (1999) 32 NYU Journal of International Law and Policy 89

Raz J, 'Authority, Law and Morality' (1985) 68 The Monist 295

Reuter P and O'Regan D, 'Smuggling Wildlife in the Americas: Scale, Methods, and Links to other Organised Crimes' (2017) 18 Global Crime 77

Revesz RL, 'A Defense of Empirical Legal Scholarship' (2002) The University of Chicago Law Review 169

Reyntjens F, 'The Privatisation and Criminalisation of Public Space in the Geopolitics of the Great Lakes Region' (2005) 43 The Journal of Modern African Studies 587

Robinson D, 'Inescapable Dyads: Why the International Criminal Court Cannot Win' (2015) 28 Leiden Journal of International Law 323
Robson V, 'The Common Approach to Article 1: The Scope of Each State's Obligation to Ensure Respect for the Geneva Conventions' (2020) 25(1) Journal of Conflict and Security Law 101
Rome L, 'The Case for Prosecuting Arms Traffickers in the International Criminal Court' (2015) 36 Cardozo Law Review 1149
Salton DM, 'Starving the Dark Markets: International Injunctions as a Means to Curb Small Arms and Light Weapons Trafficking' (2013) 46 Connecticut Law Review 369
Saul B, 'The Legal Relationship between Terrorism and Transnational Crime' (2017) 17 International Criminal Law Review 417
Scheffer D, 'Corporate Liability under the Rome Statute' (2016) 57 Harvard International Law Journal 35
Schwöbel-Patel C, 'Spectacle in International Criminal Law: The Fundraising Image of Victimhood' (2016) 4 London Review of International Law 247
—— 'The "Ideal" Victim of International Criminal Law' (2018) 29 European Journal of International Law 703
Seroussi J, 'How Do International Lawyers Handle Facts? The Role of Folk Sociological Theories at the International Criminal Court' (2018) 69 The British Journal of Sociology 962
Sirico LJ and Margulies JB, 'Citing of Law Reviews by the Supreme Court: An Empirical Study' (1986) 34 UCLA Law Review 131
Sisk GC, Heise M, and Morriss AP, 'Charting the Influences on the Judicial Mind: An Empirical Study of Judicial Reasoning' (1998) 73 New York University Law Review 1377
Smith SD, 'In Defense of Traditional Legal Scholarship: A Comment on Schlegel, Weisberg, and Dan-Cohen' (1992) 63 University of Colorado Law Review 627
Stahn C, 'Liberals vs Romantics: Challenges of an Emerging Corporate International Criminal Law' (2018) 50 Case Western Reserve Journal of International Law 91
Stavrianakis A, 'When "Anxious Scrutiny" of Arms Exports Facilitates Humanitarian Disaster' (2018) 89 The Political Quarterly 92
—— 'Controlling Weapons Circulation in a Postcolonial Militarised World' (2019) 45 Review of International Studies 57
Stewart JG, 'Atrocity, Commerce and Accountability' (2010) 8 Journal of International Criminal Justice 314
—— 'Overdetermined Atrocities' (2012) 10 Journal of International Criminal Jus*tice* 1189
Stewart JG and Kiyani A, 'The Ahistoricism of Legal Pluralism in International Criminal Law' (2017) 65 The American Journal of Comparative Law 393
Stolk S, 'A Sophisticated Beast? On the Construction of an 'Ideal' Perpetrator in the Opening Statements of International Criminal Trials' (2018) 29 European Journal of International Law 677
Tamm H, 'The Origins of Transnational Alliances: Rulers, Rebels, and Political Survival in the Congo Wars' (2016) 41 International Security 147
Tannenwald N, 'Stigmatizing the Bomb: Origins of the Nuclear Taboo' (2005) 29 International Security 5
Thurner PW and others, 'Network Interdependencies and the Evolution of the International Arms Trade' (2019) 63 Journal of Conflict Resolution 1736
Torbey C, 'The Most Egregious Arms Broker: Prosecuting Arms Embargo Violators in the International Criminal Court' (2007) 25 Wisconsin International Law Journal 335
Van den Herik L, 'The Difficulties of Exercising Extraterritorial Criminal Jurisdiction: The Acquittal of a Dutch Businessman for Crimes Committed in Liberia' (2009) 9 International Criminal Law Review 211
Van der Wilt HG, 'Genocide, Complicity in Genocide and International v. Domestic Jurisdiction: Reflections on the van Anraat Case' (2006) 4 Journal of International Criminal Justice 239
—— 'Genocide v. War Crimes in the Van Anraat Appeal' (2008) 6 Journal of International Criminal Justice 557

Van Koppen PJ and Kate JT, 'Individual Differences in Judicial Behavior: Personal Characteristics and Private Law Decision-Making' (1984) Law and Society Review 225

Van Sliedregt E, 'International Criminal Law: Over-studied and Underachieving?' (2016) 29 Leiden Journal of International Law 1

Vasiliev S, 'Watershed Moment or Same Old? Ukraine and the Future of International Criminal Justice' (2022) 20 Journal of International Criminal Justice 893

Vest H, 'Business Leaders and the Modes of Individual Criminal Responsibility under International Law' (2010) 8 Journal of International Criminal Justice 864

Villers G, 'République démocratique du Congo De la guerre aux élections: L'ascension de Joseph Kabila et la naissance de la Troisième République (janvier 2001-août 2008)' (2009) 75 Cahiers africains 114

Vinjamuri L and Snyder J, 'Advocacy and Scholarship in the Study of International War Crime Tribunals and Transitional Justice' (2004) 7 Annual Review of Political Science 345

Webb P, 'The ICC Prosecutor's Discretion Not to Proceed in the "Interests of Justice"' (2005) 50 Criminal Law Quarterly 305

—— 'Scenarios of Jurisdictional Overlap among International Courts' (2006) 19 Revue québécoise de droit international 277

Webb P and Garciandia R, 'State Responsibility for Modern Slavery: Uncovering and Bridging the Gap' (2019) 68 ICLQ 539

Webb P and Michaelsen C, 'Strengthening the Accountability of the UN Security Council' (2014) 19 Journal of Conflict and Security Law 385

Webber J, 'Culture, Legal Culture, and Legal Reasoning: A Comment on Nelken' (2004) 1 Australian Journal of Legal Philosophy 29

Weisberg R, 'Empirical Criminal Law Scholarship and the Shift to Institutions' (2013) 65 Stanford Law Review 1371

Werle G, 'Individual Criminal Responsibility in Article 25 of the ICC Statute' (2007) 5 Journal of International Criminal Justice 970

Wessels A, 'The United Nations Arms Embargo Against South Africa, 1977–1994' (2010) 29 War and Society 137

Wheeler C, 'Re-examining Corporate Liability at the International Criminal Court through the Lens of the Art 15 Communication against Chiquita Brands International' (2018) 19 Melbourne Journal of International Law 369

Williams G, 'Convictions and Fair Labelling' (1983) 42 CLJ 85

—— 'Finis for novus actus' (1989) 48 CLJ 391

Wilson RA, 'Expert Evidence on Trial: Social Researchers in the International Criminal Courtroom' (2016) 43 American Ethnologist 730

Wright Q, 'The Scope of International Criminal Law: A Conceptual Framework' (1975) 15 Virginia Journal of International Law 561

Yoroms G, 'Approaches and Challenges in ECOWAS Security Sector Reform and Governance in West Africa' (2014) 1 Journal of African Foreign Affairs 30

Zumbansen P, 'Comparative, Global and Transnational Constitutionalism: The Emergence of a Transnational Legal-Pluralist Order' (2012) 1 Global Constitutionalism 16

Zwijsen S, Kanetake M, and Ryngaert CMJ, 'State Responsibility for Arms Transfers: The Law of State Responsibility and the Arms Trade Treaty' (2020) Ars Aequi 151

Blog Posts, Websites, Unpublished Papers, and Theses

Akande D, 'Is There Still a Need for Guidelines for the Exercise of ICC Prosecutorial Discretion?' (*EJIL: Talk!*, 28 October 2009) <www.ejiltalk.org/is-there-still-a-need-for-guidelines-for-the-exercise-of-icc-prosecutorial-discretion/> accessed 4 August 2024

—— 'What Is the Meaning of 'Consensus' in International Decision Making?' (*EJIL: Talk!*, 8 April 2013) <www.ejiltalk.org/negotiations-on-arms-trade-treaty-fail-to-adopt-treaty-by-consensus-what-is-the-meaning-of-consensus-in-international-decision-making> accessed 4 August 2024

Aksenova M and Bryk L, 'Extraterritorial Obligations of Arms Exporting Corporations: New Communication to the ICC' (*Opinio Juris Blog*, 14 January 2020) <http://opiniojuris.org/

2020/01/14/extraterritorial-obligations-of-arms-exporting-corporations-new-communication-to-the-icc/> accessed 4 August 2024

Ambos K, 'Complicity in War Crimes through (Legal) Arms Supplies?' (*EJIL: Talk!*, 20 January 2020) <www.ejiltalk.org/complicity-in-war-crimes-through-legal-arms-supplies> accessed 4 August 2024

Castellanos-Jankiewicz L and Schneider M, 'Including the Arms Sector in the EU Corporate Due Diligence Directive' (*Verfassungsblog*, 19 May 2023) <https://verfassungsblog.de/including-the-arms-sector-in-the-eu-corporate-due-diligence-directive> accessed 4 August 2024

Christensen MJ, 'Academics for International Criminal Justice: The Role of Legal Scholars in Creating and Sustaining a New Legal Field' (*iCourts Working Paper Series* 2014) <http://dx.doi.org/10.2139/ssrn.2539048> accessed 4 August 2024

Clark P, 'Distant Justice Symposium: A Reply' (*Opinio Juris Blog*, 4 October 2019) <http://opiniojuris.org/2019/10/04/distant-justice-symposium-a-reply-by-phil-clark> accessed 4 August 2024

de Moraes RF, 'Our Weapons, our Problem: Arms Exports, Democracy and Civil Society in Brazil and the UK' (DPhil in International Relations, University of Oxford 2019)

Guilfoyle D, 'Reforming the International Criminal Court: Is it Time for the Assembly of State Parties to be the Adults in the Room?' (*EJIL: Talk!*, 8 May 2019) <www.ejiltalk.org/reforming-the-international-criminal-court-is-it-time-for-the-assembly-of-state-parties-to-be-the-adults-in-the-room> accessed 4 August 2024

Hopkins R, 'What Next for the Alien Tort Statute?' (*Corporate War Crimes Blog*, 30 March 2020) <https://corporatewarcrimes.com/2020/03/30/what-next-for-the-alien-tort-statute> accessed 4 August 2024

Human Rights Watch, 'New EU Law on Corporate Value Chains' (24 May 2024) <https://www.hrw.org/news/2024/05/24/questions-and-answers-new-eu-law-corporate-value-chains> accessed 4 August 2024

Krause K, *Norm-building in Security Spaces: The Emergence of the Light Weapons Problematic* (Research Group in International Security Occasional Paper, 2001) accessed 4 August 2024

Meessen KM, 'International Law of Export Control: Jurisdictional Issues' (Aspen Publishers, 1992) 19

Oxford English Dictionary (Online edn, revised December 2013)

Palmer N, 'Tensions in Domestic and International Criminal Justice' (*OUPblog*, 29 June 2015) <https://blog.oup.com/2015/06/tensions-in-domestic-and-international-criminal-justice/> accessed 4 August 2024

Payne LA and Pereira G, 'Corporate Complicity in Dictatorships' (*Oxford University Saïd Business School website*, 2014) <https://ora.ox.ac.uk/objects/uuid:fae61c56-9b8d-4f82-b731-283330bc051e/files/m2e5a9886323844ff0f901ebb3b04fc99> accessed 15 October 2024

Principles for Responsible Investment (*United Nations PRI website*, 2020)<www.unpri.org> accessed 4 August 2024

Reyntjens F, 'The Congo Wars' (*Oxford Research Encyclopedia of African History*, 1 March 2020) <https://oxfordre.com/africanhistory/> accessed 12 December 2024

Saul B, 'Terrorism in International and Transnational Criminal Law' (Sydney Law School Research Paper, 2015)

Small Arms Survey, 'Illicit Trafficking' (*Small Arms Survey website*, 2020) <www.smallarmssurvey.org/de/weapons-and-markets/transfers/illicit-trafficking.html> accessed 4 August 2024

—— 'Transfers' (*Small Arms Survey website*, 2020) <www.smallarmssurvey.org/weapons-and-markets/transfers.html> accessed 4 August 2024

Stewart JG, 'The Historical Importance of the Kouwenhoven Trial' (*Blog of James G Stewart*, 5 May 2017) <http://jamesgstewart.com/the-historical-importance-of-the-kouwenhoven-trial/> accessed 4 August 2024

—— 'Panel Discussion: International Law and Theories of Global Justice' (114th Annual Meeting of the American Society of International Law, 25 June 2020)

UNODA, 'Small Arms and Light Weapons' (*Conventional Arms Branch website*, May 2020) <http://disarmament.un.org:8080/cab/salw.html> accessed 4 August 2024

United Nations, 'Arms Exports to Israel Must Stop Immediately' (*UN Human Rights website*, 23 February 2024) <https://www.ohchr.org/en/press-releases/2024/02/arms-exports-israel-must-stop-immediately-un-experts> accessed 4 August 2024

Van Gestel R, Micklitz HW, and Maduro MP, 'Methodology in the New Legal World' (EUI Working Papers, 2012)

Van Sliedregt E and Popova A, 'Interpreting "for the purpose of facilitating" in Art 25(3)(c)?'(*Blog of James G Stewart*, 22 December 2014) <http://jamesgstewart.com/interpreting-for-the-purpose-of-facilitating-in-Article-253c/> accessed 4 August 2024

Weapons Law Encyclopaedia (*Weapons Law Encyclopaedia website*, 2020) <www.weaponslaw.org> accessed 4 August 2024

NGO Reports and Legal Opinions

Amnesty International, 'Democratic Republic of Congo: Arming the East' (Amnesty International, 4 July 2005)

—— 'Our Brothers Who Help Kill Us, Economic Exploitation and Human Rights Abuses in the East' (Amnesty International, 31 March 2003)

Batchelor P and McDonald G, 'Too Close for Comfort: An Analysis of the UN Tracing Negotiations' (UNIDIR Disarmament Forum, 2006)

Bauer S and Bromley M, *The European Union Code of Conduct on Arms Exports: Improving the Annual Report* (SIPRI 2004)

Berman EG and Lombard LN, *The Central African Republic and Small Arms: A Regional Tinderbox* (Small Arms Survey 2008)

Borrie J and Randin VM, 'Thinking Outside the Box in Multilateral Disarmament and Arms Control Negotiations' (United Nations Institute for Disarmament Research 2006)

Conflict Armament Research, 'Weapon Supplies into South Sudan's Civil War: Regional Re-Transfers and International Intermediaries' (Conflict Armament Research November 2018)

—— 'Non-State Armed Groups in the Central African Republic: Types and Sources of Documented Arms and Ammunition' (Conflict Armament Research 2015)

—— 'Weapons and Ammunition Airdropped to SPLA-iO Forces in South Sudan' (Conflict Armament Research May 2015)

Control Arms Campaign: Amnesty International, Oxfam International and International Action Network on Small Arms, '*UN Arms Embargoes: An Overview of the Last Ten Years*' (Amnesty International, 16 March 2006)

Cook D, Roberts M, and Lowther J, 'The International Wildlife Trade and Organised Crime: A Review of the Evidence and the Role of the UK' (World Wide Fund for Nature 2002)

Cuvelier J and Raeymaekers T, 'European Companies and The Coltan Trade: An Update Part 2' (International Peace Information Service September 2002) 3

Global Witness, 'The Usual Suspects. Liberia's Weapons and Mercenaries in Côte d'Ivoire and Sierra Leone. Why It's Still Possible, How it Works and How to Break the Trends' (Global Witness March 2003)

Hamilton T, 'Regulating the Arms Trade: The Potential of International Criminal Law' (International Crimes Database, Brief 17 2015)

—— 'An Arms Trade Case at the International Criminal Court: Would the Article 25(3)(c) 'Purpose' Requirement Really Matter?' (*Rethinking SLIC*, 23 September 2021) <https://rethinkingslic.org/blog/criminal-law/93-an-arms-trade-case-at-the-international-criminal-court-would-the-article-25-3-c-purpose-requirement-really-matter> accessed 4 August 2024

Hays G and Jenzen-Jones NR, 'Beyond State Control: Improvised and Craft-produced Small Arms and Light Weapons' (Small Arms Survey, November 2018)

Human Rights Watch, 'Democratic Republic of Congo and the International Criminal Court, Report on the Hearing to Confirm the Charges against Thomas Lubanga Dyilo' (Human Rights Watch, November 2006)

—— 'The Selection of Situations and Cases for Trial before the International Criminal Court: A Human Rights Watch Policy Paper' (Human Rights Watch, October 2006)

—— 'Democratic Republic of Congo: The Curse of Gold' (Human Rights Watch, 2 June 2005)

—— 'Ituri: "Covered in Blood", Ethnically Targeted Violence in Northeastern DR Congo (Human Rights Watch, July 2003)

—— 'Uganda in Eastern DRC Fueling Political and Ethnic Strife' (Human Rights Watch, March 2001)

—— 'State Responsibility in the Arms Trade and the Protection of Human Rights' (Human Rights Watch, 17 February 1999)

—— 'Human Rights Watch World Report 1998—Rwanda' (Human Rights Watch, 1 January 1998), Commentary of 2016 on the First Geneva Convention of 12 August 1949 (2016)

International Crisis Group, 'Congo at War: A Briefing of the Internal and External Players in the Central African Conflict' (International Crisis Group, 17 November 1998)

International Rescue Committee, 'Mortality in the Democratic Republic of Congo: Results from a Nationwide Survey' (Burnet Institute 2004)

Jenzen-Jones NR and McCollum I, 'Web Trafficking: Analzying the Online Trade of Small Arms and Light Weapons in Libya' (Small Arms Survey, Security Assessment in North Africa Working Paper 26, 2017)

Mack D and Wood B 'Civil Society and the Drive Towards an Arms Trade Treaty' (United Nations Institute for Disarmament Research, February 2009)

Picard M, Holtom P, and Mangan F, 'Trade Update 2019: Transfers, Transparency, and Southeast Asia Spotlight' (Small Arms Survey, December 2019)

Sands P, Clapham A, and Ní Ghrálaigh B, 'The Lawfulness of the Authorisation by the United Kingdom of Weapons and Related Items for Export to Saudi Arabia in the Context of Saudi Arabia's Military Intervention in Yemen' (*Saferworld*, 11 December 2015) <www.saferworld.org.uk/downloads/pubdocs/legal-opinion-on-uk-arms-exports-to-saudi.pdf> accessed 4 August 2024

Scheffer D, 'Amicus Curiae Brief in Support of the Issuance of a Writ of Certiorari) Presbyterian Church of Sudan, and others. v Talisman Energy, Inc. (19 May 2010) Supreme Court of the United States <http://hrp.law.harvard.edu/wp-content/uploads/2013/07/talisman-amicus-final-filed-4-30-10.pdf> accessed 4 August 2024

Schmitt M, 'Providing Arms and Materiel to Ukraine: Neutrality, Co-Belligerency, and the Use of Force' (*Articles of War*, 7 March 2022) <https://lieber.westpoint.edu/ ukraine-neutrality-co-belligerency-use-of-force/>

Small Arms Survey, 'Small Arms Ammunition Documented at Bentiu Mosque' (Small Arms Survey, May 2014)

—— 'SIPRI Yearbook 1999: Armaments, Disarmament, and International Security' (Stockholm Institute for Peace Research July 1999)

Transparency International, 'UN Should Support ICC Investigations into Links Between Corrupt Business and War Crimes in DRC (Transparency International, 4 November 2003)

Wallensteen P, Staibano C, and Eriksson M (eds), 'Making Targeted Sanctions Effective: Guidelines for the Implementation of UN Policy Options' (Uppsala University 2003)

Wood B and Peleman J, 'The Arms Fixers. Controlling the Brokers and Shipping Agents' (Peace Research Institute Oslo, 2000)

Wood B, Southward F, and Danssaert P, 'Weapons and International Law: The Arms Trade Treaty' (International Peace Information Service, 19 August 2015)

OTP Public Documents

De Smedt M, 'Speech on The Role of Companies in Conflicts within the Court's Jurisdiction' (29 October 2010) < https://www.icc-cpi.int/news/speech-head-investigation-michel-de-smedt-role-companies-conficts-within-courts-jurisdiction> accessed 4 August 2024

Moreno Ocampo L, 'Statement by the Prosecutor, Luis Moreno Ocampo, to Diplomatic Corps, The Hague, Netherlands' (12 February 2004) 4<www.legal-tools.org/doc/6dvm3d/>

OTP, 'Draft Paper on Some Policy Issues before the Office of the Prosecutor for Discussion at the Public Hearing in The Hague on 17 and 18 June 2003' (18 June 2003) <www.legal-tools.org/doc/abb9f7/> accessed 10 May 2020

OTP, 'Paper on Some Policy Issues before the Office of the Prosecutor' (5 September 2003) <www.legal-tools.org/doc/f53870/> accessed 10 May 2020

OTP, 'Policy Paper on the Interests of Justice' (1 September 2007) <www.legal-tools.org/doc/bb02e5/a6> accessed 4 August 2024

Press Articles and Online News

Doward J, 'How an Illegal Deal for 80,000 Weapons Led to the Downfall of Britain's "Lord of War"' (*The Guardian*, 2 December 2012) <www.theguardian.com/world/2012/dec/02/gary-hyde-illegal-arms-trader> accessed 22 June 2020

Greenan, P 'Jailed Arms Broker Gary Hyde's International Deals' (*BBC News website*, 5 December 2012) <https://www.bbc.com/news/uk-england-humber-20611401> accessed 22 June 2020

Human Rights Watch, 'D.R. Congo: ICC Arrest First Step to Justice' (*Human Rights Watch news release*, 17 March 2006) <www.hrw.org/news/2006/03/17/dr-congo-icc-arrest-first-step-justice> accessed 25 June 2020

Landesman, P 'Arms and the Man' (*New York Times Magazine*, 17 August 2003)

Ramjathan-Keogh K and Feinstein A, 'Why is South Africa Providing a Haven for an Arms Dealer Convicted of War Crimes?' (*Daily Maverick*, 18 March 2020) <www.dailymaverick.co.za/article/2020-03-18-why-is-south-africa-providing-a-haven-for-an-arms-dealer-convicted-of-war-crimes/#gsc.tab=0> accessed 22 June 2020

Regional Centre on Small Arms in the Great Lakes Region, the Horn of Africa and Bordering states, website < https://recsasec.org> accessed on 24 June 2020

Urry A, 'Jailed Arms Dealer Sold Guns to Police and MoD ' (*BBC News website*, 15 January 2013) <www.bbc.co.uk/news/uk-20991545> accessed 22 June 2020

Van Woudenberg A, 'Arrest All Ituri Warlords' (*Le Potentiel*, 11 March 2005)

Wakabi W and Opolot O, 'Museveni Shopped for Guns in Belarus' (*The East African*, 24 April 2000)

Index

For the benefit of digital users, indexed terms that span two pages (e.g., 52–53) may, on occasion, appear on only one of those pages.

accomplice liability doctrine 3, 11–12
actus reus 70–71, 78, 79
Arms Trade Law 48
ICC case selection 145, 149
mens rea 91
accomplices 3–5, 18, 35, 40, 64, 82, 83–84, 121
accountability
corporate 15–16, 66, 129–30
ex post facto 3, 19–20, 31, 36–37, 39, 40–41, 63, 122, 169, 170, 173, 188–89
gap 2, 17, 68
international criminal 39–41, 47, 174–75, 177–78, 188–89, 196
mass violence 148
terrorism, victims of 59
active personality principle 22
actors 6
types of 8–10
actus reus 7–8, 196
actus reus 70–90
causal relationship with arms transfer 81–83
export regulation 27–28
ICC case selection 138–40
interpretation 72–73
mens rea 101, 107
administrative fines 20
advertising 10–11
Afghanistan 10
Agency for the Safety of Air Navigation in Africa and Madagascar (ASECNA) 61–62
aggression 2, 6, 35, 36
victims of 54
AI *see* artificial intelligence (AI)
aiding or abetting 3, 16
actus reus 70, 75, 80, 81
mens rea 91–94, 101
Akande, D. 136
Aksenova, M. 15–16
Al-Qaida 59
Albania 158–59
Alliance of Democratic Forces for the Liberation of Congo (ADFL) 156–57
Allied Democratic Forces (ADF) 155–56
Ambos, K. 35–36, 88
Amnesty International 24, 174
Anderson, E. S. 65–66
Angola 10
Second Congo War 154, 158, 160, 168–69
'ant trade' 9–10, 161
see also micro-trade
Anthony, I. 13–14, 32–33
anthropology 114
see also legal culture
anti-aircraft missile systems 6–7
anti-corruption law 196
Arms Trade Law 49–50, 61
export regulation 18
anti-personnel mines 7
anti-tank guns 6–7
'any other contribution' 89
apartheid 42
armoured combat vehicles 6
arms control law 12
arms, definitional questions 7–8
arms embargoes 2, 12–13, 197
Arms Trade Law 39–49
export regulation 19–20, 30
Second Congo War 166–67
selective use of 43–45
arms manufacturing corporations 8
arms trade
already regulated, arms trade as 120–21
approach 118–24
recognizing potential cases in the DRC situation 178–80
Arms Trade Law (ATL) 3, 10, 17, 38–69
alignment 104
export regulation 18
plurality of 49–62
Arms Trade Treaty (ATT) 1–2, 6, 12, 13, 16
arms trade law 57, 60, 68
DRC situation 188–89
export regulation 18, 19, 24, 25, 29, 33–34, 35
ICC legal culture 120
limited scope of 30–31

Arms Trade Treaty (ATT) (*cont.*)
  mens rea 104, 108–9
  Second Congo War 152–53, 164–65, 166
arms transfer complicity 104–7
arms transfer conduct 6, 10–12
Articles on Responsibility of States for Internationally Wrongful Acts (ARSIWA) 50–51, 51n.84, 52–53
Artificial Intelligence (AI) 27
assault rifles 6–7
Assembly of States Parties (ASP) 135–36, 151–52
asset freezing 167, 194
attribution 15–16
Aum Shinrikyo group 34–35
Auschwitz 4
  see also Holocaust; Nazi regime
Austria 9, 20
Autesserre, S. 176

background proliferation 9
Bamako Declaration 165
banyamulenge 157
battle tanks 6
Belarus 158–59
Belgium 9
  export regulation 32–33
  Second Congo War 158–59, 161–62
Bemba, Jean-Pierre 156–57
biological technology 7
blind spots 178, 180–93, 198
Boister, N. 62
booby traps 7
Bosnia 10
Bourdieu, P. 145–47
Bout, Victor 10, 20, 22–23, 161, 172, 180, 182, 193
Brazil
  Second Congo War 158–59
  small arms transfer 9
Bredenkamp, J. 172
bribery 61
British Military Courts 4, 66
brokering
  ineffective regulation 28–29
  third state 28, 31, 54
brokers 8, 9
  definition of 9–10
  export regulation 28
  ICC legal culture 126, 131
  Second Congo War 153, 160–62, 175, 176
Bryk, L. 16
Bulgaria 158–59
bullet tracing technology 87
Burchard, C. 5, 98
Burke-White, W. W. 181
Burkina Faso 159
Burundi 154–55, 156–57, 158, 160, 165, 168–69

Cambodia 1–2, 34–35
Campaign Against the Arms Trade (CAAT) 23–24
Capone, Al 128
Casey-Maslan, S. 13
causation 15–16
  'but for' test 79–80
  criminal law concept of 79–80, 81, 82
Central African Republic (CAR) 155, 158
Chad 158
chemical technology 7
chemical weapons 34–35, 78–79
child soldiers 86
China 9, 13–14
  Arms Trade Law 44–45
  export regulation 19, 29
Chiquita corporation 56
civil society organizations 171, 180
civilian goods 7–8
Clapham, A. 13–14, 15–16, 24, 57–58
Clark, P. 113–14, 116, 181, 183, 186, 191–92
co-perpetration doctrine 84
coercive diplomacy 167–68
cognitive dissonance theory 144
Cold War 7, 34–35, 44, 154, 158–59, 168–69
colonialism 161
  see also postcolonialism
Columbian paramilitary groups 56
combat aircraft 6
commission of crimes 164
  definition of 84, 108
common purpose
  group 84–85, 107
  liability 89, 106–7
complementarity principle 18, 48, 72–73, 122, 137
complicity doctrine 3, 7–8, 17, 65–66, 73, 82, 95–96, 106
conduct *see* arms transfer conduct
Congo Free State 161–62
  see also Second Congo War
Congolese Armed Forces (FAC) 155–56, 166
conventional weapons 60–61, 86
  definition of 6
  major 6, 9, 26–27, 162
  see also non-conventional weapons
corporate accountability 15–16, 57–58, 66, 129–30
corporate social responsibility (CSR) 124

counterterrorism law 18, 38, 46–47, 49–50, 58–59, 196
  see also terrorism
coup d'état 157
credit agencies 51
crimes against humanity 1, 2, 6, 8
  export regulation 19, 20–21, 30, 35, 36
  ICC DRC Situation 188–89
  mens rea 109
  Second Congo War 174–75
Croatia 9
cross-border transfers 27
Cryer, R. 181–82, 191, 194–95
Curse of Gold report 174–75
customary international law 54, 101
cyber law 18, 49–50, 196
cyber weapons 60–61
Czech Republic 9

D'Aspremont, J. 142
Danner, A. M. 182–83
de Gurmendi, Fernández 88–89
de minimis requirement 74, 80, 83
de novo trial 21, 22
De Smedt, M. 185
defences 18
Democratic Republic of the Congo (DRC) 1, 2, 3, 9–10, 17, 197–98
  actus reus 70
  anti-DRC alliance 156–57, 158–59, 162, 168, 174
  Arms Trade Law 46, 60, 69
  export regulation 22–23
  ICC DRC Situation 177–95
  ICC legal culture 122–23
  Panel of Experts 172–74, 175–76, 179–80, 197–98
  pro-DRC alliance 155–56, 157, 158, 159, 162, 168
  Second Congo War 151–52, 153–55, 157–76
deterrence 142, 191
digital arms 60–61
digital technologies 27
diplomatic protection 50–51
directness 83–84
discretion, judicial 136, 180
Djibouti 159
DNA analysis 85
drones 27–28
drug trafficking 9, 49–50, 60, 103, 104–5, 125
dual-use items 7–8

Egypt 159
embargo busters 47–49
encouragement 73
end user documentation 12–13
environmental crime 49–50, 60
environmental law 124
Environmental, Social and Governance (ESG) 57–58
Erickson, J. L. 14, 26–27, 33
Eritrea/Ethiopia 159, 167
'essential matters' test 97–98, 108
ethics
  arms export policies 26
  investment 57–58
European Convention on Human Rights (ECHR) 56
European Court of Human Rights (ECtHR) 21
European Union (EU)
  Common Position 13, 18, 19, 33–34, 57, 68, 108–9
  corporate due diligence 57
  Council 41
  directives 59
  DRC, influence on 182–83
  embargoes 39, 48, 99, 104
  export standard 55
  Extradition Convention 104–5, 107
  Second Congo War embargoes 166–67, 168, 169, 175–76
evidence 126–28, 197
  see also forensic evidence
explosive remnants of war 7
export regulation 18–37
  see also international agreements
expressivism 66, 67
extermination 86
Extraordinary Chambers in the Courts of Cambodia (ECCC) 3, 5

Feinstein, A. 14
financial investment 57–58
Financing Terrorism Convention 58–59
force
  degree of 82–83
  exercising, manner of 82–83
  see also use of force
foreign policy constraints 25–27
forensic evidence 85
former Rwandan Armed Forces (ex-FAR) 174
France 13–14
  export controls 32–33
  export regulation 19
  ICC DRC Situation 182–83
  loi de vigilance 57
  Second Congo War 154–55, 158, 168

Gallmetzer, R. 15–16
Gardner, J. 15–16, 82, 83–84
Garland, D. 114–15, 123, 178
Geertz, C. 111–12, 146
gender-based violence 108, 151
Geneva Conventions (1949) 30, 53, 55
genocide 2, 6
  actus reus 86
  export regulation 20–21, 35, 36
  ICC DRC situation 188–89
  mens rea 99
  Second Congo War 158
Germany 9
  arms manufacturing 13–14, 19
  criminals 1
  low-value exports 11
  small arms transfer 9
global arms trade 14
Global North 164–65, 168
Global Witness 23
gravity, sufficient 191
Great Lakes Region 160, 165, 168, 182–83
  arms proliferation in the 154–55
  transfers outside 158–60
grenade launchers 6–7
Grillot, S. 168n.104
group crime, knowingly contributing to a 16, 71, 91, 94–95, 107–8, 109–10, 196–97
guarantee agencies 51
Guilfoyle, D. 105
Guinea 159
gun ownership 25–26

Habayarimana, Juvénal 154–55
habitus, concept of 145–47
Hague Conventions (1907) 53, 54
heavy machine guns 6–7
helicopters 6
Heller, K. 54
herbicides 34–35
Hiroshima 34–35
Holocaust 187–88
homicide 7
Hoover, J. 148–49
horizontal selectivity 190–93
human rights
  abuses 168
  arms exports 26–27
  business and 49–50, 66
  discourse 35
  international law 49–50
  law 14, 18, 124
  serious violations 138
  violations of 6, 33, 162
  see also international humanitarian law (*jus in bello*)
Human Rights Watch 168, 174–75, 176
human trafficking 9, 49–50, 60
humanitarian workers 143–44
humility 123–24
Hussein, Saddam 21, 99
Hutu fighters 154–55
hybrid tribunals 120–21

ICC *see* International Criminal Court (ICC)
ICC case selection 133–50
  case selection 134–35
  indeterminacy of rules 134–40
  legal reasoning 136–37
  legalism 140–49
  OTP policy 135–36
  Regulation 33 135–36
  weakly articulated legal grounds 137–40
  see also legalism
ICC DRC Situation 9–10, 134, 177–95
  context 177–78, 193–95
  horizontal selectivity 190–93
  imagined perpetrators 185–90
  imagined victims 185–90
ICC legal culture 111–32, 139, 145–49, 180–81
  complex business structures 128–30
  context 111, 131–32
  dangerous security risks 125–26
  evidence, challenges to obtaining 126–28
  ICC deference to national authorities 122–23
  ICC non-regulator status 119–20
  international criminal law 123–24
  pragmatic constraints 124–31
'ideal' perpetrators 187–88, 197
IG Farben corporation 4
illegal resource extraction
  Arms Trade Law 49–50, 60
  mandate on 170–71
  Second Congo War 158, 164, 174–75
illicit trading 65, 130–31, 196
impartiality *see* neutrality law
impunity 198
  ICC case selection 142–43, 147–48, 149–50
  ICC legal culture 123–24, 127
  Second Congo War 176
'in any other way contributes' ('*toutes autres contributions*') 77–78
India 13–14, 19
individual conduct 14–15
infinitesimal contributions 79–80
internally displaced persons (IDPs) 151
international agreements 2, 18, 29–35

Arms Trade Treaty, limited scope of 30–31
atrocity victims, accountability for 31–35
International Committee of the Red Cross (ICRC) 55
International Convention for the Suppression of Terrorist Bombings 88–89
International Court of Justice (ICJ) 51, 52–53, 90
International Covenant on Civil and Political Rights (ICCPR) 56
international crime, definition of 6
International Criminal Court (ICC)
aspirational nature 198
case selection *see* ICC case selection
complicity doctrines 3
constraints 17
DRC investigations *see* ICC DRC Situation
exceptionalism 131
inception of 1
institutional culture 3, 17, 133, 142, 149, 183, 197
legal culture *see* ICC legal culture
International Criminal Law 123–24
complicity, seriousness of 65–66
definition of 6
existing arms trade law, limitations of 63–64
integration of 45–47
potential role for 62–67
scholarship 12–17
scope of application 18
International Criminal Tribunal for Rwanda (ICTR) 3, 5, 47, 71–72, 74, 75, 114–15, 147, 181–82
International Criminal Tribunal for the former Yugoslavia (ICTY) 3, 4–5, 47, 71–72, 74, 75, 81, 87, 97
international economic law 18, 49–50, 196
international human rights law 56–58
international humanitarian law (*jus in bello*) 18, 19, 49–50, 53, 55, 108–9
International Law Commission (ILC) 50
International Military Tribunal (IMT) 3–5
International Monetary Fund (IMF) 61–62
International Rescue Committee 151
International Traffic in Arms Regulations (ITAR) 61
Interpol Red Notices 180
interpretative community 147
investment insurance agencies 51
Iran 11
export regulation 21, 34–35
mens rea 99, 104
Second Congo War 158–59, 167
Israel 9, 158–59
Gaza conflict 26
Italy 9
item categories/types 6–8, 41–43
limitations 27–28
Ituri warlord cases 183, 184–85, 186–88, 189, 191–92, 198

Jackson, M. 15–16, 101
Jackson, R. H. 1, 2, 5
Jain, N. 15–16
Japan 34–35
Joint Criminal Enterprise (JCE) 73n.10, 75, 106–7
Jørgensen, N. 15–16
journalism 197
jurisdiction 18
jurisprudence constante 72
jus ad bellum see use of force
'justice versus peace' dilemma 144

Kabila, Joseph 155, 169, 181, 182–83
Kabila, Laurent-Désiré 154–56, 163, 164–65, 168–69, 170–71, 191–92
Kadogo youth fighters 163
Kalashnikov AK47 7, 163–64
Kampala amendment 6
Katanga, Germain 86, 97, 151–52, 181
Kelsall, T. 113–14
Kennedy, D. 123–24
Kenya 125, 159
Kersten, M. 113–14
knowledge
concept of 100
constructive 109
degree of 100–3
essential matters 95–98
fact-finding 98–100
sources of 98–100
specificity of 95–98
Kony, Joseph 148
Kouwenhoven, Augustinus 22–23, 100, 148
Krupp AG 3–4
Kurdistan 64
Kutz, C. 15–16, 82

Laos 34–35
large-calibre artillery systems 6
laser weapons 7
law versus politics paradigm 116, 125, 182, 198
lawful arms trade 8, 11–12, 54, 67, 196
complicity in 65
definition of 9
League of Nations Covenant (1919) 32–33
legal certainty 72–73

legal culture 139, 145–47, 176
  concept of 111–18
  identification 117–18
  interpretation 114–15
  'law versus politics', beyond 116
  see also ICC legal culture
legal pluralism, definition of 38
legalism 140–49
  aspiration versus 142–45
  cognitive dissonance 143–45
  concepts of 140–42
  global 141
  ICC case selection 140–49
  ICC legal culture 145–47
  increasing dominance of 141–42
liberal militarism 14
Liberia 10, 22–23, 29, 100, 159
Libya 10, 47, 158
light machine guns 6–7
light weapons, definition of 6–7
Lohne, K. 113–14
Lubanga, Thomas 151–52, 157, 181, 182–84
Lustgarten, L. 13–14, 19

machetes 8, 154–55
Major Conventional Weapons (MCW) 6, 9, 26–27, 162
Malaya 34–35
mass violence 2, 142, 196
  structural causes of 119–20, 123–24, 131, 147–50
matériel 27, 41, 43
McEvoy, K. 141, 187
Mégret, F. 68
Meierhenrich, J. 114, 118, 122, 146–47
mens rea 7–8, 91–110, 196–97
  actus reus and 70–71, 74–75, 77, 78, 79, 89
  export regulation 20, 27–28, 36
  ICC case selection 137–40
Methodists 57–58
micro-traders 3, 8, 9–10, 131, 153, 177
micro-transfers 161
Middle Ages 31–32
Minin, Leonard 22–23, 29, 172
missiles 6
  launchers 6
Mkandawire, T. 163
monetary value of trades 11
Moreno-Ocampo, L. 1–7, 22–23, 148, 151–52, 176, 184–85
Mozambique 159
Muchai, A. 153–55, 159
murder 4, 86, 109, 143–44
Museveni, Yoweri 154–55
mustard gas attacks 21, 35
mutual dependence 157
Myanmar 46

Nagasaki 34–35
Nairobi Declaration 165
Nairobi Protocol 165
Namibia 158, 160
national arms export regulations 19–29
  brokering regulation, ineffective 28–29
  foreign policy constraints 25–27
  item types, limitations to specified 27–28
  national export criteria, in relation to international crimes 19–21
  Netherlands 21–23
  United Kingdom 23–25
national control systems 31
National Health Service (NHS) 60–61
Nazi regime 16–17
  concentration camps 2, 4, 34–35
  see also Holocaust
Nerlich, V. 15–16
Netherlands 21–23
  export controls 32–33
  unlawful exports as complicity 21–23
neutrality law 18, 49–50, 53–54, 196
  qualified neutrality 54
NGOs *see* Non-Governmental Organizations (NGOs)
Ngudjolo, Mathieu 181
Ní Ghrálaigh, B. 13–14, 24
Nicaragua 52–53
Niezen, R. 169–70, 187
Nigeria 29
non-armed state groups 193
non-conventional weapons 7, 34–35, 46–47
  see also conventional weapons
non-detectable fragments 7
Non-Governmental Organizations (NGOs) 2, 24, 30, 188, 189, 197
non-intervention principle 52
North Atlantic Treaty Organization (NATO) 33–34
North Korea 158–59
Nouwen, S. 113–14, 116, 143–44
Ntaganda, Bosco 181
nuclear technology 7
Nuclear Terrorism Convention 105
nuclear weapons 7, 34–35
Nuremberg Charter 75
Nuremberg trials 2, 3–4, 117, 193–94

obiter dicta views 90
Office of the Prosecutor of the International Criminal Court (OTP)
  actus reus 86–87

Arms Trade Law 46
ICC case selection 133–34
ICC DRC Situation 184, 186, 187–88, 190–91, 198
mens rea 106, 109–10
policy 135–36, 194–95
Regulations 135–36, 178–79, 180, 183
Office of the United Nations High Commissioner for Human Rights (OHCHR) 162

Organization of African Unity (OAU) 159n.55, 165
Organization of American States (OAS) 33–34
Organization for Economic Cooperation and Development (OECD) Guidelines for Multinational Enterprises 56
Organization for Security and Co-operation in Europe (OSCE) 33–34
organized crime networks 125–26, 127, 176, 196
Oxfam 24

Palestine 198
Gaza conflict 26
Palmer, N. 67, 113–15
Panel of Experts (DRC) 170–75
annexes, revision of 173
arms supplies, findings on 171–72
new mandate on arms trafficking 173–74
resource extraction mandate 170–71
Rwanda 174–75
Uganda 151–52
Panel of Experts (UN) *see* United Nations (UN)
parastatal ownership 9
paternalism 161–62
payment modes 11
Payne, L. A. 66
peace *see* threat to peace
Perlo-Freeman, S. 30
perpetrators
imagined 185–90
of international crimes 8
transferring arms from outside 88–89
Pirie, F. 140, 198
poison gas 99
politicization critiques 167–70
positive complementarity 23
Posner, E. 141
Posner, R. A. 72
postcolonialism 14
see also colonialism
principal liability 78
Principles for Responsible Investment 57–58
professional intuition 122, 131, 197
proprio motu investigations 134, 181
providing the means of commission 75
proxy warfare 157
Prunier, G. 163, 170–71
prussic acid 4
punishment, perceptions of 178

Quakers 57–58

radiological technology 7
rape 86, 109
Rassemblement congolais pour la démocratie (RCD) 155–57, 174
Rastan, R. 49, 134n.2
recklessness (*dolus eventualis*) 51, 103
refugees 151, 154–55
remoteness 79–80, 81, 82, 83–85
responsibility
attribution of 78
individual criminal 14–15, 194, 197, 198
see also state responsibility, law of
retribution 142
revolvers 6–7
Reyntjens, F. 157
rifles 6–7
risk
assessment 10–11
foreseeable 55
overriding 30
risk-based approach 104
security 125–26
Robinson, D. 192
Romania 158–59
Rome Statute 2, 3, 5–6, 13, 17, 196–97
accomplice liability 91
actus reus 70
Arms Trade Law 40, 48–49, 51, 58
basic requirements 75–77
complicit assistance 71–72
corporate bar to liability 129
export regulation 30, 35
ICC legal culture 119–20
interpretation 72–73
'most serious' crimes 191
travaux préparatoires 70, 78, 121
Rosen, L. 111–12
rule of law 146
Russia 9, 13–14, 19, 44–45, 158–59
Rwanda 1–2, 9–10, 197–98
Arms Trade Law 40, 67
ICC DRC Situation 179, 182 , –83, 193
Second Congo War 153, 154–60, 164, 165, 166, 167–69, 172, 176
Rwandan Patriotic Front (RPF) 154–55

Saage-Maaß, M. 15–16
safe tribunals 181–82
Saferworld 24
'same conduct' 48–49
sanctions 12–13, 14, 31, 39–41, 44, 194
Sands, P. 13–14, 24
Saudi Arabia 13–14, 16, 23–25, 35–36
Schabas, W. 136
Scheffer, D. 93
Schiff, B. N. 181
Schwöbel-Patel, C. 189–90
SCSL Pre-Trial Chamber (PTC) 77–78, 91–92, 134, 135, 184, 194
Scud missiles 11
Second Congo War 3, 9–10, 17, 151–76, 197–98
  actus reus 87
  anti-DRC alliance 156–57
  arms brokers, pivotal role of 160–62
  arms embargoes 166–67
  arms export regulation 164–66
  arms flows, analysis of 153–66
  Arms Trade Law 44–46, 56
  atrocity 162–64
  case study 152–53
  context 151–52, 175–76
  Global and All-Inclusive Agreement (2003) 166, 167
  politicization critiques 167–70
  pro-DRC alliance 155–56
  transnational alliances 157–58
  see also Panel of Experts (DRC)
secondary liability 78
Seekers (religious group) 145
selectivity *see* horizontal selectivity; vertical selectivity
senior leaders 191
sensu stricto 6
serious crime 191
serious injury 86
sexual slavery 86
sexual and gender-based violence 151
Shklar, J. N. 140–41
Sierra Leone 10, 22–23, 29, 167
significance requirement 81
significant arms transfers (degree of contribution) 77–80
slavery 32
  sexual 86
Slovakia 158–59
Sluiter, G. 15–16
small arms, definition of 6–7
Small Arms and Light Weapons (SALW) 6–7, 9
  brokers 9–10, 109
  category of 6–7
  export regulation 33, 34–35
  illicit trade of 173–74
  licensing 165
  Second Congo War 152, 154–55, 162, 165–66, 174
  statistical analysis 26–27
  UN Conference on 33
  see also United Nations Programme of Action on Small Arms and Light Weapons (UN PoA)
Small Arms Survey 13–14, 161
Smith, K. J. M. 15–16, 78, 95–96, 97, 100, 102–3
smuggling 19–20
social imaginaries concept 146
social networks 156
social science models 11, 14–15, 112–13
Socially Responsible Investing (SRI) 57–58
Somalia 40, 159, 167
South Africa
  Arms Trade Law 41–43
  export regulation 20, 22
  pro-DRC and anti-DRC alliances 159, 174
South Korea 9
South Sudan 28, 46
sovereignty *see* state sovereignty
Soviet Union 9
Special Court for Sierra Leone (SCSL) 3, 4–5, 22–23, 71–72, 74, 77–79, 84–85, 148
special domestic courts 120–21
Special Tribunal for Lebanon (STL) 3, 47, 58n.131
specific direction debate 101
SPLM/A in Opposition 28
Stahn, C. 18, 64, 187
Staibano, C. 14
state officials 8
state responsibility, law of 18, 50–51
  see also responsibility
state sovereignty 33, 64, 68, 149
Stavrianakis, A. 14
Stewart, J. G. 10, 15–16, 40–41, 83
Stockholm International Peace Research Institute 13–14
Stockholm Process 44
stockpile
  Cold War 158–59
  leakage 9
  management 10–11
  police 155
strict liability 20
submachine guns 6–7
subsidiary law 38, 60–62
Sudan 47, 158, 165, 198
Sudan People's Liberation Movement-in-Opposition (SPLM-iO) 28

sui generis legal system 94, 124
suicide 7
Sweden 13–14, 19, 32–33
Syria 34–35, 41
systems approach 14–15

Taliban 59
Tamm, H. 157, 158
Tan, A. 14
Tanzania 159
tax evasion 128
Taylor, C. 22–23, 29, 100, 145–46, 148
territorial integrity 51–52
terrorism 9, 13–14, 119
  gun ownership and 25–26
  UN sectoral conventions 58–59
  see also counterterrorism law
Terrorism Bombing Convention 58–59, 88–89, 105, 107
Tesch and Stabenow 4
threat to peace 40, 42, 47
tort liability 49–50
toxic gas 4
trafficking 9, 19–20
  arms/weapons 10–11, 20, 30, 48–49, 120–21, 153–54, 187–88, 193, 194
  illicit 35–36, 54
  see also drug trafficking; human trafficking
Tranparency International 180
transnational arms regulation 2
Transnational Criminal Law 17, 18
  concept of 62, 196
transnational organized crime groups 8
transport agents 131
transporters 8, 9, 153
  definition of 9–10
transshipment 10–11, 27
travel bans 167, 194
treaties *see* international agreements
treaty crimes 121
Turkey 9
Tutsi 154–55, 157

Uganda 2, 9–10, 197–98
  ICC case selection 146, 148
  ICC DRC Situation 179, 182–83, 193
  Second Congo War 153, 155–57, 158–60, 164, 165, 166, 168, 172, 174–75, 176
UK *see* United Kingdom (UK)
Ukraine 198
  conflict and neutrality law 54
União Nacional para a Independência Total de Angola (UNITA) 154, 155, 157, 167, 168
United Kingdom (UK)
  arms manufacturing 13–14, 19
  brokering laws 29
  export controls 32–33
  lawful trade, challenges to 23–25
  Supreme Court opinions 80, 102
  see also National Health Service (NHS)
United Nations (UN)
  Charter 44–45, 47, 51–52, 99
  embargo 98–100
  fact-finding bodies 46, 164
  Firearms Protocol 188–89
  Human Rights Council Working Group 57, 99
  Panel of Experts 2, 17, 22–23, 40, 56, 153, 162–63, 180, 193, 197–98
  purposes of 51–52
  Sanctions Committees 40
United Nations Convention against Transnational Organized Crime (UNTOC) 60
United Nations General Assembly (UNGA) 182
United Nations Human Rights Committee (UNHRC) 56
United Nations International Tracing Instrument (UN ITI) 33, 188–89
United Nations Office of Drugs and Crime (UNODC) 60, 120
United Nations Organization Mission in the Democratic Republic of the Congo (MONUC) 167, 182–83, 186
United Nations Programme of Action on Small Arms and Light Weapons (UN PoA) 6–7, 33, 60, 165–66, 188–89
United Nations Security Council (UNSC)
  arms traders, concern over 47
  embargo practice, criticisms of 44–45, 99, 175–76, 179
  fundamental limitations 169
  Group of Experts 194
  ICC DRC Situation 182
  multilateral embargoes 39
  permanent members 39–40
  powers, role of 153
  Resolutions 39, 40, 46–47, 100
  Second Congo War, role during 167–70, 171, 173–74, 175, 176
United States (US)
  Alien Tort Act 120
  arms manufacturing 13–14, 19
  counter-terrorism offences 59
  export controls 32–33
  gun ownership 25–26
  imprisonment for arms trafficking 20

United States (US) (*cont.*)
  low-value exports 11
  Military Tribunals 3–4
  Second Congo War 164–66, 167–69
  small arms transfer 9
  Specially Designated Nationals 100
  universal civil jurisdiction 56
universal jurisdiction, principles of 63–64
US *see* United States (US)
use of force (*jus ad bellum*) 18, 49–50, 51–53, 54, 196

van Anraat, Frans 21–23
van der Wilt, H. 66
Van Sliedregt, E. 16–17, 93
vertical selectivity 190, 192
victimhood
  concepts of 186–87
  forms of 186
  images 189–90
victims 185–90, 198
  accountability for 31–35
  ideal victims 187
  interests, centrality of 186, 188
  representation of 188
  Trust Fund for Victims 64
victor's justice 191–92
Vietnam 34–35
virtual certainty (*dolus indirectus*) 51

WannaCry ransomware 60–61
war crimes 1, 2, 4, 6, 16
  export regulation 19, 30, 35, 36
  Second Congo War 174–75
Warsaw Pact 158–59
warships 6
Wassenaar Group of states 33–34
Weapons Law Encyclopaedia 13–14
wildlife crime 49–50, 60
Wilson, R. A. 87, 99, 104, 113–15
Wood, B. 188–89
World Customs Organization (WCO) 61–62
World Trade Organization (WTO) 61–62, 124
World War I (WWI) 32–33, 34–35
World War II (WWI) 2, 3, 34–35, 151
  concentrations camps 2, 4, 34–35
  post-war cases 2
  post-war tribunals 3
  see also Nazi regime
wrongfulness 36, 65, 66

Yemen 1–2, 16, 23–25, 26, 35–36, 57–58
Yihdego, Z. 13
Yugoslavia 41, 44, 167

Zaire 40, 154–55
Zimbabwe 44–45, 158
Zumbansen, Peer 38
Zyklon B gas 2, 4